An Introduction to Discourse Analysis: The Critical Study of Language

An Introduction to Discourse Analysis: The Critical Study of Language

Contributors

Juliana Vianna da Nobrega et al.

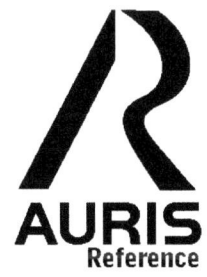

AURIS
Reference

www.aurisreference.com

An Introduction to Discourse Analysis: The Critical Study of Language

Contributors: Juliana Vianna da Nobrega et al.

Published by Auris Reference Limited
www.aurisreference.com

United Kingdom

An Introduction to Discourse Analysis: The Critical Study of Language

ISBN: 978-1-78154-745-8

British Library Cataloguing in Publication Data
A CIP record for this book is available from the British Library

Printed in the United Kingdom

Contents

List of Abbreviations

CDA	Critical Discourse Analysis
CSD	Collective Subject Discourse
CNPq	Conselho Nacional de Desenvolvimento Científico e Tecnológico , 1
ICT	Information and Communication Technologies
PTSD	`Post-traumatic stress disorder
CT	cooperative teacher
PE	physical education
CR	contrastive rhetoric
EArg	Explanation/argument
ICT	Information and Communication Technologies
RA	Reinforcement/Approval
CDA	Critical Discourse Analysis
ESL	English as a Second Language
LD	learning disabled
SPED	special education

List of Contributors

Juliana Vianna da Nobrega
Otto von Guericke University Magdeburg, Magdeburg, Germany

Maria Cristina Lima Paniago
Programa de Pós-graduação em Educação, Universidade Católica Dom Bosco, Campo Grande, Brasil

Katia Alexandra de Godoi e Silva
Programa de Pós-graduação em Educação, Universidade Católica Dom Bosco, Campo Grande, Brasil

Guo-Ping Yang
School of Foreign Languages, Beihang University, Beijing, China

Yin Chen
School of International Education and Exchange, Changzhou University, Changzhou, China

Jeppe Oute
Department of Psychology and Behavioural Sciences, Centre for Alcohol and Drug Research, Aarhus University, Aarhus, Denmark

Lotte Huniche
User Perspectives, Institute of Public Health, University of Southern Denmark, Odense, Denmark

Connie T. Nielsen
Psychiatric Department Kolding-Vejle, Region of Southern Denmark, Denmark

Anders Petersen
Department of Sociology and Social Work, Aalborg University, Aalborg, Denmark

Wadii Zayed
High Institute of Sport and Physical Education, Ksar Saîd, University la Manouba, Tunis, Tunisia
Tunisian Research Laboratory "Sport Performance Optimization", Tunis, Tunisia

Naila Bali
High Institute of Sport and Physical Education, Ksar Saîd, University la Manouba, Tunis, Tunisia
Tunisian Research Laboratory "Sport Performance Optimization", Tunis, Tunisia

Lucie Kucerova
Olomouc Department, Faculty of Education, Palacky University, Olomouc, Czech Republic

Tereza Buchtova
Olomouc Department, Faculty of Education, Palacky University, Olomouc, Czech Republic

Stefan Chudy
Olomouc Department, Faculty of Education, Palacky University, Olomouc, Czech Republic

Pavel Neumeister
Olomouc Department, Faculty of Education, Palacky University, Olomouc, Czech Republic

Preface

Discourse analysis (DA), or discourse studies, is a general term for a number of approaches to analyze written, vocal, or sign language use, or any significant semiotic event. The objects of discourse analysis—discourse, writing, conversation, communicative event—are variously defined in terms of coherent sequences of sentences, propositions, speech, or turns-at-talk. Contrary to much of traditional linguistics, discourse analysts not only study language use 'beyond the sentence boundary', but also prefer to analyze 'naturally occurring' language use, and not invented examples. The text, *An Introduction to Discourse Analysis the Critical Study of Language,* includes perspectives from a variety of approaches and disciplines, including applied linguistics, education, psychology, anthropology and communication to help students and scholars from a range of backgrounds to formulate their own views on discourse and engage in their own discourse analysis. First chapter focuses on Ronald Reagan's evil empire speech. Second chapter aims to analyze the collective discourse from members of a research and study group on their participation. Third chapter presents comparative study investigates the use of Contrastive Discourse Markers between Chinese English learners and native speakers based on corpus data. Fourth chapter aims to elucidate which political classifications of normality and mental illness that are displayed in two health political campaigns regarding anti-stigmatization and social inclusion and how such classifications co-constitute the subjectivity of individuals suffering from mental illness and their relatives. Drawing on a discourse theoretical perspective laid out by political theorists Laclau and Mouffe, we analyze how the campaigns bring into effect a weak and ineffective subject of deviance and how it is constituted by a subject of normality characterized by opposing traits. The chapter takes up the discussion of how the campaigns' articulations of the subjects of normality and deviance are imbedded in a hegemonic discourse of neoliberalism and individualism that asserts involvement as an expanded division of responsibility for the identification, classification and regulation of mentally ill subjects between public and private spheres of the Danish welfare state. Fifth chapter is about an approach to discourse analysis. Sixth chapter includes a qualitative analysis which aims to identify the advice of cooperative teachers to the student teachers for whom they are responsible for training. It's a descriptive/exploratory methodology based on observation and video recorded six physical education sessions lasting one hour each and six semi structured interviews and gave cooperative teachers the opportunity to share their perspectives on broad topics such as professional training, teaching, and characteristics of the training environment and succinct topics such as training program and their preoccupation. Last chapter presents a research investigation focused on creating a basic discourse on discipline in novice teachers.

Chapter 1

DISCOURSE ANALYSIS: RONALD REAGAN'S EVIL EMPIRE SPEECH

Juliana Vianna da Nobrega

Otto von Guericke University Magdeburg, Magdeburg, Germany

ABSTRACT

Language can be a powerful tool to convince others and make them cooperative. Cialdini (2007) has worked out several principles along which it is possible to analyze discourses in terms of their persuasiveness. Others also have contributed with tools to analyzing discourses such as Fairclough (2003). These tools are used to analyze the "Evil Empire Speech" of the US President Ronald Reagan that he held at the National Association of Evangelicals, 1983, in Orlando Florida. His historical speech was aimed at convincing the nation about the righteousness of his nuclear policy. He partly rewrote the already prepared script and included the "evil empire" part. The analysis supports that his speech was an exceptionally effective one. Reagan made his speech an example of the following principles of persuasiveness such as reciprocity, authority, commitment, liking, scarcity and social proof. He wanted support for belligerent intentions from a faithful community, which was already problematic, but he got the audience on his side through emphasizing his similarities with them, his own faithfulness, the presentation of strong examples and balancing humor and seriousness. Additionally, he introduced the striking metaphor "evil empire", which stuck to the peoples' minds and had an impact on them. He also appealed to the people through implicitly distinguishing the evil from the ones who were not evil—the US citizens. Thus, he made the American people feel better, to ensure them that they do the right thing when following him. He ranked religious people above him when he was joking about clergy men and politicians. To reinforce his authority, he borrowed the authority of various respected men through citing them. He improved his position and the power of his arguments using the philosophical wisdom of others.

HOW TO MAKE THE BEST OUT OF A SPEECH?

Life normally consists to an enormous amount of communication, so does my life as well. My own experience with group works at the University of Magdeburg showed that communication can be very difficult and time consuming but also easy, effective and efficient. I do have the same experience with presentations or lectures. Independent of whether I found the matter interesting upfront, some people turn the presentation into something that catches my attention or they make me fight with drifting away and thinking of something else. Often enough I am in the position to give speeches myself and I am sure that people think the same way of what I present them—either one or the other way.

From my point of view, some persons have the quality of nearly always doing a good job during speeches and sometimes they do it even exceptionally well. For me, one of those persons was Ronald Reagan, the president of the United States from 1981-1989.

Anyway, I find it quite challenging to find out what about his speeches make them so attractive to me and certainly to other people as well. But to know that would probably prevent me from spending much of my energy on unfruitful attempts to convince somebody of my findings. Therefore, I will dedicate myself to finding a way to properly learn more about Reagan's qualities and weaknesses in communication.

To do so I have to find out what the communication style of Reagan was and what the features of his style were that made him persuasive. This should be a well structured analysis regarding all the dimensions of communication and persuasiveness because only this focused view makes the difference from just passively listening to what he says.

The speech of Ronald Reagan will be analyzed, and the context of his speech will be outlined before the actual analysis. Upfront, I will explain the tools and at the same time theoretical background that I will use to analyze his speech. A basic part of these tools are the principles of persuasion from Robert Cialdini: reciprocation, commitment and consistency, social proof, authority, liking and scarcity (Cialdini, 2007: 1 ff.). Not each of those might be relevant, but for those which are, reasons will be given. Additionally, the Critical Discourse Analysis will be used as a means of analysis. This method will also be explained initially.

LANGUAGE AND THE PRINCIPLES OF PERSUASION

In a new functional approach, language is designed as a form of action and as a place of interaction. One can observe the effect that these expressions have in social interaction because the linguistic manifestations, which a certain speaker produces (in a real situation of communication under determined conditions of interaction), demonstrate the discursive intention of the speaker. In the linguistic system the speaker reveals his communicative propositions.

The functional use of language occurs when a language is used considering different interlocutive propositions and being adapted to various discursive contexts (Neves, 1997: 15). The speaker chooses a vocabulary with words that are adapted to his communicative intentions. This choice is not realized through a particular word but through the organization and combination of various words. Each choice, which the speaker makes, has a discursive function. The speaker chooses the words in accordance with what he wants to communicate.

The discourse is an activity that is marked by the oral ability whereas the voice and the gestures are elements, which establish a discrete and sensorial communication, and with their theatricality express and articulate meanings of the inner universe, giving everything a draping of intention to the word. The form of discourse is as important as the content. The way how a discourse is held is how it gives power and substance to the word (Vieira, 1993: 61).

The discourses are also conditioned to the context in which they are produced. The social context is the environment in which the text is produced, and the cultural context is the background where the interaction is happening. The choices obtain significance in a socio-cultural context. Because of that, it is not correct to say that an expression is right or wrong, but that this expression is (or is not) adequate in the context. Discourses are always socially situated since they take place in social environments. Furthermore, the discourse is systemically and predictably constructed that way that it relates to these contextual circumstances (Richardson, 2007: 75).

In this sense, in the process of persuasion there is a utilization of elements and techniques (by the speaker) trying to mobilize emotions in the listener, which help the speaker to reach agreement (among the listeners) and in the following change his or her behavior. There exists a specific methodology of persuasion. An art that analyzes and defines the steps through which a person tries to convince other people and that identifies its structural fundaments.

Robert Cialdini developed a theory based on the principles of persuasion, which are:

Reciprocation is about repaying what one has received from another one. People seem to be tempted to give something back when they have received a favor in advance. Furthermore, asking for very big favors would mostly immediately be rejected, but asking in the following for a smaller one raises much more the likelihood that the smaller one would be accepted.

The rule says that people should try to repay what another person has provided them. If a man does us a favor, we should do him one in return. We are obligated to the future repayment of favors, it has become a synonym for "thank you" (Cialdini, 2007: 18).

Sociologists (such as Alvin Gouldner) affirm that there is no human society that does not subscribe to the rule. It may well be that a developed system of indebtedness flowing from the rule for reciprocation is a unique property of human culture. An enormous shared and strongly held feeling of future obligation made a big difference in human social evolution, because it meant that one person could give, for example food, to another with confidence that it was not being lost. Such a system of aid (reciprocation) became possible bringing benefit to the societies that possessed it. This rule is deeply implanted in us by the process of socialization (Cialdini, 2007: 18).

A good example to illustrate this is the case of five thousand dollars of relief aid sent to Mexico from people of Ethiopia. In 1985 native officials of the Ethiopian Red Cross had decided to send the money to help the victims of that year`s earthquakes in Mexico city. A journalist asked them for an explanation about the donation and the officials answered that despite the needs prevailing in their country, the money was sent because Mexico had sent aid to Ethiopia in 1935, when it was invaded by Italy (Cialdini, 2007: 19).

Human societies are trained to comply with and believe in the reciprocity rule, and each of us knows about the social sanctions and derision applied to anyone who violates it. There is a general distaste for those who take and make no effort to give in return. In this sense, on the example illustrated it is possible to observe that the need of reciprocation had triumphed even a half century later(Cialdini, 2007: 20).

Commitment and consistency: To be consistent is another human motivation. If one can get commitment from a person in the form of a verbal or written agreement, it is much more likely that the person will do it. Cialdini calls it getting the answer 'yes'.

This principle shows that once a man has made a choice, he will encounter personal and interpersonal pressures to behave consistently with that commitment. There is a desire to be and to appear consistent with what he has already done. Those pressures will cause him to respond in ways that justify his earlier decision.

Even in ways that are clearly contrary to the human beings' own best interests the tendency to be consistent is strong enough to compel people to do what they ordinarily would not want to do. In New York City beach there was an experiment made for the psychologist Thomas Moriarty which proofed that.

In the experiment, a research accomplice would put a beach blanket down five feet from the blanket of another person, who was chosen as the experimental subject. After some minutes the accomplice would stand up and leave the blanket to stroll down the beach. A few minutes later, a second researcher, pretending to be a thief, would come, grab the radio and try to hurry away with it. The persons were very reluctant to put themselves in harm's way by challenging the thief. But when the procedure was tried with the accomplice, before taking his stroll, asking the experimental subject "watch my things", which they agreed to do, the result was different. Now, the subjects (nineteen of the twenty subjects) became virtual vigilantes and running after and stopping the thief, demanding an explanation. They were propelled by the rule for consistency (Cialdini, 2007: 59).

Social proof: People, who are not sure what to do, look for orientation in the people around them. Others do it, so they do it as well.

Persons view a behavior as more correct in a given situation to the degree that they see others performing it. The tendency to see an action as more appropriate when others are doing it normally works well. When a lot of people are doing something, it is the right thing to do. For example, advertisers like to inform the consumers when a product is the "largest-selling" because they do not have to convince them directly that the product is good, they need only say that many others think so and then, it seems proof enough (Cialdini, 2007: 117).

This tendency, to assume that an action is more correct when others are doing it, is exploited in a variety of settings. The psychologist Albert Andura has shown how people suffering from phobias can get rid of these fears in a simple fashion. He made a study of children who were exceptionally afraid of dogs. These children should watch a little boy playing happily with a dog for twenty minutes a day. After four days of exhibition it produced changes in the reactions of the fearful children and 67 percent of them were willing to climb into a playpen with a dog for playing and petting. The children were more willing to interact with a dog after the exhibition (Cialdini, 2007: 118).

Authority: People look up to authority. They find it in the form of experts, titles, clothing and status. Those factors improve credibility even though it might not always be legitimate.

Persons are trained from birth onwards that obedience to proper authority is right and disobedience is wrong. The power and value of obedience is in our culture. During the childhood children found that taking their parents advice proved beneficial because their parents have wisdom and also because they controlled punishments. As adults the pattern persists, but now other authority figures appear as judges, employers and government leaders. Their positions go together with superior access to information and power. It makes sense to comply with the wishes of these authorities even when it makes no sense at all. The obedience frequently takes place with little or no conscious deliberation. People rarely think about the pros and cons of authority's demands(Cialdini, 2007: 218).

In this sense, a good example could be the authority of physicians. Their authority is often not questioned. The various health workers well understand the level of their jobs in this structure and they see that the M.D. sits at the top. Just another doctor of higher rank would, perhaps, overrule the doctor's judgment in a case, no one else. As a consequence there is a tradition of automatic obedience to a doctor's orders among health-care staff. Professor Cohen affirms that when a physician makes a clear error no one lower in the hierarchy questions the prescription (Cialdini, 2007: 219).

Liking: People will agree more to people they like. The reasons for people to like other people can be very diverse. It might be attractiveness, similarity, etc.

There are factors that can be used to produce linking. The first one is physical attractiveness. Good-looking people have an advantage in social interaction. There are evidences of favoritism toward handsome politicians. Research demonstrated that voters do not realize their bias (Cialdini, 2007: 171). The second is similarity, people like others that are similar to them in the area of opinions, personality traits, background or life-style. The similarities may seem trivial, but they appear to work (Cialdini, 2007: 173). The third is compliment. The information that someone fancies a person can be a device for producing return linking and willing compliance. The actor McLean Stevenson described how his wife tricked him into marriage: "She said she liked me." Persons hear a positive estimation from others who want something back (Cialdini, 2007: 174). Fourth, contact and cooperation. People like things that are familiar to them. Because of its effect on liking, familiarity plays a role in decisions as, for example, the politicians people elect. In the Ohio election, a man given little chance of winning the state attorney-general race reached the victory before the election, through changing his name to a family name with political tradition in Ohio (Brown). People often do not realize that their attitude toward something has been influenced by the number of times they have been exposed to that in the past. Cooperation is a powerful cause of liking too. When people are working for the same goals, for mutual benefits, they are teammates. In an experiment researchers could observe that rival boys in a holiday camp after working together for common goals through "cooperative learning" achieved these goals. Because the success resulted from the mutual efforts (cooperation), it became difficult to maintain feelings of hostility toward those who had been teammates in the triumph (Cialdini, 2007: 181). Finally, liking through conditioning and association is presented. The simple association with something is enough to stimulate people to like or dislike something. Negative association can be exemplified in the case of a TV weatherman, who often gave bad news about the weather. The watchers did not like him and one guy even threatened to shoot him if he did not stop the rain. The positive association can be proofed through the liking of celebrities to products, for example, professional athletes are paid to connect themselves to some products even when it is irrelevant to their roles. The important thing for the advertiser is to establish a positive connection (Cialdini, 2007: 188).

Scarcity: Since people want and value scarce things more than things that are around in abundance, they would be more attentive when there is an opportunity to get such a scarce thing.

This principle has notable power in directing human action. When people note that their freedom to have something is limited, the item becomes less available and they experience an increased desire for it. Nevertheless, people do not recognize that psychological reactance has caused them to want the item more, they just know that they want it.

The idea of potential loss plays a role in human decision making. It was proofed that pamphlets using young women to check for breast cancer are more successful if they state their case in terms of what stands to be lost, for example: "You can lose several potential health benefits by failing to spend only five minutes each month doing breast self-examination." (Cialdini, 2007: 239). Something that had little appeal for the young women (breast test through self-examination) had become more attractive merely because they could lose many potential health benefits in not doing it. The scarcity principle says that opportunities seem more valuable to people when their availability is limited.

I will ratify Cialdini's theory of persuasion with Reagan's Evil Empire speech. For this reason, I will support my analysis with the method of Critical Discourse Analysis (CDA) and with Norman Fairclough in "Analyzing discourse".

CRITICAL DISCOURSE ANALYSIS

Critical Discourse Analysis as a Method in Social Scientific Research

For Fairclough Critical Discourse Analysis (CDA) is as much theory as method (Wodak/Meyer, 2001: 121). In this study, it will be referred to CDA as a method of discourse analysis. CDA is seen as a resource for critical social research that is used in combination with theoretical and analytical resources in various areas of social science.

Fairclough explains that discourse can be an element of social practice. This means that the discourse has a specific genre, which makes reference to the way of acting. The discourse is a way of representing and a style which refers to the way of being (Fairclough, 2003: 26). In the specific case treated in this paper, the genre is a public discourse, held from the former president of the United States, Ronald Reagan, at the National Association of Evangelicals in Orlando, Florida, where various reporters were present.

Fairclough (2003: 40) points out that there are three themes in social research, which should be studied. The first one is social difference. The particular social identities give way to political struggles based on the interests and identities of such particular groups. People differ in all sorts of ways and orientation. Difference is fundamental to social interaction. Reagan's discourse was based around the interests and identities of evangelical people. The second theme is the universal and the particular. The issue here is how particular identities, interests and representations can—under certain conditions—be claimed to be universal. This issue can be framed within questions of hegemony, for example, politics is seen as a struggle for hegemony, a particular way of conceptualizing power emphasizes how power depends upon achieving consent and the importance of ideology in sustaining relations of power (Fairclough, 2003: 45). The third theme is ideology. Habermas affirmed that "language is also a medium of domination and social force. It serves to legitimize organized power. In so far as the legitimations of power relations […] are not articulated […] language is also ideological" (Wodak/Meyer, 2001: 2).

Therefore, the analysis of a discourse is a preoccupation across the social sciences. Discourses are ways of representing aspects of the world. Different discourses are different points of view on the world. In the case of Reagan's speech, the new perspective on the world is a nuclear policy. This discourse is an element of social practice and will be analyzed through the Method of Critical Discourse Analysis (CDA).

The Method of Critical Discourse Analysis (CDA)

The Critical Discourse Analysis (CDA) takes into account the context of language use and, additionally, the relation between language and power. CDA theorizes social processes (within which individuals or groups create meanings in their interaction with texts) and structures which give rise to the production of a text. In this sense, three concepts are present in discourse analysis: power, history and ideology. This method of analysis considers that every discourse is historically produced and interpreted; discourses are structured by dominance and dominance structures are dominated by ideologies of powerful groups. Using CDA as a method of discourse analysis makes it possible to understand the effects of power and ideology in the production of meaning (Wodak/Meyer, 2001: 3). Thus, this method of analysis has been chosen in the present study.

Van Dijk affirms that CDA shall analyze the socio-cognitive aspect of the discourse analysis. The study of cognition is important for him while doing a critical analysis of discourse, communication and interaction (Wodak/Meyer, 2001: 97).

Cognition is understood as "personal and social cognition, beliefs and goals as well as evaluations and emotions, and any other "mental" or "memory" structures representations or processes involved in discourse interaction" (Wodak/Meyer, 2001: 98). Discourse analysis requires detailed cognitive and social analysis.

Methods of research depend on the characteristics of the context of the scholarly investigation such as aims, participants, setting, users and their beliefs and interests.

We must make choices selecting those structures that are necessary while analyzing discourses. Thus, when I analyze the way that Reagan exercised power and influence through his discourse, it only makes sense to study those properties that can vary as a function of social power as, for example, stress and intonation, word order, lexical style, coherence, topic choices, speech acts, schematic organization and rhetorical figures.

I shall explain some of the most important structures used in my analysis. Table 1 summarizes the following items that I will use in the discourse analysis. The first one is the use of the topic. The topic plays an important role in the processes of communication and interaction. The topic represents what a discourse 'is about'. Topics define what speakers orient towards and also allow for influence and manipulation. Second, there are the local meanings. They are the result of the selection made by speakers in their mental models of events. The local meanings are the kind of information that influences the mental models and therefore the attitudes and opinions of recipients. When using CDA as a method of discourse analysis, I shall observe the study of ideologically biased discourses. Moreover, it is interesting to study the use of implicit meanings because this kind of meanings is related to underlying beliefs.

Additionally, the CDA is interested in studying the structures that are less controllable by the speakers for example: intonation, rhetorical figures and all forms of spontaneous talk (i.e. pauses). These structures do not show directly underlying meanings and hence the identity of the speakers may be signaled by subtle characteristics of talk. Speakers may emphasize good things by ordering positive meanings in topics, by providing many details about good things, few details about bad things, using positive metaphors and by leaving implicit negative properties aside. In a (dominance) discourse the way of speaking not only expresses power, but also the desire to influence, to manipulate and to control the minds of the recipients.

Regarding context of the discourse, we may argue that the location of the discourse influences the speech. The characteristics of a speech change concerning the domain where it happens and according to the purposes, for example, politics or business, legislation or propaganda. Van Dijk affirms: "That is, what we say and how we say it depends on who is speaking to whom, when and where, and with what purposes" (Wodak/Meyer, 2001: 108). Context models guide us to understand what is relevant to the social situation for the speech participants. It links texts with social situations.

Event models are another point that should be observed. Van Dijk notes: "Language users not only form mental models of the situation they interact in, but also of the events or situations they speak or write about" (Wodak/Meyer, 2001: 111). The discourses are understood as coherent in relation to the mental models that the users have about the events (facts) referred to.

Van Dijk classifies three forms of social representations that are necessary to understand a discourse: 1) knowledge (personal, group, cultural); 2) attitudes (attitudes are socially shared opinions); 3) ideologies. Table 2 summarizes these findings. Discourses occur within society and therefore can only be understood in the interaction of social situation, action, actor and societal structures (Wodak/Meyer, 2001: 21).

Table 1: Items used for the discourse analysis-according to Van Dijk, Lakoff and Fairclough

1. Topics	The topic represents what the discourse "is about" (Wodak/Meyer, 2001: 101).
2. Local meanings	The local meanings are the kind of information that influences the mental models and therefore the attitudes and opinions of recipients (Wodak/Meyer, 2001: 103).
3. Metaphors	Metaphors contain modes of thought and thereby shape what we perceive as reality. Different cultures understand metaphors in different ways (Lakoff/Johnson, 1980: 22).
4. Subtle formal structures	The structures that are less controllable by speakers, as an example: intonation and pause (Wodak/Meyer, 2001: 106).
5. Context models	They guide us to understand what of the social situation is relevant for the participants of the speech. It links texts with social situations (Wodak/Meyer, 2001: 108).
5.1 Intertextuality	It is a matter of recontextualization—a movement from one context to another, entailing particular transformations consequent upon how the material that is moved, recontextualized, figures within that new context (Fairclough, 2003: 51).
5.2 Assumptions	Types of implicitness as presuppositions, logical implications or entailments, and implicatures (Fairclough, 2003: 40).
6. Event models	Van Dijk affirms: "Language users not only form mental models of the situation they interact in, but also of the events or situations they speak or write about" (Wodak/Meyer, 2001: 111).

Table 2: Social representations to understand a discourse

1. Knowledge (personal, group, cultural)
2. Attitudes (attitudes as socially shared opinions)
3. Ideologies

He concludes further that discourse analysis "is thus at the same time cognitive, social and political analysis, but focuses rather on the role discourses play, both locally and globally, in society and its structure" (Wodak/Meyer, 2001: 118). The elements will be included in the analysis together with Cialdini's criteria on persuasive speech. It should be noted that to a big extent the criteria of Cialdini and CDA have touching points. For example, the relation of power and language can also be found in authority, one of Cialdini's criteria. Furthermore, Cialdini's social proof criteria can be found in shared opinions and attitudes. Social proof goes also together with the context of the speech—where it takes place and who the auditorium is as well as the historical context. According to these different items, the analysis will be undertaken in the following. It will be started with the context of the speech and afterwards the speech will be analyzed along the remaining criteria.

RONALD REAGAN'S EVIL EMPIRE SPEECH

The Context of Reagan's Speech

The analysis of 'meanings' has to take into account the historical context, which for Reagan's speech will be outlined in short. Discourses have their own history. Chronological and sociocultural aspects produce meanings and social effects that cannot be reduced to the characteristics of the text alone. In this sense, Fowler notes that discourses are always socially situated, it occurs in a social environment and the construction of discourse "relates systematically and predictably to (these) contextual circumstances" (Richardson, 2007: 75).

Following this line of understanding, for the Critical Discourses Analysis (CDA) all discourses are historical and can only be understood with reference to their context. Moreover, CDA uses the concept of intertextuality (Wodak/Meyer, 2001: 15). As Fairclough explains: "Intertextuality is a matter of recontextualization—a movement from one context to another, entailing particular transformations consequent upon how the material that is moved, recontextualized, figures within that new context" (Fairclough, 2003: 51).

According to the National Centre for Public Policy Research (Anon.: n.d.), short before Reagan's "Evil Empire Speech" the American Congress was about to support a "nuclear freeze" policy—a bilateral nuclear disarmament policy of the US and the Soviet Union. It was born out of the idea of a disarmament researcher, Randall Forsberg, and resulted in a big "nuclear freeze" movement(Adams, 2002: 15). The Soviets supported this policy but President Reagan advised his administration against this policy and in favor of a "pro-defense" strategy. Shortly afterwards, on March 8, 1983, Ronald Reagan held his much known "Evil Empire Speech". It was directed to the National Association of Evangelicals in Orlando, Florida. The National Center for Public Policy Research further states that this speech was first written for President Reagan as a routine speech. Reagan himself added paragraphs that made this speech one of the most influencing and historical ones. I will dedicate one paragraph to his "Evil Empire Speech", which is his final point, but I will also describe how he leads to this point and make some general remarks on his whole speech. Thus the historical context is quite strong. The speech relates to the conflict between the USA and the Soviet Union during a time when nuclear armament was not seen as the single correct response. The location in which Reagan presents this speech is also a means that enforces his speech. He implicitly uses religious belief to support his speech. So he has even the church behind him, which should be an institution that represents peaceful coexistence.

The full length of Reagan's speech is around 29 minutes. It can be found in the internet (Address to the National Association of Evangelicals, 1983). The part I will analyze is the "Evil Empire" part, I mean the part where Reagan actually refers to the Soviets as an "evil empire" and where he talks about the "nuclear freeze" policy. A transcript of his speech is provided in annex 1; the "Evil Empire" part is in bold letters.

Evaluation and Description of the Elements of Reagan's Speech

Reagan's Persuasiveness—General Characteristics Related to His Speech

In my opinion the obvious purpose of Reagan's speech is to convince the auditorium about the righteousness of his nuclear policy, which he actually tackled in the final part of his speech. However, all of the other arguments leading to this final part had to be convincing as well. From my point of view Reagan was very persuasive in content and delivery of his speech for the whole length of his performance. In the following I will show why and how.

Analysts of critical discourses endorse what Habermas affirmed "language is also a medium of domination and social force. It serves to legitimize of organized power. In so far as the legitimations of power relations, [...] are not articulated, […] language is also ideological" (Wodak/Meyer, 2001: 2). This can also be observed in Reagan's speech. His speech and the setting are directed to use social force to persuade his listeners.

For a man like Ronald Reagan I want to continue with his authority, as one of the principles of persuasion. Authority and power come together. I believe that he had lots of authority alone because of the fact that he was the President of the United States at that time and with that the leader of the Western World. Therefore, his formal authority cannot be questioned. In his speech he talked about political issues, especially about the opposition to the Soviet Union. Until the date of his speech, he had had a long career as a politician for example as Governor of California and he had been for around 2 years in office as president. All of that contributes to his credibility to talk about these issues as an expert and that gives him formal and informal authority.

Wodak explains that power does not come from language, but language can be used to challenge power. Power is signaled by grammatical forms within a text and also by a person's control of a social occasion by means of the genre of a text (Wodak/Meyer, 2001: 11). Reagan's power is already given through its position as the president of the US. From this position he is able to hold different speeches than other people are able to hold. He can always borrow from the power of this position and enforce his speeches. But not only the power through one's position is of importance in speeches.

In my opinion his informal authority is strong as well because he appears very self-confident and credible at the same time. This is supported by his deep and relaxed voice and his overall calm speech. He nearly never in his 29 minutes speech makes errors or uses words to fill gaps, whereas there was no need to because there were no unintended gaps. He was credible because he was nearly flawless in speech and seemed to know what he was talking about. One example for that is that he knew all the names of the people he cited or he talked about such as Jefferson, William Penn, the Senators Denton and Hatfield, C.S. Lewis etc. Furthermore, he talked about historical events, such as the civil war in the US, he cited the Bible by saying for example "Thou shalt love thy neighbor as thyself" and he referred to details of the work of his administration and the Congress.

Analyzing Reagan's discourse one can find some basic principles of a CDA. They are: 1) language is a social phenomenon; 2) not only individuals, but also institutions and social groupings have specific meanings and values that are expressed in language in systematic ways; 3) texts are the relevant units of language in communication; 4) readers/hearers are not passive recipients in their relationship to texts; 5) there are similarities between the language of science and the language of institutions, and so on (Wodak/Meyer, 2001: 6).

In the line number 175 of the transcript of Reagan's Evil Empire speech he turned to his last point, the nuclear freeze policy that he obviously refused. How he handled this part will be discussed in a later paragraph. At this point, I will outline the structure and content until his final part and how it contributed to his persuasiveness—above all authority and liking.

In terms of his liking he first broke the ice by making jokes but still remaining credible by staying calm and not being exaggerated. Then he tackled issues and conflicts of modern life and the church such as birth control, and he always took in the position of the church. To support his authority he used clear reasoning structures. One example is a reason-claim-example-structure from line 55 - 148, when he talked about the church that had done their job (reason) well because there is a religious awakening (claim) in the US. Additionally, he gave some statistics to underline this (example).

The more detailed structure and content are as follows: He first thanked for the invitation (lines 3 - 12). Then he delivered some jokes (lines 13 - 34). From lines 35 - 108 he pointed out the good things about religion and mentioned those who are against it. He gave examples on how politics had been dealing with birth control and religious speeches of students and at the same time he emphasized his being on the side of the church (lines 109 - 143). Reagan showed how his administration had been fighting for the same ideas as the church. He delivered the example that he had made clinics, prescribing birth control drugs to underage girls, notify it to the girls' parents. From line 144 - 149, Reagan appraised the audience for their achievements supported by statistics on how religiosity had improved in America, and he pointed out that this must continue. From line 149 - 166, there was a transition phase when he talked about America's errors in the past, such as the civil war, and that hate groups should be fought against. When he came to the critical issue—his last point—he already had the audience on his side. They were prepared and would digest the coming news easily.

I have already pointed out that his liking was supported by structure and content. Other facts contribute to his liking as well. It is an honor for the National Association of Evangelicals that the president holds a speech there and, with that, supports them strongly. It is a bit like a famous person used by a company for advertising to make its brand more known. In his speech Reagan tells the people what they like to hear und is humorous at the right times. It is a good example of intertextuality. Fairclough notes that "intertextuality is inevitable selective with respect to what is included and what is excluded from the events and texts represented" (Fairclough, 2003: 55). He uses 19 times the words God or Lord, he cites the Bible and he refers to connections between politics and religion. One example for that is his statement about the reference to God which is mentioned in the First Amendment of the US Constitution (lines 92 - 96). His big and authentic smile before he opened his speech and the warm words shortly afterwards also contributed to his liking. His making jokes were already mentioned. He made two jokes and all of them were related to politicians and clergymen. In the first one he showed that he believed in prayers and in the second he made fun of politicians in general by using the example that a rare case had happened and a politician came in heaven after his death, and since this is so seldom he got the best accommodation there. During the whole speech he addressed the whole audience with his eyes so that nobody had to feel neglected.

I think that liking and social proof are very strongly related. In his speech Reagan showed to be social proof by saying that he prayed and thus is a religious man. That is something he did in the very first part of his speech. There, he even mentioned his wife and was therefore implicitly referring to marriage (example of implicitness as presuppositions), which is a sacred institution.

At different points in his speech, Reagan created scarcity and hope. One very strong example for that was (lines 52 - 54) when he directly addressed the audience and said that religious people like the audience were the hope to survive and that liberty was the "last, best hope of men". In the following he talked about the opposition —about "radically different value systems" which "are not yet a majority" (lines 54 - 64).

He also used reciprocity, which increased his persuasiveness. I have already mentioned that Reagan said how he and his administration supported the same objectives as the church did. Two examples for that were the birth-control case, where he made the clinics notify the parents, and the public religious speeches of students, which he supported. Since he had done something for church it is now the church's turn to do something for him. At various points he makes appellations for support from the audience. An example is in the part immediately before the "Evil Empire Speech" (lines 160 - 166). There he asks the audience and the church in general for help against "hate groups". I believe that he introduced these strong words—"hate groups"—also with respect to the following part, when he would talk about the Soviets.

Some natural features supported his persuasiveness as well. They could fall under different categories such as social proof and liking. He wore a dark suit and dark tie, like most of the people sitting behind him. He was a lean man, not exceptionally tall or small and seemed to me to be in good shape. Additionally to what was mentioned about his voice, it was very clear and understandable. He modulated the melody, but never exaggerated it. I want to mention some facts about his speech that leave room for interpretation whether it was positive or negative in terms of an effective speech and persuasiveness.

He never modulated the volume of his voice very much. The average length of his sentences was 21.6 words per sentence. His hand movements were very thriftily.

My final remark is dedicated to the still not mentioned principle of persuasion—commitment and consistency. It is hard to get a "yes" from the audience since the speech is not thought to be so much interactive. But I believe he got it anyway. He got it in the form of applause and people standing up to support their agreement. In the course of his speech he received a lot and very intense applauses.

Reagan's Persuasiveness—The "Evil Empire" Part

I will now turn to the last part of Reagan's speech. In the transcript in annex 1 it is written in bold. I will not touch upon the final part, which comes after the "Evil Empire" part.

The structure and content of this part contributed to his authority the same way as they had done before—by having included precise examples and matters that are important to the church. Additionally, Reagan increased his credibility by always explaining how that what he proposes was in line with the belief of the church.

In the first part for example, he pointed out the opposition of the communists against the church—again by using specific names and dates. Afterwards, Reagan talked about that he did everything he could to prevent nuclear armament—and again, he does this specifically. He mentioned the example of his proposal of cutting strategic ballistic missiles by 50%. But then he turned to talk about higher values, freedom and the belief in God (lines 175 - 185), that would justify his pro-defense attitude. In the following he talked about the "nuclear freeze" policy and how dangerous it would be at this point in time. "I would agree to a freeze, if only we could freeze the Soviets' global desires" underlines his point of view by cleverly playing with words (line 188). He lays down why a policy of strength is better to achieve the objectives of the US.

He again uses scarcity to persuade the people from his armament plans by talking about "aging forces" (line 194). With that Reagan proposes to modernize capabilities to defend the US.

One very strong example contributes to several principles of persuasiveness, namely authority, liking and social proof. At lines 204 - 205 Reagan started talking: He once was present during a speech of a young man who said he would rather see his loved girls "die now, still believing in God, than have them grow up under communism and one day die no longer believing in God".

This is an extreme example that puts the belief in God on the top of all values. Reagan strongly agrees to this man and praises him implicitly for his remark. With that he emphasizes first his own strong faith in God and second, that extreme measures are justified to protect faith.

He furthered is persuasiveness through showing another Christian quality: sympathy. He said that one should pray for those "who live in that totalitarian darkness". But afterwards Reagan clearly turned back to his line by stating that until the totalitarian regime is in place it remains to be the "focus of evil".

To build credibility for the righteousness of his plans and commitment to follow him he used a very long quotation by C.S. Lewis. According to that quotation passiveness is "the greatest evil" leading to its final result such as "concentration and labor camps". This is followed by an appellation not to be passive but to support America to become strong again. In this part he also refers to the Soviet Union as an "evil empire", that is an example of metaphor. It is observed that Reagan uses metaphors quite often and this is his strongest one. Metaphors contain modes of thought and thereby shape what we perceive as reality. Different cultures understand metaphors in a different way (Lakoff/ Johnson, 1980: 22).

SUMMARY AND CONCLUSION

Ronald Reagan's Evil Empire Speech, which he held in 1983 at the National Association of Evangelicals, was aimed at weakening the upcoming opinion that nuclear armament was not the right answer to the Russian nuclear policy. The total length of his speech was about half an hour, whereas the final part was dedicated to Reagan's political concerns, and the prior part can clearly be seen as a part that prepares the audience for that what was coming and made them digest it as well as it was possible.

To conclude my findings about President Reagan's "Evil Empire Speech", I come to an exceptionally positive result with regard to his persuasiveness. He strongly contributed to all of the principles of persuasiveness such as reciprocity, authority, commitment, liking, scarcity and social proof. He did it through his voice, a flawless speech, showing similarities with the church, his own faithfulness, the presentation of strong examples and a good balance between humor and seriousness. Additionally, he used strong metaphors especially the notion "evil empire", that stuck to the peoples' minds and had an impact on them. He also implicitly distinguishes the evil from the ones who are not evil—the US. Thus, he makes the American people feel better, to ensure that they do the right thing when following him. He also emphasizes his relation to Christianity and even more he placed religious people above him when he made a joke about clergy men and politicians. And in addition to his authority as the president of the US, he borrowed the authority of various respected men through citing them. Thus, he did not only use his power or the power of his position but also the power of other men, which were accepted for the philosophical wisdom.

ANNEX 1

Transcript of Reagan's Evil Empire Speech

www.nationalcenter.org

Reverend clergy all, Senator Hawkins, distinguished members of the Florida congressional delegation, and all of you:

I can't tell you how you have warmed my heart with your welcome. I'm delighted to be here today.

Those of you in the National Association of Evangelicals are known for your spiritual and humanitarian work. And I would be especially remiss if I didn't discharge right now one personal debt of gratitude. Thank you for your prayers. Nancy and I have felt their presence many times in many ways. And believe me, for us they've made all the difference.

The other day in the East Room of the White House at a meeting there, someone asked me whether I was aware of all the people out there who were praying for the President. And I had to say, "Yes, I am. I've felt it. I believe in intercessionary prayer."

But I couldn't help but say to that questioner after he'd asked the question that—or at least say to them that if sometimes when he was praying he got a busy signal, it was just me in there ahead of him.

[Laughter]

I think I understand how Abraham Lincoln felt when he said, "I have been driven many times to my knees by the overwhelming conviction that I had nowhere else to go."

From the joy and the good feeling of this conference, I go to a political reception.

[Laughter]

Now, I don't know why, but that bit of scheduling reminds me of a story—[laughter]—which I'll share with you.

An evangelical minister and a politician arrived at Heaven's gate one day to-gether. And St. Peter, after doing all the necessary formalities, took them in hand to show them where their quarters would be. And he took them to a small, single room with a bed, a chair, and a table and said this was for the clergyman. And the politician was a little worried about what might be in store for him. And he couldn't believe it then when St. Peter stopped in front of a beautiful mansion with lovely grounds, many servants, and told him that these would be his quarters.

And he couldn't help but ask, he said, "But wait, how—here's something wrong—how do I get this mansion while that good and holy man only gets a single room?" And St. Peter said, "You have to understand how things are up here. We've got thousands and thousands of clergy. You're the first politician who ever made it."

[Laughter]

But I don't want to contribute to a stereotype.

[Laughter]

So, I tell you there are a great many God-fearing, dedicated, noble men and women in public life, present company included. And yes, we need your help to keep us ever mindful of the ideas and the principles that brought us into the public arena in the first place. The basis of those ideals and principles is a com-mitment to freedom and personal liberty that, itself, is grounded in the much deeper realization that freedom prospers only where the blessings of God are avidly sought and humbly accepted.

The American experiment in democracy rests on this insight. Its discovery was the great triumph of our Founding Fathers, voiced by William Penn when he said, "If we will not be governed by God, we must be governed by tyrants."

Explaining the inalienable rights of men, Jefferson said, "The God who gave us life, gave us liberty at the same time."

And it was George Washington who said that "of all the dispositions and habits which lead to political prosperity, religion and morality are indispensable sup-ports."

And finally, that shrewdest of all observers of American democracy, Alexis de Tocqueville, put it eloquently after he had gone on a search for the secret of America's greatness and genius—and he said, "Not until I went into the churches of America and heard her pulpits aflame with righteousness did I understand the greatness and the genius of America. America is good. And if America ever ceases to be good, America will cease to be great."

Well, I'm pleased to be here today with you who are keeping America great by keeping her good. Only through your work and prayers and those of millions of others can we hope to survive this perilous century and keep alive this experiment in liberty—this last, best hope of man.

I want you to know that this administration is motivated by a political philosophy that sees the greatness of America in you, her people, and in your families, churches, neighborhoods, communities—the institutions that foster and nourish values like concern for others and respect for the rule of law under God.

Now, I don't have to tell you that this puts us in opposition to, or at least out of step with, a prevailing attitude of many who have turned to a modern-day secularism, discarding the tried and time-tested values upon which our very civilization is based. No matter how well intentioned, their value system is radically different from that of most Americans. And while they proclaim that they're freeing us from superstitions of the past, they've taken upon themselves the job of superintending us by government rule and regulation. Sometimes their voices are louder than ours, but they are not yet a majority.

An example of that vocal superiority is evident in a controversy now going on in Washington. And since I'm involved, I've been waiting to hear from the parents of young America. How far are they willing to go in giving to government their prerogatives as parents?

Let me state the case as briefly and simply as I can. An organization of citizens, sincerely motivated and deeply concerned about the increase in illegitimate births and abortions involving girls well below the age of consent, sometime ago established a nationwide network of clinics to offer help to these girls and, hopefully, alleviate this situation. Now, again, let me say, I do not fault their intent. However, in their well-intentioned effort, these clinics have decided to provide advice and birth control drugs and devices to underage girls without the knowledge of their parents.

For some years now, the federal government has helped with funds to subsidize these clinics. In providing for this, the Congress decreed that every effort would be made to maximize parental participation. Nevertheless, the drugs and devices are prescribed without getting parental consent or giving notification after they've done so. Girls termed "sexually active"—and that has replaced the word "promiscuous"—are given this help in order to prevent illegitimate birth or abortion.

Well, we have ordered clinics receiving federal funds to notify the parents such help has been given. One of the nation's leading newspapers has created the term "squeal rule" in editorializing against us for doing this, and we're being criticized for violating the privacy of young people. A judge has recently granted an injunction against an enforcement of our rule. I've watched TV panel shows discuss this issue, seen columnists pontificating on our error, but no one seems to mention morality as playing a part in the subject of sex.

Is all of Judeo-Christian tradition wrong? Are we to believe that something so sacred can be looked upon as a purely physical thing with no potential for emotional and psychological harm? And isn't it the parents' right to give counsel and advice to keep their children from making mistakes that may affect their entire lives?

Many of us in government would like to know what parents think about this intrusion in their family by government. We're going to fight in the courts. The right of parents and the rights of family take precedence over those of Washington-based bureaucrats and social engineers.

But the fight against parental notification is really only one example of many attempts to water down traditional values and even abrogate the original terms of American democracy. Freedom prospers when religion is vibrant and the rule of law under God is acknowledged. When our Founding Fathers passed the First Amendment, they sought to protect churches from government interference. They never intended to construct a wall of hostility between government and the concept of religious belief itself.

The evidence of this permeates our history and our government. The Declaration of Independence mentions the Supreme Being no less than four times. "In God We Trust" is engraved on our coinage. The Supreme Court opens its proceedings with a religious invocation. And the members of Congress open their sessions with a prayer. I just happen to believe the schoolchildren of the United States are entitled to the same privileges as Supreme Court Justices and Congressmen.

Last year, I sent the Congress a constitutional amendment to restore prayer to public schools. Already this session, there's growing bipartisan support for the amendment, and I am calling on the Congress to act speedily to pass it and to let our children pray.

Perhaps some of you read recently about the Lubbock school case, where a judge actually ruled that it was unconstitutional for a school district to give equal treatment to religious and nonreligious student groups, even when the group meetings were being held during the students' own time. The First Amendment never intended to require government to discriminate against religious speech.

Senators Denton and Hatfield have proposed legislation in the Congress on the whole question of prohibiting discrimination against religious forms of student speech. Such legislation could go far to restore freedom of religious speech for public school students. And I hope the Congress considers these bills quickly. And with your help, I think it's possible we could also get the constitutional amendment through the Congress this year.

More than a decade ago, a Supreme Court decision literally wiped off the books of 50 States statutes protecting the rights of unborn children. Abortion on demand now takes the lives of up to one and a half million unborn children a year. Human life legislation ending this tragedy will some day pass the Congress, and you and I must never rest until it does. Unless and until it can be proven that the unborn child is not a living entity, then its right to life, liberty, and the pursuit of happiness must be protected.

You may remember that when abortion on demand began, many, and, indeed, I'm sure many of you, warned that the practice would lead to a decline in respect for human life, that the philosophical premises used to justify abortion on demand would ultimately be used to justify other attacks on the sacredness of human life—infanticide or mercy killing. Tragically enough, those warnings proved all too true. Only last year a court permitted the death by starvation of a handicapped infant.

I have directed the Health and Human Services Department to make clear to every health care facility in the United States that the Rehabilitation Act of 1973 protects all handicapped persons against discrimination based on handicaps, including infants. And we have taken the further step of requiring that each and every recipient of Federal funds who provides health care services to infants must post and keep posted in a conspicuous place a notice stating that "discriminatory failure to feed and care for handicapped infants in this facility is prohibited by Federal law." It also lists a 24-hour, toll-free number so that nurses and others may report violations in time to save the infant's life.

In addition, recent legislation introduced in the Congress by Representative Henry Hyde of Illinois not only increases restrictions on publicly financed abortions, it also addresses this whole problem of infanticide. I urge the Congress to begin hearings and to adopt legislation that will protect the right of life to all children, including the disabled or handicapped.

Now, I'm sure that you must get discouraged at times, but you've done better than you know, perhaps. There's a great spiritual awakening in America, a renewal of the traditional values that have been the bedrock of America's goodness and greatness. One recent survey by a Washington-based research council concluded that Americans were far more religious than the people of other nations; 95 percent of those surveyed expressed a belief in God and a huge majority believed the Ten Commandments had real meaning in their lives. And another study has found that an overwhelming majority of Americans disapprove of adultery, teenage sex, pornography, abortion, and hard drugs. And this same study showed a deep reverence for the importance of family ties and religious belief.

I think the items that we've discussed here today must be a key part of the Nation's political agenda. For the first time the Congress is openly and seriously debating and dealing with the prayer and abortion issues—and that's enormous progress right there. I repeat: America is in the midst of a spiritual awakening and a moral renewal. And with your Biblical keynote, I say today, "Yes, let justice roll on like a river, righteousness like a never-failing stream."

"Now, obviously, much of this new political and social consensus I've talked about is based on a positive view of American history, one that takes pride in our country's accomplishments and record. But we must never forget that no government schemes are going to perfect man. We know that living in this world means dealing with what philosophers would call the phenomenology of evil or, as theologians would put it, the doctrine of sin.

There is sin and evil in the world, and we're enjoined by Scripture and the Lord Jesus to oppose it with all our might. Our nation, too, has a legacy of evil with which it must deal. The glory of this land has been its capacity for transcending the moral evils of our past. For example, the long struggle of minority citizens for equal rights, once a source of disunity and civil war, is now a point of pride for all Americans. We must never go back. There is no room for racism, anti-Semitism, or other forms of ethnic and racial hatred in this country.

I know that you've been horrified, as have I, by the resurgence of some hate groups preaching bigotry and prejudice. Use the mighty voice of your pulpits and the powerful standing of your churches to denounce and isolate these hate groups in our midst. The commandment given us is clear and simple: "Thou shalt love thy neighbor as thyself." But whatever sad episodes exist in our past, any objective observer must hold a positive view of American history, a history that has been the story of hopes fulfilled and dreams made into reality. Especially in this century, America has kept alight the torch of freedom, but not just for ourselves but for millions of others around the world.

And this brings me to my final point today. During my first press conference as President, in answer to a direct question, I pointed out that, as good Marxist-Leninists, the Soviet leaders have openly and publicly declared that the only morality they recognize is that which will further their cause, which is world revolution. I think I should point out I was only quoting Lenin, their guiding spirit, who said in 1920 that they repudiate all morality that proceeds from supernatural ideas—that's their name for religion—or ideas that are outside class conceptions. Morality is entirely subordinate to the interests of class war. And everything is moral that is necessary for the annihilation of the old, exploiting social order and for uniting the proletariat.

Well, I think the refusal of many influential people to accept this elementary fact of Soviet doctrine illustrates an historical reluctance to see totalitarian powers for what they are. We saw this phenomenon in the 1930's. We see it too often today. This doesn't mean we should isolate ourselves and refuse to seek an understanding with them. I intend to do everything I can to persuade them of our peaceful intent, to remind them that it was the West that refused to use its nuclear monopoly in the forties and fifties for territorial gain and which now proposes 50-percent cut in strategic ballistic missiles and the elimination of an entire class of land-based, intermediate-range nuclear missiles.

At the same time, however, they must be made to understand we will never compromise our principles and standards. We will never give away our freedom. We will never abandon our belief in God. And we will never stop searching for a genuine peace. But we can assure none of these things America stands for through the so-called nuclear freeze solutions proposed by some.

The truth is that a freeze now would be a very dangerous fraud, for that is merely the illusion of peace. The reality is that we must find peace through strength.

I would agree to a freeze if only we could freeze the Soviets' global desires. A freeze at current levels of weapons would remove any incentive for the Soviets to negotiate seriously in Geneva and virtually end our chances to achieve the major arms reductions which we have proposed. Instead, they would achieve their objectives through the freeze.

A freeze would reward the Soviet Union for its enormous and unparalleled military buildup. It would prevent the essential and long overdue modernization of United States and allied defenses and would leave our aging forces increasingly vulnerable. And an honest freeze would require extensive prior negotiations on the systems and numbers to be limited and on the measures to ensure effective verification and compliance. And the kind of a freeze that has been suggested would be virtually impossible to verify. Such a major effort would divert us completely from our current negotiations on achieving substantial reductions.

A number of years ago, I heard a young father, a very prominent young man in the entertainment world, addressing a tremendous gathering in California.

It was during the time of the Cold War, and communism and our own way of life were very much on people's minds. And he was speaking to that subject. And suddenly, though, I heard him saying, "I love my little girls more than anything"—And I said to myself, "Oh, no, don't. You can't—don't say that."

But I had underestimated him. He went on: "I would rather see my little girls die now, still believing in God, than have them grow up under communism and one day die no longer believing in God."

There were thousands of young people in that audience. They came to their feet with shouts of joy. They had instantly recognized the profound truth in what he had said, with regard to the physical and the soul and what was truly important.

Yes, let us pray for the salvation of all of those who live in that totalitarian darkness--pray they will discover the joy of knowing God. But until they do, let us be aware that while they preach the supremacy of the state, declare its omnipotence over individual man, and predict its eventual domination of all peoples on the Earth, they are the focus of evil in the modern world.

It was C.S. Lewis who, in his unforgettable "Screwtape Letters," wrote: "The greatest evil is not done now in those sordid 'dens of crime' that Dickens loved to paint. It is not even done in concentration camps and labor camps. In those we see its final result. But it is conceived and ordered (moved, seconded, carried and minuted) in clear, carpeted, warmed, and well-lighted offices, by quiet men with white collars and cut fingernails and smooth-shaven cheeks who do not need to raise their voice."

Well, because these "quiet men" do not "raise their voices"; because they sometimes speak in soothing tones of brotherhood and peace; because, like other dictators before them, they're always making "their final territorial demand," some would have us accept them at their word and accommodate ourselves to their aggressive impulses. But if history teaches anything, it teaches that simple-minded appeasement or wishful thinking about our adversaries is folly. It means the betrayal of our past, the squandering of our freedom.

So, I urge you to speak out against those who would place the United States in a position of military and moral inferiority. You know, I've always believed that old Screwtape reserved his best efforts for those of you in the church. So, in your discussions of the nuclear freeze proposals, I urge you to beware the temptation of pride—the temptation of blithely declaring yourselves above it all and label both sides equally at fault, to ignore the facts of history and the aggressive impulses of an evil empire, to simply call the arms race a giant misunderstanding and thereby remove yourself from the struggle between right and wrong and good and evil.

I ask you to resist the attempts of those who would have you withhold your support for our efforts, this administration's efforts, to keep America strong and free, while we negotiate real and verifiable reductions in the world's nuclear arsenals and one day, with God's help, their total elimination.

While America's military strength is important, let me add here that I've always maintained that the struggle now going on for the world will never be decided by bombs or rockets, by armies or military might. The real crisis we face today is a spiritual one; at root, it is a test of moral will and faith.

Whittaker Chambers, the man whose own religious conversion made him a witness to one of the terrible traumas of our time, the Hiss-Chambers case, wrote that the crisis of the Western World exists to the degree in which the West is indifferent to God, the degree to which it collaborates in communism's attempt to make man stand alone without God. And then he said, for Marxism-Leninism is actually the second oldest faith, first proclaimed in the Garden of Eden with the words of temptation, "Ye shall be as gods."

The Western world can answer this challenge, he wrote, "but only provided that its faith in God and the freedom He enjoins is as great as communism's faith in Man."

I believe we shall rise to the challenge. I believe that communism is another sad, bizarre chapter in human history whose last pages even now are being written. I believe this because the source of our strength in the quest for human freedom is not material, but spiritual. And because it knows no limitation, it must terrify and ultimately triumph over those who would enslave their fellow man. For in the words of Isaiah: "He give the power to the faint; and to them that have no might He increased strength But they that wait upon the Lord shall renew their strength; they shall mount up with wings as eagles; they shall run, and not be weary."

Yes, change your world. One of our Founding Fathers, Thomas Paine, said, "We have it within our power to begin the world over again." We can do it, doing together what no one church could do by itself.

REFERENCES

1. Cialdini, R. B. (2007). Influence: The Psychology of Persuasion. New York: Harper Collins.

2. (1983). "Evil Empire" Speech by President Reagan—Address to the National Association of Evangelicals. http://www.youtube.com/watch?v=FcSm-KAEFFA

3. National Centre for Public Policy Research (2011). Evil Empire Speech. http://www.nationalcenter.org/ReaganEvilEmpire1983.html

4. Fairclough, N. (2003). Analysing Discourse. London: Routledge.

5. Lakoff, G., & Johnson, M. (1980). Metaphors We Live by. Chicago: University of Chicago Press.

6. Neves, M. (1997). A Gramática Funcional. Sao Paulo: Martins Fontes.

7. Richardson, J. E. (2007). Analysing Newspapers. Houndmills: Palgrave Macmillan.

8. Adams, D. (2002). The American Peace Movements. http://www.culture-of-peace.info/apm/title-page.html

9. Vieira, A. (1993). Sermoes (Obras Completas do Padre Antonio Vieira) (Vol. 1). Porto: Artes Gráficas.

10. Wodak, R., & Meyer, M. (2001). Methods of Critical Discourse Analysis. London: Sage Publications.

Chapter 2

THE PARTICIPATION IN A RESEARCH AND STUDY GROUP: A COLLECTIVE DISCOURSE PERSPECTIVE

Maria Cristina Lima Paniago, Katia Alexandra de Godoi e Silva

Programa de Pós-graduação em Educação, Universidade Católica Dom Bosco, Campo Grande, Brasil

ABSTRACT

This research aims to analyze the collective discourse from members of a research and study group on their participation. In order to achieve this goal, we use a quantitative and qualitative approach. For the analysis of quantitative questions, we choose to use graphics in order to illustrate the opinion of the group members. In the analysis of qualitative questions, we choose to bring the members opinions in a single speech, using the Collective Subject Discourse methodology. Overall, the results point to the lack of time of the members to participate in the group and to the importance of deepening and glimpsing other studies about participation.

INTRODUCTION

The aim of this study is to analyze the collective discourse of the members of a research group, both with regards to a general review of the analyzed content, the participant researcher of the group, as well as their own group membership.

From this goal comes the following question: How does one develop participation in a research group?

To answer this question we used a quantitative and qualitative methodological approach, the latter based on the Collective Subject Discourse (CSD) (Lefevre & Lefevre, 2005, 2012) . In this study, these approaches are utilized as complementary, that is the two approaches can be analyzed in its various aspects, and they generate quantitative research questions to be qualitatively deepen, and vice versa. Besides this introduction, this study has five parts: the first, a history about the Group of Research and Studies in Educational Technology and Distance Education (GETED); the second, the research methodology; the third, the results and the fourth, the analysis of these results, which were analyzed in light of theoretical frameworks that could support the issues of the participatory process(Freire, 1991, 2003; Lave & Weger, 1991; Paniago, 2007) of the members the group; the last part deals with the conclusion of the study submitted.

THE GETED

The Conselho Nacional de Desenvolvimento Científico e Tecnológico (CNPq) registers the country's research groups in Brazil. Therefore, it maintains a Research Groups Directory with recording information, which is available for consultation, and it assigns a certification seal.

According to the summary statistics for the year 2010 area, CNPq has 27,523 research groups. The area of Education has 2,236 groups, which represent 8.1% of groups from all areas of knowledge.

The approach of this work lies in an initial study on the collective discourse from members of the Group of Research and Studies on Educational Technology and Distance Education (Grupo de Pesquisa e EstudosemTecnologia Educacional e Educação a Distância-GETED).

This group, certified by CNPq, was created in 2006 by the researchers PhD. Maria Cristina Lima Paniago and PhD. Arlinda Cantero Dorsa.

It aims to promote spaces for discussion, training, sharing, exchanging, questioning and developing practices, jobs, research, materials, concepts, experiences and networks related to the integration of Information and Communication Technologies (ICT) in educational settings, both in person and distance training and teaching practices. As well as, it provides theoretical and practical information to people interested in issues about educational technology and distance education, in the sense of promoting: literacy; training; and critical, reflective, proactive, participatory and collaborative technological literacy.

The GETED currently brings together 12 researchers (Universidade Católica Dom Bosco-UCDB; Universidade Estadual de Mato Grosso do Sul-UEMS; Universidade Federal de Mato Grosso do Sul-UFMS and Research Centre for Migration and Intercultural Relations-CEMRI, the Open University) and eight students (undergraduate, Masters and PhD) from UCDB and other institutions registered in CNPq. In addition, teachers from state and municipal network of Mato Grosso do Sul Education, all of them with a common interest in researching and studying ICT and their relationships in the teaching practice and Distance Education. These researchers and students meet in person meetings, which take place every 15 days, and at distance, through lectures using the Hangout and Ning tools. In addition, it maintains a closed group on Facebook social network.

METHODOLOGY

As previously announced, this study provides two data analysis approaches: quantitative and qualitative. One complements the other, since they are characterized as an effort to broaden our knowledge about discourse of GETED members.

Thus, for the part of this study we collected data at two different times: June 2014 and December 2014 using two instruments.

The data collection instrument used was the questionnaire. To Gil (1994), the questionnaire is the form most often used to collect data. It is a list of questions that the respondent alone answers, checking or writing the answers.

Thus, at the end of the first half of 2014, we call on GETED members to answer an online questionnaire using Google Docs tool, containing quantitative questions regarding to the contents discussed in the meetings, as well as related to the group's researchers. That same questionnaire also had qualitative character issues, in which group members completed the spaces to enrich their opinions with comments and suggestions (e.g. I could have used more if..., I had a certain resistance...; It was great... I did not like...; I really enjoyed... Missed..., I suggest...).

At the end of the second semester we also asked GETED members to answer a printed questionnaire which included three parts: quantitative, which addressed issues related to the content covered in the lectures, about the researchers and lecturers, and also about the participation of individual members and the group; qualitative, with spaces so that the members could enrich their opinions with comments and suggestions (e.g. I could have taken longer...; It was great...; I did not like...; Missed...); with suggestions and proposals about topics for lectures in 2015.

Before proceeding with the explanations about the part the questionnaires analyses, it is noteworthy to justify the amount of members who responded the questionnaires. Since this is a quantitative and qualitative study we considered significant the sampling of respondents, as both approaches contributed to the interpretation of the presented data, both in the first and the second questionnaires.

The sampling we work in this study is called "sampling by accessibility", that is, we select the elements to which we had access. According to Silva (2005), it is a type of non-probability sampling, because it has no relation to the statistics, so it is less accurate and it can be used in qualitative studies.

Thus, in the first questionnaire, out of twenty members from GETED, we have a five respondents sampling. We believe that this figure is due to the fact that not all group members have had time to respond to the online questionnaire.

In the second questionnaire, it had a sampling of ten respondents. This number is justified by the fact that not all group members were present at the last meeting in person.

Our assumption is that the absence of respondent members may be related to lack of time and the effective participation in the group.

In order to bring an analysis of the two questionnaires, we made a cut and we chose to treat the following issues: quantitative (in relation to the content addressed, the researcher and participation); qualitative (I could have used more if...; It was great ...; I did not like...; Missed... Suggestions...).

For the analysis of quantitative questions we chose to use graphics to illustrate the opinion of the members. In the analysis of qualitative issues we chose to bring the opinions of members in a single, collective discourse.

But how can we empirically generate a set of open questions into collective opinions?

To answer this question, we used the Collective Subject Discourse (CSD) methodology.

According to Lefevre & Lefevre (2005) and Lefevre & Lefevre (2012) , the CSD rescues the thought of a community preparing a speech about a certain topic.

To prepare the collective thought, it is necessary to add qualitatively equal individual thoughts, adding elements that make up "similar responses of different individuals", transforming the answers in a collective discourse with meaning.

The development of a collective discourse process with meaning is complex and, according toLefevre & Lefevre (2012) , transactions are necessary or methodological approaches:

- Key Expressions (KE)—selected portions of each statement that best describe the content of the testimony.
- Central Ideas (CI)—ideas that describe succinctly and accurately the meaning of the KE of each analyzed speech. The CI is also called Category.
- Collective Subject Discourse (CSD)—meeting in one speech-synthesis, drawn up in the first person singular, the KE which has the same CI.

To create the CSD, in this study, the KE were initially chosen from the related responses the two questionnaires (see item A); then the CI of each KE had been selected; and finally, the construction of the CI. Created the CI, the CSD was prepared for each CI, transforming the answers in a collective discourse.

For this study, we bring as CI, the qualitative parts of the introductory sentences of the questionnaire itself: I could have taken longer...; It was great...; I did not like...; Missed..., Suggestions...

Thus, in the text, it will be possible to identify the operations 2 and 3 (CI and CSD), as shown in the following results.

RESULTS

Data analysis refers to two questionnaires at the end of the 1st and 2nd semesters of 2014. Thus, this topic is organized in: questionnaire analysis of the 1st one and analysis of the questionnaire of the 2nd one.

Analysis of the Questionnaire of the First Semester

The questionnaire for the 1st one was divided into two parts: quantitative and qualitative.

In the quantitative part, the questionnaire addressed three aspects, which dealt with the content of the researchers and other general aspects of the group.

Regarding the content, the questionnaire encompassed issues: the time to read the suggested texts, the general assessment of the issues, the discussions held at the meetings, the contribution to the development of research on technology in Education and Distance Education, the contribution to research project of the group, the objectives achieved, the exposure of goals, provided bibliography and the approach of the discussed topics.

From the analysis of Figure 1, it can be seen that in general, about the time to read the discussed texts, 60% of the group members considered it-Good, 20% as-Very good and 20% as-Excellent. In an overall assessment, 20% of participants considered the content, as-Good, 20% as-Very good and 60% as-Excellent.

About the discussions held on the content worked, 20% pose as-Good, as 20%-Very good and 60% as-Excel- lent.

Regarding the contribution of research in ICT and distance education, 40% of the members regard as-Good and 60% as-Excellent. To contribute to the research of each member of the group, 60% put as-Good, 20% as- Very good and 60% as-Excellent.

On the presentation of the objectives, 25% say as-Good, 50% as-Very good, 25% as-Excellent. And if objectives were achieved, 20% of the members, pondered how-Regular, 20% like-Good, 20% as-Very good and 40% as-Excellent.

About the bibliography provided, 60% accept as-Good and 40% as-Excellent. Finally, the approach theme, 20% consider it-Good, 40% as-Very good and 40% as-Excellent.

In relation to the researchers, the questionnaire covered the following themes: the performance of researchers in general; encouragement to the participation of the group members; consistency in the development of the content; the form of ideas exposure.

Figure 2 shows that, on the performance of the researchers, 20% of the group members regard as-Good, 20% as-Very good and 40% as-Excellent.

Regarding the incentive to participate, the members responded that 20% consider it-Good, 40% as-Very good and 40% as-Excellent.

On the development of content, 20% of respondents believe it is-Good, 40% as-Very good and 40% as-Ex- cellent. And on the exposure of ideas, the members agree that 20% is-Good, 40% as-Very good and 40% as-Ex- cellent.

Regarding the participation, the questionnaire included: participation of the group members present at the meetings; time hours spent on contents; member own contribution.

Figure 3 shows the other issues addressed in the questionnaire: the participation of group members present at the meetings, the time hours spent on content and the member own contribution.

The participation of the group members present at the meeting, 40% of the members responded as-Good, 40% as-Very good and 20% as-Excellent.

The time hours spent on the content, 20% of the integrants consider it-Low, 20% as Good, 40% as-Very good and 20% as-Excellent.

About the member own contribution, 10% considered-Low, 40% as-Good and 50% as-Excellent.

In the qualitative part, as explained in the methodology used as CI, the beginning of qualitative questions of the questionnaire (I could have used more if...; It was great...; I did not like...; Missed... Suggestions...) and the CSD built in the first person singular, the opinions of group members, presented below.

I could have used more if... I made progress! But I could have used it more if I had participated in all meetings Also, if I had a little extra time to devote myself and exchange experiences.

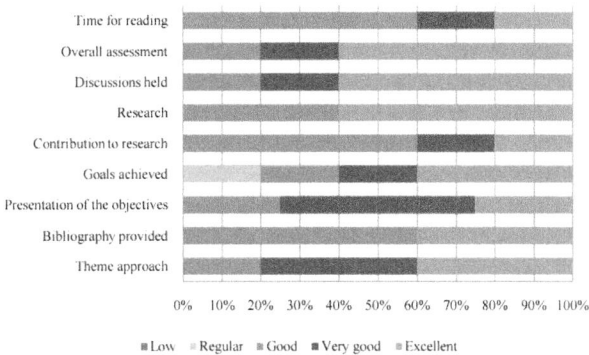

Figure 1: On the covered content.

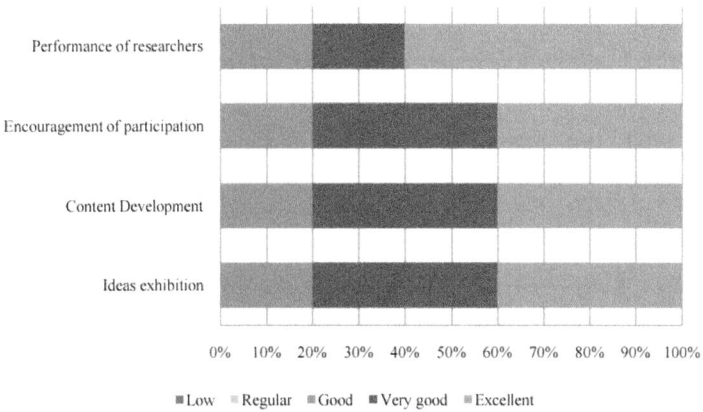

Figure 2: About the researchers.

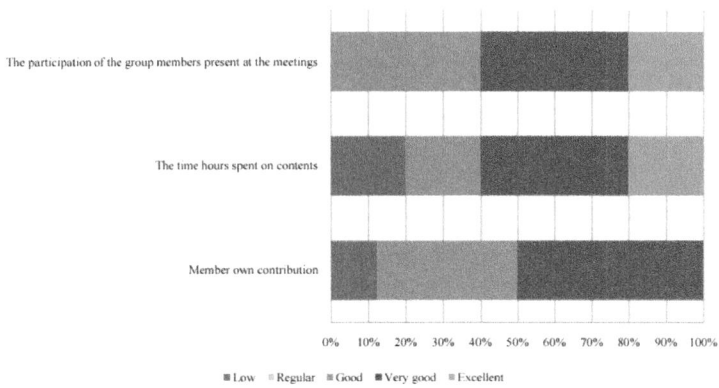

Figure 3: The participation of the group members.

It was great... Participating in the meetings, for learning and knowledge exchange.

I did not like... Not being able to participate more effectively.

Missed... Not missed anything. But I miss more communication by email and WhatsApp, because I sometimes forget to look at the Facebook group.

Suggestions... More time for studies with the group, such as readings and references on mobility and to think about new strategies of communication and information.

Analysis of the Second Questionnaire

Just as the questionnaires for the 1st half, the 2nd half of the questionnaire was divided into two parts: the quantitative and qualitative.

In the quantitative part, the questionnaire addressed three aspects, which dealt with the content of the researcher and other general aspects of the group.

Regarding the content, the questionnaire encompassed issues related to the time to read the suggested texts, the general evaluation of the issues, the discussions held at meetings, contribution to the development of research on technology in Education and on Distance Education, the contribution to the project from the member of the group, the achieved objectives, the exhibition of the goals, the provided bibliography and the themes approaches.

Figure 4 shows about the time for reading the texts, 10% of participants considered it-Low, as 40%-Very good and 50% as-Excellent.

On the overall evaluation of the subjects, 10% of participants considered it-Good, 20% as-Very good and 70% as-Excellent.

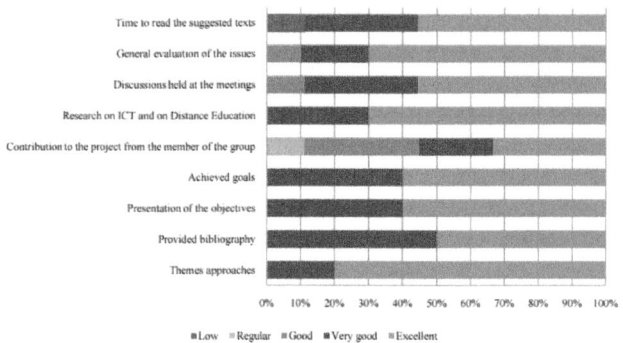

Figure 4: On the content covered.

Regarding the discussions held at the meetings, 10% of members pondered-Good, 40% as-Very good and 50% as-Excellent.

The contribution to research in the area of ICT and Distance Education, 30% of the members responded as-Very good and 70% as-Excellent. And the contribution to research from each member, 10% of the members posed as-Regular, 30% as-Good, 20% as-Very good and 40% as-Excellent.

The objectives of lectures, 40% of participants considered-Very good and 60%-Excellent. If the objectives had been achieved in the same way, 40% of participants considered-Very good and 60%-Excellent.

About the provided bibliography, 50% of members pondered-Very good and 50%-Excellent. And on the covered topics in the lectures, 20% of participants considered-Very good and 80%-Excellent.

Regarding the speakers, the questionnaire encompassed issues related to development, encouragement, consistency and exposure of ideas.

Figure 5 shows that in relation to the development of the speakers, 20% of the group members considered it-Very good and 80% as-Excellent.

Regarding the incentives, 10% of the members responded as-Good, 20% as-Very good and 70% as-Excellent.

On consistency, 100% of the members considered as-Excellent.

Regarding the own participation of the members and group participation, the survey brought the following aspects: participation of group members in the meetings; time hours spent on contents; you contributed on which way.

The graph of Figure 6 shows that in relation to the participation of group members present at the meetings, 10% of the members consider it-Good, 30% as-Very good and 60% as-Excellent.

The time hours spent on content, 10% of members rated as-Good, 70% as-Very good and 20% as-Excellent.

About their own contribution, 10% of the members regard it-Regular, 50% as-Good, 20% as-Very good and 30% as-Excellent.

In the qualitative part, as explained in the methodology used as CI, the beginning of qualitative questions of the questionnaire (I could have used more if...; It was great...; I did not like...; Missed... Suggestions...) and the DSC we built in the first person singular, the opinions of members of the group, presented below.

I could have used more if... At the times when I've been at the meetings I made progress! But I could have taken more if I had previous access to the proposed text because I could better interact and expose more my opinions. I also think that I would have taken more if it had merged lectures and studies of scientific texts in the course of the meetings.

It was great... Participation, exchanges and reflections in the meetings. Talk, discuss and meet other speakers who brought different perspectives and issues related to technology.

I did not like... From not involving myself so much this semester.

Missed... A practical part with workshops that inter-related technologies. In addition to further study, in other words, after a presentation/lecture, to have one more days to debate and reflection on the subject.

Finally, GETED members gave some suggestions about topics they would like to have in 2015. These issues are related to teacher identity in distance education, the communities of practice, digital technologies and the

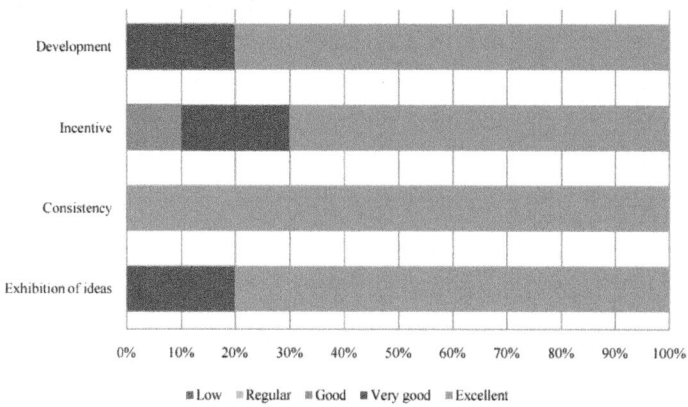

Figure 5: On the content covered.

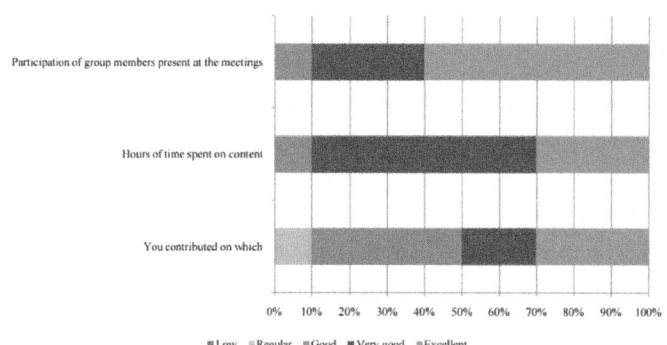

Figure 6: About participation.

students authorship, the construction of narratives, the relations between language and digital technology, qualitative analysis and interactive technologies.

ANALYSIS OF RESULTS

From the analysis of the results of the two questionnaires it can be seen, in general, that in most of these aspects (addressed content, researchers and lecturers, participation), group members considered it-Good, Very good and/ or Excellent.

In addition to this general analysis, we observed that there is a convergence point between the two questionnaires: the question of participation of GETED members.

The quantitative data showed that this participation is related to the available time to read addressed text/ content and to the own contribution of the participants in the group.

The CSD confirmed this convergence, by revealing that participants could have made more progress if they had attended all the meetings, if they had had a little too much time and greater involvement.

The word participation, according to the etymological dictionary Cunha (2010) , it means "to be part of, take part in" "to convey, inform, announce".

Bordenave (1983) explains that it is possible to "part without taking part". This is the difference between passive and active participation.

From this analysis we think that some GETED members are part of this group. However, they have not yet taken part because they believe they need more time to participate in the meetings and do the required readings, to be able to collaborate with the group.

To Freire (1991) , participation does not guarantee and cannot be reduced to a pure collaboration. It implies a "be present" and not just in it "be represented". It also implies the options, decisions and not only to make the already programmed.

Thus, Freire (2003) considers: "The participation as voice exercise, to have a voice, to interact, to decide [...]".

Lave & Weger (1991) bring another concept, from another perspective, entitled "legitimate peripheral participation". This process of participation legitimizes from the time when a member moves from the periphery of this group to its center, becoming more involved, adopting the tools and practices of the group and taking a more integral participation, which gradually increases in complexity and engagement.

From this perspective, we can also understand that although the members have not made part of the group, there may still be a process of legitimate peripheral participation in GETED.

For the peripheral participation does not mean a passive participation compared with the active participation. Legitimate peripheral participation suggests an opening, an increasing engagement process to become part of the group.

Thus, corroborating Paniago (2007), even the shares being different, the legitimate peripheral participation also has its value and can invite to reflection, as it searches learning, growth, development and a sense of involvement.

CONCLUSION

We end this brief survey aware that we bring contributions to initiate consideration about the GETED. We believe that we can offer an overview of the issues that we need to advance in the group: provide more time for reading and study, as well as encourage all members to take part in this group.

It should be noted that it is clear that the methodology with quantitative and qualitative approach should contribute to the analysis of the data.

Thus, to complete this article, we are aware that we need to deepen and envision other studies on the participation of GETED members: use other data collection instruments, such as the interview; explore other concepts emerged from the speech of the group members; study the role of the group on Facebook and Ning.

ACKNOWLEDGEMENTS

We thank the Programa Nacional de Pós-Doutora do (PNPD/Capes) for funding this study.

REFERENCES

1. Gil, A. C. (1994). Methods and Techniques of Social Research. São Paulo: Atlas.
2. Silva, M. A. F. (2005). Methods and Research Techniques. Curitiba: Ibpex.
3. Lefevre, F., & Lefevre, A. M. C. (2005). Statements and Speeches. A Proposal of Analysis in Social Research. São Paulo: Liberlivro.
4. Lefevre, F., & Lefevre, A. M. C. (2012). Social Representation Research: A Quantitative and Qualitative Approach: The Collective Subject Discourse Methodology. Brasília: Liber Livro Editora.
5. Cunha, A. G. (2010). Etymological Dictionary of the Portuguese Language. Rio de Janeiro: Lexikon Editora.

6.   Bordenave, J. D. (1983). What Is Participation? São Paulo: Editora Brasiliense.

7.   Freire, P. (1991). Education in the City. São Paulo: Editora Cortez.

8.   Freire, P. (2003). Pedagogy of the Oppressed. Rio de Janeiro: Edições Paz eTerra.

9.   Lave, J., & Weger, E. (1991). Situated Learning: Legitimate Peripheral Participation. New York: Cambridge University. http://dx.doi.org/10.1017/CBO9780511815355

10. Paniago, M. C. L. (2007). Relationships between Teachers, Students, Computer and Society in the Digital Environment, Revista Lusófona de Educação, 9, 159-171.

Chapter 3

INVESTIGATING THE ENGLISH PROFICIENCY OF LEARNERS: A CORPUS-BASED STUDY OF CONTRASTIVE DISCOURSE MARKERS IN CHINA

Guo-Ping Yang[1], Yin Chen[2]

[1]School of Foreign Languages, Beihang University, Beijing, China
[2]School of International Education and Exchange, Changzhou University, Changzhou, China

ABSTRACT

Discourse markers signal the relationship between the neighboring sentences. The present comparative study investigates the use of Contrastive Discourse Markers between Chinese English learners and native speakers based on corpus data. Special attention is allocated to but and however, since these two small words are the most popular discourse markers in Chinese English Learners and Native Speakers. Quantitative and qualitative analyses indicate that both groups prefer to employ discourse markers like but, although, (even) though, however, etc. when signaling a contrastive relationship between S1 and S2, though they have different priorities in different contextual situation; besides, but is overused significantly by Chinese English Learners to signal a contrastive relationship rather than add further information in context; lastly, Chinese English Learner usually employs however at the beginning of the sentence, while native speakers put it both at the beginning or middle of the sentences, which both signal the relationship between topics and messages. The findings also suggest that more detailed instructions should be delivered on the procedural meanings and syntactical positions of Contrastive Discourse Markers used in context.

INTRODUCTION

Discourse markers have prevailed in our language expression, which undertake the function of promoting the expression of communicative intent, and meanwhile facilitate the message interpretation of receivers. In this sense, discourse markers are regarded as a kind of metalanguage which could reflect speaker's metapragmatic awareness (Wu & Yu, 2003) and major difference between the second language learners and native speakers has to do with the frequency of individual markers (Aijmer, 2004) . It has already also been proved that the considerable underuse in the non-native group of "small words" (especially among the less nature learners) was correlated with their lack of fluency (Hasselgren, 2002) . As a matter of fact, a lot of existing researches on the second language acquisition have made kinds of comparisons between native and non-native speaker, and one of the most striking discoveries is that if an second language speaker wants to sound more like a native speaker, one way is to adopt the "conventional expressions" (e.g. Discourse Markers) used by native speakers in the native community (Liao, 2009) .

For this reason, a contrastive study between interlanguage and target language is of great significance to the acquisition of English learners in China, due to the pervasive inefficiency of English learning that a considerable gap exists in language proficiency between Chinese English learners and native speakers though they have made great efforts on language learning when they are in school. Furthermore, the findings of this contrastive study could also offer some useful pedagogical implications to language teachers and meanwhile, shed light on the essence of language learning and teaching so as to improve the efficiency of teaching process as well as the teaching effect in classroom. To sum up, the comparison involved in this study could reveal the significant differences between the interlanguage and target language and finally facilitate the understanding of language macroscopically.

Hot topic as it is, it is really difficult to work out a standard definition of discourse marker, or it is even uncertain whether we should call those small words discourse makers, which functions as a marker in discourse, as more than 27 definitions could be found in piles of documents, such as preface (Stubbs, 1983) , cue word (Rouchota, 1996) , discourse connective (Blakemore, 1987, 1992) , conversational routines (Aijmer, 1996) , pragmatic formatives/ markers (Fraser, 1985, 1996) , etc. Despite the fact that the connotation and denotation of those terminologies vary or overlap in degree, due to the distinct research approaches and purposes, more and more scholars have accepted the name of discourse marker proposed by Schifrin, who define discourse markers as sequentially dependent elements which bracket units of talk (Schiffrin, 1987) . It is generally accepted that discourse marker is a category of function words, which includes members of a number of different word classes, including adverbs, connectors, parenthetical expression, as well as particles (Risselada & Spooren, 1998), which shares a common feature that they do not convey propositional meaning but fulfill more procedural functions during the process of meaning expression and interpretation.

Theoretical Framework of Discourse Marker

Despite the fact that there is no consensus on the definition of discourse marker, the current studies on this topic mainly fall into three categories, namely, Coherence-based Framework(Schiffrin, 1987) , Relevance-based Framework (Blakemore, 1987, 1992, 2002) , as well as Syntactic/Pragmatic-based Framework (Fraser, 1985, 1996, 1999, 2006) . Schiffrin's study originates from the encoding and decoding of message and maintains that discourse markers could facilitate the interpretation of coherence relations between particular units and other surrounding units or communicative situations and they function as contextual coordinators which "indexes an utterance to the local contexts in which utterances are produced and in which they are to be interpreted" (Schiffrin, 1987: p. 326) . On the other hand, Blakemore and Fraser have established their studies based on relevance theory and syntactic pragmatic function respectively. The former believes that the major role of discourse markers is to constrain the interpretation of two utterances in context, which could alternatively derive a contextual implication, strengthen an existing assumption, or contradict an existing assumption (Blakemore, 1992) . Originating from the speech act theory, Fraser proposes that utterance is a reflection of the speakers' attitude toward communication, and an utterance is usually composed of a proposition and some lexical words which are used to signal the speaker's communicative intent. As the concept of lexical word narrowed down, the terminology is also narrowed down through the whole research process from Pragmatic Formative (Fraser, 1985) to Pragmatic Marker (Fraser, 1996) , and finally discourse marker (Fraser, 1999, 2006) . In spite of these different understandings to discourse marker, none of the three scholars listed above deny the importance as well as the function of discourse marker in meaning expression and interpretation, which lay a foundation to the present study.

Working Definition of Discourse Marker in Present Study

Since this study focuses on the signaling function of contrast between different propositions, it adopts the definition of Fraser (2006) as a working definition, namely, for a sequence of discourse segments S1-S2, each of which encodes a complete message, a lexical expression (LE doesn't contain any propositional meaning) functions as a discourse marker if, when it occurs in S2-initial position (S1-LE+S2), LE signals that a semantic relationship holds between S2 and S1 which is one of: a. elaboration; b. contrast; c. inference; d. temporality (Fraser, 2006) . Corresponding to the four different semantic relationships between S1 and S2, Fraser (2006) classified discourse markers into four distinct groups, including Elaborative Discourse Markers, Contrastive Discourse Markers, Inferential Discourse Markers, as well as Temporal Discourse Markers. This working definition reveals the true nature of discourse marker, the feature of non-proposition, and its signaling functions between two propositions, which is the main concern of present study.

Despite the fact that a significant number of previous efforts have been drawn to the theoretical discussion on the essence of discourse marker during the past decades, such as Quirk (1985), Redeker (1990), Traugott (1995), Schourup (1999), Fraser (2006) , etc., the descriptive studies on discourse markers are still comparatively limited. This paper will focus on the use of Contrastive Discourse Markers (hereafter CDM for short), a sub-class of discourse marker between Chinese English Speakers and Native English Speakers based on Corpora. Considering the uncertainty of contrast in literature, it is unsurprising that no agreement was reached before on the member of CDMs. Since the theoretical discussion of CDM is not involved in present study, this paper will only concentrate on the discourse markers that generally fall into the concept of Contrastive. Part of the frequently- used Contrastive Discourse Marker based on our intuition listed below are the major concern in present study just because it is really a useful and ordinary method in daily utterances, debates, as well as new message introduction, since CDM signals that the explicit interpretation of S2 contrasts with an interpretation of S1. The contrast included here is either between the two literally expressed propositions or between implications or between an implication and a literally expressed proposition (Feng, 2008) .but, however, (even) though, although, on the other hand, on the contrary, whereas, nonetheless, even so, alternatively, conversely, notwithstanding

RESEARCH QUESTIONS

The present study presupposes that Chinese English learners and native speakers differ in speaking styles with different preferences to discourse markers when signaling contrastive relationships. Compared with native speakers, Chinese English learners may overuse or underuse certain CDMs in expression, which makes them sound less native than native speakers even though they are proficient English users, since discourse markers are difficult for second language learners to acquire without any exposure to the target language environment. Therefore, the purpose of this study was to investigate the preference or priority to different CDMs in use between two different ethnic groups, and specifically, the following questions were addressed:

- Whether particular CDMs will take priority in the choice of different group speakers?
- Do Chinese English learners overuse or underuse one or two CDMs compared to native speakers?
- Do Chinese English learners use CDMs for the same purpose as native speakers? Is there any difference on the procedural functions of CDMs in context when a same CDM is employed in the use of two different groups?
- Do they use CDMs at the same syntactical position in the sentence? Is there any preference?

RESEARCH METHODOLOGY

The material employed in this study come from CLEC (Chinese Learner English Corpus) and FLOB (Freiburg- LOB Corpus of British English), which both covers more than a million words. The language material is pro- cessed through Wordsmith 4.0 through the function of Wordlist and Concordance.

The frequency of each CDM listed above was retrieved respectively in the two corpora to find which CDMs were comparatively more significant than others in the data in order to study the preference of different ethnic groups in language use. Two typical discourse markers were selected from the sentences retrieved in the two corpora as examples to analyze their main functions as well as their syntactical positions in the sentences of corpora, so that a clear comparison could be made on the usage of these two CDMs between Chinese English Learners and native speakers.

DATA AND FINDINGS

The concern of the whole comparative study on CDM in this paper could be summarized into one question— preference, including the preference to the choice of CDMs in the surface level when signaling the contrastive relationship between two neighboring sentences, and the preference to the position of a CDM in the surface level when it is employed in the text, as well as the preference to the procedural function of a certain marker in the deep level in utterance. In other words, this study was committed to the following question: to a certain discourse slot when indicating a contrastive relationship, which CDM should be chosen, for what purpose and where it should be put.

Preference Analysis

Twelve CDMs listed above in all are examined during the study. The frequency of each in CLEC and FLOB are recorded and the log-likelihood are calculated during the process to test the significance of each CDM in the study, the result of which are displayed together in the Table 1 so that we can detect the preference of each ethnic group at a glance.

The CDMs are arranged in a decreasing order of frequency based on the data collected from Chinese English learners, namely, but, however, (even) though, although, on the other hand, on the contrary, whereas, nonetheless, even so, alternatively, conversely, notwithstanding, and contrariwise, etc., which form a sharp contrast with its corresponding data from FLOB. The statistics have also offered another powerful circumstantial evidence to the presupposition we have mentioned above that both the Chinese English learners and native speakers differ in preference among tremendous CDMs when signaling contrastive relationships.

As to the frequency of each CDM in different group of speakers, the study reveals a similar tendency of preference on the whole in both groups when signaling contrastive relationships and the option of CDM is generally concentrated on several choices, though the frequency of each varies, if those CDMs whose frequency is less than 10 times in the corpus statistics are ignored. As a matter of fact, the CDMs tested in the study could be classed into three groups based on their frequency in both corpora: but comes first, while however, although, (even) though come as the second group, and on the other hand, on the contrary and whereas as the third group (see Table 1). Besides, the choice of CDMs to Chinese English learners are comparatively limited, as even so and nonetheless lose their traces in CLEC, even though they are also not very popular among native speakers. For this reason, the distribution of each CDM in FLOB is more reasonable than CLEC and the choice of native speakers when signaling contrastive relationship is much more diversified than Chinese English Learners though the frequency of each word varies. stands for the significance of statistics; [#] means null or the statistics here is invalid or meaningless

Eight CDMs in twelve in the study have significantly differences between two corpora. Particularly, in terms of log-likelihood ratio, Chinese English learners prefer to but, however, on the other hand, and on the contrary, while native speakers are more inclined to use (even) though, although, notwithstanding as well as alternatively. In addition, considering capacity proportion, the CDM however is much more popular among native speakers, though the absolute figure of however in CLEC outweighed in FLOB. Despite the differences, these CDMs constitute a regular corpus of signaling contrastive relationships between S1 and S2, and different speakers could choose what they need for a certain discourse slot based on the different education they received or the learning environment.

Table 1: Frequency of CDMs

CDM	Freq. in CLEC	Freq. in FLOB	Log-likelihood	Sig. ($p < 0.05$)		
But	3327	1548	847.01	0.000	***	+
However	592	566	5.77	0.016	*	+
(Even) Though	333	540	31.65	0.000	***	-
Although	428	597	14.10	0.000	***	-
On the other hand	72	54	4.61	0.032	*	+
On the contrary	31	7	18.77	0.000	***	+
Whereas	17	15	0.39	0.531		+
Conversely	4	11	2.76	0.097		-
Notwithstanding	2	9	4.17	0.041	*	-
Alternatively	1	13	11.08	0.001	***	-
Nonetheless	0	9	#NUM!	#NUM!	###	-
Even so	0	16	#NUM!	#NUM!	###	-

*stands for the significance of statistics; # means null or the statistics here is invalid or meaningless

Furthermore, if we reorder the CDMs above based on the frequency, the significant differences between these two groups will stand out (See Table 2) that both groups would give first priority to but, although, (even) though, however, etc. when signaling relationships between S1 and S2. Actually, the four CDMs outweigh all the other CDMs in the two different groups of English speakers. This conclusion coincides with the division of cancellative discourse markers in Bell (1998)who classified but, however, and though as primary core cancellatives. Besides, the marker but is overused by Chinese English Learners, which makes a sharp contrast with the use of the other three, due to a negative transfer of Chinese, since it is really a first choice to most Chinese speaker when they want to deliver some negative ideas in their mother tongue. It has also been proved byWang & Zhu (2005) , who focuses on the features of discourse marker in oral English of Chinese Speaker. Comparatively speaking, though the native speakers' choices are diversified, including but, however, (even) though, although, etc. the word but in FLOB is not employed as frequently as it in CLEC, and the frequency of the latter three words listed when added together equals to that of but in native speakers.

Last but not least, the CDMs involved in this study mainly focus on the semantic meaning CONSTRAST, including a contrast of the explicit message of S2 with the explicit or implicit message of S1, or an implication between the two sentences that the message conveyed by S1 is false, while S2 is correct. In spite of similar functions with the core meaning of contrast, the procedural meanings of those CDMs vary in sentences, which exert restrictions on the specific relationships between S1 and S2. It is generally accepted that those CDMs with least restrictions on relationships would usually be recruited in talks unless a particular requirement cannot be fulfilled. For this reason, the frequency of each CDM in corpora (See Table 2) could also be taken as a simple

Table 2: Contrast on the Frequency of CDM in Corpora

Frequency	CLEC	FLOB
3000 - 4000	But	
2000 - 3000		
1000 - 2000		But
500 - 1000	However	Although
		However
		Even though
400 - 500	Although	
300 - 400	Even though	
200 - 300		
100 - 200		
50 - 100	On the other hand	On the other hand
0 - 50	On the Contrary	
	Whereas	Even so
	Conversely	Whereas
	Notwithstanding	Alternatively
	Alternatively	Conversely
		Notwithstanding
		Alternatively

reflection on the restriction of each CDM. The CDM frequently used is less restrictive than those infrequently used. Take but and however for example, the popularity of but in both corpora results from the least restrictions it imposes than however on the relationship between S1 and S2 which is contrasted, as "but seems to identify a matter-of-fact denial, while however conveys a kind of reluctance" (Fraser & Malamud-Makowski, 1996) .

Procedural Meaning and Syntactic Position: But & However

Besides the frequency of discourse markers discussed above, the procedural meaning and syntactical position of discourse markers are another two inevitable questions, since they all work together to decide whether the sentences sounds natural or not.

In order to clarify the significant differences between Chinese English learners and native speakers, two typical CDMs but and however (600 items in all on but and however both from CLEC and FLOB selected respectively at random) are examined in this study, despite that they both signal a general relationship of contrast. However, the following two cases of but and however will not be taken into consideration of this study: "but" cannot be classified as CDM, when it means "except", thus, the phrases, such as nothing but..., have no choice but..., but to do something..., but for..., etc. are excluded from this study; "however" cannot be classified as CDM, when it is used before an adjective or adverb to emphasize that the degree or extent of something cannot change a situation or to indicate that the figure you have just mentioned may not be accurate, etc.

Discourse markers evolved from non-discourse marker sources through historical process of grammaticalization which alter their original meaning (Schourup, 1999). The non-defining feature of any discourse marker's semantic meaning will be eliminated during the process of grammaticalization until to the core meaning—an invariant semantic content of each marker. It is generally accepted that every discourse marker has only one vague core meaning, whose interpretation is in connection with the entire contextual meaning conveyed by an utterance in which a discourse marker appears and the process of meaning expression as well as utterance interpretation will contribute to the core meaning of proposed discourse marker. In this sense, discourse markers are multi-functional with a stable core function or core pragmatic function and those instantiations outside the core to be peripheral (Bell, 1998). As a matter of fact, many existing studies have argued that the general procedural meaning could be implemented in different ways to derive these meaning. For instance, Hussein (2008) summarized four different meaning encoded under the umbrella of but, including a denial-of-expectation meaning between the two conjuncts it links (Blakemore, 1987, 2002), a simple contrast of the relation between the two conjuncts (Lakoff, 1971), a correct placement for the assumption given in the first clause(Anscombre & Ducrot, 1977), and a return to the main topic of discourse. The situation goes the same to the study of however, though Fraser (1997) and Fraser and Malamud-Makowski (1996)believes however differs from but slightly.

In this study, four types of procedural meaning of but are collected from the samples of corpora (see Table 3), namely, contrasting with what you have just said, adding to what you have just said or something further in a discussion or returning to the subject, making an excuse or apologized for what you are just about to say. Two types of procedural meaning of however are collected likewise, namely, contradicting with the former message, contradicting with something said previously. It is revealed that the first two procedural meaning of but take up a dominant role both in CLEC and FLOB,

Table 3: Procedural Meaning of But and However

		But (300)				However (300)	
		CLEC	FLOB			CLEC	FLOB
Procedural meaning (Introduce something which...)	Contrasts with former message	50.67%	38.67%	Procedural meaning (Introduce something which...)	Contrasts with former message	88.67%	85.33%
	Adds further information	38.67%	48.67%		Contradicts with something said previously	12.00%	14.67%
	Returns to the subject	9.33%	12.00%				
	Make an excuse or apologize	1.33%	2.00%				

however, the importance of each procedural meaning varies slightly in Chinese English Learners and Native Speakers (see Table 3). Chinese Learners are accustomed to giving priority to but when they intend to contrast the new message of S2 with the former message from S1 (50.67%) (See Table 4), on the contrary, native speakers prefer to employ but when introducing further information (48.67%) (See Table 5). Furthermore, both Chinese learners and native speakers have got similar understanding on the procedural meaning of however, as the function of contrasting with former message outweighs the function of contradicts with something said previously in both groups.

As a matter of fact, the correct use of discourse markers involves a comprehensive understanding to the procedural functions in accordance with native speakers. The statistics in this study indicates that a natural language cannot be acquired without a subtle understanding of the core procedural meaning of discourse markers in target language.

Besides procedural meaning of CDM, syntactical position is another important factor that determines whether the language of English learner sounds nature or not. Fraser (1997) has presented a standard syntactical position of discourse marker, namely a declarative sentence, then a Discourse Marker, followed by a second declarative sentence, and summarized three types of syntactical positions of discourse markers in utterance, i.e. [S1, DM + S2], [S1. DM + S2], and [DM + S1, S2].Since it is not a theoretical discussion on discourse marker, the study here will not involve the cases of empty S1 or, even sometimes, empty S1 and S2 demonstrated in Fraser (2001) . As to the syntactical position of but, it is revealed that a large majority of both groups prefer to the structure of [S1, DM + S2], while it differs in the case of however (see Table 6 andTable 7). The structural distribution of [S1, DM + S2] and [S1. DM, + S2] in the frequency of however equals nearly in FLOB though the first structure gets a little advantage, on the contrary, the latter structure has an overwhelming superiority than the former one in Chinese English, which results from a strong negative transfer of Chinese structure suiran (although)… danshi (but)… and a lack of language flexibility after a long-term disciplined and rigid language training in China. It is not surprising that the structure of [DM + S2, S1] in but and the structure of [S1 + S2, DM] in however disappear in the samples checked here, because it does not conform to the speaking style of both groups. In general,

Table 4: but in CLEC for contrasting

success of the Three Musketeers lies in many sides, **but** I think the most important one is that

him, nearly jokingly. He was not that nervous, **but** was still embarrassed to becaught red-handed.

robot to do the job, I must say "congratulations", **but** now I can been no more the crazy noise.

also cook many good things for the ghosts to "eat", **but** in fact they eat the food all by themselves!

from shops. The Dragon Boat Festival is traditional, **but** it is full of lives. It will be handed down from

Tsinghua University have some collective characters, **but** everyone of them is unique.

Trust is often thought to be similar with "to believe", **but** in fact it's more than that.

that there are all kinds of fake commodities around us, **but** it is the fact. More and more people have

is lower than good one, and you know it is not smart, **but** you also buy it, because of its prize.

be seen that someone is too eager to do things ahead, **but** they fail in the end. Why does this happen?

Table 5: but in FLOB for adding information

car?" Sally asked suddenly. It was a car, **but** it was going in the wrong direction.

Original by the look of it, and so were the banisters, **but** someone had painted them a kind of snot green.

I smile at him and say I don't know, **but** it Really is Appalling'." But what was

see only in the tabloids' own opinion columns, **but** it's a view I've heard from a number of senior

service is going to be cut is the only news I have, **but** it won't affect you rich men in your big cars."

with devastating effect. They adored each other, **but** the odd thing was that, as Thomas aged with

not how you want to play then it's all right with me. **But** make no mistake, Marie, we belong together,

She wondered why more people weren't like him, **but**, there again, it might be difficult if everyone

briefly in the reflected lights on the dashboard. "**But** then, neither are a lot of the things I like

Table 6: Syntactical position of but and however

		but (300)				however (300)	
		CLEC	FLOB			CLEC	FLOB
	S1, DM + S2	22.00%	26.67%		S1, DM, + S2	8.667%	54.667%
Position	S1, DM + S2	78.00%	73.33%	Position	S1, DM, + S2	91.333%	45.333%
	DM + S2, S1	0.000%	0.000%		S1 + S2, DM	0.000%	0.000%

Table 7: Syntactic Structure of but and however

phone call from the President of America. "**But** you're not to tell anyone", I told her, "because I

decent music" can put you right off your groove. **But** of course an e-acutelitist door policy is supposed

bimbettes were keen on getting in on all this. **But** they were experiencing difficulties in persuading

when a person needsome pills for his sick, **but** he bought fake ones. His illness would

We may think they are common and indifferent, **but** when we buy something fake or of bad quality

in need of a medicine which to heal his sick, **but** he bought a fake medicine, so after he eating the

to expect a little romance between the two. **However**, it wasn't to be. They spent long

was certainly a cut above the Perkins family. **However,** Mrs Saunders had recently realised that her

puresnow, there are still crime, famine and war. **However,** human beings are making progress in both

except trying not to show her underwear. This bit, **however,** was going to be tricky. She bent slowly

that by a mere youth. Caution whispered to him, **however,** that the young man was nobly born,

Time goes on its way, we only use time, **however,** we don't create it. we must make it good us

Chinese English learners have a better mastery of the structure of but than that of however, which makes them sounds more natural.

Summary of Findings

The comparative study conducted here focuses on the preferences of CDMs in different language groups as well as their language habits on the syntactical position and procedural meaning of CDMs used. Special attention was allocated to but and however, since these two small words are more popular discourse markers in Chinese English Learners and Native Speakers respectively. The above analysis indicated that both groups similarly showed a strong inclination on the choice of CDMs, which concentrated on but, however, although, (even) though, despite the different frequent occurrences of each word resulted from the impact of different meta-awareness.

Besides, significant differences were found through the statistics comparisons that the proficiency of Chinese English learners still needs improving. To begin with, in comparison with the diversified selection of CDMs when signaling contrastive relationship, But is overused excessively by Chinese English Learners. The quantitative analysis reveals that superordinate termsare employed more frequently by English learners to cover the hyponymys within the same semantic meaning categories, due to a lack of knowledgeon the subtle differences of CDMs.

Furthermore, differences on the understanding of pragmatic functions of CDMs between interlanguage and target language are also reflected from the statistical differences on the procedural meanings between two groups, despite the high-frequent occurrence of but in CLEC. Considering the fact that the metapragmatic awareness of speakers, which could predict academic achievement as a kind of cognitive ability (Phillipson & Phillipson, 2012) are embodied in the selection of procedural meaning of CDMs, the data differences in comparison reflect a gap on the understanding of CDM which impedes the acquisition of native language.

Last but not least, an appropriate syntactical position of CDM symbolizes a correct acquisition of target languages in form and an observance of language rule will make the interlanguage sound more natural. Chinese English Learner usually employs however at the beginning of the sentence to contrast or contradict with former information, while native speakers put it both at the beginning or middle of the sentences or sometimes at the end of the sentence, even though no sample is selected due to a random sampling, which is used to signal both the relationship between topics and messages.

In short, the performance of language ability is high-positively correlated with the employment of DM, as Wei (2011) indicates that advanced students were generally more active than intermediate students in using markers.

CONCLUSIONS

Discourse markers are employed in communication to build discourse coherences, constrain the relationships between two neighboring sentences and facilitate the understanding of utterances. Many existing theoretical and empirical investigations on discourse marker have already revealed that discourse markers is one of the language devices used to signal the metapragmatic awareness of speakers that reflects a regulation on awareness of language, so that the utterance changes as the meta-awareness varies. For this reason, a corpus-based cross-linguis- tic study on CDM could enable us to detect the differences of different language speakers when speaking, foster a correct understanding and use of CDM in target language, and finally improve the second language proficiency of learners.

This study added empirical evidence both to the improvement of foreign language teaching as well as learning. A great significance should be attached to different types of discourse markers, including CDMs during the process of English learning and teaching. However, it should be noted that Chinese English learners is characterized with the features of interlanguage, since several CDMs, but in particular, are overused in expression. Thus, comprehensive instructions should be given to Chinese English learners so as to broaden the scope of discourse markers as well as the procedural functions and syntactical position of each discourse marker in target language. Only in this way, the utterances produced could sound more natural to native speakers.

Consequently, despite the fact that empirical study has offered a new insight into discourse markers, it was by no means intended to provide final answers to the questions addressed before, due to the random sampling in the research. In addition, the correlation between procedural meaning and syntactical position of CDMs is also not considered in the study. Therefore, the findings of this tentative empirical study are expected to be supplemented with a large scale of experimental data in the forthcoming days.

Endnote

Here DM refers to Discourse Marker. S1/S2 in this study includes not only declarative sentences but also interrogative sentences as well as imperative sentences as long as they can work together to signal the contrastive relationship.

REFERENCES

1.   Aijmer, K. (1996). Conversational Routines in English: Convention and Creativity. London, New York: Longman.

2.   Aijmer, K. (2004). Pragmatic Markers in Spoken Interlanguage. Nordic Journal of English Studies, 3, 173-190.

3.   Anscombre, C., & Ducrot, O. (1977). Deuxmais en Francais. Lingua, 43, 23-40.http://dx.doi.org/10.1016/0024-3841(77)90046-8

4.   Bell, D. M. (1998). Cancellative Discourse Markers: A Core/Periphery Approach. Pragmatics, 8, 515-541. http://dx.doi.org/10.1075/prag.8.4.03bel

5.   Blakemore, D. (1987). Semantic Constraints on Relevance. Oxford: Blackwell.

6.   Blakemore, D. (1992). Understanding Utterances. Oxford: Blackwell.

7.   Blakemore, D. (2002). Relevance and Linguistic Meaning: The Semantics and Pragmatics of Discourse Markers. Cambridge: Cambridge University Press.http://dx.doi.org/10.1017/CBO9780511486456

8.   Feng, G. W. (2008). Pragmatic Markers in Chinese. Journal of Pragmatics, 40, 1687-1718.http://dx.doi.org/10.1016/j.pragma.2008.05.012

9.   Fraser, B. (1985). Pragmatic Formatives. In J. Verschueren, & M. Bertuccelli-Papi (Eds.), The Pragmatic Perspective (pp. 179-194). Amsterdam: Benjamins

10.   Fraser, B. (1996). Pragmatic Markers. Pragmatics, 6, 167-190.http://dx.doi.org/10.1075/prag.6.2.03fra

11.   Fraser, B. (1997). Contrastive Discourse Marker in English. In Y. Ziv, &

A. Jucker (Eds.), Pragmatics and Beyond: Discourse Markers (pp. 301-326). Amsterdam: Benjamins.

12. Fraser, B. (1999). What Are Discourse Markers? Journal of Pragmatics, 31, 931-952.http://dx.doi.org/10.1016/S0378-2166(98)00101-5

13. Fraser, B. (2001). The Case of the Empty S1. Journal of Pragmatics, 33, 1625-1630.http://dx.doi.org/10.1016/S0378-2166(01)00024-8

14. Fraser, B. (2006). Toward a Theory of Discourse Markers. In F. Kerstin (Ed.), Approaches to Discourse Particles (pp. 189- 204). Amsterdam: Elsevier.

15. Fraser, B., & Malamud-Makowski, M. (1996). English and Spanish Contrastive Discourse Markers. Language Science, 18, 863-881. http://dx.doi.org/10.1016/S0388-0001(96)00052-6

16. Hasselgren, A. (2002). Learner Corpora and Language Testing: Small Words as Markers of Learner Fluency. In S. Granger, J. Hung, & S. Petch-Tyson (Eds.), Computer-Learner Corpora, Second Language Acquisition, and Foreign Language Teaching (pp. 143-173). Philadelphia, PA: John Benjamins.

17. Hussein, M. (2008). The Discourse Markers "But" in English and Standard Arabic: One Procedure and Different Implementations.http://semarch.linguistics.fas.nyu.edu/Archive/TAyOTBkM/But%20as%20a%20General%20Procedure.pdf

18. Lakoff, G. (1971). The Role of Deduction in Grammar. In J. Fillmore, & D. T. Langendoen (Eds.), Studies in Linguistic Semantics (pp. 62-70). New York: Holt, Rinehart and Winston.

19. Liao, S. (2009). Variation in the Use of Discourse Markers by Chinese Teaching Assistants in the US. Journal of Pragmatics, 41, 1313-1328. http://dx.doi.org/10.1016/j.pragma.2008.09.026

20. Phillipson, S., & Phillipson, S. N. (2012). Children's Cognitive Ability and Their Academic Achievement: The Mediation Effects of Parental Expectations. Asian Pacific Education Review, 133, 495-508. http://dx.doi.org/10.1007/s12564-011-9198-1

21. Quirk, R. (1985). A Comprehensive Grammar of the English Language. London and New York: Longman.

22. Rouchota, V. (1996). Discourse Connectives: What Do They Link? UCL Working Papers in Linguistics, 8, 1-15.

23. Redeker, G. (1990). Ideational and Pragmatic Markers of Discourse Structure. Journal of Pragmatics, 143, 367-381. http://dx.doi.org/10.1016/0378-2166(90)90095-U

24. Schiffrin, D. (1987). Discourse Markers. New York: Cambridge University Press.http://dx.doi.org/10.1017/CBO9780511611841

25. Schourup, L. (1999). Discourse Markers. Lingua, 107, 227-265.http://dx.doi.org/10.1016/S0024-3841(96)90026-1

26. Stubbs, M. (1983). Discourse Analysis: The Sociolinguistic Analysis of Natural Language. Chicago, IL: The University of Chicago Press.

27. Traugott, C. (1995). The Role of the Development of Discourse Makers in a Theory of Grammaticalization. Resource Document, Paper Presented at ICHL XII.http://www.wata.cc/forums/uploaded/136_1165014660.pdf

28. Wang, L. F., & Zhu, J. H. (2005). A Study on the Use of Discourse Markers in Chinese Students' Oral English. Foreign Languages Research, 3, 40-48.

29. Wei, M. (2011). Investigating the Oral Proficiency of English Learners in China: A Comparative Study of the Use of Pragmatic Markers. Journal of Pragmatics, 43, 3455-3472. http://dx.doi.org/10.1016/j.pragma.2011.07.014

30. Wu, Y. X., & Yu, G. D. (2003). Metapragmatic Analysis of Discourse Marker. Foreign Languages Education, 4, 16-19.

Chapter 4

THE POLITICS OF MENTAL ILLNESS AND INVOLVEMENT—A DISCOURSE ANALYSIS OF DANISH ANTI-STIGMA AND SOCIAL INCLUSION CAMPAIGNS

Jeppe Oute[1], Lotte Huniche[2], Connie T. Nielsen[3], Anders Petersen[4]

[1]Department of Psychology and Behavioural Sciences, Centre for Alcohol and Drug Research, Aarhus University, Aarhus, Denmark

[2]User Perspectives, Institute of Public Health, University of Southern Denmark, Odense, Denmark

[3]Psychiatric Department Kolding-Vejle, Region of Southern Denmark, Denmark

[4]Department of Sociology and Social Work, Aalborg University, Aalborg, Denmark

ABSTRACT

The present study is a part of a broader multisited field study on involvement of relatives in Danish psychiatry. The article aims to elucidate which political classifications of normality and mental illness that are displayed in two health political campaigns regarding anti-stigmatization and social inclusion and how such classifications co-constitute the subjectivity of individuals suffering from mental illness and their relatives. Drawing on a discourse theoretical perspective laid out by political theorists Laclau and Mouffe, we analyze how the campaigns bring into effect a weak and ineffective subject of deviance and how it is constituted by a subject of normality characterized by opposing traits. The article takes up the discussion of how the campaigns' articulations of the subjects of normality and deviance are imbedded in a hegemonic discourse of neoliberalism and individualism that asserts involvement as an expanded division of responsibility for the identification, classification and regulation of mentally ill subjects between public and private spheres of the Danish welfare state.

INTRODUCTION

This analysis investigates issues of classification and constitution of subjectivity in materials from two Danish anti-stigma and social inclusion campaigns regarding mental illness and involvement; respectively called "En af Os" and "PsykiskSårbar" which translate into "One of Us" (One of Us, 2014) and "Mentally Vulnerable" (The Social Network, 2014) . The article emerges from a broader, multisited field study, the aim of which is to shed light on the constitutive conditions for, and consequences of, involvement of relatives in psychiatric treatment and rehabilitation. In line with a multisited research strategy initially laid out by anthropologist Marcus (Marcus, 1998) and further developed by anthropologists Shore and Wright (Shore, Wright, & Però, 2011) , the main author (JO) traced discursive articulations and metaphors of mental illness and measures and ideals for involvement that connected three types of empirical sites across the Danish psychiatric system. Specifically, signs of weakness and deficits, and symbols of responsibility and effectiveness that constituted involvement were traced from the families' daily lives into the professional practices at two psychiatric hospitals and, further, to the websites of several non-governmental organizations (NGOs) and welfare state organizations amongst which a large body of policies were collected. As the campaign materials both reflected the official discourse of the two psychiatric hospitals' and the official engagements in involvement of the Danish welfare state, the campaign materials were specifically singled out for this investigation in order to elucidate the overall health political conditions for involvement and social inclusion in the psychiatric field.

Involvement campaigns form an important part of overarching political strategies for the future development of the psychiatric system and health care practice in Denmark (Danske Regioner [trans. Danish Regions], 2009) . According to the Governmental Committee on the future organization of Danish psychiatry (GCP), they reflect current developments in the national and regional prevention and treatment policy aimed at the recovery of individuals suffering from mental illness (Udvalget [trans. The Governmental Committee on the future organization of Danish psychiatry (GCP)], 2013) . According to Shore and Wright, such political campaigns may work as powerful instruments for social change that governments and NGOs use to constitute the identification, classi- fication and regulation of the subjects they seek to govern (Shore et al., 2011). As a pivotal element in these new health political developments in Danish psychiatry, the campaigns can be seen as an organizing principle that provides specific ways of conceptualizing social relations between groups of citizens, such as individuals suffering from mental illness, their relatives and health care professionals (Shore et al., 2011) . However, a policy is not necessarily considered as external, or constraining forces, and nor are they confined to texts. Instead, we will use the following understanding of policy: "As a lens through which to study processes of political transformation, the field of research becomes not a particular people or organization—far less a reified policy itself—but a 'social and political space articulated through relations of power and systems of governance'" (Shore et al., 2011: p. 11) . The analysis of political campaigns, such as "One of Us" and "Mentally Vulnerable", may therefore elucidate the political classification to which the target individuals are subjected, and how the campaigns constitute specific processes of subjectification of political citizens. Rather than considering how clinical professionals and individuals who experience distress and their relatives articulate involvement, this analysis specifically highlights what political order the campaign materials come to instigate for them (Shore et al., 2011) . As such, this article aims to elucidate which political classifications of normality and mental illness are portrayed in the campaign materials and how such classifications co-constitute the subjectivity of individuals suffering from mental illness and their relatives. In doing so, the study considers how the discourse of involvement is constituted by more resident articulations of mental illness and normality. In this sense, the analysis and the critical considerations that follow are aligned with sociological perspectives on deviance and normality rooted in the structuralist idea that different politics, ideals and values and mental illness, such as depression, are mutually constitutive of each other in a society (Kleinman, 1995; Fullagar & O'Brien, 2013; Busfield, 2000) .

The Construction of Mental Illness as a Matter of Weakness

Previous studies have pointed to the fact that dominant notions of mental illness are embedded in broader cultural constructions of weakness or vulnerability in the psychiatric field in Scandinavia. In a narrative study on involvement processes, it was identified that cohabitant relatives of depressed individuals classified their ill partner as being a weak character. The combination of the relatives' classification of their partner and the professional ways of holding the relatives responsible for psychiatric treatment constituted a moral necessity for the relatives to control the ill person's weakness. However, this rationale eventually led to conflict and relational strain in the suffering families, due to the relatives' considerable efforts to control their partner's weakness (Hansen & Buus, 2013) . Moreover, a previous discourse analysis of the most widely used Danish textbook on mental health nursing in Denmark combined with field observations and interviews with psychiatric professionals elucidated that a comparable, professional rationale about mental illness was at stake in clinical practice: In contrast to a weak, childlike and male patient, the hegemonic articulation of the nurse placed her/ him in the position of a dominant and all-knowing mother-figure; a position labelled as a "Hege-mom". This work made it clear that the subject of the patient served as a constitutive premise for the articulation of the indispensability of the subject of the nurse in the psychiatric field, because the "Hege-mom", in opposition to the subject of the doctor, is presented as someone that truly and intuitively understands the patient's personal weakness and deficiencies(Oute Hansen & Randwijk, 2015) . Moreover, based on lengthy ethnographic fieldwork in psychiatric settings, Jacobsen (Bredahl Jacobsen, 2006) and Øvre Sørensen (Øvre Sørensen, 2006) both referred to the professional discourse of psychiatric nursing staff. This discourse drew on psychoanalytic signs of the patients' weakness that constituted and legitimized a hierarchical order of ruling amongst the professionals and the psychiatric patients. In a Norwegian context, Øye et al. equally pointed out that the psychiatric care and treatment are organized based on parallel psychodynamic notions of the patient as a weak, vulnerable and childlike subject (Oeye, Bjelland, Skorpen, & Anderssen, 2009) . Furthermore Øye et al. have shown that the underlying medical-ethical rationale in the psychiatric field in Norway is based on articulations of the patient as weak or vulnerable, because national policies for this field and the medical ethical committee system signal consent to this rationale (Oeye, Bjelland, & Skorpen, 2007) . Overall, these studies point out that weakness works an inherent part of the classification of mental illness in Scandinavia. This constitutional premise frames the legitimacy of conducting care for, and control of, the weaknesses of mentally ill subjects in rather paternalistic ways. The dominant consent to the belief, that mental illness reflects personal weakness, thus works as an important premise for involvement across public and private contexts of psychiatric systems in Scandinavia. However, these notions of weakness and their constitutive effects are embedded in, and constituted by, much broader hegemonic articulations of normality in neo-liberal societies that, taken together, symbolically set the premises for what involvement can be considered to encompass. Moreover, similar studies of discourses of websites and policies have shed light on, how the understanding of mental illness as a matter of weakness is embedded in a dominant discourse about cost-effectiveness, responsibilization and self-reliance in psychiatric systems across contemporary, neo-liberal, Western societies (Carney, 2008; Fullagar, 2009; Ramon, 2008; Teghtsoonian, 2009) . However, such study has to our knowledge not been conducted in a Scandinavian context. By conducting this analysis on subjectification processes, we wish to raise questions about how such political campaigns conceptualize classifications of normality and deviance and what regulatory processes of involvement they may instigate for professionals and families experiencing mental distress. Moreover, we wish to consider the normative or moral conception of the social subject established by the discourse and the possible consequences of this conceptualization.

METHODOLOGY

The overall, multisited fieldwork took place between October 2011 and April 2013 in the Region of Southern Denmark. It began at two psychiatric outpatient clinics where individuals diagnosed with affective disorders were in treatment. Based on materials from two anti-stigma and social inclusion campaigns found at these clinical sites, signs and symbols of involvement were further traced on to the political sites consisting of numerous virtual governmental and NGOs' websites including the "One of Us" and "Mentally Vulnerable" campaigns.

The two campaigns were highly noticeable in both of the clinical sites as well as in all the political websites. For example on arrival at both of the two psychiatric hospitals, a banner for the anti-stigma and social inclusion campaign "One of Us" had been erected in a prominent position at both hospital entrances. Various advisory leaflets and postcards, targeted at patients, relatives and professionals were on display (One of Us, 2014) . The leaflets and postcards referred to the campaign website from where there was a link to "The Social Network", which had previously launched a resembling sister campaign called "Mentally Vulnerable" (The Social Network, 2014) . The materials from the "Mentally Vulnerable" campaign were included in our analysis, because the campaigns are closely related and designed to mutually reinforce each other. The large-scale political support for both of the campaigns was made evident by the organizations that gave their backing. These included the Danish Health and Medicines Authority, the Ministry of Social Affairs and Integration, Danish Regions and a wide range of psychiatric user organizations and corporate foundations, such as the Depression Association, Better Psychiatry, the Danish Mental Health Foundation and the Danish foundation called TrygFonden[1]. As the two campaigns elapse between 2009 and 2015, and are supported by multiple governing and non-governing health and social work organizations in Denmark, the eye-catching promotional stands reflected the official discourse of the psychiatric hospitals' health political engagement and efforts in involvement (Psykiatrien i Region Syddanmark [trans. Psychiatry in the Region of Southern Denmark], 2014) . Whereas the abovementioned fieldwork particularly included families with a person diagnosed with moderate to severe depression, the politically driven campaigns targeted a much wider selection of the population, including volunteers such as relatives, professionals, employers, media workers and members of NGOs and political organizations—all of whom had relations to individuals experiencing mental distress in the broadest sense (The Social Network, 2014; One of Us, 2014) .

The fact that the campaigns were prominent at the two empirical sites is an indication at these two psychiatric organizations have formally taken on, or at least support, the subjectification processes constituted by the general policy expressed through the campaigns (Psykiatrien i Region Syddanmark [trans. Psychiatry in the Region of Southern Denmark], 2014) .

Materials

We based our analysis on electronically imported text materials from the front pages and sub-menus of the websites where the campaign backgrounds and formalized materials were presented. The materials included the campaigns' official materials, which predominantly entailed descriptions of political aims and a range of individuals' statements about the aims and objectives of the campaigns. We excluded the websites' forums for users' personal stories, because our focus was on the official health political notions of normality and mental illness. From the "One of Us" campaign, we included the front page and the items: "About the Campaign", "Become wiser", "Breaking the silence" and "Become one of us" (One of Us, 2014) . From the "Mentally Vulnerable" campaign website, we included the front page, "About the social network", "The Mirror", "Vulnerable", "Relatives", "Knowledge about diagnoses" and "Activities" (The Social Network, 2014) . In total, the material consists of some 400 pages, downloaded in June 2013. Translations of Danish text materials from the websites were carried out by the first and second author and then proof read by a professional translator in cases where English versions of the materials were not available. Bearing the purpose of the article in mind, the campaign materials were read in full and then line coded into twenty-one folders. Subsequently, the folders were clustered into two categories—signifiers of weakness and signifiers of ineffectiveness—that were adjusted until the categories appeared coherent with the entirety of the material. The open-ended coding of the materials was managed using NVivo 9.0 software.

Because this critical analysis of political subjectivities and involvement processes is grounded in what can be labelled constructivist ethnography (Marcus, 1998; Shore et al., 2011) , we found it coherent to draw on a notion of discourse and subjectivity set out by political theorists Ernesto Laclau and Chantal Mouffe (Laclau & Mouffe, 2001) . Through this theoretical lens, discourse is understood as articulation encompassing "any practice establishing a relation among elements such that their identity is modified as a result of the articulatory practice" (Laclau & Mouffe, 2001: p. 105) . Discourse theory works particularly well to help clarify how articulations structure political subjectivities and social processes within the field of the social according to the dominant political classification of normality and deviance (Laclau &

Mouffe, 2001; Torfing, 1999) . Our approach to subjectivity and involvement is thus founded on the claim that "the social" can be understood as a symbolic order constitutive of the organization of meaning (Shore et al., 2011; Marcus, 1998) . As such, we consider constitutional processes, such as subjectification and involvement, as social, structural concerns (Marcus, 1998; Shore et al., 2011) . In doing so, we hypothesize that discursive structures of language, encompassing both verbal and material signs and expressions, constitute the practices of involvement. The meaning of this practice is brought into effect by dominant ways of signifying mentally ill and relative subjects (Torfing, 1999; Laclau & Mouffe, 2001) . This analytical lens relies on an anti-essentialist understanding of the subject. That is, the subjects are decentered and hence considered as positioned effects of the symbolic structure in which they contrast each other. The subjects' perspectives, practical possibilities and social mobility are thereby structured accordingly (Shore et al., 2011) .

DISCOURSE ANALYSIS

The coding and the subsequent discourse analysis clarify how a dominant notion of involvement is discursively articulated by drawing on symbols of weakness and ineffectiveness. The articulation enables a specific understanding of a subject of deviance—a subject symbolizing mentally ill people. It places the deviant subject in contrast to a subject of normality—which symbolizes a relative or significant other such as a spouse, friend or health care professional. The discourse of involvement frames how these subjectivities ought to be concerned with classification and regulation of the deviant subject.

Division of Normality and Deviance

The signifier of normality is the starting point for the articulation of the two subject positions of normality and deviance, because it implicitly indicates that there is a normal "us" and a mentally weak "them".

Pivotal examples of this signifier were identified in the slogans of the "Mentally Vulnerable" and "One of us" campaigns (The Social Network, 2014; One of Us, 2014) because they draw up boundaries between the two categories of normality and deviance. The "One of Us" slogan echoes the chorus chant "[...] gooble gobble, gooble gobble. One of us, one of us. We accept here, we accept her. One of us [...]" from the wedding feast song in Tod Browning's horror film Freaks(Browning, 1931) . In Browning's provocative horror film, the traditional figure of a trapeze beauty in a travelling circus, by the name of Cleopatra, marries a freak-little Hans, who displays a range of disabilities. Cleopatra plans to deceive and poison Hans to claim his considerable inheritance. During their wedding feast, the freaks chant the abovementioned song to invite Cleopatra to identify with their deviance. However, Cleopatra reacts with discomfort and rage, because she never intended to identify with the Freaks. She responds to their chant by degrading the deviant wedding guests with reference to discrediting classifications of them as a group. The film effectively draws up categories of "normal" and "deviant" and then proceeds to endow the deviant with the power to recast a member of the normal to become one of them. The film not only questions common ways of distinguishing between deviance and normality, it also raises the issue about who has the power to classify and regulate deviance. The campaign slogan thus highlights the fact that the slogans implicitly echo a similar contrast between normality and deviance as suggested by Browning and challenged in his film. In defining the categories of deviance and normality, the campaign articulations signify how the two opposing subject positions, the normal and the deviant, emerge through coherences of signs of weakness or strength and ineffectiveness and effectiveness.

In the following excerpt from the "One of Us" website, weakness both symbolizes the deviant subject's characteristics and signals its division from the normal subject:

"Maria Bødiker is tall, fit and healthy-looking. She seems strong and well-functioning. Her three kids look strong and well-functioning—and they are. They live in a good, well-furnished flat in one of the best parts of the town of Aarhus. So far, so good. There is just the important detail that Maria Bødiker is suffering from post-traumatic stress disorder."

The quotation suggests that the subject is characterized by weakness as an individual and an essential trait that predicts the subject's functioning, health, motherhood and everyday life, in spite of the fact that her everyday life and functioning appear to be normal. The contrast to the subject's weakness is emphasized using the verb "seem". Moreover, the final punch-line demonstrates that the subject's weakness is classified and outlined as post-traumatic stress disorder (PTSD). By emphasizing the contrast to the strength of the subject's children, it is articulated that her strength is not to be taken at face value, because she is suffering from PTSD, which constitutes Maria as a mentally ill subject. In line with the abovementioned headlines displaying the separation of normality and deviance, the mentally ill subject is discursively structured as being essentially incapable of being an effective and functioning subject [e.g., mother] and worker.

In doing so, the subject is presented as essentially weak by suggesting that its mental illness or weakness is caused by a deprivation of its true, strong self that predicts the subject's incapability to perform or function as a mother and healthy and effective citizen. As such, the articulation of a division of normality and mental deviance is articulated more specifically by drawing on signifiers of weakness, and as we shall see below, ineffectiveness.

Classification of the Weak Subject

In spite of the variations in the emergence of the signifier of weakness, weakness was implicitly laid out in contrast to a strong, normal subject in the campaign materials. A frontline example of the signifier of weakness was identified in the slogan from the "Mentally Vulnerable" campaign. Across the materials, the sign of vulnerability or weakness signalleda deeply rooted individual and essential weakness of the subject. As such, the signifier acquired its more specific meaning through the articulation of different but widely used metaphors representing weakness. One example of the kind of metaphors used in the materials comes from the "Mentally Vulnerable" campaign. The metaphysical signifier "scarred soul" reflects the assumption that the ill subject essentially suffers from a lack of strength to endure something that already has or might hurt the weak subject's being or self. Drawing on the signifier "soul", weakness is signified as a classification that concerns the subject's ontology. In this sense, the metaphorical signifiers suggest that the classification of the weak subject's self or very being relies on a contrast to the essence or core of the subject of normality that originates in a metaphysical ideal for the true being; the weak subject is thus constituted by an implicit ideal for how it ought to be. This suggests that the signifier of weakness works as a dominant sign in the articulation of how the deviant subject's being essentially suffers from an ill core. This determines its illness and its lack of abilities and competencies to live "truly" that sets it apart from the normal subject. The specific signification of such essential conditions of the deviant subject emerged as an articulation of a range of shortcomings in the subject's social and personal qualities that effectuated specific forms of regulation of the weak subject.

The weak subject is represented as lacking social qualities, such as motivation and independence, self-reliance, responsibility and the ability to manage relations appropriately. In the following quotation from the "Mentally Vulnerable" campaign the weak subject is articulated:

"I have been too slow to seek out help and have been so messed up that I drank myself into a stupor and hid away under my quilt. And I have to be way-out there before I open up but I also know that there is help at hand when I dare to be weak. […]. One must accept the help that is available. When one is suffering, you have to open yourself up—by daring to recognize that you are weak."

The excerpt suggests that the weak subject is acting socially inappropriately due to its drunkenness and isolation. However, as the subject submits itself to the subject position of the deviant by confessing its weakness and need of help, the subject's initial irresponsibility, lack of motivation and inappropriate social qualities are outlined and relieved. This becomes evident because the subject's confession to these shortcomings contrasts an implicit idealized notion of normal behaviour that constitutes the weak subject's counterpart. Thereby, the quotation elucidates that the control of the subject's weak social qualities both entails and depends on its submission to the available help so that it can be normalized. Moreover, the quotation highlights how the subject's inappropriate behaviour, lack of responsibility, motivation and self-reliance counters what is considered as normal.

This behavioural deviance of the weak subject was articulated as being constituted by a range of personal shortcomings. These shortcomings were articulated as deficits in the subject's ability to recognize, feel, think and perform responsibly and appropriately.

As such, the weakness of the deviant subject was articulated as an incapability to have an appropriate degree of self-control. These traits are articulated in the following excerpt from the "One of Us" campaign, where the deviance of the subject Bjarne is presented:

"Bjarne did not have many friends, he drank too much, his finances were in a mess, and he had a poorly functioning relationship. One day he decided to do something about it. In 2009, on his own initiative, he was diagnosed with ADHD and Asperger's syndrome. Since then, he has organized his everyday life and working life according to his strengths and weaknesses."

The quotation elucidates how Bjarne is articulated as a weak and irresponsible subject, because he lives an isolated life without many friends. His irresponsibility is signalled by his excessive drinking and his lack of control of his financial situation and his relationship. In this sense, the deviant subject is explicated in contrast to a responsible subject of normality that is supposed to take control of its weakness by recognizing that it is weak and irresponsible. As the quotation shows, the deviant subject complies with its weakness by recognizing its need to be diagnosed, freely and willingly. The proper functionality of a subject's everyday life, in terms of its marital and financial situation, is presented as resting on its ability to identify and recognize its own weaknesses. As such, the deviant subject is articulated in contrast to the subject of the normal. In this sense, the weak subject is implicitly described as someone who should be taking personal responsibility for its own well-being and effectiveness as a normal citizen by complying with a medical classification of its weakness. Because the deviant subject is compelled to recognize and identify with the classification of weakness in order to become normalized, it is effectuated as a medicalized subject complying with its recognition of the classification of its weakness. The "Mentally Vulnerable" campaign articulated how the weak subject complied with the classification of its weakness and thus its need of medical treatment:

"When I went to my GP, he found that I had clear signs of depression and he gave me antidepressants. I thought that I was cheating taking antidepressants. I could not tell anyone because I felt that I ought to do without them. But I have got to say that antidepressants are wonderful."

The quotation articulates that the weak subject is effectuated as a medicalized subject—a subject that has willingly submitted to a medical understanding of its weak core and accepted antidepressants. The subject's weakness is articulated as its "clear signs of depression". As such, the effectuation of the weak subject's medicalized position is constituted by its recognition of its weakness, and further compounded by its recognition of the need for medical regulation of its weaknesses, in that the subject "could not do" without the "wonderful" antidepressants. In this sense, the weak subject's essential lack of strength, self-control, responsibility and self-reliance legitimizes its medical regulation, because the subject's essential shortcomings predict its incapacity to function in an effective way. In this way, the regulation of the weak subject is legitimized by its lack of effectiveness.

Regulating the Weak Subject

In contrast to the normal subject, the articulation of the lack of effectiveness of weak subjects rests on an assumption that they are a stigmatized class of people excluded from taking part in societal activities, due to extensive lack of openness, knowledge and understanding of mental illness among all members of society. In the "Purpose and Vision" of the "Mentally Vulnerable" campaign, this is articulated in the following way:

"It is our wish that the dialogue and the information from the "Mentally Vulnerable" website contribute to the creation of a better understanding of mental vulnerability and not least openness—amongst the vulnerable, relatives, nursing staff, politicians, neighbours, colleagues and all others. [...] The dream is that, in the long term, we create a society where all humans—whether they have a vulnerability or not—have real opportunities to take part on equal terms with others."

The quotation suggests that the weak subject is held in a marginalized and stigmatized position in society due to lack of openness and knowledge about the subject's weakness. Thus, the quotation indicates a rationale that suggests that openness and knowledge about the classification of weakness would enhance social inclusion, recovery and equality, and would counter the stigmatization of people suffering from mental illness, if only normalized vulnerables (weak subjects acting responsibly), relatives and all other citizens could understand and classify it. By suggesting that "all other" normal subjects should aid this process of subjectification of the weak subject, the text explicates the understanding that significant others are responsible for regulating the weak subject, by subjecting it to medical classifications and treatment for its deviance.

This process of regulation of the weak subject relies on a separation between normal and deviant subjects. The division is presented by drawing on signifiers from wide-ranging political efforts to divide responsibility for the identification, classification and regulation of the weak subject between public and private spheres in the Danish welfare state. In the following excerpt from the "One of Us" campaign, the Danish Member of Parliament and former minister of Health and Prevention, Astrid Kragh is quoted:

"Perhaps due to convenience, as a society we have built a wall around mental illness that stops us from seeing, recognizing and helping the people we know who have mental problems."

The signs "seeing", "recognizing" and "helping" suggest that efforts to identify, classify and regulate the deviant subject's weakness is a moral concern regarding effective and precise diagnostic processes, treatment and normalization of the deviant. The articulation of "we" implies that normal subjects implicitly are, at least in part, supposed to be responsible for classifying and managing treatment of the weak subject in private contexts. This rationale encompasses that the responsibility for the identification, classification and regulation of weak subjects has expanded or shifted from a professional concern of the welfare state into an individual responsibility that users, relatives and employers must take on voluntarily. The discourse of involvement in the anti-stigmatization and social inclusion campaigns thus signals an expanded prevention and treatment strategy. This inherent rationale comprises efforts to divide the psychiatric labor involved with identification, classification and regulation of the weak subject between public and private contexts. By contrast to the weak subject, the discourse constitutes that the subject of the normal is considered as the subject that has true ability to "see" and "recognize" the weaknesses of the deviant subject. In this sense, the subject of the normal is constituted by its involvement with psychiatric labor related to the identification, classification and regulation of the subject of the deviant, because the weak subject is articulated as partially incapable of taking on these responsibilities competently and effectively.

In this sense, the campaigns not only set up a framework for the understanding of subjectivities of deviance and normality but also effectuate a legitimate order of ruling and control between the two subjectivities. Specifically, the regulation process of the campaigns implies that the deviant subject identifies with the classification from itself, relatives and others of significance. As such, the campaigns constitute that involvement of the subject of the normal, in direct or indirect contact with the weak subject, specifically entails a subtle but comprehensive form of social control, where the deviant subject is submitted to, and equally ought to submit itself to, constant surveillance. Conversely, the subject of the normal must commit itself to the position of the normal and thereby to the task of classifying and regulating the weakness and ineffectiveness of the deviant subject. Paradoxically, the division and symbolic effectuation of the two subjectivities excludes the subject of the weak from the class of the normal. None the less, this discursive constitution of the normal subject, and the ways in which it is involved with surveillance and control of the weak subject is articulated as legitimate.

The legitimacy of the campaigns' constitution of the process of involvement and regulation is articulated as a fundamental rationale of the campaigns. For instance, this overarching rationale gains its more precise meaning when it is articulated in the context of the expected social consequences of the stigmatization and exclusion of the weak subject, as articulated in the initial description of the ideals for the "One of Us" campaign:

"[Stigmatization] makes it hard to be ill and may be an obstacle for having a meaningful life, such as having labour market attachment. It might also prevent people from getting treatment in time. This comes at a high price. For the individual and for society."

The text highlights the campaigns' key assumption that stigmatization following lack of openness and understanding obstruct early identification and classification of weak subjects, which would counter mentally ill subjects' opportunities for having a meaningful and effective life. The articulation of the obstruction of the identification and classification suggests that the weak subject would be having a hard time creating a meaningful life, at least in part, because it is poorly integrated with the labour market, due to its lack of timely treatment. The rationale implies that the subject's opportunities for having a meaningful and cost-effective work life, rather than becoming a burden to society, rests on the subject's submission to medical classifications of its weakness and thus to compliance to medical treatment.

To sum up the elements of the discourse presented throughout this analysis, the articulations of the campaigns constitute a specific effectuation of the subject of the weak and of the subject of the normal that, at least primarily, is constituted by an overall aim to reduce societal costs by involving the subject of the normal. The discursive rationale of the campaigns relies on the suggestion that medical treatment would reduce personal and societal costs following mental illness, because the weak subject's compliance to treatment would regulate or normalize its ability to work. The discourse thus represents an effort to expand the responsibility for the identification, classification and regulation of what is implicitly understood as deviant and weak from a public and professional concern of the welfare state to a broad private and voluntary concern.

DISCUSSION

Working from a discourse theoretical perspective, this critical analysis calls for a reflection on how the understanding of mental illness is framed by symbols and signs of ineffectiveness. Below, we will broaden the discussion of the abovementioned local perspectives by arguing that the articulation of mental illness as a matter of weakness is embedded in a hegemonic discourse about cost-effectiveness, responsibilization and self-reliance in psychiatric systems across contemporary, neo-liberal, Western societies (Ramon, 2008; Carney, 2008). Subsequently, we will consider the kinds of new problems and questions that arise from this rationale.

A Hegemonic Discourse of Normality, Mental Illness and Involvement

The political scientist Jacob Torfing, who has written extensively about the theoretical foundations and implications of discourse theory and hegemony, states that: "hegemony is just another name for politics, but one which emphasizes the construction of identity, and conceives values and beliefs as an integral part of such an identity" (Torfing, 1999: p. 82). By highlighting the theoretical underpinnings for our enquiry into hegemony, Torfing continues to lay out the concept as: "the expansion of a discourse or set of discourses, into a dominant horizon of social orientation and action [...]" (Torfing, 1999: p. 101). The dominant consent to a political structure constitutive of specific values thus becomes "the result of articulation" (Torfing, 1999: p. 101). By discussing the Marxist foundations of discourse theory, Torfing warns discourse analysts about the risk of overemphasizing how hegemonic forces would constitute ideological and economic subjectivities and social order on behalf of the state when analyzing articulatory practices (Torfing, 1999). As such, our analysis requires critical reflection or, at least, a cautious attitude towards the social contingency of the discourse of mental illness and involvement. Such precautions imply reflections on how hegemonic articulations may be contested by antagonistic articulations of users', relatives' and families' voices; opposing discourses that are singled out based on the different part of the main study mentioned above. Thus, in order to clarify and disentangle the similar and diverging understandings of involvement of political intuitions, professionals and families, these discursive understandings are investigated in turn. That being said, it could have added colorful nuances to the imagery of the landscape of involvement to consider, how the campaign websites' forums of users' personal stories, which were excluded from the present analysis, could yield a contestation of the analysis of campaigns' official notions of normality and involvement. Despite these considerations, we maintain that the articulations of the campaigns signal a hegemonic discourse in the Danish psychiatric field today, because the campaigns represent the voice of several governing bodies and psychiatric institutions in Denmark.

Thus, we argue that this analysis highlights how these health political campaigns represent a hegemonic discourse about normality, mental illness and involvement. To a large extent, the rationale about mental illness as a matter of weakness rests on the consent with an ideological notion of effectiveness that constitutes how professionals, users and relatives consider and practice treatment and involvement in contemporary Danish psychiatry. Our abidance to the hegemony of the presented discourse is concerned with weakness signaling and effectuating the opposite of a notion of subjectivity deeply rooted in the moral and ideology of neo-liberalist virtues and work ethics of individualism in Western industrialized countries (Fullagar, 2009; Teghtsoonian, 2009) . These impinge on the individual's responsibility for, and capacity to be actively engaged with managing one's freedom and self-reliance and being a cost-effective citizen (Fullagar, 2009; Barry, 1996) . In this sense, the internal coherence of signs in the campaigns' discourse means that the deviant subject is presented as essentially incapable of performing responsibly, self-reliably and effectively as a citizen, because the discourse characterizes it ineffective and weak. As previously shown by the English sociologist Nikolas Rose (Rose, 2007; Rose, 1999) , the present analysis clarifies how the ideological and ethical foundations of psychiatric classifications frame the legitimization of the subtle forms of social control that have come to be an inherent part of the development of contemporary psychiatry. Thus, the analysis both sheds light on the moral landscape of contemporary understandings in society but, equally importantly, it elucidates that individualism constitutes how deviant subjects are articulated as implicitly guilty of being a societal burden. Hence, the neo-liberal and individualistic ideal of the subject of normality frames how the shortcomings and ensuing cost-ineffectiveness of the deviant subject legitimizes why and how the subject of the deviant must subject himself or herself to the processes of identification and classification of his or her lack of self-reliance, effectiveness and responsibility. Such tendencies to classify and maintain problems of living and misery as individual concerns could, however, be seen as a reflection, and perhaps even a necessity, of the neo-liberal morals of contemporary Western societies (Moncrieff, Rapley, & Dillon, 2011) . From a historical and sociological perspective, the social scientists Anders Dræby Sørensen (Dræby Sørensen, 2002) and Alain Ehrenberg (Ehrenberg, 2010) have argued that the illness of depression represents the moral negation of contemporary Western society. In a slightly provocative Danish study, Dræby Sørensen (2002) argues that depressed individuals are considered as "living dead", because they repre- sent the negation of contemporary ideals for happiness and life itself. Previously, Ehrenberg (2010) questioned the notion of mental illness by arguing that the categories of melancholia, neurasthenia, neurosis and delusions have conditioned the development of the classification of mental illness that has come to represent a lack of the neo-liberal ideals of autonomy, responsibility, capacity to act and self-realization. This highlights how the campaigns' inherent neo-liberal virtues of life itself, characterized by self-realization, autonomy and responsibility, constitute a relationship between the normality and effectiveness of the "us" and the deviance and ineffectiveness of the "them". Despite the fact that these campaigns signal the essential ideals and measures for the reformation and de-institutionalization of Danish psychiatry (Udvalget [The Governmental Committee on the future organization of Danish psychiatry (GCP)], 2013) , they paradoxically make possible an institutionalization and reproduction of an antagonistic social and moral order between the category of the normal and the category of the deviant (Torfing, 1999) . As these political articulations constitute surveillance, subjectification and medical control of the mentally ill subject in private contexts, the discourse of the policies instead legitimizes involvement as a means or managerial technology of concealed moral coercion of subjects classified as weak.

Technologies of Governance of the Weak and Ineffective

The campaigns' articulations of the involvement of ill subjects and their significant others do not work as an emancipatory effort to humanize psychiatric systems and treatment regimes in Denmark, as the "One of Us" headline might suggest. Rather, the campaigns serve as a wide-ranging, but subtle, prevention and treatment strategy aimed at governing the weak subjects at a distance by involving the normal, responsible and effective subjects, such as relatives, professionals or colleagues. The campaigns' systematic reproductive constitution of such moral order between the deviant and normal seems paradoxical, given that the campaigns are social inclusion and anti-stigma campaigns. The paradox concerns the fact that the ideological articulation of the weak and ineffective subject instead effectuates an underprivileged and stigmatized subject position of the weak. Rather than dissolving processes of stigmatization, exclusion, recovery and disenfranchisement, the campaigns both signal and frame of a very broad systemic form of stigma. This systemic or structural stigmatization entails an institutionalization of the reduction of opportunities of this particular group of people that are classified as weak and vulnerable. Then, systemic stigma is capable of structurally limiting the rights and relational possibilities of the people considered weak and vulnerable (Yang et al., 2007) . Moreover, this stigmatizing articulatory process of the subject of the weak defines the principle of its regulation, because the articulation effectuates the subjectification of the weak or inappropriate subject. Even if this type of governance and public regulation does not primarily exert direct control over those deemed as mad, the campaigns' inherent and dominant understanding of mental illness as a matter of weakness does constitute a morally flawed, ineffective subject that must rely on comprehensive but subtle social restraint from those in its surroundings. Rather than signaling a normalizing transformation of the deviant subject, this work clarifies how political campaigns legitimize systematic regulation and exclusion of the weak subject. In this sense, this critical analysis highlights what has previously been outlined in the work of multiple scholars' and social scientists and other researchers on policy, subjectivity and governance (Shore et al., 2011; Kleinman, 1995) . Such critique points out that these anti-stigma and inclusion campaigns work as neoliberal policies of governance that involve a specific constitution of the subjectivity of deviant subjects. As such, it sheds light on how the campaigns set up a framework for managing deviant subjects. The symbolic constitution of such management of deviant subjects thus signals a dominant political rationale of social control within the state of Denmark, which, paradoxically, is reproductive of the social issues it aims to resolve. Even if the headline of the "One of Us" campaign gives an immediate impression of effectuating of a more common notion of mental illness, they paradoxically imply the symbolic constitution of a rather narrow moral and ideological positioning of mentally ill subjects.

As described above, neoliberal ideology, a deficit model about mental illness and individualization work as decisive, symbolic aspects for the conception of involvement in Danish psychiatry. These aspects closely resemble the aspects and effects of recovery in psychiatry identified by UK psychologist, David Harper and sociologist, Ewen Speed (Harper & Speed, 2014) . Similar to the present analysis of Danish policy on involvement, their "uncovering of recovery" elucidates that recovery policy in the UK, US and other Western countries equates with neoliberal identity politics. Parallel to our analysis of involvement, recovery also relies on individualistic and medicalized notions of responsibility, on a deficit model about the etiology of mental illness and downplays any social context for mental distress beyond interpersonal problems (Harper & Speed, 2014) . With regard to individualization, their analysis resembles our discoveries, as they state that: "Neoliberal policies invite people to see certain problems [such as mental distress] as the responsibility of the individual rather than, for example, the state" (Harper & Speed, 2014: p. 45) . Moreover, by relying on a medical deficit model, the concepts of involvement and recovery both assert that the mental health problems are caused by weakness; characterized by a lack of ability for self-management, skills for living and working, opportunity for education, relationships, etc. All of these deficits are laid out as existing negatives with a potential to be transformed into positives; collective understandings of strengths. The meaning of the negative then depends on a positive, opposite term. Analogous to recovery (Harper & Speed, 2014) , involvement does not offer an alternative to the medicalized notion of mental illness, but rather endorses it. This is established by the fact that the campaigns reproduce and even institutionalize the use of the deficit model and an individualizing way of addressing the social inequality of stigmatized psychiatric service users. In doing so, the campaigns largely ignore an actual re-distribution of power and reproduce the structural (ideological or economic) conditions for distress.

Implications and New Directions

In conducting this analysis and subsequent discussion, we set out to clarify the social conditions for normality, deviance, subjectivity and involvement in two pivotal health political campaigns in psychiatry. By aiming to clarify the ideological and ethical foundations of the political classification of deviance and normality within the psychiatric field in Denmark, the present analysis provides a number of paradoxes concerning the reproduction of subjectivity and social order. As such, the analysis suggests that the present approach to mental health prevention may, in fact, sustain problems with mental illness. In this line of thought, the analysis indicates that the campaigns may even subject more people to the category of the weak and mentally ill. Then, this work calls for new perspectives in mental health promotion policy and research that make it possible to consider people's distress and their human condition. Accordingly, the present analysis and succeeding considerations have produced more questions than they answer. First, these clarifications raise questions about the political intentionality of the campaigns and whether or not these issues have been foreseen by the governing bodies producing them. For example, how are we to understand that Danish user organizations such as Better Psychiatry, which support the campaigns, represent such discrediting discourse about mental illness, when they specifically aim to improve the rights and possibilities of relatives and users (Bedre Psykiatri, 2014 [trans. Better Psykiatry])? Given that Danish user organizations draw on such discrediting discourse, who will represent users' voices and resistance in Danish psychiatry and how can user voices be heard and supported in both Danish policy and future research? In contrast, the British Psychological Society has recently put out a stigma-combatting policy by the name of "Understanding Psychosis and Schizophrenia— why people sometimes hear voices, believe things that others find strange or appear out of touch with reality, and what can help" (Division of Clinical Psychology, 2014) . For instance, in the report it is articulated that it concentrates: "… on the psychological and social aspects, both in terms of how we understand these experiences and also what can help when they become distressing" (Division of Clinical Psychology, 2014: p. 5) . Second, what does the campaigns' constitution of the reproduction of the subjects of deviance mean for the statistical prevalence and overall wellbeing of mentally ill people in Denmark? Third, because managerial policies, such as the present campaigns, provide a framework for professional practice (Shore et al., 2011) , the clarification of the campaigns' organizing rationale points to the necessity of scrutinizing what social consequences the constitution of subjectivity might have and how such rationales may be negotiated in clinical practice as well as in families experiencing distress. For example, several Scandinavian studies highlight that the signifier of weakness serves as a dominant sign in the professional discourse of mental illness. The professional discourse constitutes a similar paradox, as the patient is simultaneously considered as weak and incompetent and personally responsible for its actions. As such, the professionals can legitimately demand that the patient submits him/herself to their classification of his/her weakness and treatment needs (Oute Hansen & Randwijk, 2015) . This work therefore raises queries about if or how the professional discourse of weakness can connect with such psycho-ideological classification of the campaigns. Such insight could shed further light on the hegemony and effects of political and professional discourse on mental illness within clinical practice today. Moreover, what happens if cohabitant relatives of depressed individuals could share such notions of their partner's weakness and subsequently take on responsibility for treatment and emotional care (Hansen & Buus, 2013) ? This analysis then points to the importance of a deeper understanding of when or how weakness connects with families' organization, division of labour and development of psychosocial burdens of living with mental illness and distress.

ACKNOWLEDGEMENTS

This study was supported by grants from the Research Foundation of mental health in the Region of Southern Denmark, Danish Nurses' Organization, Novo Nordisk Foundation, Health Foundation and the Faculty of Health Sciences, University of Southern Denmark. We owe great appreciation to Christian van Randwijk for his numerous insightful comments on this paper. We declare that we have no conflict of interest.

REFERENCES

1. Barry, A. (1996). Foucault and Political Reason: Liberalism, Neoliberalism and Rationalities of Government. Chicago: University of Chicago Press.

2. Bredahl Jacobsen, C. (2006). Paradoksal psykiatri: Etnografiske analyser af samspillet mellem plejepersonale og patienter i dansk restpsykiatri. Copenhagen: Institute of Anthropology, University of Copenhagen.

3. Browning, T. (1931). Freaks. 117. Ref Type: Motion Picture.

4. Busfield, J. (2000). Introduction: Rethinking the Sociology of Mental Health. Sociology of Health & Illness, 22, 543-558.http://dx.doi.org/10.1111/1467-9566.00219

5. Carney, T. (2008). The Mental Health Service Crisis of Neoliberalism— An Antipodean Perspective. International Journal of Law and Psychiatry, 31, 101-115. http://dx.doi.org/10.1016/j.ijlp.2008.02.001

6. Danske Regioner [Danish Regions] (2009). En psykiatri i verdensklasse: Regionernes visioner for fremtidens psykiatri. Kobenhavn: Danske Regioner.

7. Division of Clinical Psychology (2014). Understanding Psychosis and Schizophrenia—Why People Sometimes Hear Voices, Believe Things That Others Find Strange or Appear out of Touch with Reality, and What Can Help.

8. Dræby Sorensen, A. (2002). Den biologiske psykiatris renæssance og det antidepressive menneske. Slagmark, 159-183.

9. Ehrenberg, A. (2010). The Weariness of the Self: Diagnosing the History of Depression in the Contemporary Age. 345.

10. Fullagar, S., & O'Brien, W. (2013). Problematizing the Neurochemical Subject of Anti-Depressant Treatment: The Limits of Biomedical Responses to Women's Emotional Distress. Health (London), 17, 57-74. http://dx.doi.org/10.1177/1363459312447255

11. Fullagar, S. (2009). Negotiating the Neurochemical Self: Anti-Depressant Consumption in Women's Recovery from Depression. Health, 13, 389-406. http://dx.doi.org/10.1177/1363459308101809

12. Hansen, J. O., & Buus, N. (2013). Living with a Depressed Person in

Denmark: A Qualitative Study. International Journal of Social Psychiatry, 59, 401-406. http://dx.doi.org/10.1177/0020764012438478

13. Harper, D., & Speed, E. (2014). Uncovering Recovery: The Resistible Rise of Recovery and Resilience. In E. Speed, J. Moncrieff, & M. Rapley (Eds.), De-Medicalizing Misery II (pp. 40-57). London: Palgrave Macmillan. http://dx.doi.org/10.1057/9781137304667.0008

14. Kleinman, A. (1995). Writing at the Margin: Discourse between Anthropology and Medicine. Berkeley, CA: University of California Press.

15. Laclau, E., & Mouffe, C. (2001). Hegemony and Socialist Strategy: Towards a Radical Democratic Politics (2nd ed.). London: Verso.

16. Marcus, G. E. (1998). Ethnography through Thick and Thin. Princeton, NJ: Princeton University Press.

17. Moncrieff, J., Rapley, M., & Dillon, J. (2011). De-Medicalizing Misery: Psychiatry, Psychology and the Human Condition. Basingstoke: Palgrave Macmillan.

18. Oeye, C., Bjelland, A. K., & Skorpen, A. (2007). Doing Participant Observation in a Psychiatric Hospital—Research Ethics Resumed. Social Science & Medicine, 65, 2296-2306.http://dx.doi.org/10.1016/j.socscimed.2007.07.016

19. Oeye, C., Bjelland, A. K., Skorpen, A., & Anderssen, N. (2009). Raising Adults as Children? A Report on Milieu Therapy in a Psychiatric Ward in Norway. Issues in Mental Health Nursing, 30, 151-158. http://dx.doi.org/10.1080/01612840802557246

20. One of Us (2014). En af os [One of Us]. www.enafos.dk

21. Oute, J., & Randwijk, C. V. (2015). "We Will Be Taking Over Now"—A Discourse Analysis of Subject Positions in Danish Psychiatry. Issues in Mental Health Nursing, Accepted for Publication.

22. Ovre Sorensen, N. (2006). I virkeligheden udenfor: Et dobbelt perspektiv pa sygeplejerskers arbejde i en psykiatrisk institution. En analyse af magt, styringsog selvstyrings teknikker. Roskilde: Institut for uddannelsesforskning, Forskerskolen i Livslang Læring, Roskilde Universitetscenter.

23. Psykiatrien i Region Syddanmark [trans. Psychiatry in the Region of Southern Denmark] (2014). Psykiatrien i Region Syddanmark. www.psykiatrieniregionsyddanmark.dk

24. Ramon, S. (2008). Neoliberalism and Its Implications for Mental Health in the UK. International Journal of Law and Psychiatry, 31, 116-125. http://

dx.doi.org/10.1016/j.ijlp.2008.02.006

25. Rose, N. (1999). Governing the Soul: The Shaping of the Private Self (2nd ed.) London: Free Association Books.

26. Rose, N. (2007). The Politics of Life Itself: Biomedicine, Power and Subjectivity in the Twenty-First Century. Princeton, NJ: Princeton University Press. http://dx.doi.org/10.1515/9781400827503

27. Shore, C., Wright, S., & Però, D. (2011). Policy Worlds: Anthropology and the Analysis of Contemporary Power. New York: Berghahn Books.

28. Teghtsoonian, K. (2009). Depression and Mental Health in Neoliberal Times: A Critical Analysis of Policy and Discourse. Social Science & Medicine, 69, 28-35. http://dx.doi.org/10.1016/j.socscimed.2009.03.037

29. The Social Network (2014). Psykisk saarbar [Mentally Vulnerable]. www. Psykisksaarbar.dk

30. Torfing, J. (1999). New Theories of Discourse: Laclau, Mouffe, and Zizek. Oxford: Blackwell Publishers.

31. Udvalget, O. P. [The Governmental Committee on the Future Organization of Danish Psychiatry (GCP)] (2013). Enmoderne, Aaben og inkluderende indsats for mennesker med psykiske lidelser: Rapport fra Regeringens Udvalg om Psykiatri [A Modern, Open and Inclusive Effort for People with Mental Illnesses: A Rapport from the Danish Governmental Psychiatry Committee]. Regeringens Udvalg om Psykiatri.

32. Yang, L. H., Kleinman, A., Link, B. G., Phelan, J. C., Lee, S., & Good, B. (2007). Culture and Stigma: Adding Moral Experience to Stigma Theory. Social Science & Medicine, 64, 1524-1535.

Chapter 5

DISCOURSE ANALYSIS: WHAT MAKES IT CRITICAL?

INTRODUCTION

This paper is about my approach to discourse analysis (Gee, 2005, 2007). It is also about the question: What makes discourse analysis "critical discourse analysis"? At the outset, I want to make a distinction that is important from a linguistic point of view: a distinction between utterance-type meaning and utterance-token meaning (Levinson, 2000). Any word, phrase, or structure has a general range of possible meanings, what we might call its meaning range. This is its utterance-type meaning. For example, the word "cat" has to do, broadly, with the felines, and the (syntactic) structure "subject of a sentence" has to do, broadly, with naming a "topic" in the sense of "what is being talked about." However, words and phrases take on much more specific meanings in actual contexts of use. These are utterance-token meanings or what I will call "situated meaning." Thus, in a situation where we say something like "The world's big cats are all endangered," "cat" means things like lions and tigers; in a situation where we are discussing mythology and say something like "The cat was a sacred symbol to the ancient Egyptians," "cat" means real and pictured cats as symbols; and in a situation where we are discussing breakable decorative objects on our mantel and say something like "The cat broke," "cat" means a statue of cat.

Subjects of sentences are always "topic-like" (this is their utterance-type meaning); in different situations of use, subjects take on a range of more specific meanings. In a debate, if I say "The constitution only protects the rich," the subject of the sentence ("the constitution") is an entity about which a claim is being made; if a friend of yours has just arrived and I usher her in saying "Mary's here," the subject of the sentence ("Mary") is a center of interest or attention; and in a situation where I am commiserating with a friend and say something like "You really got cheated by that guy," the subject of the sentence ("you") is a center of empathy (signaled also by the fact that the normal subject of the active version of the sentence—"That guy really cheated you"—has been "demoted" from subject position through use of the "get-passive").

THE UTTERANCE-TYPE MEANING TASK

Discourse analysis of any type, whether critical or not, can undertake one or both of two tasks, one related to utterance-type (general) meaning and one related to situated meaning. One task, then, is what we can call the utterance-type meaning task. This task involves the study of correlations between form and function in language at the level of utterance-type meanings (general meanings). "Form" here means things like morphemes, words, phrases, or other syntactic structures (e.g., the subject position of a sentence). "Function" means meaning or the communicative purpose a form carries out. The other task is what we can call the utterance-token meaning or situated meaning task. This task involves the study of correlations between form and function in language at the level of utterance-token meanings. Essentially, this task involves discovering the situation-specific or situated meanings of forms used in specific contexts of use. Failing to distinguish between these two tasks can be dangerous, since very different issues of validity for discourse analysis come up with each of these tasks, as we will see below. Let me start with an example of the utterance-type meaning task.

Specific forms in a language are prototypically used as tools to carry out certain communicative functions (that is, to express certain meanings). For example, consider the sentence labeled (1) below (adapted from Gagnon, 1987, p. 65): 1. Though the Whig and Tory parties were both narrowly confined to the privileged classes, they represented different factions and tendencies. This sentence is made up of two clauses, an independent (or main) clause ("they represented different factions and tendencies") and a dependent clause ("Though the Whig and Tory parties were both narrowly confined to the privileged classes"). These are statements about form. An independent clause has as one of its functions (at the utterance-type level) that it expresses an assertion; that is, it expresses a claim that the speaker/writer is making. A dependent clause has as one of its functions that it expresses information that is not asserted, but, rather, assumed or taken-for-granted. These are statements about function (meaning). Normally (that is, technically speaking, in the "unmarked" case), in English, dependent clauses follow independent clauses. Thus, the sentence (1) above might more normally appear as: "The Whig and Tory parties represented different factions, though they were both narrowly confined to the privileged classes." In (1) the dependent clause has been fronted (placed in front of the whole sentence). This is a statement about form. Such fronting has as one of its functions that the information in the clause is thematized (Halliday, 1994), that is, the information is treated as a launching-off point or thematically important context from which to consider the claim in the following dependent clause. This is a statement about function.

To sum up, in respect to form-functioning mapping at the utterance-type level, we can say that sentence (1) renders its dependent clause ("Though the Whig and Tory parties were both narrowly confined to the privileged classes") a taken-for-granted, assumed, unargued for (i.e., unasserted), though important (thematized) context from which to consider the main claim in the independent clause ("they represented different factions and tendencies"). The dependent clause is, we might say, a concession. Other historians might prefer to make this concession the main asserted point and, thus, would use a different grammar, perhaps saying something like: "Though they represented different factions and tendencies, the Whig and Tory parties were both narrowly confined to the privileged classes."

At a fundamental level, all types of discourse analysis involve claims (however tacitly they may be acknowledged) about form-function matching at the utterance-type level. This is so because, if one is making claims about a piece of language, even at a much more situated and contextualized level (which we will see in a moment), but these claims violate what we know about how form and function are related to each other in language at the utterance-type level, then these claims are quite suspect, unless there is evidence that the speaker or writer is trying to violate these sorts of basic grammatical relationships in the language (e.g., in poetry). As I have already said, the meanings with which forms are correlated at the utterance-type level are rather general (meanings like "assertion," "takenfor-granted information," "contrast," etc.). In reality, they represent only the meaning potential or meaning range of a form or structure, as we have said. The more specific or situated meanings that a form carries in a given context of use must be figured out by an engagement with our next task, the utterance-token or situated meaning task.

The Situated Meaning Task

A second task that any form of discourse analysis, critical or otherwise, can undertake is what I called above the utterance-token or situated meaning task. For simplicity's sake, I will now just call this "the situated meaning task." When we actually utter or write a sentence it has a situated meaning (Gee, 2004, 2005). Situated meanings arise because particular language forms take on specific or situated meanings in specific different contexts of use. Consider the word "coffee" as a very simple example of how situated meaning differs from utterance-type meaning. "Coffee" is an arbitrary form (other languages use different sounding words for coffee) that correlates with meanings having to do with the substance coffee (this is its meaning potential). At a more specific level, however, we have to use context to determine what the word means in any situated way. In one context, "coffee" may mean a brown liquid

("The coffee spilled, go get a mop"); in another one it may mean grains of a certain sort ("The coffee spilled, go get a broom"); in another it may mean containers ("The coffee spilled, stack it again"); and it can mean other things in other contexts, such as berries of a certain sort, a certain flavor, or a skin color. We can even use the word with a novel situated meaning, as in "You give me a coffee high" or "Big Coffee is as bad as Big Oil as corporate actors." To see a further example of situated meanings at work, consider sentence (1) again ("Though the Whig and Tory parties were both narrowly confined to the privileged classes, they represented different factions"). We said above that an independent clause represents an assertion (a claim that something is true).

But this general form-function correlation can mean different specifi c things in actual contexts of use, and can, indeed, even be mitigated or undercut altogether. For example, in one context, say between two like-minded historians, the claim that the Whig and Tory parties represented different factions may just be taken as a reminder of a "fact" they both agree on. On the other hand, between two quite diverse historians, the same claim may be taken as a challenge (despite YOUR claim that shared class interests mean no real difference in political parties, the Whig and Tory parties in 17th-century England were really different). And, of course, on stage as part of a drama, the claim about the Whig and Tory parties is not even a "real" assertion, but a "pretend" one. Furthermore, the words "privileged," "contending," and "factions" will take on different specific meanings in different contexts. For example, in one context, "privileged" might mean "rich," while in another context it might mean "educated" or "cultured" or "politically connected" or "born into a family with high status" or some combination of the above or something else altogether. To analyze Gagnon's sentence or his whole text, or any part of it, at the level of situated meanings—that is, in order to carry out the situated meaning task— would require a close study of some of the relevant contexts within which that text is placed and which it, in turn, helps to create.

This might mean inspecting the parts of Gagnon's text that precede or follow a part of the text we want to analyze. It might mean inspecting other texts related to Gagnon's. It might mean studying debates among different types of historians and debates about educational standards and policy (since Gagnon's text was meant to argue for a view about what history ought to be taught in schools). It might mean studying these debates historically across time and in terms of the actual situations Gagnon and his text were caught up in (e.g., debates about new school history standards in Massachusetts, a state where Gagnon once helped write a version of the standards). It might mean many other things, as well. Obviously, there is no space in a chapter of this scope to develop such an analysis. The issue of validity for analyses of situated meaning is quite different than the issue of validity for analyses of utterance-type meanings. We saw above that the issue of validity for analyses of utterance-type meanings basically comes down to choosing and defending a particular grammatical theory of how form and function relate in language at the level of utterance-type meanings, as well as, of course, offering correct grammatical and semantic descriptions of one's data. On the other hand, the issue of validity for analyses of situated meaning is much harder. In fact, it involves a very deep problem known as "the frame problem" (Gee, 2005).

The Frame Problem

The frame problem is this: Any aspect of context can affect the meaning of an (oral or written) utterance. Context, however, is indefinitely large, ranging from local matters like the positioning of bodies and eye gaze, through people's beliefs, to historical, institutional, and cultural settings. No matter how much of the context we have considered in offering an interpretation of an utterance, there is always the possibility of considering other and additional aspects of the context, and these new considerations may change how we interpret the utterance. Where do we cut off consideration of context? How can we be sure any interpretation is "right," if considering further aspects of the context might well change that interpretation? Let me give an example of a case where changing how much of the context of an utterance we consider changes significantly the interpretation we give to that utterance. Take a claim like "Many children die in Africa before they are fi ve years old because they get infectious diseases like malaria." What is the appropriate amount of context within which to assess this claim? We could consider just medical facts, a narrow context. And in the context the claim seems unexceptional.

But widen the context and consider the wider context described below: Malaria, an infectious disease, is one of the most severe public health problems worldwide. It is a leading cause of death and disease in many developing countries, where young children and pregnant women are the groups most affected. Worldwide, one death in three is from an infectious or communicable disease. However, almost all these deaths occur in the non-industrialized world. Health inequality effects not just how people live, but often dictates how and at what age they die. [see http://www.cdc. gov/malaria/impact/index. htm and http://ucatlas.ucsc.edu/cause.php]

This context would seem to say that so many children in Africa die early not because of infectious diseases but because of poverty and economic underdevelopment. While this widening of the context does not necessarily render the claim "Many children die in Africa before they are five years old because they get infectious diseases like malaria" false, it, at least, suggests that a narrow construal of "because" here (limiting it to physical and medical causes) effaces the workings of poverty and economics. The frame problem is both a problem and a tool. It is a problem because our discourse analytic interpretations (just like people's everyday interpretations of language) are always vulnerable to changing as we widen the context within which we interpret a piece of language. It is a tool because we can use it—widening the context—to see what information and values are being left unsaid or effaced in a piece of language. The frame problem, of course, raises problems about validity for discourse analysis. We cannot really argue an analysis is valid unless we keep widening the context in which we consider a piece of language until the widening appears to make no difference to our interpretation. At that point, we can stop and make our claims (open, of course, to later falsification as in all empirical inquiry).

Critical Discourse Analysis

Some forms of discourse analysis add a third task to the two (the utterancetype meaning task and the situated meaning task) discussed so far. They study, as well, the ways in which either or both of language-form correlations at the utterance-type level (task 1) and situated meanings (task 2) are associated with social practices (task 3). While non-critical approaches can and do, indeed, study social practices, critical approaches and non-critical ones take a different approach to social practices and how to study them. Non-critical approaches (e.g., see Pomerantz & Fehr, 1997) tend to treat social practices solely in terms of patterns of social interaction (e.g., how people use language to "pull off" a job interview). Thus, consider again the sentence from Gagnon we discussed above.Though the Whig and Tory parties were both narrowly confined to the privileged classes, they represented different factions and tendencies.

A non-critical form of discourse analysis could well point out the fact that using "Though the Whig and Tory parties were both narrowly confined to the privileged classes" as a dependent (and, thus, assumed and unasserted) clause sets up a social relationship with the reader in terms of which the reader should accept, as given and assumed, that distinctions of wealth in a society are less central to the development of democracy than political differences within elites in the society (which the main asserted clause is about). Critical approaches, however, go further and treat social practices, not just in terms of social relationships, but also in terms of their implications for things like status, solidarity, the distribution of social goods, and power (e.g., how language in a job interview functions as a gate-keeping device, allowing some sorts of people access and denying it to others). In fact, critical discourse analysis argues that language-in-use is always part and parcel of, and partially constitutive of, specific social practices, and that social practices always have implications for inherently political things like status, solidarity, the distribution of social goods, and power.

So the issue becomes this: Is it enough to leave the analysis of the social at the level of how talk and texts function in social interactions or do we need to go further and consider, as well, how talk and text function politically in social interactions? Does the latter task render discourse analysis—and thus, perforce, critical discourse analysis—"unscientific" or "unacademic," a mere matter of "advocacy"?

Consider sentence (1) again. There are historians who think that class conflict—conflict between haves and have notes—drives history. They would say that that the fact that the Whig and Tory parties were narrowly confined to the privileged classes is a key fact about the political situation of 17th-century England (though Gagnon places it in a subordinate clause). This fact, they will say, drove change because it led to the non-elites fighting for representation. What Gagnon has done is put what these historians see as the key point in a subordinate clause and treated it as assumed and backgrounded information that, while important, does not challenge his main claim that the Whig and Tory parties represented different factions (and, thus, for Gagnon were in the forefront of the development of democracy in Western society). His formulation is a move not only in an academic argument with such historians but in political debates about what and how history ought to be taught in school.

It might mean studying these debates historically across time and in terms of the actual situations Gagnon and his text were caught up in (e.g., debates about new school history standards in Massachusetts, a state where Gagnon once helped write a version of the standards). It might mean many other things, as well. Obviously, there is no space in a chapter of this scope to develop such an analysis. The issue of validity for analyses of situated meaning is quite different than the issue of validity for analyses of utterance-type meanings. We saw above that the issue of validity for analyses of utterance-type meanings basically comes down to choosing and defending a particular grammatical theory of how form and function relate in language at the level of utterance-type meanings, as well as, of course, offering correct grammatical and semantic descriptions of one's data. On the other hand, the issue of validity for analyses of situated meaning is much harder. In fact, it involves a very deep problem known as "the frame problem" (Gee, 2005)

The Frame Problem

The frame problem is this: Any aspect of context can affect the meaning of an (oral or written) utterance. Context, however, is indefinitely large, ranging from local matters like the positioning of bodies and eye gaze, through people's beliefs, to historical, institutional, and cultural settings. No matter how much of the context we have considered in offering an interpretation of an utterance, there is always the possibility of considering other and additional aspects of the context, and these new considerations may change how we interpret the utterance. Where do we cut off consideration of context? How can we be sure any interpretation is "right," if considering further aspects of the context might well change that interpretation? Let me give an example of a case where changing how much of the context of an utterance we consider changes signifi cantly the interpretation we give to that utterance. Take a claim like "Many children die in Africa before they are fi ve years old because they get infectious diseases like malaria." What is the appropriate amount of context within which to assess this claim? We could consider just medical facts, a narrow context. And in the context the claim seems unexceptional. But widen the context and consider the wider context described below:

Malaria, an infectious disease, is one of the most severe public health problems worldwide. It is a leading cause of death and disease in many developing countries, where young children and pregnant women are the groups most affected. Worldwide, one death in three is from an infectious or communicable disease. However, almost all these deaths occur in the non-industrialized world. Health inequality effects not just how people live, but often dictates how and at what age they die. [see http://www.cdc. gov/malaria/ impact/index.htm and http://ucatlas.ucsc.edu/cause.php]   This context would seem to say that so many children in Africa die early not because of infectious diseases but because of poverty and economic underdevelopment. While this widening of the context does not necessarily render the claim "Many children die in Africa before they are five years old because they get infectious diseases like malaria" false, it, at least, suggests that a narrow construal of "because" here (limiting it to physical and medical causes) effaces the workings of poverty and economics. The frame problem is both a problem and a tool. It is a problem because our discourse analytic interpretations (just like people's everyday interpretations of language) are always vulnerable to changing as we widen the context within which we interpret a piece of language. It is a tool because we can use it—widening the context—to see what information and values are being left unsaid or effaced in a piece of language. The frame problem, of course, raises problems about validity for discourse analysis. We cannot really argue an analysis is valid unless we keep widening the context in which we consider a piece of language until the widening appears to make no difference to our interpretation. At that point, we can stop and make our claims (open, of course, to later falsifi cation as in all empirical inquiry).

Critical Discourse Analysis

Some forms of discourse analysis add a third task to the two (the utterancetype meaning task and the situated meaning task) discussed so far. They study, as well, the ways in which either or both of language-form correlations at the utterance-type level (task 1) and situated meanings (task 2) are associated with social practices (task 3). While non-critical approaches can and do, indeed, study social practices, critical approaches and non-critical ones take a different approach to social practices and how to study them. Non-critical approaches (e.g., see Pomerantz & Fehr, 1997) tend to treat social practices solely in terms of patterns of social interaction (e.g., how people use language to "pull off" a job interview). Thus, consider again the sentence from Gagnon we discussed above:

Though the Whig and Tory parties were both narrowly confi ned to the privileged classes, they represented different factions and tendencies. A non-critical form of discourse analysis could well point out the fact that using "Though the Whig and Tory parties were both narrowly confi ned to the privileged classes" as a dependent (and, thus, assumed and unasserted) clause sets up a social relationship with the reader in terms of which the reader should accept, as given and assumed, that distinctions of wealth in a society are less central to the development of democracy than political differences within elites in the society (which the main asserted clause is about).

Critical approaches, however, go further and treat social practices, not just in terms of social relationships, but also in terms of their implications for things like status, solidarity, the distribution of social goods, and power (e.g., how language in a job interview functions as a gate-keeping device, allowing some sorts of people access and denying it to others). In fact, critical discourse analysis argues that language-in-use is always part and parcel of, and partially constitutive of, specific social practices, and that social practices always have implications for inherently political things like status, solidarity, the distribution of social goods, and power. So the issue becomes this: Is it enough to leave the analysis of the social at the level of how talk and texts function in social interactions or do we need to go further and consider, as well, how talk and text function politically in social interactions? Does the latter task render discourse analysis—and thus, perforce, critical discourse analysis—"unscientific" or "unacademic," a mere matter of "advocacy"? Consider sentence (1) again. There are historians who think that class con- flict—conflict between haves and have nots—drives history. They would say that that the fact that the Whig and Tory parties were narrowly confined to the privileged classes is a key fact about the political situation of 17th-century England (though Gagnon places it in a subordinate clause).

This fact, they will say, drove change because it led to the non-elites fighting for representation. What Gagnon has done is put what these historians see as the key point in a subordinate clause and treated it as assumed and back-grounded information that, while important, does not challenge his main claim that the Whig and Tory parties represented different factions (and, thus, for Gagnon were in the forefront of the development of democracy in Western society). His formulation is a move not only in an academic argument with such historians but in political debates about what and how history ought to be taught in school. This is an essential aspect to understanding not just what Gagnon is saying, but what he is trying to do. It moves us beyond social in-teractions between writer and reader and to value-laden positions that are "po-litical." Claims like Gagnon's do not come out of nowhere. They are part of ongoing dialogue or debate (as Bakhtin, 1986) and are understood within that dialogue or debate. Thus, a full discourse analysis must discuss such matters and must, in that sense, be critical. When I discuss the "building tasks" in the next section, I will offer yet another, more general, reason why all language use is "political" and, thus, why discourse analysis ought to be critical. I will also define what I mean by "politics" and "political."

Building Task I mentioned in the last section that in sentence (1) Gagnon was not just saying something, but doing something: that is, engaging in a debate and making a move in that debate, as well as trying to influence how and what history is taught in the schools. But language in use always performs actions in the world. Some of these actions are verbal actions in the sense that they require language to carry them out. This includes actions like promising, asking a question, giving an order, or making a request. Some of the actions that we use language to carry out are not verbal. They could be done without language, though it most cases it is easier to do them with language than without.

This includes actions like encouraging people, insulting them, manipulating them, and making them believe certain things. The actions we accomplish using language allow us to build (or destroy) things in the world, things like state history standards, marriages, or committee meetings. We do not usually just engage in a single isolated action and leave it at that. Rather, we have plans and goals and engage in series of related actions in related contexts over long periods of time. These longer-term chains of action are usually done in order to build something in the world (like an institution or a marriage) or to sustain it across time. We continually and actively build and rebuild our worlds, not just through language, but through language used in tandem with actions, interactions, nonlinguistic symbol systems, objects, tools, technologies, and distinctive ways of thinking, valuing, feeling, and believing. Sometimes what we build is quite similar to what we have built before (e.g., sustaining a good marriage); sometimes it is not (e.g., starting a new career).

So language-in-use is a tool, not just for saying and doing things, but also, used alongside other non-verbal tools, to build things in the world. Whenever we speak or write, we always and simultaneously build one of seven things or seven areas of "reality." We often build more than one of these simultaneously through the same words and deeds. Let's call these seven things the "seven building tasks" of language (Gee, 2011). In turn, since we use language to build these seven things, a discourse analyst can ask seven different questions about any piece of language-in-use. This gives us, in turn, seven tools for discourse analysis. Below, I list the seven building tasks.

Significance:

We use language to make things significant in certain ways. As the saying goes, we make "mountains out of mole hills." Things are not trivial or important all by themselves. We humans make them trivial or important or something in between. Gagnon made "The Whig and Tory parties were narrowly confined to the privileged classes" less significant than the supposed fact that "they represented different factions and tendencies." Other historians would have made the fact that the Whig and Tory parties narrowly represented elites in society more significant.

Activities (Practices)

We use language to carry out actions like promising and encouraging and a great many others. However, we humans also enact what I will call larger activities, using the word in a special and restricted way. By an "activity" I mean a socially recognized and institutionally or culturally supported endeavor that usually involves sequencing or combining actions in certain specified ways. Encouraging a student is an action; mentoring the student is an activity. Telling someone something about linguistics is an action (informing); lecturing on linguistics is an activity. Often the term "practice" is used for what I am calling an activity.

We use language to get recognized as engaging in a certain sort of activity.

A graduate student who has lost her advisor after some time in a graduate program and asks a professor "Will you be my advisor?" is making a request (an action we do with language). But she is also engaged in the activity of seeking a new graduate advisor in graduate school. This requires more than just the request. There is more that needs to be said and done. For instance, the student has to be able to talk about her background in the program, her knowledge and skills, and her accomplishments in ways that impress the advisor without seeming too arrogant or exaggerated.

Identities

We use language to get recognized as taking on a certain identity or role: that is, to build an identity here and now. For example, I talk and act in one way and I am speaking and acting as the chair of the committee; at the next moment I speak and talk in a different way and I am speaking and acting as just one peer/ colleague speaking to another. Even if I have an official appointment as chair of the committee, I am not always taken as acting as the chair, even during meetings.

Doctors talk and act to their patients differently when they are being doctors and when they are talking as acquaintances or friends, even in their offices. In fact, traditional authoritarian doctors and new humanistic doctors talk and act to the patients differently, are different types of doctors. Humanistic doctors try to talk less technically and more inclusively to their patients. One and the same doctor can even switch between the two identities at different points or in different activities in his or her treatment of a patient.

RELATIONSHIPS:

We use language to build and sustain relationships of all different kinds. We use language to build relationships with other people and with groups and institutions. For example, in a committee meeting, as chair of the committee, if I say "Prof. Smith, I'm very sorry to have to move us on to the next agenda item," I am constructing a relatively formal and deferential relationship with Prof. Smith. On the other hand, suppose I say, "Ed, it's time to move on." Now I am constructing a relatively informal and less deferential relationship with the same person. Speaking and acting a certain way across time with Prof. Smith or Ed will build a certain sort of relationship with him or multiple relationships with him for different contexts.

POLITICS (THE DISTRIBUTION OF SOCIAL GOODS)

I use the term "politics" in a special way. By "politics" I do not mean government and political parties. I mean any situation where the distribution of social goods is at stake. By "social goods" I mean anything a social group or society takes as a good worth having. We use language to build and destroy social goods. For example, for most groups, treating people with respect in certain circumstances is a social good and treating them with disrespect is not. Speaking and acting respectfully and deferentially in these circumstances is to create and distribute a social good. There are other circumstances where people want to be treated not deferentially, but with solidarity and bonding. Speaking and acting toward someone who wants my friendship with solidarity and bonding is in that circumstance to create and distribute a social good. Why do I refer to this as "politics"? Because the distribution of social goods and claims about them—goods like a person being taken as acceptable, normal, important, respected, an "insider" or an "outsider," or as being connected to acceptable, normal, or important things (in the right circumstances)—are ultimately what give people power and status in a society (or not).

People obviously disagree about what are social goods in various circumstances. They obviously sometimes fight over the distribution of social goods and demand their share of them. Let me give an example that shows that how we construct our sentences has implications for building or destroying social goods. If I say "Microsoft loaded its new operating system with bugs," I treat Microsoft as purposeful and responsible, perhaps even culpable. I am withholding a social good from them as an institution, namely respect and a good reputation.

If I say, on the other hand, "Microsoft's new operating system is loaded with bugs," I treat Microsoft as less purposeful and responsible, less culpable. I am still withholding social goods, but not as much as before. If I say, "Like any highly innovative piece of new software, Microsoft's new operating system is loaded with bugs," I have mitigated my withholding of social goods further and even offered Microsoft social goods, namely treating them as innovative and as not really responsible for the bugs. How I phrase the matter has implications for social goods like guilt and blame, legal responsibility or lack of it, or Microsoft's bad or good motives, and Microsoft's reputation.

CONNECTIONS

Things in the world can be seen as connected and relevant to each other (or not) in a great many different ways. For example, people argued over the connection Iraq had to 9/11. That Iraq had no direct connection was eventually conceded by almost everyone, but some people continued to argue that as a "sponsor of state terrorism" they had an indirect connection. Others disputed this connection. If I say "Malaria kills many people in poor countries," I have connected malaria and poverty. If I say "Malaria kills many people across the globe," I have not connected them. Some connections exist in the world regardless of what we say and do (like malaria and poverty).

Nonetheless, we can still render these connections visible or not in our language. Other connections do not exist so clearly in the world until we have worked— partly through how we use language—to make them real in some sense, at least in terms of having real effects in the world. For example, in debates over health care reform in the United States, one regularly hears that government-sponsored health care is a form of socialism. It is debatable whether government subsidies for health care and socialism go together in reality (for example, nearly no one now—though they used to—says Medicare, a government-run program for the elderly, is a form of socialism or wants to get rid of it), but they are so often connected in some of the media in the United States that many people do see them as connected.

SIGN SYSTEMS AND KNOWLEDGE

We use language to build up or tear down various sign systems (communicational systems) and ways of knowing the world. There are many different languages (e.g., Spanish, Russian, and English). There are many different varieties of any one language (e.g., different dialects, as well as language varieties like the language of lawyers, the language of biologists, and the language of hip-hop artists). There are communicative systems that are not language (e.g., equations, graphs, images) or at least not just language (e.g., hip-hop, poetry, ads with pictures and words). These are all different sign systems.

All these different sign systems are important to the people who participate in them. People are often deeply connected to and committed to their dialect. Lawyers are committed to talking like lawyers. Hip-hop fans are passionate. There are even violent arguments over where and when Spanish should be spoken in the United States. Physicists believe the language of mathematics is superior to languages like English for explicit communication.

Furthermore, different sign systems represent different views of knowledge and belief. As we said, physicists believe the language of mathematics is superior to English for producing and communicating knowledge about the physical world. Poets believe poetry is a higher form of knowing and insight, as do, in another sense, people who use religious varieties of language. Speakers of Black Vernacular English believe there are some things that can be expressed or felt in that dialect better than they can in Standard English. So, too, Spanish-English bilinguals favor one language or the other for different topics or emotions. Statisticians believe statistics is a deep way of understanding reality, while some qualitative researchers do not, or, at least, believe the language of statistics has spread too far in our understanding of the social world.

We can use language to make certain sign systems and certain forms of knowledge and belief better or worse, relevant or privileged, "real" or not in given situations; that is, we can build privilege or prestige for one sign system or way of claiming knowledge over another. For example, I can talk and act so as to make the knowledge and language of lawyers relevant (privileged) or not over "everyday language" or over "non-lawyerly academic language" in our committee discussion of facilitating the admission of more minority students. I can talk and act as if Spanish is an inferior language, or not. I can talk and act so as to make the language and actions of "controlled studies" (e.g., "controlled studies of classroom") what constitutes "real evidence" or "real science," or not. I can talk and act so as to constitute the language of creationism as "scientific" and as a competitor with the language of evolution, or not.

The Sign System and Knowledge Building task is clearly related to the Politics task, since constructing privilege for a sign system or way of knowing the world is to create and offer a social good. But the domain of sign systems (including the world's languages) and ways of knowing are especially important domains. Consider the effort people have spent trying to build or destroy "design science" (creationism) as an "acceptable" and "true" way of talking and acting.

EXAMPLE

To see the seven building tasks at work, consider the data below. This is a teacher being interviewed. She was asked if she ever discusses social issues in her classroom, issues to do with power, race, or class. [A comma means a nonfinal intonation contour; a period means a final falling intonation contour; a question mark means a final rising intonation contour; "I" stands for "interviewer"]:

Uh I talk about housing,

We talk about the [????] we talk about a lot of the low income things, I said "Hey wait a minute," I said, "Do you think the city's gonna take care of an area that you don't take care of yourself"? [I: uh huh] I said, "How [many of] you [have] been up [NAME] Street"? They raise their hands, I say "How about [NAME] Ave.?" That's where those gigantic houses are. I said, "How many pieces of furniture are sitting in the front yard"? [I: mm hm] "Well, none." I said "How much trash is lying around"? "None." I said, "How many houses are spray painted"? "How many of them have kicked in, you know have broken down cars."

I do not have space here for a full analysis of this data. I will just comment shortly on each task. A full analysis would require tying each point I make below to specific uses of language in the data. The Significance Building Task: The teacher makes the neighborhood conditions significant in demarcating richer and poorer people. She does not make the social and economic conditions in which they live significant (e.g., there are more broken-down cars in poor neighborhoods, because poor people cannot afford to put them in expensive repair shops). The Activities Building Task: The teacher enacts a dialogue she has with her class. This dialogue enacts the activity of a certain form of advice giving (what to do and not do for success in society). Indeed, this data was preceded by the teacher talking about an Ann Landers advice column on how to dress for a job interview that she reads to her students.

The Identities Building Task: The teacher creates through her language an identity for her kids as people who are associated with "low income things" and who contrast with people in richer neighborhoods. She holds a view, which she makes clear elsewhere, that class is behavior, and if people change how they behave and dress, they become "middle class" people and not ones associated with "low income things."

The Relationships Building Task: In her enacted dialogue the teacher sets up a relationship to her students where she is a world-wise middle-class advice giver that can change their lives through her advice. Elsewhere she makes clear that poor children cannot get proper nurturing and advice from their parents and so it becomes the role of the teacher to give this to them. The Politics Building Task: The teacher is engaged in a form of "blaming the victim" (i.e., you and your "low income" behaviors are the cause of your own failure, not larger social and economic conditions). She is, thus, denying the children in her class the social good of not being associated with "low income things," as well as the social good associated with those "gigantic houses" in the rich neighborhood. The teacher develops in her language a specific politics of poverty and wealth that has to do with behavior and not the possession, say, of wealth and wealthy houses. [By the way, I am not saying the teacher is "wrong" or "right." Saying people are just victims of large social forces over which they have no control is also not highly motivating for people.]

The Connections Building Task: The teacher connects "low income things" and a list of neighborhood behaviors (e.g., trash lying around). At a deeper level she connects the appearance of a neighborhood with both its wealth and the "nature" of its people (because it is the people who make the appearances, not the social conditions—e.g., no regular trash pickup—because they are associated with "low income things" and behaviors and can change those behaviors). The Sign Systems and Knowledge Building Task: The teacher's language privileges one way to know the world, namely by observing behavior and appearances. This can be contrasted with some sociological ways of knowing the world that argue that behavior and appearances are the outcome of larger social, economic, and political forces. For the teacher, poverty is not first and foremost a socio-economic category. It is first and foremost a behavioral category under the control of the people themselves. I want to stress that I have not offered a discourse analysis of the data. I have offered some conclusions that I believe could be drawn from the data if an analyst asked what grammatical and discourse features of the language are carrying out which of our seven building tasks and in what ways. We have to tie grammatical and discourse features (linguistic features) to the sorts of meanings each task entails.

Theoretical Tools of Inquiry

We turn now to four tools that are centered in theories from different academic areas about how language ties to the world and to culture (Gee, 2005). First, we will draw on theories from a variety of areas (cultural anthropology, cultural psychology, sociolinguistics, and philosophy) about how meaning goes well beyond human minds and language to involve objects, tools, technologies, and networks of people collaborating with each other. Here we will introduce the notion of "Discourses" with a capital "D" (so-called "big 'D' Discourses").

Second, we will draw on a theory from sociolinguistics about how different styles or varieties of using language work to allow humans to carry out different types of social work and enact different socially situated identities. We will introduce the notion of "social languages" and argue that any language (like English or Russian) is composed of a great many different social languages. Third, we will draw on a theory from cognitive psychology about how meaning works. We will use the notion of "situated meanings" and argue that we humans actively build meanings "on line" when we use language in specific situations. Fourth, we will draw on a theory from psychological anthropology about how humans form and use theories to give language meaning and understand each other and the world. Here we will introduce the notion of "figured worlds." Figured worlds are narratives and images different social and cultural groups of people use to make sense of the world. They function as simplified models of how things work when they are "normal" and "natural" from the perspective of a particular social and cultural group.

Discourses

People talk and act not just as individuals, but as members of various sorts of social and cultural groups. The social groups with which we share conventions about how to use and interpret language are many and varied. These groups include cultures; ethnic groups; professions like doctors, lawyers, teachers, and carpenters; academic disciplines; interest-driven groups like bird watchers and video gamers; and organizations like street gangs, the military, and sports teams. There are yet many other sorts of social groups. All of them has distinctive ways with words associated with distinctive identities and activities. There is no one word for all these sorts of groups within which we humans act out distinctive identities and activities. People have tried various names for them: "cultures" (Street, 1995, broadening the term), "communities of practice" (Lave & Wenger, 1991), "speech communities," (Labov, 1972a, 1972b), "discourse communities" (Bizzell, 1992), "activity systems" (Engeström, Miettinen & Punamäki, 1999), "actor-actant networks" (Latour, 2005), "collectives" (Latour, 2004), "affinity spaces" or "affinity groups" (Gee, 2004), and others. Each label is meant to capture just some such groups or just some aspects of such groups

I use the term "Discourse" with a capital "D" (so-called "big 'D' Discourses"). I use this term because such groups continue through time—for the most part, they were here before we arrived on earth and will be here after we leave—and we can see them as communicating (discoursing) with each other through time and history, using us as their temporary mouthpieces. I use the term "discourse," with a little "d," to mean language in use or stretches of oral or written language in use ("texts"). When we enact an identity in the world, we do not just use language all by itself to do this. We use language, but we also use distinctive ways of acting, interacting with others, believing, valuing, dressing, and using various sorts of objects and tools in various sorts of distinctive environments.

If you want to show me you are a basketball player, you cannot just talk the talk; you have to walk the walk and do that with a basketball on a basketball court in front of other people. If you want to get recognized as a devout Catholic, you cannot just talk the "right" way about the "right" things; you also have to engage in certain actions (like going to Mass) with the "right" people (e.g., priests) in the "right" places (e.g., church) and you have to display the "right" sorts of beliefs (e.g., the virgin birth of Christ from his mother Mary) and values (e.g., deference to the Pope). The same is true of trying to get recognized as a "Native American," a "good student," a "tough policeman," or a "competent doctor." You need to talk the talk and walk the walk. A Discourse with a capital "D" is composed of distinctive ways of speaking/listening and often, too, writing/reading coupled with distinctive ways of acting, interacting, valuing, feeling, dressing, thinking, believing, with other people and with various objects, tools, and technologies, so as to enact specific socially recognizable identities. Discourses are about being "kinds of people" (Hacking, 1986). There are different ways to be an African American or Latino of a certain sort or kind. Thus, there are different kinds of African Americans or any other cultural group. Being a policeman is to act out a kind of person. So is being a "tough cop," which is to talk and act as sub-kind of person within the kind of being a policeman. Being a SPED student ("Special Ed") is one way to be a kind of student; it is one kind of student. There are kinds within kinds.

Kinds of people (Hacking, 1986) appear in history and some disappear. At one time in history in England and the United States you could be recognized as a witch if you talked the talked and walked the walk (and you might in some cases do so unintentionally). Now it is much harder to get recognized as a witch in many of the places where it was once much easier, though there are still places in the world where you can get recognized as a witch. That "kind of person" has pretty much disappeared in England and the United States. The whole point of taking about Discourses is to focus on the fact that when people mean things to each other, there is always more than language at stake. To mean anything to someone else (or even to myself) I have to communicate who I am (in the sense of what socially situated identity am I taking on here and now). I also have to communicate what I am doing in terms of what socially situated activity I am seeking to carry out (Wieder & Pratt, 1990), since Discourses (being and doing kinds of people) exist in part to allow people to carry out certain distinctive activities (e.g., arresting people for a policeman, taking communion for a Catholic, getting an "A" for a good student). Language is not enough for this. We have to get our minds and deeds "right," as well. We also have to get ourselves appropriately in synch with various objects, tools, places, technologies, and other people. Being in a Discourse is being able to engage in a particular sort of "dance" with words, deeds, values, feelings, other people, objects, tools, technologies, places, and times so as to get recognized as a distinctive sort of who doing a distinctive sort of what. Being able to understand a Discourse is being able to recognize such "dances."

Discourses are not units or tight boxes with neat boundaries. Rather they are ways of recognizing and getting recognized as certain sorts of whos doing certain sorts of whats. One and the same "dance" can get recognized in multiple ways, in partial ways, in contradictory ways, in disputed ways, in negotiable ways, and so on and so forth through all the multiplicities and problematics that work on postmodernism has made so popular. Discourses are matters of enactment and recognition, then. All recognition processes involve satisfying a variety of constraints in probabilistic and sometimes partial ways. For example, something recognized as a "weapon" (e.g., a baseball bat or a fireplace poker) may share some features with prototypical weapons (like a gun, sword, or club) and not share other features. And there may be debate about the matter. Furthermore, the very same thing might be recognized as a weapon in one context and not in another. So, too, with being in and out of Discourses, for example enacting and recognizing being-doing a certain type of street gang member, Special Ed student, or particle physicist. While there are an endless array of Discourses in the world, nearly all human beings, except under extraordinary conditions, acquire an initial Discourse within whatever constitutes their primary socializing unit early in life. Early in life, we all learn a culturally distinctive way of being an "everyday person" as a member of our family and community. We can call this our "primary Discourse." Our primary Discourse gives us our initial and often enduring sense of self and sets the foundations of our culturally specific vernacular language (our "everyday language"), the language in which we speak and act as "everyday" (nonspecialized) people. As a person grows up, lots of interesting things can happen to his or her primary Discourse. Primary Discourses can change, hybridize with other Discourses, and they can even die. In any case, for the vast majority of us, our primary Discourse, through all its transformations, serves us throughout life as what I will call our "lifeworld Discourse" (Habermas, 1984). Our lifeworld Discourse is the way that we use language, feel and think, act and interact, and so forth, in order to be an "everyday" (nonspecialized) person. In our pluralistic world there is much adjustment and negotiation as people seek to meet in the terrain of the lifeworld, given that lifeworlds are culturally distinctive (that is, different groups of people have different ways of being-doing "everyday people").

All the Discourses we acquire later in life, beyond our primary Discourse, we acquire within a more "public sphere" than our initial socializing group. We can call these "secondary Discourses." They are acquired within institutions that are part and parcel of wider communities, whether these be religious groups, community organizations, schools, businesses, or governments. The notion of Discourses tells us discourse analysts that language—what we are specialists in—is only part of the picture. If we want to explicate the workings of identity and social practices in society (which is the point of discourse analysis for me), we have to put the language we analyze back into the context of Discourses at work (play?) in society across time and space.

Social Languages

People do not speak any language "in general." They always speak a specific variety of a language (which might actually mix together more than one language like English or Spanish) and they use different varieties in different contexts. There are social and regional varieties of language that are called "dialects." However, we are going to concentrate here on what I will call "social languages" (many linguists use the term "register" in a somewhat similar way, e.g., Halliday & Hasan, 1989). Social languages are a important aspect of the language part of Discourses (remember that Discourses involve more than just language). To understand what a speaker says, a listener needs to know who is speaking. But it is not enough to know, for example, that Mary Smith is the speaker. I need to know what identity Mary is speaking out of. Is she speaking to me as a teacher, a feminist, a friend, a colleague, an avid bird watcher, a political liberal, or one of a great many other possible identities or roles?

Listeners need to know who speakers are. Is my doctor saying I look "stressed" just as a friend or is he speaking as a doctor? When the police officer says "I think you should move your car," is she speaking as a police officer and ordering me to move the car or speaking as a helpful fellow citizen giving me advice? I will define social languages as styles or varieties of a language (or a mixture of languages) that enact and are associated with a particular social identity. All languages, like English or French, are composed of many (a great many) different social languages. Social languages are what we learn and what we speak. Here are some examples of social languages: the language of medicine, literature, street gangs, sociology, law, rap, or informal dinner-time talk among friends.

Even within these large categories there are subvarieties. Not all types of gangs or sociologists speak the same when they are speaking as gang members or sociologists. To know any specific social language is to know how its characteristic lexical and grammatical resources are combined to enact specific socially situated identities (that is, being, at a given time and place, a lawyer, a gang member, a politician, a literary humanist, a "bench chemist," a radical feminist, an "everyday person," or whatever). To know a particular social language is either to be able to "do" a particular identity or to be able to recognize such an identity, when we do not want to or cannot actively participate. Dialects like Southern English, Black Vernacular English, and working-class English (all of which come in different subvarieties) can be seen as social languages as well. Southern English is a way to mark oneself as a southerner. Black Vernacular English is a way to mark oneself as an African American of a certain sort. Let me give an example.A young woman, telling the same story to her parents and to her boyfriend, says to her parents at dinner: "Well, when I thought about it, I don't know, it seemed to me that Gregory should be considered the most offensive character," but later to her boyfriend she says: "What an ass that guy was, you know, her boyfriend." In the first case, she uses distinctive lexical and grammatical resources to enact "a dutiful and intelligent daughter having dinner with her proud parents" and in the other case to enact "a girlfriend being intimate with her boyfriend." Note, by the way, that the particular labels I use here are not important. Many social languages have no names and names need not be used by people overtly. People who use a given social language may differ on what they call it. The point just is that people must have some, however tentative, unspoken, and problematic, idea of who is speaking in the sense of what social identity is at play

Situated Meanings

We have already talked about this tool above when we talked about the situated meaning task. In actual situations of use, words and structures take specifi c meanings, meanings we will call "situated meaning." We gave examples of situated meanings above. But there is one important aspect to add here. When speakers speak they assume that listeners share enough knowledge, beliefs, values, and experiences with them to be able to situate the meanings of their words. Listeners situate the meanings of words by consulting what the speaker has said, the context in which it has been said, and (if they actually have it) the wealth of shared background the speaker assumes they have. So take the following remark:

yet I believe [Milton] Friedman is right that thoroughgoing restrictions on economic freedom would turn out to be inconsistent with democracy. (http://www.becker-posner-blog.com/archives/2006/11/on_milton_fried. html)

If you do not know neoliberal theories of economics (which Milton Friedman helped innovate and implement in countries across the world), you have no idea what to make of how "democracy" is being used here. You do not know how to situate its meaning. Given only the utterance-type (general) meaning of "democracy" as representative government with elections, the remark, on its face, would seem to be senseless: surely an elected government could pass laws that restricted economic freedoms and this would seem to be an example of democracy at work. The remark is only consistent if you know how to situate the meaning of "democracy" in it, and you only how to do this if you share with the author (which he assumes you do) knowledge about neoliberal economics. Neoliberal economics is a Discourse. Many people know how to recognize and get recognized as "neoliberals." So speakers assume that in situating meaning we share knowledge about Discourses in society with them. They also assume that we share knowledge of "cultural models" or "fi gured worlds" with them. And to this we now turn.

Figured Worlds Is the Pope a bachelor (Fillmore, 1975)? Though the Pope is an unmarried man—and "bachelor" as a word is defined as "an unmarried man"—we are reluctant to call the Pope a bachelor. Why? The reason is that we do not use words just based on their definitions or what we called earlier their "utterancetype (general) meanings." We use words based, as well, on stories, theories, or models in our minds about what is "normal" or "typical" or "the way the world should be or is."

It is typical in our world that men marry women. A man who is somewhat past the typical age when people marry, we call a "bachelor," assuming he is open to marriage but has either chosen to wait or has not found the "right" person. The Pope is both well past the normal age for marriage and has vowed never to marry. He just does not fit the typical story in our heads. We use words based on such typical stories unless something in the context makes us think the situation is not typical. If the issue of gay marriage or the chauvinism of calling men "bachelors" and women "spinsters" comes up, then we have to think more overtly about matters and abandon, if only for the time, our typical picture. Indeed, things can change in society enough that what counts as a typical story changes or becomes contested. People may even stop using words like "bachelor" based on the typical story and form a new typical story—and, thus, start calling marriage-eligible women "bachelors" as well.

We use such typical pictures so that we can go on about the business of communicating, acting, and living without having to consciously think about everything—all the possible details and exceptions—all the time. This is good for getting things done, but sometimes bad in the ways in which such typical stories can marginalize people and things that are not taken as "normal" or "typical" in the story. What counts as a typical story for people differs by their sociocultural affiliations. For example, some parents confronted by a demanding 2-year-old who angrily refuses to go to bed when his or her parents say to take the child's behavior as sign of growth towards autonomy because they accept a typical story like this: Children are born dependent on their parents and then grow towards individual autonomy or independence. On their way to autonomy, they act out demanding independence when they may not yet be ready for it, but this is still a sign of development and growth (Harkness, Super, & Keefer, 1992).

Other parents confronted by the same behavior take the behavior as a sign of the child's willfulness because they accept a typical story like this: Children are born selfish and need to be taught to think of others and collaborate with the family rather than demand their own way (Harkness et al. 1992; Philipsen, 1975). It is, perhaps, not surprising that this latter typical story is more common among working-class parents and families where mutual support among family and friends is important. The former story is more common among middleand upper-middle-class families with many more financial resources where people are expected to grow into adults who have the resources to go it more on their own.

Such typical stories are not "right" or "wrong." (for example, children are, of course, born dependent on their parents, but are children primarily inherently selfish and in need of being taught how to cooperate with others or are they inherently reliant on caregivers and in need of learning to be independent? These are different viewpoints that are probably both true in some sense, but one or the other can be stressed and form the main parenting style in the home).

They are simplified theories of the world that are meant to help people go on about the business of life when one is not allowed the time to think through and research everything before acting. Even theories in science are simplified views of the world meant to help scientists cope without having to deal with the full complexity of the world all at once.

These typical stories have been given many different names. They have been called "folk theories," "frames," "scenarios," "scripts," "mental models," "cultural models," "Discourse models," and "figured worlds" (and each of these terms has its own nuances; see Gee, 2004, 2005, for discussion and citations). Such typical stories are stored in our heads (and we will see in a moment that they are not always only in our heads) in the form of images, metaphors, and narratives.

We will use the term "figured world" here for these typical stories. The term figured world" has been defined as follows: A socially and culturally constructed realm of interpretation in which particular characters and actors are recognized, significance is assigned to certain acts, and particular outcomes are valued over others. Each is a simplified world populated by a set of agents who engage in a limited range of meaningful acts or changes of state as moved by a specific set of forces. (Holland, Lachicotte, Skinner, & Cain, 1998, p. 52). A figured world is a picture of a simplified world that captures what is taken to be typical or normal. What is taken to be typical or normal, of course, varies by context and by people's sociocultural affiliations (as we saw in the example of acting out 2-year-olds above). To give another example, consider the figured world (or typical story) that might arise in someone's mind if they think about an elementary school classroom: Typical participants include one teacher (a female) and a group of kids of roughly the same age, and some support staff including teachers who help kids with special problems (e.g., learning disabilities, reading problems, or who are learning English as a second language), sometimes by pulling them out of the classroom. The kids are sitting in desks in rows facing the teacher, who is doing most of the talking and sometimes asks the kids questions to which she knows the answers. There are activities like filling out sheets of paper with math problems on them. There are regular tests, some of them state standardized tests. There is an institution surrounding the teacher that includes a principal and other teachers as well as curriculum directors and mandates from officials. Parents are quasi "outsiders" to this institution. There are labels for individual kids, labels such as "SPED" (special education), "LD" (learning disabled), and "ESL" (English as a Second Language). This figured world—with its typical participants, activities, forms of language, and object and environments—is, of course, realized in many actual classrooms. However, there are many exceptions, as well, but they do not normally come to mind when we think and talk about schools. In fact, every aspect of this figured world is heavily contested in some current school reforms (e.g., age grading, lots of testing, skill sheets, too much teacher talk, children in rows). The taken-for-granted nature of the figured world, however, often stands in the way of change. Reforms just do not seem "normal" or "right" or "the ways things should be." For example, today it is not uncommon that young children can teach adults things about digital technology, but the child teaching and the teacher learning violates our typical story. It also violates the values and structures of authority this typical story incorporates.

I have said that these typical stories—what we are calling figured worlds—are in our heads. But that is not strictly true. Often they are partly in our heads and partly out in the world in books and other media and in other people's heads, people we can talk to. The figured world in which children are born dependent and development is progress towards individual autonomy and independence for adults who can manage their own lives based on their own resources is a model that is found in lots of child-raising self-help books and in the talk and actions of many parents who are professionals (e.g., doctors, lawyers, professors, executives, and so forth) with whom we can interact if we live in the right neighborhood. When people "figure" a world, that is, imagine what the world looks like from a certain perspective of what is "normal" or "typical" (as in the classroom example above), they are imaging pictures of Discourses or aspects of Discourses at work in the world. They are imaging typical identities and activities within typical environments.

Situated meanings, social languages, figured worlds, and Discourses move us from the ground of specific uses of language in specific contexts (situated meanings) up to the world of identities and institutions in time and space (Discourses) through varieties of language (social languages) and people's takenfor-granted theories of the world (figured worlds). This progression is, in my view, the point of discourse (or, better d/Discourse) analysis. Since Discourses and their interactions in time and space are inherently about the distribution of social goods (i.e., kinds of people and their places in society), discourse analysis is or should be inherently "critical" and even "political.

NARRATIVES OF EXCLUSION AND THE CONSTRUC-TION OF THE SELF

Schooling prior to higher education in Mexico comprises four levels: preschool (3 years), elementary or primaria (6 years), secundaria (3 years), and bachillerato (3 years, equivalent to grades 10 to 12 in U.S. schools). Bachillerato is not compulsory. Students who have access to this level are expected to pass every subject if they want to remain in school. Although schools provide a second opportunity through make-up exams to students who do not obtain a passing grade, if they fail to pass these exams they are automatically expelled from school, a process described in school records as "baja académica" or "academic dropout." Studies show that this phenomenon occurs predominantly during the first year of bachillerato (Álvarez, 2009; Miramontes, 2003; Romo & Fresán, 2002); however, little is known about the way teachers and students experience this process and the school cultures and positions that enable the identity of "academic failure" and expulsion. In this chapter I focus on narratives of personal experience by Mexican high school students facing imminent expulsion, and compare them to the narratives of their more successful peers at the end of their senior years.

The data for this study is a subset of data gathered during a 3-year longitudinal study in which I and a team of researchers and research assistants collected information regarding the literacy practices of one peri-urban and four urban high schools in selected school subjects. The study encompassed classroom observations in all five sites over the course of one class generation (2004–2007), as well as interviews with teachers, school administrators, and selected students from the groups observed. Student interviews took place at two distinct times: I interviewed students who were failing one or more school subjects at the end of their first year of bachillerato (equivalent to 10th grade, first year of the study), and successful students, identified by a high GPA, at the end of their senior year (third year of the study).

Overall, I interviewed 27 first-year students, 28 third-year students, and 7 third-year students enrolled in the International Baccalaureate, a curricular program offered as a separate track in one of the school sites. I chose the narratives for the analysis that follows because they all share two very revealing Overall, I interviewed 27 first-year students, 28 third-year students, and 7 third-year students enrolled in the International Baccalaureate, a curricular program offered as a separate track in one of the school sites. I chose the narratives for the analysis that follows because they all share two very revealing aspects about the construction of students' selves and their school personae: thematically, they depict episodes of positioning involving teachers and school authorities; and structurally, they evolve around a school conflict and its resolution. In particular, I identify and comment on the figured worlds that render these students' experiences meaningful and the role they play in the experience of "not understanding" and/or not passing a school subject, and the concomitant school identities of academic failure, in the case of first-year students, and academic success, in the case of third-year students. I contend that, as an analytical tool, figured worlds can be viewed as an interface between discourse and Discourse, between linguistic structure and social order. To frame my analysis I provide some figures and information about Mexico's education system and extrapolate to education in general.

Background

In 2005 only 41% of 14- to 17-year-olds in Mexico were enrolled in bachilleratos (Instituto Nacional de Evaluación Educativa, 2006); of these, 60% were able to graduate on time (INEGI, 2005). The low enrollment and graduation rate at this level are symptomatic of Mexico's educational system, where youth face difficult entrance exams, dropout rates are attributable to social, financial, academic, and institutional reasons, and the educational programs vary enormously across regions and student populations. In spite of these staggering numbers, there is a pervasive Discourse on the part of institutions about school achievement that attributes student failure to students' actions and "incompetence."

This Discourse is sustained under a meritocratic premise of equal access and opportunities to succeed regardless of students' background, social class, or gender. However, studies show that the uneven distribution of economic, social, and cultural capital among Mexican youth correlates directly to their success at this school level (Villa, 2007; Zorrilla, 2008). Thus, students with different trajectories and resources occupy different positions within the Discourse upon entering secondary and higher education: whereas those who have had access to the necessary resources to "present" themselves as rightful members may indeed be perceived as more "competent," many students who gain institutional entrance are systematically excluded (especially students from working-class families) from the benefits of a good education, and positioned as incompetent or undeserving.

Gentili (2009) explains this phenomenon as a result of the power struggles that have characterized the expansion of education in most Latin American countries. For underprivileged students, argues Gentili, this has translated into educational programs that "invite" these students to abandon school, or that actively expel them while putting the blame on them for not succeeding. It is not sufficient to stay in school, concludes Gentili, if a person doesn't feel that she/he belongs there. "Not belonging" may arise as a consequence of lacking the necessary resources (social languages, skills and knowledge) and the identities (Discourses, positions) to fully participate within the specialized domains of school. This situation is not limited to Latin America. As Bourdieu and Passeron (1994) and many others have argued, academic language is "no one's mother tongue" (p. 8), and for working-class children in particular, "the divorce between the language of the family and the language of school only serves to reinforce the feeling that the education system belongs to another world" (p. 9). While Bourdieu and Passeron refer specifically to the inevitable "semantic fog" (p. 10) that students have to deal with when they don't have access to the linguistic code of the teachers, I would like to elaborate on this metaphor and suggest that, in addition to the lack of linguistic and cultural resources, students are also deprived of ways of seeing the world from particular standpoints such as those of specialized domains. For instance, Kress (2001) describes the process in which students of particular subjects are expected to learn to see the world of nature through the "world of culture and its conventions" (p. 402). For Kress, teaching students to learn new ways of seeing requires more than linguistic communication (more than discourse, in Gee's parlance), which in the case he describes is used as an "ancillary mode of communication" (p. 402). Similarly, Boaler's (2000) research about students learning math in English schools shows that, for the students interviewed, secondary mathematics was something "of another world," a world that held no meaning or appeal to them (emphasis in original, p. 392).

It is worth mentioning that, in a previous study about academic failure in one of the schools where I carried out my research, Miramontes (2003) found that students who had failed chemistry described this subject as "from another planet" (p. 76), a feeling that was exacerbated by a discourse that was "foreign" and inaccessible to them. Furthermore, Miramontes found that these students' chemistry teachers assumed their students were not "qualified" to understand their class (p. 93), but felt no responsibility for the situation, thereby revealing a school culture that tacitly accepted a "tolerable" number of flunked (and expelled) students per class.

Describing school subjects as "otherworldly" and with particular ways of speaking and perceiving is one way to convey the figured worlds evoked by different disciplines, each with its own specialized (social) language and "distinctive ways of speaking/listening, writing/reading coupled with distinctive ways of acting, interacting, valuing, feeling, thinking, believing," that is, with the different Discourses that allow the enactment of "specific socially recognizable identities" (Gee, this volume, p. xx). As part of the "shared repertoire" (Wenger, 1998) that students would need in order to fully participate in the specialized domains of school subjects, figured worlds are probably one of the most potent reifications for making sense of one's position and creating meaning within the domain.

Narratives, Figured Worlds and Positioning

For the (critical) discourse analyst, narratives of personal experience provide powerful insights into the figured worlds that render experience meaningful. Furthermore, they encode the different voices (Bakhtin, 1981) that make up a person's "space of authoring" (Holland, Lachiotte, Skinner, & Cain, 1998), and thus leave traces of Discourses, positioning, and identities. When someone narrates a personal experience, that person makes herself "an object for another and for oneself . . . But it is also possible to reflect our attitude toward ourselves as objects . . . In this case, our own discourse becomes an object and acquires a second—its own—voice" (Bakhtin, 1986, p. 110).

According to Bruner (1986), narrative thinking is one mode of human cognition; in fact, narratives play a crucial role in the way people make sense of their worlds (Bruner, 1986; Gee, 1989, 1999). As Casey (1995) points out, narrative research is "distinctly interdisciplinary" (p. 22). In using narratives of personal experience as the material for my analysis I want to locate this chapter, following Casey (1995), under the overarching work of narrative research; but I want to distinguish it from other forms of narrative inquiry such as what has been lately described as "narrative analysis" (Coulter & Smith, 2009).

Whereas the former includes the analysis of narratives to explore the relationship between form and function, the latter produces narratives as a way of knowing. Perhaps one of the best analyses that explores the relationship between form and function in narratives is the seminal work of Labov and Waletzky (1967). In it, the authors identified five structural elements of narratives: orientation, complication, evaluation, resolution, and coda, to which Labov later (1972) added a sixth initial element: the abstract. Labov and Waletyzky also established two main functions of narratives: referential and evaluative. Similarly, Wertsch (2002) distinguishes between the referential and the dialogic functions of narrative.

Wertsch alludes to both "empirical" and "fictional" narratives (p. 57), while Labov and Waletzky (1967) concentrate on narratives of events that "did in fact occur" (p. 30) and that are told in the sequence in which they actually happened.

For Labov and Waletzky narratives constitute a method of recapitulating past experience that matches "a verbal sequence of clauses to the sequence of events that actually occurred" (p. 20). The referential function refers to the sequence of events in the narrative, but a narrative that only carries this function may seem pointless and difficult to follow. It is the evaluative function that gives meaning to narratives; Labov and Waletzky explain it by showing how in most narratives of personal experience the narrator suspends the action before the resolution in order to infuse the narrative with evaluative elements that reveal the attitude of the narrator towards the experience narrated in the text. Gee (1999) sums it up by defining the evaluation in narratives as "the material that makes clear why the story is interesting and tellable" (p. 112). Because most narratives respond to a particular stimulus, it is important to consider "the social context in which the narrative occurs" (Labov & Waletzky, 1967, p. 13) and the particular stimulus the narrative responds to. The identification of the evaluative elements of narratives (evaluative function) is one of the most important contributions of Labov and Waletzky's analysis, because these elements encapsulate the point of any narrative.

For Wertsch, the dialogical function refers to "the relationship between one narrative and another . . . [and recognizes] that narratives do not exist in isolation and do not serve as neutral cognitive instruments" (p. 59). Skinner, Valsiner, & Holland (2001) take this argument a little further and, in direct reference to Bakhtin's notion of dialogism, point out the role of others people's voices in the construction of narratives, to which the author takes "a position from which meaning is made—a position that enters a dialogue and takes a particular stance in addressing and answering others and the world" (para. 10, p. 5). Considering the referential, evaluative, and dialogical functions in the narratives of the students interviewed for this study can help shed light on the school cultures and d/Discourses that construct students as "incompetent" or "competent," positions that may lead to either expulsion and academic failure, or permanence and academic success.

Several authors agree that narratives, as cultural artifacts, fall under some kind of distinctive genre, underlying structure, or unconscious realm of interpretation: a "charter narrative" for Amsterdam and Bruner (2000), a "narrative template" for Wertsch (2002), a "master narrative" according to Jameson (1981), or a "master myth" for Gee (1996). For Amsterdam and Bruner (2000) narrative genres "are mental models representing possible ways in which events in the human world can go" (p. 133, emphasis in original). Correspondingly, Gee (1996) argues that "cultural models" or "simplified worlds in which prototypical events unfold" (p. 78) are paramount in rendering discourse meaningful. This description is akin to Holland et al.'s (1998) conceptualization of figured worlds. Figured worlds are historical phenomena that recruit, distribute, divide, and relate participants; they are social encounters in "which participants' positions matter" (. . . and relate participants to landscapes) "giving the landscape human voice and tone" (Holland et al., 1998, p. 41). Most importantly, figured worlds take shape within and grant shape to the coproduction of activities, discourses, performances, and artifacts. A figured world is peopled by the figures, characters, and types who carry out its tasks and who also have styles of interacting within, distinguishable perspectives on, and orientations toward it. (p. 51)

Through figured worlds, narratives of personal experience reveal important aspects about the "discourses and practices that describe" the self (Holland et al., 1998, p. 27). In fact, Gergen describes these texts not as "personal impulses made social but social processes realized on the site of the personal" (in Holland et al., 1998, p. 292). As a tool of inquiry, figured worlds can help us to understand the interface between discourse (language in use) and Discourse (a socially enacted identity). That is, figured worlds, as "socially and culturally constructed realm(s) of interpretation" (Holland et al., 1998, p. 52), provide the basis for making choices when assigning meaning to language and social practices (Gee, 1996). For the purposes of this study, this may be grasped through experiences in which social positions and identities are "offered" to particular persons, or what Holland and Leander (2004) refer to as "episodes of positioning."

Methods and analysis

Data

After carefully reviewing school records, I contacted first-year students who had failed one or more school subjects and explained to them the purpose of the study. All the students voluntarily agreed to be interviewed. The same procedure was followed 2 years later when I approached third-year students, the selection criteria for these students being that they have a high GPA. Most students were interviewed on the school grounds.1 All of the interviews were tape-recorded and fully transcribed with the students' authorization. One of the questions I asked students was to relate a particular experience they felt they could talk about concerning problems they had faced at school, and I asked them to elaborate on how they had coped. This was a question that I purposefully included to elicit narratives and explore issues of agency and the construction of the self. In most cases this elicited narratives that captured episodes of positioning involving their teachers and other school authorities.

Procedures and Analysis

After several readings of the data, I chose 11 narratives for analysis, 6 by firstyear students and 5 by third-year students (3 from the general program and 2 from the International Baccalaureate). I chose these narratives because they fit two criteria according to Labov and Waletzky's (1967) definition of a narrative of personal experience: the sequence of the narrative clauses matched the temporal sequence of the experience, and they were fully formed narratives in terms of evaluative elements. I will comment on the overall themes and structures of the interviews with samples from several of them, but will provide a more detailed analysis based on two narratives, one from a first-year student and one from a third-year student. It is important to mention the obvious but complex issue of the language in which the narratives were produced. Since all of the students interviewed are native speakers of Spanish and the study took place in Mexico, all the interviews were conducted in Spanish. For the purposes of this chapter this posed a problem: Sequence and grammar are very important when analyzing discourse; furthermore, certain idioms and linguistic expressions may not lend themselves to translation. Fairclough (1995) contends that "to include textual analysis of translated data as part of the analysis of a discursive event . . . [is] a procedure which is open to serious objections." (p. 190).

He further recommends that "discourse analysis papers should reproduce and analyse textual samples in the original language, despite the added difficulty for readers" (p. 191). Mindful of these shortcomings, I decided to work with the Spanish originals and translate them into English once I had coded and analyzed every original transcript. This gave me a greater insight into the cultural meanings and the different voices in the narrative. Because a purpose in the analysis was to identify the figured worlds encoded in the narratives, in the English versions I tried to remain faithful to the registers of the participants and the cultural and linguistic gist of the originals, an objective that I believe I accomplished to a certain degree, but not entirely. For instance, the Spanish expression no séqué is strikingly consistent in all the interviews: It is used at particular times in the interviews when students revoice the speech of others, mainly teachers and administrators. In Spanish this phrase expresses a cognitive activity: knowing (a literal translation would be "I don't know what"). This became a central aspect in the analysis and informed my repeated readings of the transcripts, thereby allowing me to identify the different ways students captured the alien voice of authority. It is a clear example of the relationship between linguistic form (cognitive statement) and social function (disavowal of authoritarian voice). However, since I wanted to translate the particular gist every time it was used, the expression took different forms in the English text such as "or something" in Narrative 1, and "stuff like that" in Narratives 1 and 2. In spite of these limitations, I tried to convey the force of these utterances through the analysis. All the interviews were double checked for accuracy by a bilingual linguist whose first language is English. In all cases I provide the Spanish original with the English translation.

The length of each transcript was an average of 15 doubled-spaced pages, but in all cases narratives were clearly identifiable in the transcripts because they were responses to a particular question or "stimulus": a problem each student had faced while at school.

Following Labov and Waletzky (1967), I divided each narrative into clauses and, after several readings, identified the overall structure and color-coded the referential function (sequence of events) and evaluative function (evaluative clauses). The referential function provided the basis for identifying the underlying genre of the narrative, while the evaluative function shed light on the figured worlds that gave meaning to the experience narrated in the text. Because narratives are thick with other people's voices I looked for traces of figured worlds at two levels: dialogical and structural. I considered as dialogical the figured worlds in which the text was clearly doublevoiced in Bakhtin's sense. For instance, I coded the following statement as a dialogical figured world: "If the teachers don't arrive during the first 30 minutes then everyone can leave" (lines 6–7, Narrative 1). In this case, the student echoes the words of others (school authorities) and captures a figured world of rules and rights for teachers and students. Once I had identified the figured worlds at the dialogical level in the narratives I went back to the full transcripts of all the interviews to search for new textual evidence that would help me get a clearer picture of those figured worlds and the voices echoed through the narrative. This helped me corroborate what figured worlds were shared by the students, and to understand the different ways students faced the episodes of positioning involving the school authorities. In the analysis I provide two types of textual data: two narratives (Narratives 1–2) and five excerpts that illustrate particular figured worlds, d/Discourses, and episodes of positioning (Texts 1–5).

I considered the figured world at the structural level the "charter narrative" or narrative genre of the text; that is, the overall structure of the events narrated in the text. Since all the narratives concern problems faced by the students and how they resolved them, at this level the figured world expresses the storylines that modeled their sense of self and reveals issues of agency and self-objectification.

Interpretations

No Matter How Much I Study, I Don't Understand

One of the most striking findings was that, in all five schools, not understanding a school subject was described by both first- and third-year students as the inability to grasp a world that had no meaning for the students, a situation that was aggravated by the teachers' authoritarian Discourse and concomitant positionings. Jaime,2 a first-year struggling student, expressed his frustration as follows:

	Spanish original	English translation
1	J: Química, a eso no le entiendo	J: Chemistry, that I don't understand
2	GLB: ¿Qué es lo que no le entiendes?	GLB: What is it that you don't understand?
3	J: A.. unir moléculas y todo ese rollo, ni	J: To . . . combine molecules and all that stuff, I
4	sé ni.. cómo es..	don't even know what it looks like
5	GLB: ¿ni qué?	GLB: You don't know what?
6	J: No sé cómo es	J: What it looks like

Text 1: Not Understanding

Jaime's words exemplify an instance in which the world of nature is seen "through the world of culture and its conventions," a culture, or rather a world, Jaime is unable to figure and understand. Expressing frustration with the same subject in a different school, another student, Ana, commented on her teacher's inability to communicate with the students:

	Spanish original	English translation
1	A: Se pone a hablar como si hablara	A: He [the teacher] begins to talk as if he was
2	solo. No, no se pone a decirle a los	talking to himself. He doesn't, doesn't tell the
3	alumnos cosas, o sea, se pone a hablar	students anything, like, he just talks and he
4	y no habla con nadie, con nadie,	doesn't talk to anyone, not to anyone,
5	parece que está hablando con él	it seems that he's talking to himself
6	mismo	

Text 2: Monologic Discourse

These two instances capture a figured world that is alien to the students and a teacher whose voice is lost in his own monologue. In the first instance, Jaime is unable to grasp the meaning of a linguistic code that describes objects and processes he can't perceive; in the second, Ana refers to a context in which the communicative function of language is lost. These examples are consistent with Miramontes' (2003) findings about the alien world of chemistry for students and the utter indifference of teachers. The following text by a different student (Luisa) further delineates the school culture and the roles assumed by teachers and students in this type of school environment:

Spanish original	English translation
1 L: Te ponen un ejemplo y te dan otro	L: They [the teachers] give you an example and
2 tema y otra vez, ¿no? pues ya lo	give you another topic, and then again, right?
3 miramos el tema y te explican, te	Well we see the topic and they explain it, and
4 ponen un ejemplo y te dan otro tema y	then they give you another example and another
5 otra vez, ¿no? y te dan otro ejemplo y	topic, and then once again, right? And they give
6 otro tema. Te dan como cinco temas en	you another example and another topic. And they
7 la misma clase y al siguiente día, la	give like five topics in one class, and the next
8 siguiente clase que te toca otra vez te	day, the next class, they give you five more
9 dan cinco temas. . . .	topics.
10 Y en química cuenta 90 % de examen,	And in chemistry he calculates 90% of the grade
11 y yo creo que eso es imposible. Pero	based on the final, and I think that's impossible.
12 pues el maestro así lo hace y, y pues	But he's the teacher and that's how he does it
13 nadie le puede decir nada porque pues	and, and well, there's nobody that can tell him
14 él tiene la autoridad ahí.	anything because he has the authority there.

Text 3: Authoritarian Discourse

In this text the student's voice captures two episodes of positioning: In the first, the teacher covers a prescribed content in the curriculum regardless of students' comprehension of those topics; in the second, the teacher arbitrarily assigns a final grade without taking into consideration the curriculum. In both instances, students are the objects of the authoritarian Discourse of the teachers. This text also revoices an institutional figured world of school positions (the authority of the teacher, the powerlessness of the students) that is in clear contraposition to an internal figured world of rights and obligations ("he calculates 90% of the grade based on the final, and I think that's impossible"). This contradiction is expressed formally through evaluative clauses that are linked by the adversative conjunction "but," a form that in evaluative clauses can signal contrasting figured worlds. In the first evaluative clause, the cognitive I-statement ("I think that's impossible") captures an agentic voice that questions the teachers actions, while the second ("but he's the teacher and . . . nobody can tell him anything") expresses the frustration of being silenced by the authority embodied in the teacher. These examples of students' d/Discourse speak of a school culture of indifference towards students' alienation, which thereby fosters the institutional construction of academic failure. Further, they exemplify the lack of meaning of a specialized discourse when students are denied access to particular ways of seeing the cultural objects and processes that render the discourse meaningful.

He Told Us: "You All Failed"

Not understanding, not having access to figured worlds that have been consistently denied, and not having a voice at school leads to failure, which in turn, leads to expulsion. The following narrative by Brenda, a 16-year-old who had been recently expelled at the time the interview took place, will show the different figured worlds, Discourses and identities this student had to navigate while at school.

	Spanish Original	English Translation
1	Y todos, pues sí reprobamos un chorro,	And everyone well, yeah, a lot of us didn't pass,
2	pues, porque no.. porque no, no calificaba tareas, ni trabajos.	because he didn't, he didn't grade our assignments or homework.
3	Sí nos dejaba tareas,	He did give us homework
4	pero no las revisaba nunca.	but he never checked it.
5	Nunca las revisó.	Never checked it.
6	Tengo los . . . tengo los cuadernos, este . . . y	I have my . . . I have my notebooks and well,
7	no, no tengo nada revisado, una hojita, nada más tengo así.	I don't have anything checked, just one little piece of paper.
8	G: ¿Nunca le dijeron al maestro?	GLB: Did you ever tell the teacher?
9	B: ¡Sí!, y nos decía: "No" que "no sé qué,	B: Yes! And he would say: "No" or something,

10	sí los voy a calificar."	"I will grade them."
11	Porque una vez, pues, todos se le pusieron al profe.	Because once, well, they all confronted him.
12	Porque nos quiso poner muchas faltas . . .	Because he wanted to give us a lot of absences..
13	es que un día el llegó . . . llegó al . . .	because once he got to . . . he got . . .
14	nos tocaba clase de once a una,	we had a class from 11:00 to 1:00,
15	creo, de . . . sí, de once a una,	I think, and yeah, 11:00 to 1:00.
16	entonces, has de cuenta que, según cuando, sí no llegan los profesores en media hora	So like, if the teachers don't arrive during the first 30 minutes
17	todos se pueden ir.	then everyone can leave.
18	Y todos nos esperamos ahí	And we all waited there
19	y no llegaba	and he didn't come,
20	y pasó una hora	and an hour passed
21	y no llegaba,	and he didn't come,
22	y todos nos fuimos,	and everyone left,
23	se quedaron nada más como cinco,	only about five stayed
24	se me hace,	I think,
25	no me acuerdo cuántos,	I don't remember how many,
26	y todos se fueron	and everyone else left
27	y el profesor llegó a las doce.	and at 12:00 the teacher arrived.
28	Y llegó	And he arrived
29	y dio la clase,	and he taught his class,
30	dio la clase y les puso falta	and he gave an absence
31	a los que se habían ido.	to everyone who had left.
32	Y al siguiente día, pues, todos le dijimos	And the next day well, we all asked him why
33	que por qué nos había puesto falta.	he gave us an absence.
34	Dice:	And he said
35	"No, es que ustedes se fueron,"	"it's because you left."
36	pero le dijimos, pues, "que en media hora	But we said well, if half an hour (passes)
37	se supone que no . . ."	we're supposed to.."
38	y este, y dijo:	and he said
39	"No, pero que me tienen que esperar",	"no, you have to wait for me"
40	dijo.	he said.
41	Y es culpa de él,	And it's his fault
42	porque ni siquiera había dicho	because he didn't even tell us

43	que iba a alguna parte,	that he was going somewhere,
44	y entonces nos dijo	and then he said
45	que no se acordaba	he didn't remember
46	que tenía clase,	that he had a class,
47	que pensó	that he thought
48	que empezaba a las doce.	it was at 12:00.
49	Y nos puso falta a todos.	And he gave an absence to everyone.
50	Y pues nos afectaba en ese momento para el examen,	And that would affect our grade for the exam,
51	o nos bajaba puntos.	or he would lower our grade.
52	Y según él decía que el examen contaba el ochenta,	And according to him the final was worth 80% of the grade,
53	creo,	I think,
54	y no es cierto,	but that's not true,
55	¡contaba el cien!	it was 100%!
56	Aparte de que nada más nos contaba el examen,	On top of basing our final grade only on the exam
57	nos bajaba puntos.	he would lower our score (because of the absences).
58	GLB: ¿Y cómo distribuyó la calificación final?	GLB: And how did he calculate your final grade?
59	¿Eran los tres parciales más el final?	Did you have three midterms and a final?
60	B: Más el final. Sí porque no, ya después no nos, es que nunca nos, a veces . . . ese	B: Plus the final. Right because no, later he would not, cause he never . . . sometimes . . .
61	examen no nos los entregó.	that test he never gave it back to us.
62	Ni los (tipo A) no los entregaba.	He didn't return our final either . . .
63	Nada más decía	He would only say
64	que todos estábamos reprobados,	that we had all flunked the class,
65	pero no nos los entregaba.	but he didn't give us back our exams.
66	GLB: ¿Y les dijo que estaban reprobados?	GLB: And he told you that you had all failed?
67	B: Ajá, de por ejemplo, "profe, ¿quiénes pasaron el examen?"	B: Yeah for instance "teacher, who passed the exam?"
68	yo dije	I said (to myself),
69	"tan siquiera lo voy a pasar con ocho,"	"at least I'm going to get a B,"
70	y le dije yo a mi mamá . . .	and I told my mom
71	y me dijo:	and she said:
72	"Bueno, ojalá y pues lo pases".	"Well, I hope that you pass."
73	Y no, que nos va diciendo:	But no, then he told us:

74	"No, todos están reprobados."	"No, you all failed."
75	G: ¿Y qué sucedió?	GLB: And what happened then?
76	B: Éramos como diez, yo creo, más o menos.	B: There were about ten of us, I think, more or less.
77	G: ¿Y no le pidieron el examen?	GLB: And did you ask him for the exam?
78	B: Después . . . no, nadie se lo pidió.	B: Later . . . no, nobody asked him.
79	Después yo le dije a mi amá,	Afterwards I told my mom,
80	y cuando fue . . .	and when she went [to school]
81	y nos dijo la orientadora:	and the student counselor told us
82	"No, es que ya es demasiado tarde para pedirlo", que no sé qué.	"No, it's too late to ask for it" and stuff like that
83	G: ¿Y si hubieras pasado esa materia sí te hubieras quedado? B: Sí.	GLB: And if you had passed that class would you have stayed in school? B: Yeah.

Narrative 1: Not Passing a Class

This interview took place at Brenda's home at the end of the school year, when she had just been informed she would no longer be able to attend school. The daughter of a single mother, Brenda's lived in a working-class neighborhood. In her narrative, Brenda recalls a particular incident in which the majority of the students in her class confronted their chemistry teacher for not respecting the schools norms and rules and for his lack of accountability. The narrative conveys the teacher's unfair grading practices and the consequences for students. The narrative begins with an "abstract" of the experience in Labov's (1972) sense ("a lot of us didn't pass"). Lines 2 to 7 are all evaluative clauses and encode the figured worlds of obligations for students (doing assignments) and teachers' prerogatives (grading at will or not grading at all). In line 10 Brenda uses direct speech to revoice the teacher's commitment to grade their work. But this line is preceded by a quote that reveals Brenda's attitude toward her teacher's discourse (line 9: And he would say: "No" or something). She marks the teacher's words with a phrase showing that some of the original language is lost and further marks those words as suspect or unreliable. Line 11 recapitulates what the narrative will be about (confronting the teacher), and it's followed by an evaluative clause. Lines 13 and 14 are complicating action, a sequence that is suspended by the evaluative clauses that follow. These encode a figured world of a school that sets rules and rights for both teachers and students: it evokes the way things are supposed to be. Lines 18 to 37 continue the sequence of events, including the confrontation between students and the teacher. In this confrontation students appeal to the dialogical figured world expressed in line 16, that is, the voice of school authorities regarding teacher's and students' punctuality and absences

In describing these events, it is interesting that Brenda's use of the third person plural at the beginning of the narrative (line 11: "Because once, well, they all confronted him") switches to the first person plural in line 32: "and the next day, we all asked him why"). It is as though at the beginning Brenda is speaking with the assumed voice of an outsider, a person who no longer belongs to the world she relives through the narrative; but in recalling this experience she regains her school persona and the collective voice of the group. Lines 35 through 39 are all in direct speech and show the confrontation between the students and the teacher, each echoing two opposing figured worlds: the institutional world of what ought to be for the students and the figured world of authority for the teacher. This is a clear episode of positioning, an instance in which the students are "invited" to comply with the rules of the teacher or else suffer the consequences. The evaluative clauses that follow ("and it's his fault because he didn't even tell us that he was going somewhere") suspend once more the sequence and capture the authorial voice of Brenda. Lines 44 to 49 continue the sequence of events and we hear more evaluative elements through line 57. Again, lines 60 to 65 are evaluative clauses emphasized by several repetitions. These elements provide a clearer picture of the figured world encoded in Text 3, a figured world enacted through the teacher's actions and authoritarian

Discourse

Line 69 captures the inner speech of Brenda, an important point in the narrative since it reveals her expectations to enact the identity of academic competence so far denied to her. In line 72 Brenda uses direct speech to revoice the wishes of her mother (a direct echo of her own wishes and expectations), and lines 73 and 74 express the outcome and one of the most dramatic episodes of positioning in the narrative: the teacher telling the students that they had all failed his class. Perhaps more dramatic is the lack of agency the concluding elements of the narrative reveal: Constantly being cast in a position with no voice or say in school matters, the students learn that the teacher (and school) is not accountable for their actions and the students unwillingly accept it without even asking for the exam (lines 77 and 78). In a final twist, even the mother is unable to find an answer from the school authorities, and Brenda and her family suffer the consequences.

The figured worlds described so far are clearly double-voiced, dialogical models that are set in motion by distinct actions (or inactions) by the participants. Brenda is thus caught up between the figured world of "what ought to be for the students" and the figured world of what "must be" for the teachers. Although Brenda unwillingly complies with this authoritarian Discourse (with its positions and identities), it is clear that she learns to distrust the discourse (the means of communication) and disavow this language with its representational quality. This is expressed when she revoices her teacher's discourse through direct speech (line 9: "And he would say: 'No' or something") or indirect speech (line 58: "according to him the final was worth 80%"), and even when she quotes the school authorities at the end of the narrative: "the student counselor told us 'no, it's too late' and stuff like that" (lines 81–82). As I mentioned earlier, this is expressed in the Spanish original (no sé qué) through a cognitive statement (not knowing) that disavows the representational function of an alien d/Discourse.

It is a language that is lost and becomes suspect or unreliable. This is something that was common in all the narratives of first-year and some narratives of thirdyear students. The following extract (Text 4) by a first-year student exemplifies best the attitude of these students toward the representational function of this institutional d/Discourse, an alien discourse imbued with authority but that clearly is not internally persuasive or authoritative for the students:

	Spanish original	English translation
1	Pues yo creo que, la verdad sí me gusta	Well I think that, actually, I do like
2	Química. Esa materia sí es muy bonita,	chemistry. This subject is very attractive
3	porque es todo lo que nos rodea y bla, bla, bla, bla,	*because it's everything that surrounds us and blah, blah, blah,*

Text 4: Representational Function of Language

Maybe That's Why I Was Able to Remember

Extending Bakhtin's notion of authoritative discourse, Morson (2004) distinguishes between authoritarian and authoritative discourse and reflects on how each affects students' learning, including learning "our sense of ourselves" (p. 318). For Morson, authoritarian discourse is distinctively monologic, such as the discourse authoritarian regimes impose on their own publicly sanctioned interpretation of history. Authoritative discourse, on the other hand, may or may not be authoritarian. Morson argues that authoritative discourse may try to insulate itself from dialogue with reverential tones, a special script, and all the other signs of the authority fused to it, but at the margins dialogue waits with a challenge: you may be right, but you have to convince me. Once the authoritative word responds to that challenge, it ceases to be fully authoritative. . . . Every educator crosses this line when she or he gives reasons for a truth. (p. 319)

1	C: entonces cuando llegué a segundo de	C: so, when I was in eighth grade, I think,
2	secundaria, creo, un maestro muy bueno y	[I had] very good teacher and with him,
3	este, y con la primera vez que me explicó lo	the first time that he explained it to me I
4	entendí bien rápido, y se me hacía así como	understood right away and I would think,
5	que a veces, ay qué tonto, porque, tú, tal vez,	how stupid, they had explained that same
6	me explicaron pues ese mismo procedi-	procedure before but I didn't get it until
7	miento pero no lo comprendía hasta que ese	that teacher taught me, and so [before] it
8	profesor no me lo enseñó, entonces fue un	was a problem because as time went by I
9	problema porque conforme iba pasando el	would think, it's like, I'll know everything
10	tiempo yo decía es que sí como no, voy a	else but I won't be able to do fractions, I
11	saber todo lo demás y no voy a poder hacer	thought, kind of illogical.
12	fracciones, se me hacía como que ilógico.	
13	GLB: ¿Y te acuerdas de algo en particular de	GLB: And do you remember something in particular about the way that teacher helped
14	la forma como te explicó ese maestro que	you to understand?

15	haya contribuido a que comprendieras?	
16	C: Tal vez porque estaba en el pizarrón y	C: Maybe because when he was at the
17	este, y ponía y te preguntaba, ¿sabes hacer	blackboard, and he would write and he
18	esto? y no pues que sí, ah, pues, y te lo	would ask you, do you know how to do
19	explicaba, no sé, tan detalladamente así, te	this? And well yes or no, and then ok he
20	marcaba súper bien, te encerraba los números	would explain it to you, I don't know, with
21	que, te encerraba por ejemplo, te encerraba	a lot of detail, he would highlight really

22	donde iba a empezar a hacer el	well, he would circle the numbers and like,
23	procedimiento a desglosarlo como para que	he would circle where he was going to
24	vieras de por qué salió, te lo ponía aparte, te	begin the procedure and then he would
25	lo explicaba y luego te preguntaba, y te decía	break it up so that you could understand
26	te hacía ver y se regresaba, como se iba y se	why he would come up with a result, he
27	regresaba, se iba y se regresaba cada paso,	would highlight that and he would explain
28	como que a lo mejor eso hizo que se me	it and then he would ask you, and he would
29	grabara más.	tell you, *he would make you see* and he
30		would go back and forth, back and forth,
31		step by step and, maybe that's why I was
32		able to remember.

In the two narratives discussed above we see instances of the authoritarian Discourse of the teachers in which there are no signs or attempt to engage students in dialogue. This is reinforced by a school culture that treats certain students as "expendable," especially those students who have been denied access to particular discourses (specialized languages), figured worlds (ways to perceive objects, people, and activities) and Discourses (ways to enact a particular identity) of "academic competence." The following sample by Carlos, a middle-class, third-year student, provides a different scenario. In this case the student explains his frustration at not being able to learn how to do fractions, in spite of receiving help and support from his father, whom he depicts as very knowledgeable. The episode describes the moment when he finally "understood"

Text 5: Learning To Do fractions

What this student describes is the authoritative discourse of the teacher becoming internally persuasive for the student through the teacher's engagement with him and the resources he uses to make an alien figured world accessible for the student, best captured with the expression "he would make you see." It is a case of what Lave and Wenger (1991) define as legitimate peripheral participation. This type of experience is completely absent in the narratives by first-year students, as the previous examples showed.

I Was Not Going to Let That Happen

The second narrative I want to discuss is by Gabriela, a middle-class student enrolled in the International Baccalaureate. In it she describes an episode of positioning by a teacher whom she confronted:

	Spanish original	English translation
1	GLB: ¿Puedes contar algún problema que hayas tenido en tus clases?	GLB: Can you tell a particular problem you had in your classes

2	G: Por ejemplo sistemas de información, tuvimos un problema	G: Yes, for instance in information systems we had a problem,
3	de que nos dejó un proyecto,	we had to do a project,
4	de hacer un vídeo como si fuera un comercial,	we had to produce a video like a commercial,
5	entonces lo hicimos,	so we did it,
6	pero mm, yo siempre soy, soy perfeccionista	but mm I'm always, I'm a perfectionist
7	o sea trato de hacer las cosas lo mejor que se pueda,	or I try to do things as best as I can,
8	entonces yo lo edité, el video y . . .	so I edited it, the video
9	la profesora dijo	and the teacher said
10	"sí que me editen," no sé qué,	"yes, edit it" and stuff like that.
11	pero al final de cuentas todos mis compañeros lo trajeron sin editar,	But at the end all my classmates brought it in without any editing,
12	o sea nada más tomaron el video,	like, they just took the video
13	lo entregaron	and turned it in,
14	y yo por querer editarlo lo traje tarde	and I, by trying to edit it turned it in late
15	y la profesora no me lo quiso recibir,	and the teacher wouldn't take it,
16	me quería reprobar,	she wanted to fail me
17	y pues no,o sea yo no me iba a dejar reprobar así nada más porque sí,	and well no, I mean I was not going to let that happen just like that,
18	fui y hablé con la profesora Magda y con el subdirector	so I went and spoke with [a teacher] and with the vice-principal,
19	y ya le dijeron que no fuera tan drástica,	and they told her not to be so drastic,
20	que me calificara mi práctica,	to grade my assignment,
21	y le di el trabajo,	and I gave it to her,
22	valía 5 puntos	it was worth 5 points
23	y me quedé en 7,	and she gave me a C,
24	pero pues 7 es aprobatoria, gran diferencia entre el 5.	but well, C is a passing grade, big difference than an F.

Narrative 2

For the analysis of this narrative I want to concentrate in the evaluative clauses expressed in lines 6, 7, 11, 12, 17, and 24, because these lines capture the figured worlds that give meaning to the student's experience and text. In lines 6 and 7 she uses an "I-statement" (Gee, 1999) that positions her as a thoughtful and responsible student, a figured world about herself in relation to the rest of her classmates; it is a figured world that is taken up and elaborated again in lines 12 and 14 where she evaluates her classmates actions ("just took the video") as opposed to her own ("by trying to edit it"). In line 17 she expresses a figured world about teachers not unlike those of her less successful peers: a world of authoritarian teachers who arbitrarily "fail" students. Similarly, she disavows this language when she revoices the teacher's speech (line 10: "The teacher said 'yes, edit it' and stuff like that"). Consistent with her figured world about herself, line 17 captures her own agentic school persona, a positional identity quite different from first-year, working-class students who, in spite of evident signs of solidarity among themselves and their collective actions, in their agentic selves were severely curtailed by the school teachers and authorities. Gabriela seeks support not only from another teacher but from the vice-principal as well, a support that is granted and allows her to reverse the teacher's arbitrary decision. In this episode Gabriela uses a narrative strategy identified by Labov and Waletzky (1967) as an effective method for evaluating the whole experience: the judgment of a third person absent from the experience (line 19: "they told her not to be so drastic"). The sequence of events being evaluated describes the experience of a middle-class student enrolled in the most prestigious program in the school (the International Baccalaureate), and because the person evaluating Gabriela's experience is the school's vice-principal, we see how schools construct and position students in very different and opposing ways. In this case, school authorities side with Gabriela against the arbitrary decisions of their own personnel.

Narrative Structure and the Construction of the Self

So far I've commented on how the polyphony expressed in narratives of personal experience capture different figured worlds, voices, and d/Discourses the authors have to "orchestrate" in their own voice (Bakhtin, 1981; Holland et al., 1998). There is another way we can look at figured worlds in narratives, what I previously described as the "charter narrative" or structural figured world. A good way to look at the structural figured world is to focus on the referential function of narratives: In Narrative 1 the sequence of events portrays collective human agency being curtailed by institutional forces, a model that may very well be a variation of fatalism.

In Narrative 2 the sequence of events appears to be the result of individual human action, in particular the agency of the narrator. Because these are narratives of personal experience, the "charter narrative" provides a good insight into self-objectification, since "self is a popular fiction, a 'figurative reification,' by means of which we account for our and others' actions"

(Holland et al., 1998, p. 293). In a similar vein, Amsterdam and Bruner (2000) explain how narrative genres "model" (p. 117) characteristic plights of groups of people that share the same culture. This happens because "cultures convert their plights and aspirations in narrative forms that represent both the culture's ordinary legitimacies and possible threats to them" (p. 117). In this sense, these authors argue that narratives function not simply to make experience communicable and thereby increase cultural solidarity, but also to give a certain practical predictability to the plights of communal life and a certain direction to the efforts needed to resolve them. (p. 117).

In Narrative 1 we see a student who constructs herself through her relationships with others and through the eyes of others who imprint on her their own gaze and positioning. It is a "sociocentric" self (Holland & Kipnis, 1994), a self that seeks the collaboration of others like her and expresses her solidarity through collective action. However, the figured world encoded in the narrative plot is of a self with limited possibilities for agency and action. It is a self that, regardless of her collective or individual action, is rendered powerless by the enforcement of an authoritarian school Discourse. This is quite the opposite of the second narrative. Here we find an "egocentric" and agentive self, expressed through a charter narrative that echoes the autonomous subject of modernity, a subject in charge of her own destiny and a byproduct of school cultures that construct students differently.

Final Remarks

I want to conclude this chapter with a reflection on method. As Gee (this volume) convincingly argues, for the critical discourse analyst the issue of frame is crucial. The narratives discussed in this chapter were chosen after careful readings of hundreds of pages. The analysis was always done in a two-way direction: the selected texts illuminated the overall picture afforded by the interviews and vice versa. Having two distinct groups of participants provided many contrastive elements, which were consistent throughout the data: the collective voice of first-year students versus the "autonomous" subjects of third-year students; the authoritarian Discourse imposed on first-year students versus the enabling authoritative Discourse described by third-year students. The figured worlds that articulate these experiences, an articulation between language and social order, provide clear evidence of what Bourdieu (1980) calls the "institutionalization of difference," that is, the strategies institutions such as schools use to enforce statutory and symbolic barriers between people and groups.

A CRITICAL DISCOURSE ANALYSIS OF NEOCOLONIAL-ISM IN PATRICIA MCCORMICK'S SOLD

These are the lacerating words of Lakshmi, the 13-year-old protagonist in Patricia McCormick's Sold, a 2006 National Book Award Finalist in young people's literature. Sold into prostitution by a drunken, greedy, and destitute stepfather, Lakshmi travels from a pastoral Nepali village to the infamous red-light district of Kolkata, India. These are also the opening words of a speech on human trafficking, delivered by Mr. Gary Lewis, Representative, United Nations Office of Drugs and Crime at the 53rd Commonwealth Parliamentary Conference held in New Delhi, 2007 (Lewis, 2007). One might say that literature is one of the many "storylines" or Discourse models which people use "to make sense of the world and their experiences in it" (Gee, 2006, p. 61).

In this chapter I take on the problematic nature of literature that is written by North Americans about "third world"1 countries. Literature about the world is typically envisioned as a bridge that spans the differences between cultures and nations, as a window that opens minds to the world's diversity and global challenges, and as a mirror that encourages reflection (Bishop, 1990; Botelho and Rudman, 2009; Hadaway, 2007; Lepman, 1969; Stan, 2002). My intention is to dismantle the window's frame, survey the pillars of these connecting bridges, and hold up a critical mirror that examines our assumptions about these structures and the concepts they entail (Lakshmanan, 2009). Literature's global reach is further enhanced by technology. Today, authors' and publishers' websites offer links to international organizations such as Amnesty International or the International Labor Organization. In teaching guides and scholarly articles, literature is also presented as a springboard for engaging students' participation in social activism abroad (McKenna, 2007; Yokota & Kolar, 2008). Referring to "transformative models" of reading, Marian J. McKenna (2007) writes that literature about the world should not only "teach students about the world in which they live but also . . . transform them into engaged, active citizens" (p. 166).

Emerging from a framework of critical multiculturalism, reading becomes a means to engage with concerns about the subjugation of race, class, and gender (Botelho & Rudman, 2009). This is particularly true of literature on contemporary South Asia, which is often written with a view to informing readers about existing social injustices. I argue that critical literary analysis should not be limited to an examination of power relations that inhere in race, class, or gender differences in the text. Rather, a critical lens should also be directed at power relations that emanate from the text to its global implications. Only then can one become aware of the ideological positions being offered to the reader, and how these could affect international relations (Lakshmanan,

2009). I propose that before literature about the world is used to activate social justice in the world, readers need to delve below the surface content of a text, and discern how the form of language, narration, and visuals constructs knowledge practices, mediates relationships, and directs a certain ideological discourse on how individual/social transformation happens or should happen. In this chapter I will examine Sold (2006) by Patricia McCormick, in order to demonstrate the connection between literary discourse (as ways of representing, being, and participating in the world), the marketed visuals on a book's cover, and knowledge practices. Patricia McCormick is well known for her previous novels, Cut (2000) on self-inflicted "cutting," and My Brother's Keeper (2005) on drug addiction. Both of these novels are based in the United States. Sold, instead, is set in Nepal and India. Here, McCormick captures the searing reality of child trafficking in the sex trade. It is the result of several interviews during the author's month-long stay in these countries. Written in free verse, and the first-person voice of a diary, Lakshmi's story unfolds in a series of crisply edited poetic vignettes. In an interview posted on her website (www. patriciamccormick.com), McCormick states her "inspiration" to tell this story:

I believe that young adults want to know what's happening to their peers on the other side of the world, but that media accounts, by their very nature, cannot usually go beyond the surface. To me there is nothing more powerful— or permanent—than the impact of a book. (McCormick, para. 2).

Literature as a privileged mode of knowing the "other" side of the world begs a deeper study of how its knowledge practices are embedded in a discursive formation that extends beyond the text. Keeping in mind the institutionalization of literature, by way of marketing and education, my analysis relates the text to the author's intention, the cover image, and the publisher's (Hyperion) discussion guide (Zimmer, n.d.), which is freely available on the internet. By way of method, I take up James Paul Gee's (2006) idea that we collaboratively use language and other semiotic systems to "build" seven interrelated and intertextual tasks to construe situations and the world around us (p. 104). Based on Gee's model, I am guided by the question: How does the enactment of significance, activities, identities, relationships, connections, and knowledge practices condition the political discourse on individual/ social change in literature written by North Americans about "third world" developing countries? In this respect, I am guided by Norman Fairclough's (1995) comment that "no proper understanding of contemporary discursive practices is possible that does not attend to the matrix of change" (p. 19).

The Text and Context

The novel opens with the line, "One more rainy season and our roof will be gone, says Ama." We soon realize that in spite of the idyllic surrounding of a verdant Himalayan slope, where the "yellow pumpkin blossoms will close, drunk on the sunshine" (p. 9), poverty is endemic. Every season is marked by "women's work and women's woes":

This is the season when the women bury the children who die of fever. . . . This is the season when they bury the children who die from the coughing disease. (pp. 10–11).

Lakshmi's story is set against this predetermined rhythm of poverty, death, and womanhood. Beset by debts and alcoholism, her stepfather sells her to a prostitution ring. Lakshmi, who is convinced that she is going to work in the big city as a maid, dreams that thanks to her efforts, her mother will fi nally have a tin roof when the rains come, and money for "rice and curds, milk and sugar. Enough for a coat for the baby and a sweater." But the reader knows that her stepfather will gamble away the money at the tea-shop, or buy another contraption, like the defunct motorcycle he bought when her mother pawned her earrings. Sold for 800 rupees, Lakshmi is accompanied by "aunts" and "unclehusbands" across the Indo-Nepali border, and into the teeming heartland of India "where the lying-down people look like the dead. And the standing-up ones, like the walking dead." She is fi nally re-sold, at a tremendous profi t, to "Happiness House," a brothel in the Calcutta (known as Kolkata since 2001) red-light district. Lakshmi is locked in a room, beaten and starved, but she will not give in. A vignette titled "After fi ve days" has only one line: "After fi ve days of no food and water I don't even dream." The blank page beneath says it all. Finally, a drugged glass of buttermilk does what hunger and confi nement could not, and her fi rst customer "rolls off" her. Drugged for several days, imprisoned in the room, men come and go: "They crush my bones with their weight. They split me open. Then they disappear." Yet Lakshmi's spirit is not entirely broken. In "Happiness House" she also discovers friendship, the awe of watching The Bold and the Beautiful, the sparkle of Coca-Cola, and the liberating joy of a yellow pencil. Ultimately, she is rescued, by an American.

I chose Sold for three reasons, each addressing the overlapping public and private contexts in which literature operates. Context is understood as the "the mentally represented structure of those properties of the social situation that are relevant for the production and comprehension of discourse" (van Dijk, 1998, p. 356). First, the book's themes are directly related to the global Discourse on poverty, sexual exploitation, gender, and the tension between culture and modernity. Second, the Discourse models associated with the text gain institutional privilege because of the marketing, circulation, and consumption associated with "award-winning" books.2 Third, as a woman of South Asian origin, I am driven by the need to unravel the archive of texts and images which have come to inscribe my own identity. As Seyla Benhabib puts it, "To be and to become a self is to insert oneself into webs of interlocution" and "our agency consists in our capacity to weave out of these narratives our individual life stories"(2002, p. 15). Yet, I am more than aware that this personal impetus can also obfuscate my vision. While there can be no shying away from my suspicion of any relic of a colonial civilizing mission, the theoretical framework and methodology of critical discourse analysis (CDA) afford me some distance between the text and myself. But most importantly, CDA allows me to examine how semiotic signs (language and visuals) and narrative patterns represent and construct our relationship to "the other side of the world." It bears repetition that my purpose is not to undermine the factual, moral, and humanitarian validity of a book that seeks to broaden the reader's awareness of the relationship between human trafficking, poverty, and culturally fostered gender inequities. Rather, I would argue that in spite of the indisputable commitment to human rights and the pedagogical need to foster empathy and further social justice, a critical stance needs to be alert to the morphing of hegemonic processes in the "third worlding" of social action.

Literature, Critical Discourse Analysis, Social Semiotics, and Post/Neocolonialism

Literature as discourse has been studied by numerous scholars (Eagleton, 1991; Fowler, 1977, 1981; Hodge, 1990; Hodge & Kress, 1993; Said, 1979; Stephens, 1992; van Dijk, 1985). As Terry Eagleton (1991) puts it, literature is about "who is saying what to whom for what purposes" (p 9). As a discourse, or a certain way of relating to the world, literature is a social practice that resounds with the implied reader precisely because it is enmeshed in a society's way of representing, being, and participating in the world. This, however, does not exclude the possibility that literature can be a vector for a transformative counterdiscourse. Indeed, in the international arena, the pen has sometimes proved an

active player in international relations. Alan Paton's Cry, The Beloved Country (1948) brought apartheid to world consciousness just as Salman Rushdie's The Satanic Verses (1989) plunged the literary narrative into the maelstrom of global conflict. If anything, recent events validate that language, the narrative, and semiotic signs such as visuals, cartoons, and clothing cannot be extricated from identity and the enactment of a certain political relationship to the contemporary world.

Viewed in this light, one can surmise that literature about other nations and cultures is embedded with a multimodal compass, directing a new generation on how to participate in the world. This nexus between text, semiotic signs, and being in the world is best captured in Gee's (2006) theorizing of discourse in Discourse, or D/discourse. The former (discourse) refers to how language is used to "enact activities and identities" (p. 7). But, social or ontological meaning is not made through language (or image) alone. The author's intention, the awards conferred, how a book is cited and researched, how it is taught, and the blogs it generates, are all instances of the macro Discourses (with a capital "D") that coalesce to make the production, marketing, and consumption of the book a social practice. Hence, analyzing literature as D/discourse does not distinguish between the literary text, the non-literary, and social practice. The writing, production, reading, and interpretation of the text are also political acts.

By political, I mean, in Gee's words, how "power, status, value or worth" are distributed (2006, p. 2). Any critical analysis and interpretation of a text written about a "third world" situation would be incomplete without the perspectives of postcolonial theories on power relations. Postcolonial theory, which emerged in the 1980s, addresses the dominant Discourses used to view non-Western people. It is essentially about the problematic relationship between social and historical conditions, representation, knowledge construction, the constitution of the subject, and effective practices. Edward Said, Homi Bhabha, and Gayatri Chakravorty Spivak are considered central to the field of colonial discourse analysis (Childs & Williams, 1997), which was heralded by Said's seminal book, Orientalism (1979). Said melds the Gramscian notion of hegemony with a Foucaldian understanding of discourse to examine the discursive practices of the European construction of the "oriental," and its hegemonic complicity with Western imperialism. He describes Orientalism as "an accepted grid for filtering through the Orient into Western consciousness" (p. 6).

In Culture and Imperialism (1994), he further develops his argument, maintaining that the novel articulates a prevailing "structure of attitude and references," thereby indicating both the limitations and possibilities of these structures. With respect to Orientalism (1979), Said has been widely critiqued for his essentialist binary opposition between East and West. Homi Bhabha (1994), instead, introduces terms like cultural hybridity, liminality, colonial mimicry, and ambivalence, to argue for a more fluid notion of cultural production in the colonial encounter.

Though postcolonialism is a response to a history of colonial rule, it cannot be dislocated from the present actuation of neocolonial political and economic hegemony. In fact, as Spivak famously remarked, "We live in a post-colonial neo-colonized world" (1990, p. 166). In this sense, postcolonialism "names a politics and philosophy of activism that contests that disparity [of inequality and dependence], and so continues in a new way the anti-colonial struggles of the past" (Young, 2003, p. 4). In addition, rather than an obscure theory advanced by ivory-tower intellectuals, the Subaltern Study group, (Ranajit Guha, Gayatri Chakravorty Spivak and Gyan Prakash) have elaborated a politics of the subaltern, or a "postcolonialism from below" (Young, 2003, p. 6). This perspective urges me to remain alert to any effacement of the autonomy and agency of the subaltern woman.

Method

The frame of this analysis is limited to the book's text, the visual on its cover, the author's interview on her website, her mode of observing and recording, and the publisher's discussion guide (available at http://www. hyperionbooksforchildren.com). James Paul Gee's (2006) seven building tasks provided a common lens that directed my analysis of how the form and patterning of semiotic signs construct identities, relationships, and power relations. Gee proposes that when we use language, actions, interactions, and non-linguistic semiotic systems, we build seven "areas of reality" (2006, pp. 10–11). These interrelated tasks are significance, activities, identities, relationships, politics, connections, sign systems, and knowledge (henceforth italicized). My analysis is derived from the questions Gee proposes for each task.3 Applying Gee's seven building tasks to correlate an ensemble of signifying vectors permitted me to chart the regularity of a recognizable dominant Discourse on relationships with the developing world. For example, if the cover engendered a certain kind of relationship between the image and the viewer, then it was legitimate to ask what kind of relationship is furthered in the author's interview, the text's linguistic markers, and the publisher's discussion guide. My premise is that ideology is patterned in the orchestration of different domains of activity that are related to a text.

My analysis began with decoding how the book cover produces social relationships and construes the identity of the "third world" woman. It would be remiss not to mention that it was the disturbing image on the book's cover that fi rst beckoned me to read the book. Specifi cally, I applied Gunther Kress and Theo van Leeuwen's (1996, 2001) social semiotic methodology. Kress and van Leeuwen bring to CDA an examination of how the elements of design articulate a discourse through the representations made available, the social interaction enacted, and the way in which the representational and interactive elements relate to each other. I sought the theoretical juncture between Kress and van Leeuwen's method and Gee's "seven building tasks" by asking which building task does the sign system of design, color, composition, image, or semiotic mode exemplify. My underlying assumption was that through a critical decoding of book covers, we can ask ourselves what global relationships are being marketed and offered for consumption. Having explored the social semiotics of the book cover,

I then proceeded to the textual analysis of the book, shuttling back and forth from the cover to the text, the author's interview, and the discussion guide. Patricia McCormick's interview is taken as an indication of the book's intended activity. As van Dijk (1998), succinctly puts it, "a fully fl edged theory of discourse and context is impossible without assuming the relevance of intentions of speakers or writers as part of the 'cognitive' dimension of the context" (p. 217). Throughout the analysis I kept in mind Fairclough's advice that "textual analysis should mean analysis of the texture of texts, their form and organization, and not just commentaries on the 'content' of texts which ignore texture" (1995, p. 4).

Sold is told in a series of 177 vignettes, ranging from a couple of pages, to a few lines. The capitalized title of each vignette succinctly captures its essence, whether it is a concept (THE DIFFERENCE BETWEEN A SON AND A DAUGHTER), an event (A TRADE), or a description (ON THE BUS). Some vignettes are barely a couple of lines. "A PRONOUNCEMENT," the episode before Lakshmi is drugged into submission, has three sentences: "One day Mumtaz came to my door without her strap. 'I have decided to let you live,' she says. Then she is gone, leaving me to ponder what will happen next" (p. 118). The rest of the page is blank, leaving both Lakshmi and the reader to wonder "what will happen next."

In order to decode how the texture of form and content relate to a macro Discourse on the "other side of the world," I focused on vignettes with repetitive linguistic patterns that are also mirrored in another episode. I worked from the hypothesis that this intentional doubling of linguistic form underscored and connected certain topics. These units were taken as examples of signifi cance (Gee's fi rst building task), which poses the question: "How is this piece of language being used to make certain things signifi cant or not and in what ways?" Two sets of vignettes were identifi ed: A NEW WORLD (number 42) on rural Nepal and NEXT (number 47) on urban India (Figure 4.1). In both vignettes, Lakshmi's view of her spatial setting is described through the following syntactical construction: indeterminate article + noun + gerund/ present indicative. For example, as Lakshmi travels through the countryside, she sees "a man pulling a wild boar on a rope." Six such phrases illustrate the Himalayan villages. Similarly, when she enters the city, she looks at "a man scooping hot popcorn into a paper cone, next to . . . ." Conveying the frenetic urban pace, there are a total of twenty descriptive phrases, all patterned in a similar manner. Since my analysis deals with what linguistic patterning can tell us about an implied relationship with the Third World context, I categorize these vignettes as concerned with contextual relationships (see Figure 4.1).

The second set of mirrored vignettes were EVERYTHING I NEED TO KNOW (number 11) on culturally mandated behavioral norms for girls, and EVERYTHING I NEED TO KNOW NOW (number 95) on the ploys of prostitution (Figure 4.2). While the previous set of vignettes dealt with the context of spatial setting, these focused on time and causality, as indicated in the syntactical form before-now-never-always and the conditional if/then clause. In EVERYTHING I NEED TO KNOW, Lakshmi's mother tells her "Before today . . . you could run as free as a leaf. . . . Now . . . you must carry yourself with modesty." In EVERYTHING I NEED TO KNOW NOW, Lakshmi is told that "Before . . . Mumtaz sent the customers to you. . . . Now you must do what it takes to make them choose you." Similar parallelisms were noted in if/then conditional clauses, and the use of strong modal verbs.

I then used Gee's seven building tasks to categorize these four vignettes (Figure 4.2). The fi rst set (Figure 4.1), which describes rural and urban settings, were taken as examples of an enactment of relationship and connection to the activity Lakshmi is watching. Since the phrases under consideration are all object clauses (Lakshmi stares at x), identity and politics were not considered. The second set of vignettes had to do with codes of behavior as mandated by cultural traditions and profession. Here, the gendered activity of being a girl or female prostitute defi nes Lakshmi's identity and ways of knowing and believing. It is a political discourse since these rule books distribute social goods believed to be of power and status, in this case the male and money (Gee, 2006, p. 2). Finally, keeping in mind that the conclusion of a "problem" novel often conveys a preferred outcome (Stephens, 1992), I analyzed the last vignette, THE WORDS HARISH TAUGHT ME.

As a further layer of investigation, I examined the book's cover and the above mentioned vignettes for evidence of what Edward Said identifi ed as stylistic fi lters that typify an "Orientalist" perspective: repetitive tropes, synecdoches, establishing binary differences and hierarchy by portraying the subject as "incapable of defi ning itself" (1979, pp. 300–301), and imagery and metaphors that classify, generalize, and accommodate the "strange" by making it familiar (pp. 58–59). Bhabha's (1994) notion of cultural production in a third borderline space was also kept in mind.

Vignette number & page	Title of vignette	Dominant linguistic patterns
42 (pp. 58–59)	A NEW WORLD	Contextual relationship Indeterminate article + noun + gerund/present indicative
47 (pp.65–66)	NEXT	Contextual relationship Indeterminate article + noun + gerund/present indicative

Figure 4.1 Building tasks: *relationship, connections, activity*

Vignette number & page	Title of vignette	Dominant linguistic patterns
11 (pp.15–16)	EVERYTHING I NEED TO KNOW	Time & Causality Before-now-never Conditional causality: If/then
95 (pp. 141–143)	EVERYTHING I NEED TO KNOW NOW	Time & Causality Before-now-always Conditional causality: If/then

Figure 4.2: Building tasks: activity, identity, knowing and believing, political

Filters that typify an "Orientalist" perspective: repetitive tropes, synecdoches, establishing binary differences and hierarchy by portraying the subject as "incapable of defining itself" (1979, pp. 300–301), and imagery and metaphors that classify, generalize, and accommodate the "strange" by making it familiar (pp. 58–59). Bhabha's (1994) notion of cultural production in a third borderline space was also kept in mind. Finally, following Fairclough's (1992) advice, my study is directed by the need to identify, describe, and interpret what he referred to as cruces or moments of crisis. These discursive struggles alert me to shifts in hegemonic articulations. For an understanding of hegemony, I draw from Laclau and Mouffe (1985). Torfing's (1999) rendering of their definition is pivotal to the conclusions I reach:

We can define hegemony as the expansion of discourse, or set of discourses, into a dominant horizon of social orientation and action by means of articulating unfixed elements into partially fixed moments in a context crisscrossed by antagonistic forces. This definition of hegemony has a general validity for analyzing processes of disarticulation and rearticulation that aim to establish and maintain political as well as moral-intellectual leadership. Thus, the concept of hegemony refers not only to the privileged position of a nation-state in a group of nation-states, but more generally to construction of a predominant discursive formation. (p. 101)

In Sold, the novel's conflict of "antagonistic forces" and the concluding "fixed moment" when Lakshmi finally articulates her identity enabled me to reach conclusions regarding hegemonic processes that further a political D/discourse on America's global role. Gee's seven building tasks offered a heuristic that helped to unscramble the discursive conditions which lead to narrative conclusions that support American social activism and moral leadership in "third world" developing countries.

Reading a Book by its Cover

Gazing at us is the face of a young girl (Figure 4.3). Her mouth is covered by a shawl, or the end of a sari. The bright saffron yellow background, with a lightly printed geometric pattern, contrasts sharply with this sepia-washed photograph. The capitalized title "SOLD" hovers in the middle, directly above the girl's head. From a marketing point of view, the jacket "advertises" the book's content in an aesthetically unique image that will capture the consumer's attention. In doing so, it has to activate a whole chain of connections, values, and judgments. Therefore, even before we open the book, our Discourse models have been positioned to "read" it for discourses shared in our "community of practice." According to Kress and van Leeuwen (1996, 2001), elements of design, such as the layout, color, text, typography, provenance, perspective, and mode, are all expressions of this discourse.

Figure 4.3: "Sold"

Kress and van Leeuwen remind us that pictorial structures of design not only reflect reality butf are "bound up with the social institutions within which the pictures are produced, circulated, and read. They are ideological" (1996, p. 45). As a discourse, or a certain way of representation, design is a sign system of knowledge that conveys a certain kind of relationship between the visual and the viewer. There are three dominant elements in this design: text, color, and image.

At the center is the title, Sold.

The solid red typography alludes to a stamp, a repeatable stamp; much like a label you would find on a sold item. It is not the individuality of handwriting. As a word, the use of the passive voice (x is sold by y), which excludes agency, indicates how this thematic action will take place. A closer look at the printed saffron yellow background reveals several interdiscursive connections. To begin with, it evokes cultural connotations, directing the onlooker to a South Asian scenario. Significantly, saffron yellow is directly associated with the Indian subcontinent. It calls to mind the robes of Hindu and Buddhist monks and the deep saffron (kesari) on the Indian flag symbolizes courage, sacrifice, and the spirit of renunciation. All at once, we have interdiscursive connections with religion, cultural values, and political identity. Even so, while one may read connotations onto the background, it is important to remember what it is not. It is not deictic of any specific place in India or Nepal. The backdrop of regional and cultural connotations is emptied of any specificity. Context, it would seem, remains on the surface of evocative generalities. eneralities.

Clearly the focus is on the photograph of the girl. There are three participants in the communicative interaction ensuing from the photograph: the onlooker, the subject of the photograph (who is not acknowledged), and the photographer (duly credited).

As a sign system, photographs are a "mechanical analogue of reality" (Barthes, 1977, p. 18) and experience. Since a photograph thereby carries the validity of testimony, truth, and objectivity, the onlooker's trust is strengthened. But, as a signifier, the retro black and white photograph activates connections to the old, not contemporary, and hence not modern. The photograph also activates certain kinds of relationships between the viewer and the viewed. In fact, some very significant questions arise if the photo is viewed from the position of the photographer (shared by us): Who could see this person in this way? What sort of person would I have to be to occupy that space? And if we remember Susan Sontag's (2003) observation that "photographs objectify: they turn an event or a person into something that can be possessed" (p. 81), we may well ask: What does it mean to objectify those who cannot respond? These are questions that relate to the viewer's position of power.

An even closer look at the photograph reveals several semiotic signs: the cultural provenance of clothing, and the embodied modes of gesture and gaze. Kress and van Leeuwen (2001) refer to provenance as signifieds that are "'imported' from some other domain (some other place, time, social group, culture) to signify a complex of ideas and values which are associated with that 'other' domain by those who do the importing" (p. 72). When signs of provenance are consistently repeated, they fossilize into what Roland Barthes (1972) refers to as the metalanguage of representation. The woman's head cover (burkha, chador, nijab) is a persistent example of provenance in representations of the exotic or repressed Oriental woman. When one considers this unrelenting and selective representation, the image of a girl's covered head and mouth certainly signifies cultural practice, but at the second stage of Barthes' metalanguage, it alludes to being voiceless (Barthes, 1972). Hence, the provenance of clothing and an embodied gesture have become a synecdoche for a discourse on repressive cultural practices and female disenfranchisement (Said, 1979). The gaze instead, is strongly experiential, evoking sympathy, engagement, or at the very least, a voyeuristic curiosity. It is not the dreamy long-distance gaze of reverie. It is a middle-distance gaze "out of the frame," that verges on the stare. Certainly, she is not looking at the future, but at us, engaging the onlooker in a relationship.

It seems to speak, in lieu of the covered mouth. Much has been written about the gaze. According to Kress and van Leeuwen (1996), the gaze is more interactional than representational (p. 90). They distinguish between offer and demand in a gaze. An indirect address would represent an offer, whereas a direct address represents a demand for the viewer to enter into a relationship with the person (pp. 126–127). Other studies consider the frontal or oblique direction of the gaze from behind the camera. John Tagg (1988, p. 189) argues that frontality is a technique of documentation. Reminiscent of the ethnographer's lens, it offers up what is represented for evaluation. Tagg describes how historically, the frontal portrait is a "code for social inferiority" (p. 37). If one conceptualizes the photograph in these terms, then the image on the cover goes beyond its exteriority, and enters a Discourse on how identities are construed, and practices of intercultural relationship.

Taken as a dynamic composite of text-image-color, the cover has a narrative and discursive function. To begin with, it speaks about a young girl who has been sold. But, when the discourse of visual sign systems is dismantled, the construct of the "third world" woman's identity becomes evident. She is the notso-modern, voiceless, or at best muffled subaltern, who demands (Kress & van Leeuwen, 1996) a relationship of engagement and evaluation (Tagg, 1988). But is this a dominant discourse model that cuts across different genres of activity? Kress and van Leeuwen emphasize that "language and visual communication can in many cases express the same kind of relations, albeit in many different ways" (1996, p. 211). With this in mind, I added layers of textual analyses that investigate the relationship between the cover image, vignettes identified as significant, the author's interview, and discussion guides.

"Everything I Need to Know" about the "Other Side of the World"
The novel opens with the innocence of childhood. Much like Mary and her little lamb, Lakshmi goes to school followed by her goat Tali. Everything changes after her "fi rst blood." Now a woman, her mother schools her in "EVERYTHING I NEED TO KNOW" (pp. 15–16):

Before [italics added] today, Ama says, you could run as free as a leaf in the wind. Now [italics added], she says, you must carry yourself with modesty, bow your head in the presence of men, and cover yourself with your shawl. (p. 15)

Recalling the shawl-covered girl in the photograph, her look of demand or evaluation is now changed to a downcast gaze of submission. The axis of time (before, now, never) is accompanied by varying degrees of modal verbs. Before she "could," now she "must," and the future is locked in the assertion of a categorical, unconditional and non-modalized "never." In this how-to-behave list of rules, Lakshmi must:

Never [italics added] look a man in the eye. Never allow yourself to be alone with a man who is not family. And never look at growing pumpkins or cucumbers when you are bleeding. Otherwise they will rot. (p. 15)

Once she is married, the mother's sociocultural rule book adopts a conditional if/then sequence, in which every activity is conditioned by the male. In this case, the reader knows that the antecedent (if) is not hypothetical, nor is the consequence (then) contingent on a previous event. Instead, the conditional clause alludes to a given causality of circumstantial context.

If [italics added] he burps at the end of the meal, it is a sign that you have pleased him. If he turns to you in the night, you must give yourself up to him, in the hopes that you will bear him a son. (p. 15)

After a series of instructions on breastfeeding a son as against a daughter, the vignette concludes with Lakshmi asking her mother:

"Why," I say, "must women suffer so?"

"This has always been our fate,"

she says.

"Simply to endure," she says,

"is to triumph." (p. 16)

Like the photograph on the cover, the use of the present tense is anchored in the "here" and "now" and the reader/viewer becomes a participant in the protagonist's activity (Traugott & Pratt, 1980). In fact, just as Lakshmi asked, "Why must women suffer so?" the text demands the reader's engagement and evaluation of these codes of behavior. The mother's reply becomes emblematic of the book's representation of culturally determined female suffering. The sentence "Simply to endure is to triumph" appears italicized on the inner jacket of the book. Evoking the stereotypical notion of Hindu passivity, determinism and fatalism, temporality (before-now-always) and causality (if-then) are imprisoned in a sociocultural system which obliterates the experiential difference between passivity ("to endure") and agency ("to triumph"). This timeless obliteration of the human actor is linguistically endorsed by the statement "simply to endure is to triumph," in which a categorical universality is rendered by the present tense copula "is" (Said, 1979, p. 72), and the implicit nominalization of endurance and triumph, shifts the discourse from one of conditional human agency, to the collapsing of the actor into the action itself (Hodge & Kress, 1993, pp. 22–26).

These episodes are directly related to at least three of Gee's building tasks: identity, and ways of knowing and believing, and activities. Lakshmi's identity and ways of knowing and believing are defi ned through the activities of a girl of a certain culture and socioeconomic status. Gee's seventh building task on knowledge poses the question: "How does this piece of language privilege or disprivilege . . . different ways of knowing and believing or claims to knowledge and belief?" (Gee, 2006, p. 13). While culture, superstition (looking at cucumbers and pumpkins), and gender roles dictate Lakshmi's ways of knowing and believing, what about the reader? The reader too, is limited by the character's referential frame and point of view. Point of view, as Fowler noted (1977, p. 52), constitutes perspective in literature. The stylistic choice of a fi rst-person narrative is not incidental. In the author's interview she states:

I knew immediately that I wanted to do what no one else had done so far: tell this heartbreaking story from the point view of one individual girl [italics added]. (McCormick, para. 1)

Stephens (1992) reminds us that total identifi cation with a focalizing character blurs the distance between author-narrator-reader, making the reader susceptible to implicit ideologies (pp. 67–69). In novels written from the perspective of a child, who is not privy to the heterogeneity of societies, the fi rstperson narrative fi lters the complexity of context. Point of view also accounts for an estrangement from the context. In Sold, Lakshmi, the author, and the reader all view Nepal and India as outsiders. As the author says on her webpage interview: "It helped that I was a foreigner on the busy streets of Kathmandu and Calcutta, because I was as bewildered and awestruck by these places as Lakshmi in the novel" (McCormick, ¶ 3). Thus, while the use of the fi rst person effectively focuses the reader's identifi cation and empathy on Lakshmi's experience, thereby fulfi lling the demand of the haunting gaze on the cover, the individualized perspective limits the reader's peripheral view, enacting relationships (Gee's fourth task) that are distanced and non-dialogic. This dislocated4 mode of relating to the context is brought out in the episode "A NEW WORLD."

Lakshmi is sold to a go-between Auntie. As they walk past the Himalayan countryside, people "gape" at them (a common complaint of foreigners). Recalling the piercing gaze of the girl on the cover, Lakshmi too "stares" at "all the things" she has never seen before.

A man pulling a wild boar on a rope.

A herd of yak hauling sacks of salt.

A mail runner ringing a cluster of bells as he nears a village.

A rope footbridge strung like a spiderweb.

A river that runs white. And a man with teeth entirely of gold. (p. 58)

Seven pages later, the cinematic panning is repeated when Lakshmi is plunged into an alien Indian city. Craning her neck, Lakshmi looks at:

a man scooping hot popcorn into a paper cone, next to

a barber lathering an old man's face, next to

a boy plucking the feathers from a lifeless chicken . . . (p. 65)

In both passages, the repeated indefi nite article "a" foregrounds each line, suggesting a dislocated and distanced relationship between the author/ narrator and pastoral Nepal or urban India (Hodge & Kress, 1993, pp. 87–89). Compare this with the use of a more contextually situated defi nite article: "The river runs white," "The man with teeth entirely of gold." That would have been an insider's point of view. I suggest that the technology of viewing and recording reality mediates ways of knowing, writing, and relating to context. McCormick writes on her website,"trained as an investigative reporter, I took notes and photos observing the sights, smells, foods, sounds, and the custom-details to give the book authenticity" (¶ 3). Transposed to language-use, what we have is a series of disjointed photographic images. This is another aspect of Kress and Leeuwen's (2001) notion of provenance, which typically points to where signs come from, but in an "unsystematic, ad hoc manner, which is often communicated as a pastiche or list" (p. 73). With a sharp focus on individuals and their actions, the contextual frame of reference is blurred into blankness. Rather than leading the reader into the visual space, zooming in from large to small (or the reverse), this technique quickly transitions from one scene to another, mimicking a series of photographs. The panning of street life continues for the rest of the page, till Lakshmi wonders:

> In this swarming, hurry-up city,
> what will happen
> next
> to me. ("Next," pp. 65–66)

By the end of the vignette, the locative connector, "next to," takes on the added function of a temporal "next," shifting the expository narration, to the happening of plot. This is achieved by the spatial splitting of "next" and "to me." Organization of words and the use of empty space can be considered as a sign system which highlights the relationship between the text and the reader. Referring to the several episodes which are only a few lines, McCormick comments, "I also think the 'white space' between vignettes calls on the reader to engage his or her imagination in the story-telling process to fi ll in the blanks." In this regard, Terry Eagleton's comment on imagination comes to mind:

The imagination is the faculty by which you can empathize with others—by which, for example, you can feel your way into the unknown territory of another culture . . . But this leaves unresolved the question of where you, as opposed to they, are actually standing. . . . (2000, p. 45)

The episode ends with two words: "to me." As a passive form, it forebodes the actions the protagonist will undergo. Drugged and beaten into submission, Lakshmi is now schooled in the rules, routines, and ruses of prostitution. In the episode "EVERYTHING I NEED TO KNOW NOW," (pp. 141–142) Shahanna instructs her:

Before [italics added] when you were in the locked room, Shahanna says, Mumtaz sent the customers to you. Now [italics added], if you want to pay off your debt, you must do what it takes to make them choose you . . . Always wash yourself with a wet rag after the man is fi nished . . . . . . If [italics added] a customer likes you, he may give you a sweet . . . If a customer likes you, he may give you a tip . . .

The temporal axis of "before-now-always" and the use of conditional clauses mirror the earlier episode "EVERYTHING I NEED TO KNOW" when her mother instructed her on what a woman should and should not do. The similar patterning of these episodes prompts connections between the two activities. In fact, on publisher Hyperion's discussion guide, students are asked to: "Discuss the vignette entitled 'Everything I Need to Know Now.' What do you think of the cultural mandates that she must live by? Compare it to the vignette of the same title that appears later when she is in the city. How does it represent all the changes in her life?" Gee's building task on connections asks: "How does this piece of language connect or disconnect things; how does it make one thing relevant or irrelevant to another?" (p. 13). Both episodes are about female existence and identity. But, in the fi rst episode gender roles are connected to cultural sanctions, whereas in the second episode the subservience and conditional causality of a woman's existence is connected to the gendered economics of sex trade. The marked parallelism in the form of the two episodes draws connections between these two domains: "cultural mandates" and "sex trade." This latent intersection elides economic factors; parents sell their children because of poverty, not because of culture. The fusion of culture and exploitation is underscored by the shawl as a connecting signifi er. While the earlier episode (EVERYTHING I NEED TO KNOW) referred to the cultural function of the shawl, it now takes on the dubious roles of a marketing lure, a protective shield, and fi nally a possible noose. As the girls "paint their faces," one of them explains to Lakshmi another semiotic performance of the shawl:

There are special things you need to know about how to use your shawl,she says.

Flick the ends of your shawl in a come-closer gesture and

You will bring the shy men to your bed . . .

. . . Draw your shawl to your chin, bend your neck like a peacock.

This will bring the older men to your bed . . .

Press your shawl to your chin with the back of your hand . . .

when you must bring a dirty man to your bed. (pp. 142–143)

The reader can now conjecture as to why the girl in the photograph covers her mouth. Perhaps it was not a gesture of voiceless submission, but of repulsion. The passage concludes ominously with another use of the shawl.

There is another way to use a shawl, she says . . .

. . . That new girl, the one in your old room, she says.

Yesterday morning Mumtaz found her hanging from the rafters. (p. 143)

Clearly, the D/discourse is about the annihilating exploitation of women. Culturally prescribed gender roles and economic enslavement are to blame. In her foundational 1984 paper "Under Western Eyes: Feminist Scholarship and Colonial Discourse," Chandra Talpade Mohanty (cited in Brydon, 2000) suggests that "the singular, monolithic notion of patriarchy or male dominance leads to the construction of a similarly reductive and homogeneous notion of what I call the 'Third World Difference' – that stable, ahistorical something that apparently oppresses most if not all the women in these countries" (p.

1185). Ratna Kapur (2005), who also writes from a framework of postcolonial feminism, examines how traffi cking and violence against women and sexuality in the context of human rights have served to reinforce the fi rst world/third world divide. She comments that the prevalent characterization of sex workers as victims of a culturally endorsed practice, and the persistence of economic exploitation, is an approach "located on an East/West binary and assumes that choice is possible in the West, while economic oppression in Asia is so all encompassing, that the very possibility of choice or agency is negated" (p. 76).5 hile undoubtedly the "fetishism" of selective and homogenous representations persists, in a world of cultural hybridity (Bhabha, 1994) and sensitivity to what Abdul JanMohamed (1986) referred to as the Manichaean allegory, a critical analysis of D/discourse cannot be limited to ferreting out generalizations, differences, and equivalences in a text (such as South Asian culture = male dominance); instead, an analysis of power relations needs to identify and describe how these ethical, cultural, and existential models are resisted and changed within the text. In short, who has the power to engender change? How does Lakshmi break the shackles of a culture portrayed as "simply to endure is to triumph"? How does she discount the calculations of poverty and dependence? How does she get and use voice?

"I Know This Voice. It is My American."

As the book progresses, Sold actually presents the hybridity of two cultures operating in India and Nepal: South Asian culture and the globalization of American culture and commodities. In the Himalayan village, culture is a mélange of Hindu festivals, cultural practices, and superstitions. But in "Happiness House," American cultural icons become far more active. Though "posters of gods" plaster the walls, the practice of religion is not portrayed. Instead, the girls watch The Bold and the Beautiful. Shahanna comments, "It's from America. It's our favorite show" (p. 136). Similarly, a bottle of Coca-Cola holds promises of happiness. Lakshmi is curious about this drink since "the people who drink it on TV are happy when its tiny fi reworks go off in their mouths" (p. 235). McCormick is equally wary of falling into facile moral binaries of east/west. Lakshmi's customers include a gentle Indian, a drunken American, and an American who promises to take her away to a shelter for girls.

However, despite the author's careful calibration of the good, bad, and ugly, the power to change Lakshmi's situation does not come from within South Asian society. It is not one of the many South Asian grassroots movements (included in the author's acknowledgements) that comes to Lakshmi's rescue, but an American. I argue that the latent message is that South Asian society offers little potential for positive change. Instead, the American abroad is at the center of a transformative discourse on literacy and the articulation of individual identity. For the women of the brothel, literacy is a curse. As Harish, the little boy who befriends Lakshmi, cautions: "If they fi nd out you can read and write, they will think you are planning to escape" (p. 171). Harish goes to a "singing-and-playing school" run by a "kind" American lady. In this value-added package of friendship-innocence-literacy-freedom-America, he represents the mediator between the disempowered subaltern and American goodwill. It is he who secretly teaches Lakshmi Hindi and even English, while reassuring her that she can trust Americans, despite Anita's warning:

The Americans will try to trick you into running away . . . .

Don't be fooled. They will shame you and make you walk naked through the streets. (p. 142)

Soon Lakshmi learns "American words" from a storybook given to Harish by the American lady. She can now say:

Big Bird,
Elmo,
ice cream,
soccer. (p. 174)

Literacy is firmly grounded in the tropes of American childhood. Unlike the dubious aspirations of The Bold and the Beautiful, this is the "good" humanist export of American culture (a Hindi version of Sesame Street, called Galli Galli Sim Sim, was released in 2006, the year Sold was published). We are given to understand that it is thanks to Harish that the Americans organize a police raid. And it is Harish who teaches Lakshmi the words of self-awareness:

"My name is Lakshmi," . . .
"I am from Nepal.
I am thirteen years old." (p. 192)

These are the words she repeats to herself, and these are the words of freedom, that she announces to her liberators. The use of italics in both passages draws the reader's attention to a connection between two Discourses: the positive icons of American childhood and the enunciation of her identity. In short, Lakshmi's identity is articulated in terms of America and literacy. Laclau and Mouffe (1985) describe hegemonic discourses as the result of articulation, where articulation is a "practice establishing relations among elements such that their identity is modified as a result of articulatory practice" (p. 105). Torfing (1999) succinctly adds that "articulations that take place in a context of antagonistic struggles and conflicts are defined as hegemonic articulations" (p. 298). Lakshmi's selfdefining articulation is a hegemonic discourse in so far as it is contingent on the resolution of a discursive struggle between two political forces: the American as friend or foe. The role of the "good" American abroad culminates in the final episode titled "THE WORDS HARISH TAUGHT ME."

Stephens (1992) reminds us that "Intentionality can only be fully attributed to a text from the perspective of the close" and "Endings reaffirm what society regards as important issues and preferred outcomes" (pp. 42–43). Seen from this perspective, closures often indicate an ideological conclusion to the book's discourse. It is a year since Lakshmi left her village. After "days of waiting for the American" who had promised to liberate her, the book concludes with a raid, and Lakshmi's reassurance that "her" American has arrived:

I know this voice. It is my American . . .

It is an American, I whisper . . .

The American is shouting something . . .

he is calling out to me . . .

I cannot go to my American . . .

But I can still hear the American . . .

The American calls out . . .

My American is leaving . . .

Something inside me breaks open, and I run down the steps . . .

I see my American. There are other men with him, Indian men, and the American lady from the picture. "My name is Lakshmi", I say. "I am from Nepal. I am fourteen years old."(p. 263)

This is a political ending. Gee's fifth building task is politics. Gee asks: "What is the politics of the situation, who has what status and power over when and where? (2006, p. 174). In this brief concluding episode of three pages, the word "American" occurs nine times. Notably, it is a political Discourse on the trustworthy commitment of the good American abroad, and not about collective or indigenous social change. This liberal humanist focus on individual agency as evidence of a possible challenge to systems and its eventual transformation dismisses the context of the social, economic, and historical. Most importantly, the narrative of the American as liberator discounts homegrown movements. The reality on the ground says otherwise. In the book's coda of acknowledgements, McCormick writes:

This book could not have been written without the help of Ruchira Gupta and Anuradha Koriala, who paved the way for me to visit the Maiti Nepal shelter for women and children in Kathmandu; the village of Goldbungha in the Himalayas, and the Deepika Social Welfare Center for Women and Children in the red-light district of Calcutta.

It is unfortunate that considering the courageous work done by several Nepali and Indian women, Sold portrays the "third world" woman as one whose liberation and identity cannot emerge from within her own society and culture. One can of course dismiss the American presence as a necessary narrative ploy that makes the text relevant to an implied American reader. It can also be read as an instructive narrative about a nation's export of goodwill, individual freedom, and enlightened modernity. From a humanitarian point of view, one may argue that the right to protect (R2P) is above and beyond nations, cultures, and ideologies. Others may contend that imagination is an artistic license which should not be confl ated with political nuances.

Whether the novel's conclusion is a response to an implied market, a reflection of political models (not necessarily mutually exclusive), or is validated by its firm ethical footing, the question still remains as to how knowing and understanding "the other world" finds its resolution in praiseworthy American intervention. It is a moot question if one considers the current scenario of international relations. As Homi Bhabha (1990) puts it, the people are "constructed in the performance of narrative" (p. 299). The people are also constructed through the performance of education. In an attempt to investigate how institutions (in this case the publisher) further the educational "performance" of a narrative, I turned to publisher Hyperion's discussion guide. Students are asked to consider: "What was the most disturbing part of this story for you? What facts crawled under your skin and continue to haunt you? Do you think there is anything you can do to help? What?" It appears that emotive empathy with the protagonist is the privileged way of understanding what happens beneath the surface. Even "facts" crawl "under your skin," grafting the "other side of the world." I suggest that the pedagogical enterprise of privileging ways of knowing that heighten individuation and relationships that are de-contextualized may induce empathy with a human condition, but an enthusiasm for individuals as the source of meaning, action, and change, is untenable because the supporting framework of political and socioeconomic assumptions is not accounted for.

Constructing the "Third World"

Narrative This chapter began with the question: How does the enactment of significance, activities, identities, relationships, connections, and knowledge practices condition the political discourse on individual/social change in literature written by North Americans about "third world" developing countries? Operationalizing Gee's seven building tasks used to "create or build the world of activities" (2006, p. 10) has helped me reveal the discursive conditions which lead us to accept a D/discourse in which emancipatory change comes primarily from an American presence.

First, I would conclude that an analysis of the book cover, text, and discussion guides reveals that the hegemonic political discourse on individual/social change in developing countries is contingent on the positive equivalence of a chain of activities: friendship-literacy-enunciation of consciousness-the American-liberation. Second, the effi cacy of this chain of equivalence (to use a Laclauian term) depends on an oppositional relationship with another set. For example, in Sold, connections are drawn between culture-gender disempowerment-poverty-sexual exploitation. These connections negate the possibility of change from within the "third world." Operating from this premise, the promise of individual/social transformation is now open to a neocolonial discourse which portrays the subaltern third-worlder's identity as "incapable of defi ning itself" (Said, 1979, p. 301) in an autonomous frame of reference. Roderick McGillis' description of neocolonialism comes to mind: "neocolonialism manifests itself as both a depiction of minority cultures as inveterately other and inferior in some ways to the dominant European or Eurocentric culture" (2000, p. xxiv). Third, when the macro signifi cance deals with human rights violations, questioning who has the power to engender change or how the subaltern is voiced becomes irrelevant. In such cases, it would even be immoral to talk about covert political deployment. This de-politicization of Discourse models is furthered in educational knowledge practices that promote affective engagement and a heightened individuation that is de-contextualized and un-problematized. By foregrounding personal engagement, the underlying political discourse is obscured. And by continuing the dichotomy between West and the rest, "the other side of the world" is then once again proved to be incompetent. Nonetheless, it bears repeating that the importance of literature lies precisely in its potential to provoke a dialogue that is willing to confront ambiguities, fathom complexities, and challenge comfortable assumptions. This chapter is an attempt to stir, and bring to the surface, the kind of refl ection from which such learning is launched.

Conclusion

Learning has been described as a "community of practice" (Lave & Wenger, 2002) or a "way of talking about the shared historical and social resources, frameworks, and perspectives that can sustain mutual engagement in action"

(Wenger, 1998, p. 5). If learning activates communal identity, the problem for global relationships is clear. How does one veer away from the pitfalls of divisive parochialism? Or, as Gee (2008) observes, "with the notion of a 'community' we can't go any further until we have defined who is in and who is not, since otherwise we can't identify the community" (p. 88). When reading and re-reading Sold, I was constantly reminded that in the case of literature about the world, transformative learning is the willingness to question the "communities of practice" we are entrenched in, and identify how the text and image defines "who is in and who is not" part of that shared "engagement in action."

Reading Sold through a postcolonial and neocolonial lens would have immediately directed me to the exclusion of the "third world's" potential in engaging with the telos of human emancipation. So why combine it with CDA? To begin with, CDA and multimodal analysis strengthen postcolonial/ neocolonial discourse analysis, giving it a systematic process-oriented methodology that can translate theory into a critical praxis of reading. In fact, CDA, social semiotic theories, and postcolonial theories form a compatible set of analytical tools, sharing a common concern with the imbrications between discourse, ideology, power, identity, and practice. Combined, this 'tool-kit' can lay bare how a book's D/discourse places the reader in naturalized subject positions of power with respect to the disenfranchised. Finally, a 'third world' perspective satisfies what Fairclough described as socially transformative learning: "a relatively high degree of dialogicality and orientation to difference" (2004, p. 233). CDA, postcolonial and neocolonial theories are all concerned with the exercise of power. Yet, while analyzing Sold, I became aware that power circulates ubiquitously, both within the text and in the interpreter. In the book, Lakshmi's father, the brothel owner, and the American all exercised power over her identity. In tandem with each of these narrative sites of power, I too weighed in with the loci of my identities: the independent woman, the Indian-American, the third-worlder, the educator, and the researcher. As a woman, my sentiments tugged me unequivocally toward female empowerment, in whatever way that may come about. As an Indian-American who has lived in the United States for 16 years, I still harbor the innate pride of a third-worlder who is always aware of a selective and enduring genealogy in the representation of the "third world" woman. Growing up in post-independence India, I belonged to a generation which knew about US journalist Katherine Mayo's justifi cation of British rule and her searing attack on Indian nationalism. In her infamous book Mother India (1927), Mayo gave a detailed account of public health in India and more explicitly the sexual practices of the Indian woman. Mahatma Gandhi famously referred to Mayo's book as the "drain-inspector's report." What remains of this dubious legacy is the specter of how others choose to see the South Asian woman. As a teacher of children's and young adult literature about the world, I grapple with the daunting task of balancing universal values with a principle of difference and autonomy. And as a critic, I am acutely aware that the bridge between analysis and interpretation is always suspect. It is a diffi cult position to be in. Yet, it is the awareness of the multiple and frequently confl icting sites of our identities that strengthens how we analyze, learn, and interpret. Weaving into the text and out of ourselves, we can bring context and complexity to the way we look at the world.

Notes

- Young (2003) has this to say about the contemporary use of the term "third world": "At the Bandung Conference of 1955, 29 mostly newly independent African and Asian countries . . . initiated what became known as the non-aligned movement. They saw themselves as an independent power bloc, with a new 'third world' perspective on political, economic, and cultural global priorities"(p. 17). This was a time when the world was divided into two major political systems, capitalism (the fi rst world) and socialism (the second world).

- American Library Association's 2007 Top Ten Best Books for Young Adults; Booklist Editors' Choice (Youth), 2006; Children's Literature Council's Choice, 2007; National Book Award fi nalist, 2006; Publishers Weekly, Best 100 Books of 2006; YALSA Best Books for Young Adults 2007.

- In An Introduction to Discourse Analysis: Theory and Method, Gee (2006) states that, "a discourse analyst can ask seven different questions about any piece of language-inuse" (p. 11). These are: Signifi cance: "How is this piece of language being used to make certain things signifi - cant or not and in what ways?" Activities: "What activity or activities is this piece of language being used to enact (i.e. get others to recognize as going on?" Identities: "What identity or identities is this piece of language being used to enact (i.e. get others to recognize as operative?" Relationships: "What sort of relationship or relationships is this piece of language seeking to enact with others (present or not)?" Politics: "What perspective on social goods is this piece of language communicating (i.e. what is being communicated as to what is taken to be 'normal,' 'right,' 'good,' 'correct,' 'proper,' 'appropriate,' 'valuable,' 'the way things are,' 'the way things ought to be,' 'the high status or low status,' 'like me or not like me,' and so forth?" Connections: "How does this piece of language connect or disconnect things; how does it make one thing relevant or irrelevant to another?" Sign systems and knowledge: "How does this piece of knowledge privilege or disprivilege specifi c sign systems (e.g. Spanish vs. English, technical language vs. everyday language, words vs. images, words vs. equations) or different ways of knowing and believing or claims to knowledge and belief?"(Gee, 2006, pp. 11–13).

- Torfi ng (1999) describes dislocation as the "destabilization of a discourse that results from the emergence of events which cannot be domesticated, symbolized or integrated within the discourse in question" (p. 301).

- A salient example of collective agency is the Kolkata based sex workers' union. In 1995, the Durbar Mahila Samanwaya Committee (DMSC) formed a forum of transgender, male, and female sex workers and their children. Demanding their right to form a trade union, they lobbied for their basic human rights, security for their children, old age support and better working conditions. As their program director put it, "They work with their bodies and hence they want workers' rights" (The Times of India, 2005). The DMSC's "Sex Workers Manifesto" has been taken up by other sex workers' unions in India. A copy can be downloaded from the website of Network of Sex Work Projects (www.nswp.org/rights/dmsc), an international organization operating in 40 countries.

FIGURED WORLDS AND DISCOURSES OF MASCULIN-ITY: BEING A BOY IN A LITERACY CLASSROOM

Theories about masculinities (e.g., Coles, 2009; Connell, 2005; Jackson & Salisbury, 1996) suggest that there are multiple Discourses (Gee, 1996; 2007; this volume) or ways of being and doing masculinity. Discourses of masculinity are constructed and reconstructed over time within different social and cultural groups. These groups (e.g., families, sports teams, street gangs, literacy professors, high school English teachers) share conventions about language and activities such as speaking, writing, reading, acting, interacting, valuing, dressing, and so on. In this chapter, we explore the activities and language conventions within the Discourses of a Mexican American adolescent who was aspiring to be a certain kind of popular male athlete and literacy student. Masculinity theories recognize that masculinities and femininities are constituted in relation to one another, and that some Discourses1 of being masculine hold more social status and power than others, depending on the particular social contexts (Coles, 2009; Connell, 2005; Jackson & Salisbury, 1996; Reed, 1999). Often, however, Discourses of masculinity are represented as stable and nonnegotiable. For example, machismo, a concept associated with Hispanic masculinity, has been represented as a rigid set of practices such as domination of women, aggression, confrontational behavior, and a strict division of labor in the household (Klein, 2000). Recent research (e.g., Klein, 2000; Arciniega, Anderson, Tovar-Blank & Tracey, 2008) found that there are varying degrees and dimensions of machismo, and Hispanic men are far more complicated and diverse than the generalized concept of machismo might suggest. Still, the beliefs associated with the ideals of machismo linger and serve to perpetuate rigid stereotypes about Hispanic men.

Critical discourse analysis allows for the study of the Discourses of masculinity through an analysis of social practices. In this chapter, we (two middleclass White females) adapted Gee's (2005; this volume) guidelines for critical discourse analysis to explore how Chavo's (a middle-class, Mexican American, 18-year-old male) constructions of masculinity shaped his participation in school literacy activities and the way that school literacy activities and classroom contexts, in turn, shaped his understandings of what it meant to be a boy in a literacy classroom.

Chavo was aware, as early as middle school, of the different Discourses of masculinity (e.g., popular male athlete, nerd, skater) that existed at his school. To be recognized as a member of the popular male athlete Discourse—a Discourse to which he aspired—he took steps to hide his good grades and learned ways to pass English courses without reading the required texts. Chavo's story is not unique among adolescent boys. What is unique was his ability to articulate the practices/activities of masculinity and literacy that he believed would help others recognize him as a certain kind of young man. Chavo was 1 of 21 adolescent males who participated in a narrative inquiry that explored what was happening with and to them in a variety of literacy classrooms in the southwestern United States (Young, Hardenbrook, Esch, Hansen, & Griffith, 2003). Our purposes in highlighting Chavo's literacy stories in this chapter are twofold: (a) to complicate simplistic notions of male stereotypes; and (b) to make visible the ways in which critical discourse analysis can allow us to understand the multiple Discourses that inform our beliefs and understandings of masculinities and literacy participation

During the year-long study in which Chavo was a participant, Marsh (aka Young), along with four other researchers, observed seven adolescent literacy classrooms (e.g., English, reading, humanities, and writing) and selected three male focal students from each site to observe and interview. We interviewed these male students and their teachers and parents about their literacy and gender beliefs and practices. We also wrote weekly fi eld notes about the literacy class in general and the ways that the focal students participated in it more specifi cally.

Meant to add to the growing body of research about boys, masculinities, and literacies, the purpose of the study (Young et al., 2003) was to gain an understanding of what it is like to be a boy in an adolescent literacy classroom. This research was timely given the resurgence of concern over boys' achievement, especially literacy achievement, in schools (e.g., Beaupre, 2003; Lesko, 2000; Smith & Wilhelm, 2002). These concerns rose to near panic status in the United States after the rash of school violence in late 1990s; statistics showing declines in school achievement (Hedges & Nowell, 1995) and male college attendance (e.g., Fonda, 2000; Goodman, 2002) were publicized, and boys' high school reading and writing standardized test scores fell (Beaupre, 2003). For example, Sommers (2000) suggested that we are waging a war against boys, and Faludi (1999) wrote about betraying our boys and men. Our study was particularly concerned with the trouble some boys seemed to be having in the area of school literacy. For instance, according to the National Center for Education Statistics (2000), boys were three to five times more likely than girls to be placed in learning/reading disabilities classes. Boys in elementary through high school scored lower than girls on standardized measures of reading achievement (Hedges & Nowell, 1995), and were less likely than girls to enroll in advanced placement (AP) courses in language, literature, and history (College Board, 2007). Still, almost 10 years later, our research remains timely as concerns about boys' achievement and the existence of a gender gap continue to garner the attention of the media (Cook, 2006; Tyre, 2006) and educational researchers

(Downey & Vogt-Yuan, 2005; Hammett & Sanford, 2008). However, recent National Assessment of Educational Progress (NAEP) results (Mead, 2006) do not support the notion that boys' achievement is continuing to fall. For example, fourth- and eighth-grade reading assessment scores on the 2003 test show improvement. These data, however, are less clear for older boys, with 17-year-old boys' scores falling, but the gap between boys and girls was not much different than it was in the 1970s. Boys' graduation rates are also lower than those of their female counterparts, and these differences are magnified among Black students (Lloyd, 2007).

Some educators, journalists, and lawmakers called for (and still call for) quick fixes that rely on equal opportunity approaches to curriculum (Brozo & Gaskins, 2009; Skelton, 1998). Solutions include returning the so-called femininized literacy classrooms back to the boys by hiring more male teachers, providing all-male classrooms and more male literacy role models, and using more boy books, which focus on stereotypical male interests (Brozo & Gaskins, 2009; Scieszka, 2003). These calls for reform tend to narrowly define masculinity and do not take into account race, class, and the long history of the boy problem in schools (Griffith, 2009; Tatum, 2008a; Tatum, 2008b;

Tyack & Hansot, 1990). They also tend to reinforce stereotypical gender roles by pitting boys' literacy needs against girls' (AAUW, 2009) and promoting a "boys will be boys" ideology (Kimmel, 2000, p. 7). In addition, these solutions have not adequately addressed the social complexities inherent in Discourses of masculinity and school literacy practices.

Discussions that theorize masculinities are taking place within literacy education (e.g., Alloway, 2007; Blair & Sanford, 2004; Madill, 2009; Martino & Kehler, 2007; Tatum, 2008a, 2008b; Young, 2000). These discussions about the practices of masculinity enable us to explore the ways that race, ethnicity, and social class complicate the picture of boys' literacy achievements and school behaviors (Griffi th, 2009; Kimmel, 2000; Tatum, 2008b). They make visible the practices of masculinity and includes masculinity in our discussions about gender (Kimmel, 2000). Discussions of masculinity also make visible the infl uence of social contexts and diversity on how boys do and think about gender and literacy and can inform our thinking about ways to engage boys in school literacy. It is our intention to highlight some of these complexities through the analyses presented in this chapter.

The Gender Order and Discourses of Masculinity

Certain social practices/activities and Discourses of masculinity come with more social status, potential power, and social goods than others. R. W. Connell (1987) used the term "gender order" (p. 91) to describe the hierarchies present between and among the different ways of being masculine and feminine. He theorized that the Discourses of masculinity interact with institutional and societal relations to negotiate and construct hierarchies and differences. These differences and hierarchies are known as the gender order and are infl uenced by race, class, age, and sexual orientation. In addition, the gender order is not static; it is constantly changing and creating relations of power between men and women and among men. The gender order describes the political nature of Discourses of masculinity and is important to keep in mind when thinking about boys and literacy because it works to limit the way boys and men participate in literate activities in and out of school. For instance, boys and men who strive for membership in a more dominant Discourse (one that defi nes a real man) may adopt particular literacy practices that they believe will identify them as a member of that particular real man Discourse. These practices might include liking books with action-fi lled plots, identifying with male characters not female ones, and selecting books and other texts written by and about men; or they might include withholding all participation in school literacy practices. In other words, boys who wish to be viewed as a boy of a certain sort (e.g., jocks, nerds, skaters, gays) must "talk the talk" and "walk the walk" (Gee, 2005, p. 21). They must learn to read (or not read), write (or not write), and so on like others who claim membership in that particular Discourse of masculinity. This learning takes place as they interact with others over time within particular social contexts.

Critical Discourse Analysis

This research depicts stories recalled by Chavo, his mother, and his humanities teacher of Chavo's lived literacy experiences. The stories were told to me (fi rst author, Marsh) during individual semi-structured interviews with Chavo, his mother, and his teacher, and they refl ect my observations in Chavo's seniorlevel honors humanities classroom over a 6-month period and my informal observations of him in the sports arena for several years. As I constructed the stories for this chapter, I used four theoretical tools of inquiry suggested by Gee (2005; this volume) for critical discourse analysis. The four tools I used were (a) Discourses, (b) social languages, (c) situated meanings, and (d) fi gured worlds. Although all of these were useful in helping me understand the Discourses that infl uenced Chavo, because of page limitations I focus primarily on fi gured worlds for this analysis.

The fi rst tool, Discourses, framed the study. I sought to identify the Discourses in which Chavo, his mother, and teacher were members and understand how these Discourses informed their ways of thinking, speaking, reading, acting, and so on. The other theoretical tools assisted me in this process and offered questions to guide my thinking about the data. The questions, adapted from Gee (2005), helped me look closely at the words, how they were put together within different social contexts.

The theoretical tools of social languages and situated meanings assisted my analysis. Social language is the way a person speaks or writes to enact a particular identity (e.g., Chavo's use of the phase it sucks when he described the humanities class to his teammates so that he appeared to be a certain kind of guy). Situated meanings or utterance-token meanings (see Gee, this volume),

refer to the multiple connotations words take on in different contexts. As I read the data, I asked questions to help me understand the situated meanings constructed and the social languages used during our interviews and informal chats. These questions included the following adapted from Gee (2005): What social language did Chavo use in his conversation during the interview? How did this social language represent him? How did the contexts shape the meaning of his responses? What sorts of discourse patterns indicate this? In this way, I considered how social language and the situated meanings constructed during the interviews infl uenced the way participants used language to represent themselves and their ideas. For example, during an interview, Chavo told me that the humanities class "isn't motivational." He used language that defi ned him as a student within the context of a formal interview with a professor. Using the terms isn't motivational helped me to recognize him as an experienced student—one who knew the lingo of school and one who blamed the course for his disinterest. One reasonable meaning that I could infer from this statement was that Chavo did not like the class, but he did not want to come out and tell me this during the interview. Perhaps he was unsure if I would report back to his teacher or mother. Perhaps he did not want me to think less of him as a student, so he blamed the course. Interestingly, in speaking about the same class to a soccer teammate who was considering signing up for it the following year, I overhead Chavo tell him that the course "sucked." The term sucked in this context helped his teammate recognize him as a fellow teenage athlete who did not like English courses, especially this one. As with isn't motivational, the terms class sucked also placed the blame for his disinterest and dislike for the course on the course, but in more popular terms. In both instances, Chavo used social language to enact a particular kind of identity situated within different social contexts—one as a student talking to a professor, one as a fellow male athlete.

Figured worlds is the fourth analytical tool suggested by Gee (this volume) and the major analytical tool used during this analysis. Applying the concept of fi gured worlds helped me make visible and understand how Chavo's constructions of masculinity shaped his literacy practices and how, in turn, his literacy practices shaped his understandings of what it meant to be a boy in a literacy classroom. Figured worlds, similar to cultural models (Gee, this volume), are everyday storylines or theories that help individuals determine what is normal and typical within a particular Discourse. It is the beliefs, values, and attitudes held that inform what we say and how we act, read, and interact. Figured worlds are not static; they change as we interact, read, experience, observe, and adapt to new situations, and they mean different things to members of different Discourse communities. For example, the fi gured world storyline boys will be boys means something slightly different to mothers, young boys, adolescents, coaches, and teachers. Using fi gured worlds as a tool of inquiry led me to ask interpretive questions such as: What fi gured worlds were relevant to Chavo, his mother, and his teacher? How consistent are the fi gured worlds throughout the study? How do fi gured worlds relevant to Chavo, his mother, and his teacher reproduce, transform, and create

Discourses and the social practices associated with being male in adolescent literacy classrooms? To construct stories about Chavo's literacy practices/ activities, I fi rst read and reread the data many times and asked the questions of the data related to Gee's theoretical tools (2005; this volume). I selected snippets from the interview transcripts and observational data that seemed to answer my research question about what it was like for Chavo to participate in literacy classrooms and how his constructions of masculinity might have shaped his participation in school literacy. I organized the transcripts into lines and stanzas as defi ned by Gee (2005). Each line consisted of a single idea unit or a small piece of information, and a set of connected lines that were about a theme, perspective, topic, or image was considered a stanza. In other words, I left large portions of the transcripts intact and did not rearrange the lines of the transcripts. I titled each stanza to help me determine themes and perspectives of the speakers. The following is a stanza I titled Chavo Used to Read. It represents an idea unit represented by a snippet of intact transcript.

Chavo Used to Read

In sixth grade, ah,we had a list of all the honors' books and

> I had my mom go pick up like four or fi ve of those during the summer.

> In sixth grade and

> I read them all and then seventh and eighth grade

> I just, I don't know, I just decided not to do that anymore.

I then constructed a 27-stanza narrative that wove together transcripts from interviews I conducted with Chavo, his mother, and his teacher. Using Chavo's transcripts as the foundation for each stanza, I selected transcripts from Chavo's mother and teacher that informed Chavo's words. This sort of multi-vocal transcript provided me with a fuller picture of Chavo and his fi gured worlds. It allowed me to ask analytical questions of the data and to make hypotheses about how the activities and beliefs about masculinity of each speaker were constitutive. I then separated the stanzas back by speaker in an effort to represent different perspectives about Chavo's literacy and masculinity. In the following section, I present stories about Chavo's literacies and masculinities in the words of Chavo's mother, teacher, and Chavo himself. I constructed stories using the word-for-word transcripts of the interviews with his mother, his teacher, and Chavo. I took out sound representations such as "um," "ah," and false starts to make the text more easily read (Institute of Oral History, 2001). I also deleted my interview questions that elicited these responses. I reorganized the stanzas for the purpose of connecting ideas or themes, but did not rearrange the lines within each stanza, thus leaving most of the transcripts intact. Then within each story of Chavo, I took apart the transcript again and looked carefully at the form and function of the words spoken by each participant. For example, to understand the fi gured worlds that were relevant to Theresa, Chavo's mother, about her son's literate life,

I found that her use of reported speech (dialogue used in retellings of events such as I said . . ., he said . . .) served as evidence to support the fi gured worlds informing her beliefs. I then isolated the reported speech and organized it into stanzas. This microanalysis of the transcripts helped me see more clearly how Theresa perceived Chavo's literacy experiences and facilitated my interpretation of the function that reported speech played in Theresa's story of Chavo. Likewise, in Ms. Brown's story of Chavo, I found her use of two descriptive nominalizations (compound nouns used to name a certain kind of person, place, thing—e.g., a literature kid or a man's man) and reported speech to be powerful in determining the fi gured worlds important to her. For Chavo's story, I focused my analysis on his use of I-statements (e.g., I know, I read) during the microanalysis of his transcripts. In each case, I isolated the specifi c words (e.g., nominalizations or I-statements) and thought carefully about what they were telling me about fi gured worlds and Discourse.

Stories of Chavo's Adolescent Literacy Experiences

From His Mother's Perspective

Chavo's mother, Theresa, is Hispanic and the mother of four sons. Chavo is the next to youngest. For many years, she stayed at home with the boys and participated in their school and after-school activities. She recalled that Chavo spent long hours putting puzzles together when he was preschool age, and that he loved to sit on her lap and be read to when he was young. He would snuggle up to her and ask her to read his favorite books. In fact, he was so interested in reading at an early age that she taught him to read before he entered kindergarten. Later when he was a bit older, Chavo's father took over the nightly reading by reading aloud to Chavo and his three brothers from classic and popular novels.

Literacy was an important part of Chavo's household. Both parents are strong readers, and the family always deemed education an essential aspect of their lives. As young children, Chavo and the brother closest in age to him played creatively, much of the time without toys, making up their own stories and games. As they grew up, they played outside sports with the neighborhood boys and engaged in computer games together and alone. When Chavo entered high school and his younger brother was in middle school, Theresa went back to school to become a licensed social worker. Chavo saw her reading and studying during the years in which she pursued her master's degree. He also observed his Euro-American father, a public health physician and university instructor, studying his medical journals, writing a textbook, and grading medical student papers. Chavo was surrounded at home by people who read and wrote, and never lacked literacy-related texts and tools—books, magazines, newspapers, computers, paper, and so on. In fact, Theresa reported that Chavo read the sports section of the newspaper every day. The following snapshot presented in

Theresa's voice is a brief overview of her memories about Chavo's past participation in school literacy activities.

Figured World 1: Chavo Was Not Challenged at School

Chavo Used to Read

In sixth grade, ah,we had a list of all the honors' books and

I had my mom go pick up like four or fi ve of those during the summer.

In sixth grade and

I read them all and then seventh and eighth grade

I just, I don't know, I just decided not to do that anymore."

And I said, "He may be doing that but I am telling you the quality of his work has really gone down."

III.

I tried to convince Chavo that he ought to go to St. Anthony's (a Catholicboys' prep school) so he would be challenged.

And instead, we compromised by taking honors classes at the high school.

And he actually got into the [high school honors] program and he did very well.

IV.

But I think that as time went onand he got interested in cross-country,

I think that he lost the interest [in academics].

It [running] was very, very satisfying to him.

I think a lot of that has to do with the factthat he was very much more interested [in running],

It is very demanding and it physically wears you out.

But I think the other half of that is that,

I don't think that he really had a challenge.

And all honors meant was that it was more homework.

It wasn't necessarily more interesting.

Figured World 2: Being male has nothing to do with it

I think that with Chavo, because of his really deep love for learning,

I don't think that [being a boy] ever mattered to him, what anyone would say, or kid him about doing his homework, or being a

good student.

He thrives on being a good student.

I mean, that is a really big thing for him to be able to accomplish.

But, when I think of him being male, I think that he very early fi gured out that, fi rst of all that he loved to learn these things, but second of all, because of his rules, he knew that in order for him to

play sports, he was gonna have to make the grades.

I think that made sense to him . . .

And I think the overall riding factor in that was that he does have a real huge

love for learning.

Two figured worlds seemed to inform Theresa's perspective about Chavo's literacy and academic achievement. The fi rst one, and perhaps the most striking, was the fi gured world that teachers are responsible for making school challenging and motivating for all students. Chavo began school as a motivated student and always tried to do his best. He was a good student and knew that a good student followed the rules. He had a love for reading that was facilitated at home. Beginning in eighth grade, things started to change for Chavo. His mother believed that this was at least in part due to the fact that his teachers did not challenge him to achieve more than the status quo. He learned quickly by the middle school teachers' responses to his work that he could get an A without working very hard or even doing the same quality work he had produced in the past. Theresa went to the school to point out this observation and was greeted by a teacher who did not seem to understand her concerns because, after all, Chavo was still making A's.

What Chavo did fi nd challenging in high school was running cross-country. Cross-country challenged him physically and mentally. He ran long crosscountry courses through the deserts of the Southwest, over terrain full of cacti, snakes, and rocks in hot August and September temperatures. Theresa observed her son running and perceived that running competitively was very satisfying and challenging for her son. He was animated after running and was a cheerleader for his teammates who ran slower than he.

The second fi gured world relevant to Theresa's thinking about Chavo's literacy was that gender had nothing to do with his participation in school literacy and other academics. She believed that peer pressure from the other kids in school had nothing to do with Chavo's doing or not doing his work. The only thing about being male that may have infl uenced Chavo, according to his mother, was his respect for rules—specifi cally, the rule that stated he had to make good grades to play high school sports. To identify and describe the fi gured worlds that were relevant to Theresa, I looked closely at what she said and listened to how she said it. The tone of her voice changed as she told stories about Chavo's literacy. Her voice was warm with the memories of Chavo learning to read and becoming a reader and good student. When retelling about Chavo's middle school years, her voice refl ected the anger and disappointment she felt about Chavo's experiences with some of his teachers. She spoke quickly and with much animation as she retold his middle school, emphasizing her belief that teachers had a responsibility to make school challenging and motivating.

Another way Theresa represented relevant fi gured worlds was through her use of dialogue or reported speech within her interview with me. Reported speech served several functions (Myers, 1999), including giving evidence, making stories more vivid and interesting, and shifting the focus of attention from the speaker. As Theresa told stories about Chavo's past literacy experiences, she included reported speech that depicted her past experiences with Chavo and his teachers and provided evidence of the fi gured worlds relevant to her. For example, when she described her meeting with his teachers, she selected speech that best represented her belief that teachers should present challenging learning opportunities for students (e.g., "You know, you're losing him because he's not being challenged") and her belief that the teachers did not believe in the same way (e.g., "He's still making very high grades"; "They [the teachers] don't care, I'm still getting A's"). Her use of reported speech was powerful and served to emphasize and support her beliefs.

From Chavo's Teacher's Perspective

Chavo's honors humanities teacher was Ms. Brown. She was a 30-year veteran English teacher and chair of the English department. Her passion for the humanities and teaching was evident in and out of the classroom. She was a humanities major in college until she realized she needed to broaden her fi eld to English if she wanted a teaching position. She told stories of the Greeks and Romans with such intensity and excitement that often I forgot to write fi eld notes about what her students were doing at the moment. I was enthralled by her stories and found her to be an engaging storyteller. Most notable was her desire for her students to love the humanities. She believed that humanities was more than literature—it was a world of ideas.

Many of the students in her class were leaders in the school and most were very high achievers. She expected high-quality written and oral participation from these students and usually got it. Ms. Brown was very proud of her students, and she believed that most had been raised as renaissance people. By this she meant that they were raised to believe they could be good at anything regardless of their gender. Because of this, she posited, gender was not a factor in determining how the students participated in this class. She believed that the boys participated "every bit as much as her girls," and she explained the lack of boys in the class (6 of the 25 students were male) as a consequence of other senior English course offerings such as regular senior English and creative writing. However, she held other notions about who were and were not humanities or literature kids that were not so visible.

Figured world 3: Chavo Is Not a Literature Kid

I.

Nothing, I know nothing about Chavo.

I said to Chavo about a month or six weeks ago I said "Chavo, I know you don't like this class."

I said, "You remind me so much of my daughter, she didn't like it either and I know your mother's making you stay in here."

I said, "but would you just smile at me once in a while." =

II.

He must be so bored with this stuff.

He would never, you know, I don't know if Chavo reads on his own, but I would venture to guess if it's not a sports magazine or a soccer journal, he doesn't.

He is not a literature kid from my perspective.

He's gotta B in the class.

No, it's not an easy class.

And he does his work

104 Josephine Marsh and Jayne C. Lammers But he doesn't love it.

It's not awful.

It's just not inspired.

III.

Chavo has never voluntarily participated in the discussions all year.

He has never opened his mouth unless I call on him and then he gets all spazzled.

So I don't do that anymore because I don't want to embarrass him.

I'm just trying to bring him in.

So, now I just wait, but he's been more jovial.

He's smiling a bit more.

But he is defi nitely not a humanities kid.

IV.

And I don't know if it's because he's a boy or not . . .

My daughter is not a boy, she's quite tomboyish (chuckle) [she did not like the humanities class] So I don't know whether that's just gender.

I'd say with my daughter, (laughingly) she had too many headers [soccer term for passing the ball with one's head] and maybe that's Chavo's problem.

No, he doesn't seem, not bright, he's just not interested.

V.

It's not like there's not precedent, my two best discussers are boys.

It's not like he couldn't if he wanted to. I don't know that it's a gender issue.

Unless all boys are interested in math and science and all girls are interested in literacy, but I don't think that's true anymore.

I just think that it's a Chavo issue.

I don't think it's gender . . .

He is my least enthusiastic student.

One of the fi gured worlds that seemed relevant to Ms. Brown was that not all kids were literature or humanities kids. Along with that model, like Chavo's mother, Ms. Brown held the cultural model that gender had nothing to do with participation or enrollment in the honor humanities class. Ms. Brown appeared to have a picture in her mind about who were and were not literature or humanities kids. They could be male or female; in fact, she believed her best discussers were male. She also knew who were not literature or humanities kids—her daughter, a tomboyish athlete, was not a humanities kid, and neither was Chavo. Her belief that certain kids were or were not literature kids seemed strong and most likely infl uenced her interaction with these students. For example, she stopped trying to get Chavo involved in class after seemingly embarrassing him by asking him questions. She fi nally just asked him to smile once in a while. She denied that being male might have infl uenced how Chavo participated or that being male had anything to do with the lack of boys in her class. She believed that Chavo's disinterest in the class and his lack of participation was a Chavo issue, nothing more, and she explained that the low number of boys enrolled in her class was due to the number of senior English courses available.

To represent the fi gured worlds relevant to her, Ms. Brown, like Theresa, used reported speech to describe an interaction with Chavo and as supporting evidence for the fi gured world that some kids are not literature kids. Most powerful in her representation of fi gured worlds is her use of two descriptive nominalizations—literature kid and humanities kid—during the interview. By describing Chavo as not being a humanities kid or literature kid, she compiled lots of information into a compound noun. It is hard to know the exact information that went into the creations of nominalizations by Ms. Brown (Fairclough, 2003; Gee, 2005); we would need to know more about Ms. Brown's expectations and experiences as an English teacher to completely understand. We are left wondering what the exact characteristics of a literature kid or humanities kid are, and characteristics of not being one. All we really know is that Chavo was not a literature kid, he was the most unenthusiastic kid in the class, and his work lacked inspiration. Nominalizations tend to turn concretes into new abstract entities (Fairclough, 2003; Gee, 2005), like literature or humanities kids. Using the nominalizations effectively named him without clearly defi ning the process or attributes of being or not being a literature/humanities kid.

From Chavo's Perspective

Chavo entered the senior honors humanities classroom with a face of stone each day. All expression of affect was erased from his face. He walked in and sat down quietly. His face told me (and his teacher) that he did not want to be 1 of the 6 males in a class of 25 high school honors students. His facial expressions were supported by his actions in the classroom. He rarely spoke in class or entered one of the many whole-group discussions. He slouched in his seat, looked down or around, and seldom looked at the teacher. Often he closed his eyes or put his head on his desk.

It was hard for me to believe that this was the same guy who was captain of the cross-country and soccer teams. My two sons were on the same high school soccer team as Chavo, so I had observed him for 3 years as a student athlete. He was a leader and motivator. He was a role model for the other guys on and off the soccer fi eld. He quietly led through mutual respect, loyalty, and friendship. The difference in his demeanor in the classroom and on the soccer fi eld intrigued me. After a few months of weekly classroom observations, I invited him to be part of the study. I wanted to investigate what it was like for Chavo to be a student in this high school literacy classroom and explore how his constructions of masculinity might have shaped his participation in it.

Figured world 4: Athletes Don't Read Books

I.

In sixth grade,

We had a list of all the honors' books and I had my mom go pick up like four or fi ve of those during the summer.

I read them all.

And then seventh and eighth grade, I just, I don't know, I just decided not to do that [read the summer honors' books] anymore.

Where the Red Fern Grows [was one of the summer honor books] I couldn't put it down, like I'd go home and read . . .

But non-stop and then when it ended I seriously did not want the book to end.

I was so caught up in the characters I felt like I knew 'em and stuff II.

I think, I found sports more interesting [than reading] and doing stuff.

I mean like in a house full of guys you can always fi nd some kind of athletic activity to do.

Whether it's playing basketball or Nintendo or the backyard swimming.

And especially where we live, there's always kids like in our neighborhood.

And then we'd ride bikes, play tag, all kinds of stuff.

So somehow I just lost reading as a priority.

III.

I think also once you get involved in sports like you're s'pose to be known as like an athlete.

It's just like a lot of the [athletes] really don't even want to like talk about reading or so don't even read.

So you just kind of get caught up into that somewhere along the line, I guess.

IV.

I still tried to get good grades, got straight A's in middle school.

And I just wouldn't like be loud about it or brag about it.

V.

The kids just like to harass each other in middle school Yeah, if he's a good athlete like he's better than other people I get kind of mad about that.

And then also I, if he is good at something else, I probl'y, I guess probl'y, I'd harass him now [in high school].

VI.

[The last book I read] was Grapes of Wrath [in 11th grade] That's when I stopped [reading]

Because we had a quiz on it And then I got like a D on it and I had read the whole book.

It was picky questions, really picky and that's a thick book . . .

I decided, I could just skip reading and get the same grade.

And that's when I totally stopped [reading].

We read current events every week in Economics. I always read the sports page.

Figured world 5: Guys Participate Differently than Girls I.

Well, I don't participate in that class [honors humanities] at all.

I don't really want to, and I probably won't want to for the rest of the year.

I mean I don't know, I don't feel uncomfortable around those people because I've been in the same class with them since sixth grade.

But it's just different, like, when I'm with the sports team or whatever, like that really motivates me and stuff like that.

This class isn't motivational.

II.

Ms. Brown thinks it's important that everyone is heard.

So sometime or another you have to participate.

I don't know, it [being called on] makes me feel kind of like, it puts me on the spot, really.

And it kind of makes me feel like I'm a little bit less, or kind of, I don't know, like she doesn't think I know the answer.

And that is usually the case.

I don't think she should be doing it.

I think that she's trying to make us feel involved.

III.

Since there are less of us [guys], I feel overpowered by the women.

And our teacher is a woman.

I really think that she's like a big time supporter of women.

How it's their turn to get the spotlight, all this stuff.

She's always talking about women's rights.

And, I just think she's more, this might not be true, I just see that she's more lenient towards the girls. Like if they're all involved in after-school activities, not necessary sports but other stuff,

Well since they're involved in other stuff that's academically like more challenging,

They seem to get a lot more exceptions.

They turn in work late.

I feel like I can't even ask her if I can turn in something late because it's dealing with a sport and

 I think she'll just tell me no.

IV.

They [guys in class] say how they feel.

All the girls just think whatever the teacher says they'll just do it.

Some of us [boys] speak out against that.

A lot of guys don't like to do the work, especially their senior year.

V.

Well, the fi rst semester like I sat in the back of the room.

Which was, I don't know, I wasn't really with any of my friends or whatever.

And there's a bunch of girls back there and so I was like having to listen to them and everything.

And so I switched seats.

Now I'm sitting with Dave and Peter and Johnny.

And I think we all basically feel the same about that class.

[I'm] more comfortable around them cause they're my friends.

And then I don't know, it could be that they're males, you know, 'cause over on the other side there wasn't (any males).

I was sitting next to a bunch of girls and I felt really uncomfortable.

These stories portray the fi gured worlds relevant to Chavo's life that seem to guide the choices Chavo made about his participation in reading and being an athlete. One of the figured worlds was that male adolescent athletes do not read (or admit to reading) and they do not excel in school academics (or let anyone know if they did). Kids would harass you if they found out you were good in both, he believed. No one liked someone good in sports and academics. Chavo made decisions about his literacy practices based on this figured world. Even after good experiences reading the summer honors books in sixth grade,

Chavo decided not to participate in the honors summer reading again and said that somehow he lost reading. It appeared that he lost reading to outside play and sports, but not entirely. He read the sports page every morning, read current events, and he read at least some of the required books for school until he learned in 11th grade that reading the book was not necessarily linked to success on a test about that book.

Chavo was a good student and a good athlete. This presented a tension for him. As early as middle school, Chavo learned how to cover up that he was a good student to be identified as a male athlete. In middle school, he learned

to keep his grades quiet. In honors humanities, he addressed this tension by acting bored and disinterested and refusing to participate in class discussions while quietly maintaining a B average. I am left to wonder how he earned the B without reading at least some of the required texts or paying some attention in class. Perhaps turning in all the written assignments and being present in class was enough. Perhaps he secretly read the materials. Perhaps not. Chavo did not openly participate in the humanities, nor did he think he ever would. His actions in class made it clear that the class was not motivating to him. Sports motivated him, the humanities did not.

Chavo believed that girls and guys participated differently in the humanities classroom. This belief was informed by the fi gured worlds he held about male athletes, literacy, and school and contributed to the way he participated in the humanities classroom. In this particular class, there were significantly more female than male students. This fact probably fed into his belief that girls participated in humanities more than boys. He reported that he did not feel comfortable sitting among a "bunch of girls." Yet he sat in this location for almost an entire semester. The girls, he said, always agreed with the teacher, whereas the guys would speak out against the teacher's point of view or about a given assignment. Eventually, Chavo moved (there was never any restriction about where to sit) to sit by some of the guys. These guys questioned Ms. Brown, and Chavo perceived that they felt the same way about the class as he did. They were also athletes and wore their varsity letter jackets whenever the weather permitted. Interestingly, moving next to these guys did not change his participation in class discussions. However, I observed that Chavo did speak to the guys during class and worked collaboratively with them on certain assignments.

Another way Chavo thought the girls were different than the guys was the teacher's response to them. He perceived that the teacher was more lenient toward the girls about late assignments, for example, because they were involved in after-school activities that might not be related to sports. He never tested this belief and continued to believe that the girls got more exceptions than the guys in the class without ever asking Ms. Brown for an extension himself. He perceived that the teacher honored academic and service after-school activities more than those that dealt with athletics. In both stories, what was most apparent in the form of Chavo's words was the strength of his convictions and the personal responsibility he took for his views and actions. Chavo's use of strong I-statements (e.g., I think, I read; Gee, 2005) made more visible to me the fi gured worlds that were relevant to him. In other words, how he answered my interview questions, the structure or form of his language, helped uncover what fi gured worlds were relevant to him.

Whereas Gee and Crawford (1998) used I-statements to look at differences in the talk of middle-class and working-class youth, I found I-statements to be useful in uncovering fi gured worlds. In the 119 lines of the selected transcript, Chavo used 53 I-statements. I categorized the I-statements based on the kind of verb that followed the pronoun, I. The vast majority of I-statements were either cognitive (16) or action (24) as defi ned by Gee (2005).

Following Gee, Idefined cognitive statements as statements made about his thinking and knowing. I-statements such as I don't know, I decided, I think, and I guess fell into this category. His cognitive statements provided information, knowledge, and opinions about his beliefs and experiences with literacy. They served to explain and state his opinions about his past literacy experiences and interactions.

Chavo used nearly twice as many action statements as he did cognitive statements. His use of action-oriented I-statements tells more about his historical story of being a male athlete who lost reading. His I-statements—such as I had my mom, I read, I'd go home and read, I found, I'd harass, I stopped reading, I switched, I'm sitting—paint a picture of Chavo as a young enthusiastic reader who gradually changed as he learned others' expectations of him as a male athlete and student, and the social practices of the Discourse of male athlete to which he aspired. The action I-statements he used demonstrated how he took responsibility for his actions. Chavo's use of I-statements led me to believe that he perceived himself to be in control, that he consciously made decisions about his identity, and that he strongly believed that popular male athletes do not read (at least in public). He also believed that guys and girls participated differently in literacy classrooms.

When describing his experiences in the humanities class, much of his speech was laced with emotions and feelings as he reported his literacy experiences to me. Words and phrases such as harass, uncomfortable, feel kind of on the spot, feel like I'm a little bit less, make us feel involved, feel overpowered by women, more comfortable, and I feel like I can't even ask her exemplify the diffi culties young men like Chavo may feel as they navigate the terrain of being male and participating in school literacy. It is interesting that he is so aware of and open about his feelings and emotions associated with being a male student in the class.

From the Researcher's Perspective

The Situated Meanings of Being Chavo

My story of Chavo is from the perspective of a White, middle-class university researcher, the mother of two of Chavo's teammates, and a past high school literacy teacher. My perspective is infl uenced by the stories told by Chavo, his mother, and his teachers and my past research and reading on masculinities and literacy. I have a great interest in boys, literacy, and the influence that Discourses associated with sports have on literacy and schooling, in part, because of my two sons. I have watched as one of my sons quit reading as a high school student and as the other never developed a love or respect for reading. I also remember the boys who hid in the back of my classroom to read paperback books and magazines when I was a reading teacher at an alternative high school. I have long wondered about boys and literacy and have read with great interest theories of masculinities and boys and literacy.

What I find so interesting in the stories of Chavo is the power of fi gured worlds to shape beliefs and actions related to literacy and masculinities. Chavo

defined masculinity as having to do with strength, courage, sticking up for what

you believe, and responsibility as the following transcript depicts:

Someone who shows like strength and courage, and Has the ability to stick up for what they believe.

And someone who is willing to do whatever it takes . . . like on an everyday basis.

Like when you're older going to work everyday, that kind of thing.

Of just going to school everyday and just getting what you have to do and like getting it done

My dad (epitomizes masculinity) Because . . .

he could be getting paid a lot of money [as a doctor in private practice], but instead he is working for people that really can't afford the health insurance and stuff. He's working for those kind of people and manages to find money to provide for his family. Sometimes he worked on weekends, he did what he had to do to support his family. And if we ever have a problem we go to him. . . .

The Discourse of masculinity exemplified by his father played an important role in Chavo's constructions of masculinity and being a student. He learned to incorporate and emulate this model of masculinity within the Discourses of which he claimed membership. The attributes of masculinity—strength, courage, sticking up for your beliefs, and responsibility— were evident in how he represented himself through language and social practices/activities. Chavo's muscular body, brown skin, and big dark eyes provided him the look of an athlete. He worked out regularly in the school weight room and ran to stay in optimal shape. He pushed himself in the weight room and bragged to his teammates about the number of pounds he could lift. On occasion, I observed him and his teammates measuring their biceps to compare arm sizes and amount of growth. His clothing also helped others recognize him as a certain kind of young man (Harris, 1995). He selected clothes to wear such as tight T-shirts and baggy shorts or athletic wear, which accented his muscular, athletic body. If that did not do it, he wore team garb and his varsity jacket to school with many letters and awards sewn onto it. No one could mistake it, he was an athlete.

Chavo acted the part. In addition to being a good athlete, he was known to be a tough competitor and good leader. He was well liked and respected by his peers, as evidenced by being voted captain of two sports teams—soccer and cross-country. He took responsibility for leading the cross-country teams to a state championship—this required both physical and emotional strength. As he positioned himself as a popular athlete, Chavo earned the respect of his peers and worked to not be recognized as a good student. Yet he was. His mother knew he was and was frustrated that his teachers did not challenge him. His humanities teacher did not know him as a good student, but made assumptions based on his status as an honor student. He started hiding his inclination to be a good student in middle school when he stopped reading honors books and stayed quiet about his grades as he learned the practices of the Discourse of popular boy athlete at his school. By his senior year in high school, he was an expert at doing his version of popular male athlete and student. No one would doubt that he was bored and did not like humanities. His whole body told the story, and he never spoke during class discussions. Yet he took responsibility for doing what had to be done to make a good grade. He exemplified the practices of masculinity he revered in both the humanities classroom and the athletic arena.

Surprisingly, Chavo, the good student, became visible during the last month of school. He won the contest for the best end-of-year humanities project. The project was designed to synthesize and extend what they had learned about humanities. The students selected a modern-day thinker, artist, and activist and made video or computer presentations about a common cultural theme the three shared. Chavo and the two guys he sat next to in humanities focused their presentation on three people associated with sports—Jerry Colangelo (great thinker who brought professional sports to Phoenix), Michael Jordan (great artist), and Chris Berman (a sports anchor and activist)—and demonstrated how they contributed to a culture that treated sports in similar ways as the ancient people did religion. His group worked long hours on the script and video presentation to integrate what they had learned about human thought and culture with modern-day cultural concerns and emphasis on sports. His voice was the narrator on the video, giving rise to Ms. Brown exclaiming after the video showing, "I haven't heard you speak that many words all year." Chavo's group's project was deemed "the best" by his classmates and teacher. He was recognized with a monetary prize and the grade of A on the project. One is left to wonder whether this is the kind of challenging curriculum his mother hoped for and what might have happened if Chavo had been asked to do similar kinds of literacy activities before the last month of school.

Chavo's mother and teacher embraced a figured world in which gender does not matter. However, for Chavo gender, or his beliefs about what it meant to be masculine in a literacy classroom, played a role in the decisions he made about his participation in the literacy classroom. This was especially evident in the humanities class, where he reported feeling overpowered by women in the class and did not like the way the girls acted in class. The sheer numbers of female students made him uncomfortable. He believed there were differences in how girls and guys approached literacy courses. He participated in the way that he thought would best represent him as masculine. For example, he felt it was important to stick to his beliefs, although they were different from the teacher's. He did not think the girls did this. For him, the Discourse of popular athlete included being masculine—strong, courageous, responsible, and having strong convictions. He demonstrated these qualities in the class as he resisted his teacher's enthusiasm for humanities and his mother's belief in reading, all the while making good grades and excelling in a class project.

In addition to strong beliefs that gender did not matter, Chavo's mother, teacher, and Chavo held firm notions of what counted as acceptable literacy practices. Even though he pronounced he did not read anymore, he confessed to reading the newspaper daily, particularly the sports pages. This apparently did not count as reading, but was an acceptable literacy activity within this particular Discourse of popular male athlete.

It is important to note that in my analysis of Chavo there is only a hint about influences of social class and ethnicity. Chavo's mother is Mexican American and she and her husband share many of the same middle-class values and expectations as Chavo's teacher and myself, the researcher. Chavo's brown skin, dark hair, and Hispanic heritage did not come up in any of the interviews, although I suspect it is always present in his interactions with others. I wish I had asked Chavo's mother how she thought her Hispanic heritage might have influenced the teachers' response to her when she requested more challenging curriculum for Chavo and how she thought it influenced Chavo's beliefs about his own masculinity and literacy practice. I also wish I had found out from Chavo how he thought being Mexican American might have influenced the Discourses of masculinity and of being a literacy student for which he aspired. Further, I wish I knew how it influenced Chavo's past teachers' academic expectations and interactions with him. These unanswered questions are limitations to my analysis, and answers to these questions are needed to fully understand how Chavo learned to be a boy in a literacy classroom and multiple ways of being masculine.

Note 1

I use big "D" Discourse in the tradition of Gee to mean ways of reading, writing, acting, valuing, dressing, and so on to be recognized as a certain sort of person.

SEMIOTIC ASPECTS OF SOCIAL TRANSFORMATION AND LEARNING

A common critique of CDA is that it has not often attended to matters of learning. Learning, in this chapter, is addressed as a performativity of texts—both spoken and written. Social practices such as teaching and learning are mediated by structures and events and are networked in particular ways through orders of discourse. Orders of discourse comprised genres, discourses, and styles or "ways of interacting," "ways of representing," and "ways of being." This chapter theoretically reflects on semiotic aspects of social transformation and learning. Its particular focus is one gap in my work in Critical Discourse Analysis (CDA), which a number of contributors in this volume have pointed out: It has not addressed questions of learning. So my objective is to incorporate a view of learning into the version of CDA that has been developing in my more recent work (Chiapello & Fairclough, 2002; Chouliaraki & Fairclough, 1999; Fairclough, 2000a, 2000b, 2001, 2003; Fairclough, Jessop, & Sayer, 2003). I approach the question of learning indirectly in terms of the more general and in a sense more fundamental question of the performativity of texts or, in critical realist terms (Fairclough, Jessop, & Sayer, 2004), their causal effects on nonsemiotic elements of the material, social, and mental worlds and the conditions of possibility for the performativity of texts. I use the term semiosis rather than discourse to refer in a general way to language and other semiotic modes such as visual image, and the term text for semiotic elements of social events, be they written, spoken, or combining different semiotic modes as in the case of TV texts.

Semiotic Aspects of Social Structures, Social Practices, and Social Events

Let me begin with the question of social ontology. I assume that both (abstract) social structures and (concrete) social events are real parts of the social world that have to be analyzed separately as well as in terms of their relation to each other—a position of analytical dualism (Archer, 1995, 2000; Fairclough et al., 2004).

Social structures are abstract entities. One can think of a social structure (such as an economic structure, a social class or kinship system, or a language) as defining a potential—a set of possibilities. However, the relationship between what is structurally possible and what actually happens, between structures and events, is a complex one. Events are not in any simple or direct way the effects of abstract social structures. Their relationship is mediated—there are intermediate organizational entities between structures and events. Let us call these social practices. Examples would be practices of teaching and practices of management in educational institutions. Social practices can be thought of as ways to control the selection of certain structural possibilities and the exclusion of others, and the retention of these selections over time in particular areas of social life. Social practices are networked together in particular and shifting ways. For instance, there has recently been a shift in the way in which practices of teaching and research are networked together with practices of management in institutions of higher education—a managerialization (or more generally marketization; Fairclough, 1993) of higher education. Semiosis is an element of the social at all levels. Schematically:

Social structures: languages

Social practices: orders of discourse

Social events: texts

Languages can be regarded as among the abstract social structures to which I refer here. A language defines a certain potential, certain possibilities, and excludes others—certain ways of combining linguistic elements are possible, others are not (e.g., the book is possible as a phrase in English, book the is not). Yet texts as elements of social events are not simply the effects of the potentials defined by languages. We need to recognize intermediate organizational entities of a specifically linguistic sort—the linguistic elements of networks of social practices. I call these orders of discourse (see Chouliaraki & Fairclough, 1999; Fairclough, 1992). An order of discourse is a network of social practices in its language aspect. The elements of orders of discourse are not things like nouns and sentences (elements of linguistic structures), but discourses, genres, and styles (I differentiate them shortly). These elements, and particular combinations or articulations of these elements, select certain possibilities defined by languages and exclude others—they control linguistic variability for particular areas of social life. Thus, orders of discourse can be seen as the social organization and control of linguistic variation.

There is a further point to make: As we move from abstract structures toward concrete events, it becomes increasingly difficult to separate language from other social elements. In the terminology of Althusser, language becomes increasingly overdetermined by other social elements. At the level of abstract structures, we can talk more or less exclusively about language—more or less because functional theories of language see even the grammars of languages as socially shaped (Halliday, 1978).

The way I defined orders of discourse makes it clear that at this intermediate level we are dealing with a much greater overdetermination of language by other social elements—orders of discourse are the social organization and control of linguistic variation, and their elements (discourses, genres, styles) are correspondingly not purely linguistic categories, but categories that cut across the division between language and nonlanguage, semiosis and the nonsemiotic. When we come to texts as elements of social events, the overdetermination of language by other social elements becomes massive: Texts are not just effects of linguistic structures and orders of discourse, but are also effects of other social structures and of social practices in all their aspects, so it becomes difficult to separate out the factors shaping texts.

Semiosis as an Element of Social Practices: Genres, Discourses, and Styles

Social events and, at a more abstract level, social practices can be seen as articulations of different types of social elements. They articulate semiosis (hence language) together with other nonsemiotic social elements. We might see any social practice as an articulation of the following elements:

Action and interaction

Social relations

Persons (with beliefs, attitudes, histories, etc.)

The material world

Semiosis

For instance, classroom teaching articulates together particular ways of using language (on the part of both teachers and learners) with particular forms of action and interaction, the social relations and persons of the classroom, and the structuring and use of the classroom as a physical space.

We can say that semiosis figures in three main ways in social practices:

Genres (ways of acting)

Discourses (ways of representing)

Styles (ways of being)

One way of acting and interacting is through speaking or writing, so semiosis figures first as part of the action. We can distinguish different genres as different ways of (inter)acting discoursally—interviewing is a genre, for example. Second, semiosis figures in the representations, which are always a part of social practices—representations of the material world, of other social practices, reflexive self-representations of the practice in question. Representation is clearly a semiotic matter, and we can distinguish different discourses, which may represent the same area of the world from different perspectives or positions. An example of a discourse in the latter sense would be the political discourse of New Labour, as opposed to the political discourse of old Labour, or the political discourse of Thatcherism (Fairclough, 2000b). Third and finally, semiosis figures alongside bodily behavior in constituting particular ways of being, particular social or personal identities. I call the semiotic aspect of this a style.

An example would be the style of a particular type of manager—the way a particular type of manager uses language as a resource for self-identifying. Genres, discourses, and styles are realized in features of textual meaning and form, and we can distinguish three main aspects of textual meanings and their formal realizations (similar to the macrofunctions distinguished by Halliday, 1994) corresponding to them: actional, representational, and identificational meanings. These meanings are always simultaneously in play in texts and parts of texts.

Social Effects of Texts and on Texts

I have begun to discuss the causal effects of social structures and social practices on texts. We can see texts as shaped by two sets of causal powers and by the tension between them: on the one hand, social structures and social practices; and on the other hand, the agency of people involved in the events of which they are a part. Texts are the situated interactional accomplishments of social agents whose agency is enabled and constrained by social structures and social practices. Neither a broadly interactional perspective nor a broadly structural perspective (the latter now including social practices) on texts can be dispensed with, but neither is sufficient without the other.

We also have to recognize that texts are involved in processes of meaning making and that texts have causal effects (i.e., they bring about changes) that are mediated by meaning making. Most immediately, texts can bring about changes in our knowledge, beliefs, attitudes, values, experience, and so forth. We learn from our involvement with and in texts, and texturing (the process of making texts as a facet of social action and interaction) is integral to learning. Yet texts also have causal effects of a less immediate sort—for instance, one might argue that prolonged experience of advertising and other commercial texts contributes to shaping people's identities as consumers or their gender identities. Texts can also have a range of other social, political, and material effects—texts can start wars, for instance, or contribute to changes in economic processes and structures, or in the shape of cities. In summary, texts have causal effects on, and contribute to changes in, persons (beliefs, attitudes, etc.), actions, social relations, and the material world.

We need to be clear what sort of causality this is. It is not a simple mechanical causality—we cannot, for instance, claim that particular features of texts automatically bring about particular changes in people's knowledge or behavior or particular social, political, or material effects. Nor is causality the same as regularity: There may be no regular cause–effect pattern associated with a particular type of text or particular features of texts, but that does not mean that there are no causal effects.1 Texts can have causal effects without them necessarily being regular effects because many other factors in the context determine whether.particular texts as parts of particular events actually have such effects, and this can lead to a particular text having a variety of effects.

Contemporary social science has been widely influenced by social constructivism—the claim that the (social) world is socially constructed. Many theories of social constructivism emphasize the role of texts (language, discourse, semiosis) in the construction of the social world. These theories tend to be idealist rather than realist. A realist would argue that, although aspects of the social world such as social institutions are ultimately socially constructed, once constructed they are realities that affect and limit the textual (or discursive) construction of the social. We need to distinguish construction from construal, which social constructivists often do not: We may textually construe (represent, imagine, etc.) the social world in particular ways, but whether our representations or construals have the effect of changing its construction depends on various contextual factors, including the way social reality already is, who is construing it, and so forth. So we can accept a moderate version of the claim that the social world is textually constructed, but not an extreme version (Sayer, 2000).

A major causal effect of texts that has been a major concern for Critical Discourse Analysis is ideological effects—the effects of texts in inculcating and sustaining ideologies. I see ideologies as primarily representations of aspects of the world that can be shown to contribute to establishing and maintaining relations of power, domination, and exploitation—primarily because such representations can be enacted in ways of interacting socially and inculcated in ways of being in people's identities. Let us take an example: the pervasive claim that in the new global economy countries must be highly competitive to survive (something like this is presupposed in this extract from a speech by Tony Blair to the Confederation of British Industry: "Competition on quality can't be done by Government alone. The whole nation must put its shoulder to the wheel"). One could see such claims (and the neoliberal discourse with which they are associated) as enacted in new, more businesslike ways of administering organizations like universities and inculcated in new managerial styles. We can only arrive at a judgment about whether such claims are ideological by looking at the causal effects they have in particular areas of social life—for instance, factories or universities, asking whether they contribute to sustaining power relations (e.g., by making employees more amenable to managers' demands).

Dialectical Relations

The relations between elements of a social event or social practice, including the relation between semiosis and nonsemiotic elements, are dialectical relations. We can say that elements are different, cannot be reduced to another, require separate sorts of analysis, and yet are not discrete. In Harvey's (1996) terms, each element internalizes other elements. What I said earlier about overdetermination can be seen in terms of the internalization of nonsemiotic elements in semiotic elements (texts, orders of discourse).

What I said about the causal effects of texts can be seen in terms of the internalization of semiotic elements in nonsemiotic elements. We can see claims about the socially constructive effects of semiosis, including the moderate social constructivism advocated earlier, as presupposing the dialectical internalization of semiosis in the nonsemiotic—presupposing, for instance, that discourses can be materialized (internalized within the material world) in the design of urban spaces. We can also see claims about how people learn in the course of communicative interaction (such as the claims in the chapters of this volume) as presupposing the dialectical internalization of semiosis in the nonsemiotic. What people learn in and through text and talk, in and through the process of texturing as we might put it (making text and talk within making meaning), is not merely (new) ways of texturing, but also new ways of acting, relating, being, and intervening in the material world, which are not purely semiotic in character. A theory of individual or organizational learning needs to address the questions of retention—of the capacity to recontextualize what is learned, to enact it, inculcate it, and materialize it.

Dialectical relations obtain intrasemiotically as well as between semiotic and nonsemiotic elements. For instance, processes of organizational learning often begin (and especially so in what has been conceived of as the contemporary information society or knowledge society) with the recontextualization within organizations of discourses from outside—an obvious example these days is the discourse of new public management (Salskov-Iversen, Hansen, & Bislev, 2000). Yet such discourses may (the modality is important in view of the moderate version of social constructivism advocated before) be enacted as new ways of acting and interacting, inculcated as new ways of being, as well as materialized in, for instance, new buildings and plants. Enactment is both semiotic and nonsemiotic: The discourse of new public management may be enacted as new management procedures, which semiotically include new genres (e.g., new ways of conducting meetings within an organization). Inculcation is also both semiotic and nonsemiotic: The discourse of new public management may be inculcated in new managers, new types of leaders, which is partly a matter of new styles (hence partly semiotic), but also partly a matter of new forms of embodiment. Bodily dispositions are open to semioticization (as indeed are buildings), but that does not mean they have a purely semiotic character—it is precisely a facet of the dialectical internalization of the semiotic in the nonsemiotic. What this example (and the case study by Salskov-Iversen et al.) also points to is the dialectic between colonization and appropriation in processes of social transformation and learning: Recontextualizing the new discourse is both opening an organization (and its individual members) up to a process of colonization (and to ideological effects) and, insofar as the new discourse is transformed, in locally specific ways by being worked into a distinctive relation with other (existing) discourses—a process of appropriation.

Let us come back to the modality of the claim that discourses may be enacted, inculcated, and materialized. There are social conditions of possibility for social transformation and learning, which are in part semiotic conditions of possibility (Fairclough et al., 2003). In the example of new public management discourse, for instance, the semiotic conditions of possibility for the recontextualization and dialectical enactment, inculcation, and materialization of the discourse within particular organizations refer to the order of discourse:

the configuration of discourses, genres, and styles, which is in place not only within a particular organization, but in the social field within which it is located and the relations between the orders of discourse of different fields. To cut through the complexities involved here, we can say broadly that the openness of an organization to transformations led by a new discourse, and the openness of the organization and its members to learning, depend on the extent to which there is a discourse or configuration of discourses in place within the organization and the field for which the dialectic of enactment, inculcation, and materialization is fully carried through, and the capacity for autonomy with respect to other fields (not, of course, a purely semiotic matter).

Emergence and Learning

The CDA of texts includes both interdiscursive analysis of the genres, discourses, and styles drawn on and how different genres, discourses, and styles are articulated together (textured together), and analysis of how such mixes of genres, discourses, and styles are realized in the meanings and forms of texts (which entails linguistic analysis and other forms of semiotic analysis, such as analysis of visual images or body language). The chapters in this volume by Rogers, and Lewis and Ketter, for instance, point to the significance in talk of interdiscursivity, discourse hybridity, for learning. In the critical realist frame I have been drawing on, one can see this as the basis for semiotic emergence, the making of new meanings. Yet as Lewis and Ketter indicate, the possibilities for emergence depend on the relative dialogicality of text and talk—the orientation to difference. We can schematically differentiate five orientations to difference, with the proviso that this is not a typology of texts—individual texts and talk may combine them in various ways (Fairclough, 2003):

(a) an openness to, acceptance of, and recognition of difference; an exploration

of difference, as in dialogue in the richest sense of the term

(b) an accentuation of difference, conflict, and polemic—a struggle over

meaning, norms, and power

(c) an attempt to resolve or overcome difference

(d) a bracketing of difference, a focus on commonality, solidarity

(e) consensus, a normalization and acceptance of differences of power, which

brackets or suppresses differences of meaning and over norms

Scenario (e) in particular is inimical to emergence. Dialogicality and orientation to difference depend on the sort of broadly structural conditions

I pointed to in the previous section—conditions to do with social practices, fields, and relations between fields, which have a partly semiotic character (in terms of orders

of discourse). However, as suggested earlier, the causal powers that shape texts are the powers of agency as well as of structure—whatever the state of the field and the relations between fields, we can ask about both latitudes for agency and their differential uptake by different agents, including agents involved in the sort of critical educational research reflected in the chapters of this volume.

A relatively high degree of dialogicality and orientation to difference can be seen as favoring the emergence of meaning through interdiscursive hybridity, although to talk about learning there needs to be some evidence of continuity and development (provided by longitudinal aspects of the research reported in this book) and retention (which one might see as requiring evidence of transfer and recontextualization, from one context to others). Learning can be seen as a form of social transformation in itself, but as a necessary but insufficient condition of social transformation on a broader scale. Learning through text and talk can be interpreted as part of what I referred to earlier as the semiotic conditions for social transformation.

Critical Research, Learning, and Social Transformation

In assessing the possibilities for and limitations of critical educational research motivated by emancipatory (e.g., antiracist) agendas for learning and social transformation, one needs to consider both factors of a broadly structural character and factors to do with agency. With respect to the former, educational research can be seen as part of a network of social practices that constitutes an apparatus of governance (in part semiotically constituted as an order of discourse; Fairclough, 2003)—a network that includes practices of classroom teaching, educational management, educational research, and (national, state, local, etc.), government, and policy making (Bernstein, 1990). The nature and workings of the apparatus are internally as well as externally contested—critical educational researchers are, for instance, often seeking to create more open and equal relations between academic research and classroom teaching. One issue they must consider is what I referred to earlier as the social conditions of possibility for social transformation and learning, which include latitudes for agency within educational research. These issues can be partly addressed from a semiotic perspective in terms of latitudes for agents in social research to develop, recontextualize, and seek to enact and inculcate new discourses. But there are also considerations to do with forms of agency in recontextualizing contexts (e.g., questions of the dialogicality of interactions between educational researchers and teachers). Once again neither a structural nor an interactional perspective can be dispensed with, but neither is sufficient without the other.

Note 1

The reduction of causality to regularity is only one view of causality—what is often referred to as Humean causality, the view of causality associated with the philosopher David Hume (Fairclough, Jessop, & Sayer, 2003; Sayer, 2000).

LEARNING AS SOCIAL INTERACTION: INTERDIS-CURSIVITY IN A TEACHER AND RESEARCHER STUDY GROUP

In this chapter, we closely examine the interactions of a long-term teacher and researcher study group focusing on the reading and teaching of multicultural literature in a rural middle school setting. Over the 4-year span of the study, the group included 10 members—all White females—the two of us as researcherparticipants and eight teachers of grades 5 to 9. The purpose of the group was for participating teachers to read and discuss multicultural young adult literature in ways that would help them to make decisions about whether and how to teach these works in their community. (See Appendix A for book list.) In order to do this, our work together over the years focused not only on issues related to the teaching of literature but, more importantly, on our individual and collective assumptions about race, identity, and multicultural education in terms of how these assumptions shape decisions about text selection and teaching approaches. This study builds on earlier phases of our research that examined how our discussions of multicultural young adult literature were shaped by community contexts and by constructions of racial identity (Lewis, Ketter & Fabos, 2001; Ketter & Lewis, 2001). In this work, we identifi ed the fi xed practices in which all members of the group engaged, practices that seemed to create barriers to our learning and dialogue. We came to see how these practices were created and reinforced by the social and political contexts of the particular setting. For this phase of our longitudinal study, we were interested in understanding the nature of learning over time among members of the study group. In addition, we wanted to know how interaction patterns in the group sustained or disrupted fi xed discourses in ways that shaped the group's learning.

Review of Literature

Three areas of scholarship inform this research: sociocultural theories of learning, critical theories of language, and critical multiculturalism as it relates to the reading and teaching of multicultural literature. Our theoretical framework views learning not as primarily a mental act but as a social act dependent upon interaction among people and their tools and technologies (Gee, 1999; Lave, 1996; Rogoff, 1995; Wenger, 1999). Based on her research on learning communities outside of schools, Lave argues that learning is about constructing "identities in practice" (1996, p. 157). Wenger (1999) also views learning as arising from the identity work that occurs through participation in communities of practice, communities "created over time by the sustained pursuit of a shared enterprise" (p. 45). Identities practiced in such communities are always a work in progress shaped by individual and collective efforts to create coherence through participation in varied social contexts. Barton and Hamilton (2005) argue that the scholarship on communities of practice does not suf- fi ciently examine the mediating nature of language in reifying and reshaping communities. Our study shows how language works in these ways in one community of practice—a book group. Explicitly connecting a theory of language with a theory of learning, Hicks (1996) asserts that learning involves the learner in appropriating and reconstructing the discourses within his or her social world. Grounding her use of the term "appropriation" in the work of Bakhtin (1981, 1986), she argues that his emphasis on the dialogic nature of utterances supports a generative use of the concept of appropriation. Central to Bakhtin's theory of language is the sociocultural constitution of utterance, with a speaker's utterance embedding prior and anticipated utterances. Hicks argues that this process represents a rearticulation rather than a recapitulation of existing discourses.

This theoretical argument is important to our study because we are interested in examining what Fairclough (1992) refers to as "interdiscursivity," defi ned as the presence or trace of one discourse within another.1 Interdiscursive texts, according to Fairclough, can lead to dynamic rearticulations of otherwise stable discourses. In this way, such hybrid discourses have transformative potential that, in our view, connects language to learning. Related to Fairclough's notion of interdiscursivity is Wenger's description of the interdiscursive demands placed on anyone who enters a new community of practice whose discursive practices may confl ict or contrast with those of another community in which the participant has been a long-time actor. All communities of practice bring with them unarticulated but shared knowledge—ways of acting and generic expectations that prescribe or make convenient certain ways of writing, thinking and speaking and preclude others. Hence, those who join a new community of practice often initially operate on the boundaries of that community, a boundary where the participants must negotiate with intersecting and often confl icting discursive practices (Wenger, 1999). Wenger argues that these boundary locations are exactly where new knowledge is produced and identities can be transformed.

An examination of how the teachers and researchers in this group are challenged to rearticulate and reconstruct available and often confl icting discourses, including one another's, has implications for what it means to learn in a professional development community. Moreover, such a view corresponds to recent research on professional development that underscores the benefi ts of teachers forming learning communities that provide intellectual renewal (Grossman, Wineburg, & Woolworth, 2001), productive confl ict (Achinstein, 2002) and the structures necessary to form critical relationships (Gallego, Hollingsworth, & Whitenack, 2001). In their study of a long-term learning community of English and social studies teachers, Grossman et al. (2001) found that whereas group members initially shared their individual content expertise, more substantial learning over time was evident when individual perspectives and espistemological positions were internalized by other members.

Beyond these features of professional development, Lawrence and Tatum (1997, p. 63) argue that White teachers engaged in professional development related to multicultural education must examine their own racial identities in order to be effective educators. This argument is particularly compelling in light of the demographic statistics that reveal the persistence of a majority White teaching force, suggesting the continued need to examine issues of racial identity in teacher education and professional development. Moreover, the epistemology of racism constitutes the very conditions upon which knowledge is enacted and evaluated within dominant institutions such as public schools (Scheurich &Young, 1997). In the 1990s, many theorists of race and ethnicity argued that White people normalize Whiteness and the privilege it represents For example, in her study of White teachers' responses to workshops on multicultural education, Sleeter (1993) found that teachers typically denied that racial identity was a signifi cant factor in their teaching. White teachers did not expect to examine Whites as a racialized group when attending workshops. Instead, preservice and practicing teachers were accustomed to focusing on groups they perceived as "other," groups about which they wanted information. In this way, race and ethnicity were marked as "foreign" and teachers were positioned as cultural tourists (Kincheloe & Steinberg, 1997; Purves, 1997). Recent scholarship has cautioned that antiracist and critical pedagogies in teacher education can result in alienation, shame, self-righteousness, or anger (Marx & Pennington, 2003; Thompson, 2003; Trainor, 2008); rather than a productive sense of responsibility or solidarity (Flynn, Lensmire, & Lewis, 2009; Sheets, 2003)

According to many scholars, reading multicultural literature in ways that consciously consider the cultural and sociopolitical infl uences that shape authorship and interpretation can challenge a reader's perception of self and other (Florio-Ruane, 2001, Medina, 2010). Fang, Fu and Lamme (1999) argue that multicultural literature "should be considered sociocultural and political texts (Taxel, 1992) for fostering students' understanding of the historical and material forces underpinning the construction of cultural identities" (p. 270). Yet teachers are rarely taught to read children's and young adult literature as political texts, nor are they encouraged to read bibliographic resources with a critical eye (Harris, 1993). The meanings and purposes that teachers assign to the teaching of literature infl uence and refl ect how young adult literature functions politically and theoretically in any context, but these political and theoretical functions are often disregarded in curricular conversations (Barrera, 1992).

Methods and Analysis

Given our research focus on learning over time, we have found it useful to combine a view of learning grounded in the literature on "communities of practice," with social and critical theories of language. Doing so has provided us with the theoretical and methodological tools to better understand how our interactions produce and at times disrupt a particular set of discourses. Whereas earlier phases of this research used ethnographic tools to help us fully understand the context of this rural school district and community related to the teachers' responses to multicultural texts, this study employs critical discourse analysis (CDA) to help us understand the longitudinal nature of our learning. Using CDA, we studied key transcripts over the 4-year period to examine the ways that participants took up particular world views, patterns of talk, and systems of thought as they related to multicultural literature and to the meaning and purposes of multicultural education. Teaming critical discourse analysis with ethnographic research allowed us to establish invaluable contexts for the sort of knowledge CDA extracts from texts.

Although eight teachers participated over the 4 years of the study, fi ve teachers formed the consistent core of the study group. These language arts and reading teachers teach fi fth-, sixth-, and eighth-grade students at a middle school that has an all-European American faculty and two administrators who are both White males. The student body of the middle school is over 94% European American and 25% of the students receive free or reduced-cost meals. We researcher-participants are White middle-class women who have both taught language arts and reading in the public schools before going on to work at the university and college where we are now respectively employed. We acted as participant/observers in the study group and saw ourselves as viable contributors to the process of text selection and procedures for discussing the texts. We secured funds to purchase one class set of multicultural books for each participant teacher and to pay for the books we read for all but one year of the study.

To establish the ethnographic context for the CDA we used for this part of the study, we called on the wealth of data we collected and coded using the NUD*IST qualitative research program over the 4 years of the study. The ethnographic context included a careful analysis of our own positions within the study group and community related to status, affi liation, and ideological stances. Data included audiotaped sessions of the literature discussions, audiotaped interviews with participants and 11 community informants, written responses to surveys, an audiotaped focus group discussion of group dynamics, and both observational and refl ective fi eld notes. After each session, we recorded our observations and analyses separately in order to insure that they were fi rst articulated without the infl uence of the other researcher. We also taped several key research meetings in which we examined how our roles as researchers and as participants played out in the literature discussions (Alvermann, Commeyras, Young, Randall, & Hinson, 1997).

To analyze the groups' interactions in this phase of the study, we used a method of critical discourse analysis suggested by Fairclough (1992) and Chouliaraki and Fairclough (1999). Specifi cally, we examined 15 transcripts taken from the entire span of the study (six from the fi rst 2 years and nine from the last 2 years). It was important that we analyze more transcripts from the latter part of the study, given our research focus on change over time. We chose the transcripts that were most salient to our research question about learning and social interaction. The ones that struck us as having the most potential in this regard were transcripts that included segments in which we either sustained or disrupted discourses that had become fi xed interactional positions taken up repeatedly by members of the group. We reasoned that to understand learning over time, we would need to closely examine segments of talk that contained statements and ideological positions that repeatedly surfaced in the transcripts and compare those segments to others that moved us beyond these reifi ed positions. Given our long-term involvement with this study group and our multilayered analyses of the transcripts, we were able to use the knowledge gained from earlier phases of this research to locate the transcripts containing such segments. For instance, in our earlier work (Lewis, Ketter, & Fabos, 2001), we had identifi ed statements and ideological positions in our talk that reinforced norms of Whiteness through the use of language that universalizes across experiences. This insight—the result of both qualitative coding procedures and the tools of discourse analysis—was useful to us as we selected the 15 transcripts to be closely examined in this new phase of our research. Once we identifi ed the 15 transcripts, we divided each transcript into episodes, with each episode representing a series of turns that all relate to the same topic or theme (Marshall, Smagorinsky, & Smith 1995; Florio-Ruane, 2001). We then examined each episode to identify fi rst its prominent discourses. Chouliaraki and Fairclough (1999, p. 63) defi ne "discourse" as "the construction of some aspect of reality from a particular perspective." However, in our efforts to identify prominent discourses in the transcripts, we found it useful to draw on Luke's (2000, p. 456) defi nition of discourse as "systematic clusters of themes, statements, ideas, and ideologies [that] come into play in the text." In this vein, we searched the transcripts for regular clusters of themes, statements, and ideologies. Again, this process was aided by our extensive involvement in the study group and its surrounding community as well as our previous analyses of the transcripts. Identifying the recurrent and somewhat fi xed themes, statements, and ideologies present in these transcripts led us to formulate the coding categories for "discourse" listed in Appendix B.

One dominant discourse we identifi ed in our discussions was that of liberal humanism. In an article advocating for Critical Race Theory's method of counter storytelling as a way of addressing the discomfort and defensiveness that arises in classroom discussion about race, Williams (2004) identifi es two narra- tives that contribute to discomfort and resistance in such discussions. Williams argues that the fi rst narrative, "Individualism trumps social forces," is somewhat unique to the United States and ties it to meritocratic ideals upon which our country was founded (p. 185). The second narrative, that Whiteness is not a race, plays out in the discourses we describe here as an assumption that Whiteness is the norm and that race only "matters" when we are discussing those who are not White. In our analysis of the transcripts, we found that these narratives, which we identify as a discourse of liberal humanism, were often paired with a discourse that we researchers espoused—that of critical multiculturalism with a focus on recognizing Whiteness as a race and uncovering the systems or structures of inequality that act as barriers to individual achievement. Because CDA requires an in-depth examination of language in use, we have limited the focus of this chapter to these two discourses as they repeatedly surfaced over time. We decided to focus on the intersection of these discourses because they represent an epistemological confl ict that was central to our discussions and persisted over time. The discourse of liberal humanism represents the individual as uni- fi ed, coherent, and possessing freedom of choice. The discourse of critical multiculturalism represents the individual as a socially, culturally, and historically produced subject. The intersection of these discourses often suggested confl icting world views that had implications for how we interpreted and evaluated multicultural texts. Once intersections of the two discourses were located in the 15 transcripts, we chose episodes for close analysis that would be most salient to our research questions.

We cross-coded these episodes using the categories of genre and voice as defi ned by Chouliaraki and Fairclough (1999, p. 63) as follows:

(1) Genre is "the language (and other semiosis) tied to a particular social activity . . ."

(2) Voice is "the sort of language used for a particular category of people and closely linked to their identity . . ."

An analysis of genre included an analysis of participant structures with regard to turn-taking. We established the other categories for genre by considering all the features of our activity setting. Given the overarching genre of "book group," we made repeated passes through the transcripts to identify norms and expectations that were established in this social and linguistic setting, a process that led us to formulate the codes for the category of "genre" that appear in Appendix B. Most of the coding categories listed under "voice" (Appendix B) are adapted from Fairclough (1989, 1992) and Chouliaraki and Fairclough (1999), who suggest that these features of language are particularly salient to issues of power and identity in the construction of social reality.

The following example demonstrates how discourse was cross-coded with genre and voice. Rather than use an example directly related to a novel we have yet to discuss in this chapter, we include instead an example of a conversation peripheral to one of our readings. The conversation centers on whether or not people are inclined to prefer associating with their own race. We have omitted comments by all participants other than two, Barb and Carol, to provide a brief example of how features of genre and voice intersect and serve to coordinate particular discourses.

Barb But I think you go, you go to a major university and you see Black students sitting with Black students and Asian students sitting with Asian mstudents. You tend to (.) hang around people that have like similar

backgrounds (.) to you= Carol Right.

Barb =it, it seems like I mean don't we hang around the same kind of people that we= . . .

Barb Yeah, you just, you just do that. . . .

Carol But I think, I think people feel threatened also.. . .

Barb I don't think it's threatened, it's just that you don't understand it. I mean it, it is a different culture, I mean/ Carol But I, I think/ Barb =it just is. . . .

Carol But I also think when you're talking about this, I think they feel threatened for the very reason that we're talking about this, because you have now you have two kids who like each other who may eventually marry, so you have that, the cross cultures again and some people that frightens, to have, to have (.) the mixing up of races. It does frighten them. [spoken softly] (..)You know, so, I think sometimes fear comes into it. [very softly]

The pronouns in this exchange frequently shift even within speaker turns. Barb uses pronouns that will draw her listeners into the stories and ideas she is relating. Her frequent use of the indefinite form of "you" creates a bond with her listener ("You tend to hang around people that have similar backgrounds to you."). She asks a rhetorical question for the sake of affirmation and uses the indefinite form of "we" to stand in for 'everybody' ("Don't we hang around the same kind of people that we ="). These are features of voice that serve to naturalize the discourses being promoted. It is natural, her talk suggests, for everybody to feel this way about being with people who have similar backgrounds. Carol's pronoun use, on the other hand, first creates bonds with her listeners and then distances her from her subject. Consider, for example, some of the shifts in her final turn:

. . . because now you have two kids who like each other who may eventually marry, so you have that, the cross cultures again and some people that frightens, to have, to have (.) the mixing up of races. It does frighten them. You know, so, I think sometimes fear comes into it.

First Carol creates a bond with her audience through the use of "you," but then she distances herself from those other people who are threatened by interracial relationships. As in this example, CDA helps us to discover how our fi xed discourses persisted through or were interrupted by the interaction patterns and voices we enacted as the group evolved. Focusing closely on genre, discourse, and voice in these portions of text allowed us to identify subtle processes not readily apparent in more holistic readings of text. Underlying our analysis is the assumption that fi xed discourses are most likely to be interrupted when more dialogic (Bakhtin, 1981) conversations occur. These moments may be marked by hybridized discourses, discourses that indicate shifts in the socially situated identities of the participants and in which newly constructed perspectives or ideologies are embedded.

Findings

We begin this section with a brief discussion of the overarching discourses and genres that characterized our conversations about multicultural literature. We then move to a more nuanced analysis of transcripts from the early and middle years of our study to reveal the ways in which our binary discourses and our interaction patterns evolve over time. This paper covers a span of study group years from June 1997 to April of 2000.

Overarching Discourses and Genres

Across the 15 transcripts, there is a tendency on the part of the middle school teachers to see the inequity characters experience in novels (and real life) as resulting from individual choices or circumstances rather than from structural or systemic forces. Public schools have long been and continue to be institutions that define as democratic a championing of individual achievement and individual responsibility and thus discount counter theories charging that institutions and their established cultural practices oppress and disempower the poor, immigrants, and people of color (Spring, 2004). According to numerous studies, this view is typical of White preservice and practicing teachers (Beach, 1997; Fang, Fu, & Lamme, 1999; Naidoo, 1994; Rogers & Soter, 1997; Sleeter, 1993). The teachers also demonstrated a related tendency to attribute the cause of the character's oppression to poor parenting or "abnormal" social practices rather than to structural barriers or institutionalized racism, a move that Bonilla-Silva labels "biologization of culture" (2001, pp. 147–149). We argue that the liberal humanist discursive practices reinforced and reinscribed through the teachers' participation in their public school's community of practice conflicted with the more social constructionist practices typical of our institutions and the research community of practice in which we are active members. For example, the transcripts suggest a tendency on our part to see the inequities depicted in these novels as examples of structural racism and to focus on the social or cultural rather than the individual experience. This finding is in keeping with research on perceptions about racism conducted by Gee (2005) in which teachers' responses focused on individual acts and professors' responses focused on institutional racism.

From the beginning this group was a hybrid social and linguistic activity or genre: part book group, part professional development, and part academic seminar. It was a site on the boundary between conflicting communities of practice that challenged all participants to search for coherence and stability in the face of our shifting identities as teachers and readers. From the academic community of practice, the group borrowed from a seminar format with we researchers leading the discussion of texts. As a book group, it was part informal discussion similar to book groups meetings held in people's living rooms, where, in fact, we did meet on several occasions. As professional development, the talk frequently focused on how the books might be used in a classroom or whether they were appropriate for a particular age level or group of students, topics not typical of adult book group discussions and more likely to occur in workshops or seminars meant for the continuing education of practicing teachers. In our earlier study, we found that the middle school teacher participants viewed us as having a kind of outside authority they did not, and we viewed the middle school participants as having an "insider" authority arising from their daily interactions with students and other teachers. In keeping with the seminar genre (seminar "leaders"), we were commonly the speakers who introduced a topic or began the discussion, particularly in the early years of the study. We had a tendency to make what we call "teacherly moves," although we did not consciously plan these moves. Included in this category were probing questions, requests for elaboration, intertextual references, and the citing of authorities (e.g. scholars, children's book authors, colleagues).

As researchers connected to the university, we often felt as though we were looked upon for expertise at the same time that our expertise was viewed as impractical or erudite. We brought to the group an orientation toward critical multiculturalism that shaped the discussions in ways that were alternately taken up, ignored, or resisted. We used verbal and nonverbal cues to signal our shifting affiliations and statuses. We would look down when saying something that we believed might sound too academic or politically radical, for instance, and we often adjusted our vocabulary so that it would not be mired in the jargon of our disciplines. We stumbled over sentences that we would have spoken articulately in our university or college settings, not intentionally, but because our hyper-awareness of power and status relations within the group troubled our speech. We assume that the teachers may have been doing some of the same, working out their own issues related to status and power among themselves, much as one of the teachers put it when she talked about feeling intimidated by another teacher in the group based on their long history of professional relations. Although we usually were not conscious of these performances at the time, they repeatedly surfaced during our independent analyses of transcripts and in our reflective fieldnotes.

The Early Transcripts: Polite Opposition

Our early book discussions reveal the emergence of the two intersecting, and often opposing, discourses: liberal humanism and critical multiculturalism. We begin with an excerpt from our discussion of An Island Like You: Stories from the Barrio (Cofer, 1995), our third book discussion in the first year of the study. A theme that runs through this collection of short stories about life in a Puerto Rican community in Paterson, New Jersey, is that of adolescents trying to find a comfortable identity in the face of competing views of who they are or should be, some stemming from their own community and some imposed by normative definitions of beauty and success mired in Eurocentric institutions and sensibilities. In this excerpt, Cynthia initiates a turn in which she tries to illustrate that racism and oppression have cut this barrio off from the rest of the country, but this move is resisted by Denise, who identifies with what it must feel like to be an individual in the barrio.2

Cynthia: It's interesting what you said about the universality of it, too, because I think that is so much there, and that's why it's such a good book to use with kids. At the same time, it's called "An Island like You" and I know that's a reference to the grandparents, but I think it's also sort of a claustrophobic sense of being apart from the rest of the world that so many of the characters feel. The barrio is sort of a part of the rest of the world. . . . There's this universality, but there's also this incredible difference.

Denise: And the poem at the beginning says "alone in a crowd." And, you know, I think that's something kind of like an island, I mean you're the only one who feels that way or the only one that thinks that way or the only one who's had that experience, and you don't connect with people.

This exchange was characteristic of many early exchanges in which either Cynthia or Jean makes a statement to focus on how the race or ethnicity of the characters marginalizes them. In this case, Cynthia was offering a response to an earlier comment made by Denise suggesting that the stories are about common, universal experiences. Here, Cynthia began by affirming Denise's stance but quickly moved to what is, in effect, an argument against Denise's view that the characters' experiences are universal. Denise responded by indirectly asking us to identify with the experience—one we presumably all have had—of being a lone individual in the midst of others who do not understand the individual's experience. She used "you" in a way that works to persuade her listeners to identify with the lone individual as she herself does ("you're the only one,"

"you don't connect"). Her take on the book title and the poem that serves as the book's prologue was a decidedly psychological one whereas Cynthia's was sociological and cultural.

Perhaps most interesting is the language used to signal agreement, despite the disagreement at the root of the exchange. Cynthia began by affirming Denise's earlier comment valuing this book for its universality and suggested that it is these universal qualities that make it a good book to share with kids. This being only our third book discussion, Cynthia voiced her disagreement in a manner that was likely to be palatable and fairly indirect, couched in an overall sense of affirmation and agreement. Not wanting to claim any particular authority, she introduced her disagreement with the phrase "at the same time," which suggests that the two discourses can coexist, side by side, with no contradiction, rather than a phrase such as "on the other hand," which would point to the incompatibility of the two discourses. Similarly, Denise initiated her response to Cynthia's comment with the conjunction "and," which suggests a continuation of Cynthia's idea and an implicit agreement; however, she quickly shifted to her focus on the individual, using the pronoun "you" and the repetition "only one" which create a bond with her listeners by pulling them into the experience of the lone individual.

Later in the same discussion, we can see the same dynamic at work, this time between Denise and Jean.

Denise: But, I think that self-esteem—and going back to some of the characters in this book—is such a vital thing for students. I just see kids with low self-esteem that are, really have big problems.

Jean: And it's interesting since self-esteem issues arise out of racism they experience, you know, a lot these kids, like the Mateo boy, and, um, Luis and Arturo, to some extent, especially, I think, and the girls too.

Here, again, the teacher, Denise, in the exchange was focusing on the individual psyche of the characters (and by association, her students), whereas the researcher, Jean, was focusing on the structure of racism as it affects self-esteem. And again, we see Jean begin her turn with the appearance of agreement ("And it's interesting since self-esteem") but then shift quickly into the discourse of structural inequity (racism).

In terms of genre, we coded Jean's initial clause, "And it's interesting," in two categories: "politeness/etiquette" and "teacherly move." She avoided disagreeing with Denise in any direct way as she might have had she known her better or not been concerned about appearing to be in control of the discussion. She did not begin her turn with something on the order of "It's important to understand that the lack of self-esteem arises out of the racism these characters experience," a statement which would have made her sound like a teacher who is correcting Denise's response. Yet, we believe that beginning her turn with "And it's interesting" represented another kind of teacherly move—one that we've both often used with our own students when we want to detract from our own power by affi rming the student's point even as we disagree. This is a way of "honoring a response" of a speaker while arguing against it or restating it to make a different point. Such moves are beyond mere politeness or attempts to downplay difference because the "teacher" is attempting to refi ne or reinterpret an idea for the participant who presented it.

We are not suggesting that our use of language (the teachers' or our own) was an intentional ploy to achieve a certain affect, for we doubt this was the case. It is the form and function of the text that is of interest to us and how the form and function constructs and is constructed by the situated identities of the speaker. That is, we are interested in how social identities are achieved through moment-to-moment interaction and how these interactions are shaped by particular identities. The process, as Fairclough (1992) and Gee (2005) make clear, is dialectic.

In our discussion of Scorpians (Myers, 1988), the sixth book our group read together, similar dynamics were at work. When discussing Scorpians, a book about an African American youth caught up in a gang to which he does not want to belong, all of us worked to connect at an emotional level, perhaps to offset the effects of the opposing discourses we espoused. Here, again, Jean began with a comment that pointed to structural inequity as it is passed on from generation to generation. Denise, on the other hand, responded through identification with the boy who suffers in the story. Since by this point in our discussion, it had already become clear that our discourses about the literature differ, we worked to agree at an emotional level. All of us agreed from the start of this discussion that the characters in the stories suffer, that they are forced into situations that present difficult if not impossible choices even if we disagree about the context that creates that suffering.

Jean: But you just see this, I kept thinking about this kind of trap that doesn't seem to, it doesn't seem to be different from generation to generation. And one of the poignant things about this book that I thought was very well done was because it wasn't overdone, but two times she talks about when, when the older son was born . . . how she has all this hope.

Denise: Yes. There was just no hope. I mean, how, there was no way out. There was just no way out, you know, and even this kid that picks on him at school. He doesn't want to fight with this kid. He just wants to ignore him. He wants him just to go away. And yet, he's not, you know, that, the other kid is not going to allow that to happen, and so then, what do you do if you're that kid? And you're constantly being picked on. And how many of our kids are victimized like that? And then they end up striking back and then they get in trouble and then they get a reputation and then people expect them to be bad. Just like all his teachers.

Cynthia: Right. Such a cycle.

Affective bonding is clear in this exchange through our direct reference to the emotional nature of our responses to the work. In Jean's turn, she referred to the "poignancy" of the mother's hope when her older son is born, and Denise spoke of empathizing with the students who get in trouble and then can't shake their bad reputations. This was an emotional issue for Denise, whom we have found to be the consummate child advocate—always seeing the best in her students and believing that kids have enormous capability to respond to literature in deep and thoughtful ways. When Jean co-taught with

Denise on several occasions, she found that Denise often raised the concern that teachers make judgments about students based on what other teachers say, or what they know about the students' families. She often spoke with outrage about a situation in which a teacher told one of her students that he was too "dumb to make it to college."

The use of intensifiers, repetition, and pronoun usage also signify emotionality or affective speech. For example, in her turn, Denise used intensifiers such as "just" and "constantly" to index her empathy with the character. She also switched to "you" in the fourth line, indicating her own empathy with the character she imagined and also to include the others as participants in her distress about how the boy is victimized. She referred to the victims she imagines as "our" kids, including all the participants as caretakers or guardians of the kids she describes.

Cynthia affirmed her response with agreement and restatement. "Right. Such a cycle." Although her response echoed Denise's response with the intensifier "such" and affirmation of her feelings, she was also returning to Jean's initiating turn in the episode focusing in the structural forces at work, passed on, in cyclical fashion from generation to generation. Denise, on the other hand, focused on individual experiences and choices in her analysis of the "victim's" experience. This pattern repeats itself in another turn between Denise and Cynthia. Cynthia had just asked if the lack of hope in the book would make it too difficult to share with adolescents. Sarah's response initiated the following exchange:

Sarah: You don't, you wouldn't want to be preachy about it and say, "Look you guys, this is what could happen to you if you don't toe the line.

Denise: I think the, I think the, uh, no, I think the value of the book is for kids to see what other kids in other subcultures are going through.

Every day of their life. I think we're so removed from that here. I mean that. Maybe we're not.

Cynthia: Yes. And it makes those, those, these kids seem very human and very. And to have, they have ethics and morals and /

Although Sarah sounds as though she would not want to use the book as a cautionary tale, she often talked about young adult literature in just those terms, believing that it should present kids with moral and ethical truths they can live by. She tended to view students as incapable of getting beyond sur-

face responses to texts and often asked group members how she could help her fifth-grade students "dig deeper" under the surface of the literature they read. This is in contrast to Denise, who, as described earlier, had every confidence that her eighth-grade students could think deeply and thoughtfully about the books they read. In response to Sarah, then, Denise somewhat tentatively offered her belief about the value of teaching this book. Although she seems to second guess herself at the end of this turn ("Maybe we're not"), she uses intensifiers like "every day" and "so" and "I mean" to express her distress that these "other" teens, who are "in other subcultures" do not have the advantages Denise sees her students enjoying. Cynthia's first response was "Yes." Again she affirmed Denise's response at an emotional level but then presented a different argument in that she emphasized the way that the characters in the book can be normalized rather than viewed as "other." Features of voice here are very interesting because Denise uses "othering" pronouns—"they and we"—and Cynthia began by repeating this pattern, but then changed it: "those, those, these kids."

In this excerpt, Denise signifi ed the other adolescents for whom she'd like her students to have empathy. This way of viewing the Other can lead to a moral judgment or paternalism or a desire to protect the innocence of the adolescents in this community. Although it is tempting for us to read her remarks in this way, we would like now to offer an alternative reading, one that is more generous and in keeping with Denise's strong affi nity for her students and general advocacy for youth. Asked to come up with a reason for teaching this book to kids in her community, and wanting to emphatically divorce herself from any sense of this book as a cautionary tale, she made what we believe to be an attempt to situate the characters in this book within an unjust system of oppression and inequity. She referred to this system through her use of the word "subcultures," which marks a movement away from viewing the characters as individuals who make what appear sometimes to be bad choices. My response, on the other hand, can be read as a shift to a focus on the kids rather than the structures that shape them.

This exchange is an example of interdiscursivity as defi ned earlier – a trace or presence of one discourse within another. In this case, one can read the discourse of the individual in Denise's remark (the individuals who are her students can learn from what the other individuals experience every day) and the discourse of structural inequity in my remark (the underlying assumption being that it is necessary to represent as human those who have been systematically represented as "other" and as malevolent). Embedded in each of these remarks, however, are alternate discourses: an understanding about the structural nature of subcultures in Denise's remark and an understanding about the importance of foregrounding the individual, with moral and ethical dilemmas, in my remark. This pattern of interdiscursivity becomes more pronounced in later transcripts, and we argue that such hybrid language opens spaces for learning as we have defi ned it—the appropriation and reconstruction of discourses within one's social world. Fixed practices are most likely to be interrupted when more dialogic conversations occur resulting in subtle shifts in the social identities of the participants.

The Middle Transcripts: Interdiscursive Moments

In our analysis of transcripts from the middle years of this study, we found marked changes in the categories of genre and voice as they intersected with the discourses of liberal humanism (individual) and critical multiculturalism (structural forces). To demonstrate these changes, we focus this section on a lengthy exchange from our discussion of American Eyes: New Asian American Short Stories for Young Adults (Carlson, 1994) that took place in April of 2000. This collection of short stories by Asian American writers explores issues of assimilation and acculturation among young Asian Pacific Americans. We focus on two episodes from the book group discussion, and include nearly the entire episode in each case in order to make some points about the structure of participation in each episode.

We begin with an episode that starts with Carol, a teacher who taught gifted education and had been a member of the group for a little over 2 years at the time of this discussion. Carol is unique in the group because she had experience teaching in a rural south Texas community with a population of working-class Latinos. Her experience was often refl ected in her analysis of a character's motivation and, in particular, her perceptions of the confl icts those from a minority culture experience in schooling and society at large. At this point, we were discussing a story about a fi rst-generation Japanese adolescent who revisits Little Tokyo in Los Angeles, where his recently deceased father had taken him many times as a child (Oba, 1994).

- Carol: And it's so funny, too, I think all the way through that that, um, all the way through the book, the trade off that they have to be an American and not give up whatever culture is offered, whatever their culture offers them. I'm not explaining this right, but each one of them has kind of a different way, like, like, when you were talking about that seeing ghosts, you know, calling back his uncle, and accepting that he would really appear, and the boy who went back, tried to go back to that Japanese part, yeah, yeah, to fi nd the different stores and everything and they were gone, and, I don't know/ . . .

Sarah: Oh, that was sad.

Cynthia: And he wasn't accepted in the store [restaurant].

Carol: Right. Exactly. Exactly. When he sat there waiting for him Sarah: Yes ( )

Cynthia: That was sad.

Sarah: Um hmm. It was.

Sarah: Was that the story where they repeated this phrase a couple times, "If you lived here you'd be home"? [All affirm]

Sarah: There's something about that phrase.. . .

Cynthia: His father has died, right, and his mother is filling her life by making origami. That's a great image.

Sarah: All over the house.

Carol: And she left the neighborhood, too, so it's like there aren't any connections ,back with that neighborhood anymore.

The episode started with Carol struggling to explain her sense that these characters are caught between American culture and the culture of their ancestry. One could argue that Carol's use of the word "American" reveals an experiential value (Fairclough, 1989) or ideological stance toward first generation ethnic minorities that marks them as immigrants or non-Americans and assumes White people as unmarked "Americans." Yet, in the context of her entire turn, it seems more likely that the phrase "American culture" refers to "dominant" American culture, and that Carol is interested in how this individual's life is shaped by a larger social and cultural framework. Another interdiscursive moment, this speaker turn holds traces of both discourses under discussion— the individual and the structural. Given that before Carol's turn, we had been discussing something entirely different (nuclear family narratives), Carol took control of the topic, a move not typical of the teachers in the early transcripts. Also related to the genre of "book talk," Carol claimed a particular stance at the same time that she seemed either unwilling to claim it or unsure of herself. She began this rather serious statement about the characters' cultural positioning with the seemingly contradictory "And it's so funny, too," perhaps as a way to undercut the seriousness of what she was about to say. A few sentences later, she undercut her claim to authority by stating "I'm not explaining this right." We found that when teacher participants in the group began to frame their responses in terms of the discourse of structural forces, they did so with some degree of inarticulateness, using more filler words and sometimes apologizing for their manner of speaking ("I'm not explaining this right"). This inarticulate voice was far from ineffective, however, because it signaled a shift in discourse as participants constructed new perspectives. Carol did not simply appropriate a way of thinking more associated with Cynthia or Jean. Instead, she reconstructed this world view in her own way, one that centered as much on the individual as it did on the social constitution of the individual.

We include most of the turns that were part of this episode because they reveal both the animated, collaborative talk that we displayed by this time in our group's evolution, and because this series of turns serves as an extended example of interdiscursive talk that weaves in and out of both discourses. For instance, although all of the turns add a bit of detail to create a sense of immediacy and sadness about the predicament of this individual adolescent boy, three of the turns reinforce the structural nature of his predicament. Cynthia reminded others that the boy was not accepted as more than a tourist in

one of the Japanese restaurants he entered, searching for a past he had lost. Carol agreed and added an image of the boy waiting to be acknowledged in the restaurant. And, finally, Carol underscored the lack of cultural affiliation the boy experiences. Throughout this set of cohesive turns, we follow up on each other's comments, almost finishing each other's sentences and building on previous turns. The next episode followed directly after the one just discussed. It, too, represents an instance of interdiscursivity, but one that works quite differently than the first episode. Sarah began by asking a question about White privilege, but did so from a position of dominance that served to marginalize those whom she refers to as "people who are different."

- Sarah: I wonder how many White people are aware in their day-to-day life how much other people are trying to be like them? You know, people who are different. I never think of that until I read these stories and see about how important all these things are—the language, the hair color, all of those things—that striving for those things, that we don't even think about it. Why, why do people feel they have to be just like that in order to be of worth?

Cynthia: Yeah, I don't see them as striving for it, I see them as (pause) wanting Sarah: envy?

Cynthia: the privilege that comes with that Sarah: Oh, okay.

Cynthia: and the power that comes with these things and feeling like they're completely denigrated and treated with prejudice because they don't have it. That seems like it's more directed towards us than towards the self to me, but what do others think?

It was difficult for us to be generous in our response to Sarah's initial turn in this episode, coming as it did nearly three years into the study group at a time when we had hoped we had progressed beyond such comments. In our view, her first sentence was inscribed with the very White privilege her comment, at some level, sought to challenge. Moreover, by indexing White people as "them," she seems not to acknowledge her own implication in this system of privilege. Later in the turn, Sarah uses repetition of an article ("the" language, "the" hair color, "all of those things") to refer to characteristics of

White people that she believes are seen as desirable. Her use of "the" and shift from "these things" to "those things" further serves to distance her from this system of privilege.

Indeed, there are some characters in American Eyes who measure themselves against Eurocentric standards of beauty; however, they do so with an awareness of the power differences that privilege these standards. One can read into Sarah's turn the now familiar discourse of liberal humanism (and the individual psyche). She was concerned that this "striving" toward White characteristics could be damaging to one's self-worth.

Cynthia channeled her frustration into a response that directly opposed Sarah's discourse of Whiteness, attempting to disrupt the way that Sarah conflated White privilege with what she perceived as the desire to be White. Even as Cynthia paused to consider the best way to finish her sentence about not seeing people of color as "striving" to be White, Sarah jumped in to finish Cynthia's sentence with the word she thought would fit—"envy," further revealing her belief that White people serve as objects of desire for people of color. Earlier in the life of our book group, as is evident from our analyses of genre and voice in the exchanges included in the section on early transcripts, Cynthia most likely would have made her point less directly. For instance, she might have found some common point of agreement before moving on to disagree, or, possibly concerned about sounding too authoritative, she might have found herself pulling back—speaking inarticulately, using filler words, half-spoken sentences, and seeming not to want to claim her position. Such was not the case by this time in the study group, however, and so, after a quick affirmation ("yeah"), she explicitly states her opposition, claiming her position, in part, through the use of repetition ("I don't see them as striving for it, I see them as . . ."). She continued to draw on the features of book talk genre that we've labeled as "teacherly moves" and "disagreement" for several turns, strongly stating her position. Finally, having had control of the floor for three turns, Cynthia opens the floor to others in a very teacherly manner ("but what do others think?"). She spoke those words, as teachers sometimes do, as though she were completely open to other perspectives, but we now suspect that everything about her words and intonation suggested otherwise. Vocabulary such as "privilege," "power," "completely denigrated," and "prejudice," make the discourse of critical multiculturalism very clear, and this discourse, it seemed to us when we first analyzed this episode, stands in stark contrast to Sarah's discourse of liberal humanism and self-worth.

However, as we have read and reread Sarah's words, placing them in the context of our historical understanding of Sarah and her position in our group, we have come to see her contribution differently. Sarah was reared in a

Midwestern town where she lived in what she described as a "working-class town with much prejudice, including [her] parents." Many times in our years together, she commented, often derisively, about the way her home community would have treated a particular character. She was proud of her participation in this group, calling it a "class," and reporting that her friends, family, and fellow teachers asked her questions about why she belonged to the group and what its value was to her. She kept count of the books we read and shared short articles and bibliographic entries about multicultural literature taken from teaching magazines. This year, the fifth year of the study, the group is continuing their monthly meetings without us, and Sarah, who has just retired from teaching, is organizing and audio-taping the meetings and leading the book selection process.

Sarah's role in the group was most always tentative. Her turns were often questions, asking for advice or elaboration, usually directed to Cynthia or Jean. She also had a habit of echoing the end of someone's sentence and then nodding her agreement. She represented herself in interviews as someone who did not know as much about interpreting literature as others in the group (since she was elementary trained and the others were trained in secondary English). Her social identity as a member of this group was tentative and insecure, whereas her social identity as derived from participation in the group was elevated. She often referred to the strong bonds we had developed as a collegial learning community.

This history of identities, relationships, and connections (Gee, 2005) moved us to re-see Sarah's turn about "other people" striving to be like White people. In the context of Sarah's evolution in this group, we began to realize that the lens through which we interpreted Sarah's words was shaped by the way our academic discourse community talks about race. Thus, we did not consider that Sarah's words could be read as an awareness of Whiteness as a race rather than a taken-for-granted norm. As she put it, "I never think of that until I read these stories and see about how important all these things are—the language, the hair color, and all of those things—that striving for those things that we don't even think about it." Here she moved in a new direction, tentatively considering the construction of race in relation to self and other, before the next sentence when she returned to a focus on the psychology of individual self-worth. This move was in keeping with research findings (Helms, 1990; Lawrence & Tatum, 1997) suggesting that becoming aware of one's own Whiteness is an early stage of White racial identity development.

Although Sarah could be said to "other" those who are "different," she also represents White people as other in her first sentence. Later in the turn, she used the pronoun "we" to refer to White people, but in the first sentence, she referred to White people with the pronouns "their" and "them," setting herself apart from those White people who live their lives day to day naturalizing race. She, on the other hand, had begun to denaturalize race, and reading the literature under discussion has helped her to do so. Sarah's way of representing the discourse of structural inequality was different than ours. She embedded the discourse within a story—the story of her thinking and reading processes.

After Cynthia asked what others thought, hoping, at the time, that someone else would challenge Sarah, Carol continued the episode with a turn that displayed a common feature of the book talk genre—the personal story.

Carol: I think it is whatever that country puts up as their ideal. I know that my friend who came from Bolivia had, has, fair skin and, um, golden eyes, and dark hair. And his skin is not, and he would be my color— he's not, like, very fair. And he was looked down upon, I mean literally, to the point where he was carrying a knife in school to scare them away, because he was not dark. So, it's just, he wasn't Indian enough looking.

Denise: He didn't fit in. That must be a sad state of affairs.

Carol: Right, and he was looked upon as a foreigner even though he was Bolivian. And his mother came from Chile.

Here, as in the case of Sarah's turn, the personal story is being used in ways that are quite different than one might expect. Rather than feeding into the discourse of the individual, Carol told a story from which we listeners were expected to extract significance: it is the larger structures of privilege that determine who will be marginalized, and those structures are somewhat arbitrary (changing from country to country). Perhaps having read Sarah's comment as a privileging of Whiteness, Carol's story served to contest that privilege. Some readers might suggest that her discourse is too quick to assume that the structure of power and privilege is arbitrary rather than historical, political, and economic. However, coming on the tail of Sarah's comment, it serves an important purpose in this local scene—to gently challenge within the framework of story. And Carol sticks with this position in her last turn, despite Denise's attempt to focus on the individual circumstance of Carol's friend ("He didn't fi t in.").

The Intersection of Genre, Discourse, and Voice

In the early transcripts, the individual/structural binary was constructed through generic features of talk in our book group, such as politeness and affirmation. We researchers denied our authority even as we controlled most topics and made indirect teacherly moves. Although our talk was constituted in a range of social languages, those social languages emerged out of the discourses we brought to the table from our respective social worlds (e.g. liberal humanism for the teachers; critical multiculturalism for us). Our language bridged these binary discourses through elements of voice that downplayed them—through the use of pronouns, filler words, and intensifiers that created bonds and promoted affect. In the middle transcripts, the individual/structural discourses were less distinct. Elements of genre intersected with these discourses in ways that blurred their boundaries. For instance, the use of personal story, an oftencited feature of "book talk" genre (Florio-Ruane, 2001; Long, 1986; Marshall, Smagorinsky, & Smith, 1995) that serves to accentuate the individual, here instead provided a form through which teachers gave shape to the structural.

Although we researchers still at times resorted to teacherly moves as a feature of our book talk, we did so with more explicitness, making our agendas clear (a feature that is even more accentuated in later transcripts). Disagreements among members were more explicit as well. One teacher, for instance, disagreed so strongly with Jean's statement that racism was the root cause of an African American character's incarceration that she strongly retorted "Now wait, wait, wait! You think that's what he's thinking? Or is that what we're reading into it." More often, during this middle period, a teacher participant would challenge another teacher's reading of the text more effectively than we did because the teacher's use of hybrid discourses (individual/structural) was accomplished through the use of a familiar and affective genre such as personal story. Our analyses of the data in this study point to the central role interdiscursivity plays in learning. If we view learning as the appropriation and reconstruction of one's social world, then it stands to reason that interdiscursive language would be critical to this process. For it is through the presence of one discourse in another that a generative rather than fixed appropriation becomes possible. In this vein, the members of our study group take up one another's genres, discourses, and voices over time in ways that create rather than replicate, thus opening spaces for new ways of constructing a teaching and learning self.

Notes

1.   1 Fairclough's use of the term "interdiscursivity," also referred to as "constitutive intertextuality," draws heavily from Kristeva's (1986) use of the term "intertextuality" in her explication of Bakhtin's (1981, 1986) dialogic theory of social languages and genres.

2.   2 The following conventions are used in the presentation of transcripts: [text] indicates descriptive text added to clarify elements of the transcript; text indicates overlapping speech; ( ) indicates unintelligible

words; . . . indicates extracts edited out of the transcript; / indicates interrupted or dropped utterances.

3. 3 We are interested in studying how the teachers' learning in the study group might shape their work with each other and with their students now that we have left the site. Currently the study group is continuing without us—a group that includes fi ve of the core teachers plus two new teachers. The teachers have agreed to provide us with audiotapes of their discussions, which will allow us to study instances of interdiscursivity as they occur without our participation. We are also interested in how our study group may have shaped discussions of multicultural texts in the teachers' classrooms. To this end, we are currently analyzing interviews with the teachers that speak to this subject as well as the artifacts and narratives related to their teaching that the teachers brought to our study group meetings. In addition, Jean has taught three collaborative units with Denise in her eighth-grade classroom. The data from this collaboration will provide more information about the role of interdiscursivity in learning as it plays out in the classroom context.

LANGUAGE, POWER, AND PARTICIPATION: USING CRITICAL DISCOURSE ANALYSIS TO MAKE SENSE OF PUBLIC POLICY

State and federal policymakers in the U.S. have never been more concerned with reading than they are today. Nationwide we have seen a tremendous increase in state legislation around reading and phonics (Allington, 2002; Paterson, 2000). At the federal level we are experiencing what some refer to as a "policy epidemic" (Hopkins, 2001, p. 4). The No Child Left Behind (NCLB) Act and Reading First legislation provided $1 billion a year for reading education beginning in 2002 and ended in 2007.1 These changes mark a significant shift that has taken place not only around reading, but also around the role of elected officials in defining how to teach. Traditionally, issues of pedagogy and teaching content have been left to teachers and administrators. These more recent trends in policymaking, however, take a different approach—one that pushes against constitutional rights for local, school-based control.

These shifts have not taken place in a vacuum. Newspapers across the country report that all children must be reading on grade level by grade 3, that there is a crisis in education, and that scientific research should be the basis for most if not all decision making. Despite the omnipresence of this agenda and the apparent persuasiveness of the media and agenda setters, we need to complicate these discourse practices of cultural models and expertise. Instead of simply assuming that they are both stable and correct, we need to reach the text, discourse practices, and social practices behind them (see Coles, 2000; Edmondson, 2000; Rogers, Mosley, & Kramer, 2009). By combining the works of Fairclough (1992, 2003) and Bernstein (2000), this chapter explores the use of Critical Discourse Analysis (CDA) as a tool in the critical analysis of public policy. Through the close analysis of changes in reading policies in California between 1995 and 1997, this research seeks deeper understandings of how power and policy are interrelated.2

As Fairclough suggested, policies define how we are to act and by what rules we must abide. Through public policy we come to be socialized in many ways into what is thinkable and unthinkable (Bernstein, 2000). Policy and political discourse represents the authoritative allocations of values and goals and socially situated representations of the world (Ball, 1990; Fairclough, 1995a). These cultural models (Gee, 1996, 1999) or understandings about the world position people in specific ways. Although it is easy to point to the evidence of power in policymaking and policy documents, it is quite another thing to be able to show how that power is generated, the role individuals play in that power structure, and the implications that those lines of power have for policy consumers. Given this complex web, a critical analysis of policy is necessary— one that pushes past questions of efficiency and outcomes to questions of "how power is used to define the parameters of particular questions, to set the rules for particular practices, and to shape particular agendas" (Edmondson, 2002, p. 114).

Prunty (1985) defined policy as an agenda or set of objectives that legitimizes the values, beliefs, and attitudes of its authors. He argued that issues of how problems arise and appear on agendas, how issues are developed, how policy is developed, and how policy is implemented are each important features for critical policy analysis.

Kingdon's (1995) framework for policy analysis speaks to this view of analysis, offering explicit analyses of the contexts, constructs, and social roles played by those inside and outside of policymaking. Although Kingdon's framework addresses much of what Prunty called for in the critical analysis of policy, it does not engage us in critical social analysis or inquiries into how such political power constructs (and is constructed by) larger social practices. Critical analyses of policy include inquiry into underlying issues of power and ideology embedded within the definition of the perceived problem and solution. Although more recent analyses of reading policies in the United States make explicit the political nature of policymaking, they do not lead us to examine how political power with respect to dominant voices actually flows throughout (or drives, as the case may be) the policy domain (Woodside-Jiron, 2003). Helpful in thinking about the different layers of inquiry necessary in this sort of policy analysis is Fairclough's (1992, 2003) frame for CDA.

CDA, Bernstein, and Policy Analysis in California

Fairclough and CDA

Fairclough (1992, 2003) named discourse as a mode of action—one that is socially constitutive. He identified texts, discourse practices, and social practices and how they each come together to carry constructive effects. In his framework, he adopted a Hallidayian (Halliday, 1978) definition of text as spoken as well as written language. Discourse practices involve the processes of text production, distribution, and consumption. Social practices represent discourse as ideology and power.

As Rogers (this volume) points out, local, institutional, and societal levels of interpretation necessarily take place at each of the three levels of analysis in CDA: text, discourse practice, and social interaction. I argue here that placing these domains in relation to one another is complex and requires a sys- tematic theory and analysis of relationships. What is often missing in CDA are the specific analytic procedures—something that Bernstein's framework and Fairclough's more recent works (2003) offer to CDA.

Bernstein and the Pedagogic Device

Bernstein's (2000) work sheds light on this issue by offering a specific theory of relationship among the various levels of discourse under study. Specifically, Bernstein presented the Pedagogic device reflecting the relationship between regulative and instructional discourses. In his framework, Bernstein presented regulative discourse as the moral discourse that creates order, relations, and identity and ultimately controls instructional discourse. Instructional discourse is that which creates specialized skills and their relationship to each other. Bernstein suggested that the regulative discourse ultimately controls the instructional discourse. By placing these discourses in detailed relation to one another and examining how the regulative discourse actually shapes the instructional discourse, we begin to understand the pedagogic device or specific power relations between the two. The charge to the researcher combining this frame with Fairclough's CDA is to thoughtfully and systematically identify these discourses (i.e., texts, discourse practices, social practices) as regulative, instructional, and pedagogic so they can be examined in relationship to one another, offering a more complete understanding of the social analysis present in CDA (see Table 8.1). This analytic approach offers a way for the critical policy analyst to explore not only the presence of power structures in social change, but also how, specifically, power structures influence social change.

Table 8.1: Combining Lenses to Inform Critical Discourse Analysis

Fairclough/Chouliaraki	Bernstein	Implications for Research/Reflexivity
Local context: Interactions or outcomes of the institutional context	Instructional discourse: What is thinkable/ unthinkable	Places where things are being redefined for the larger public (language/text). Issues of genre or ways of interacting
Institutional context: Social and political institutions that frame the local context	Regulative discourse: Dominant forces, voices, or decision makers	Governing bodies that name those redefinitions (organization/ discourse practice). Issues of discourse or representing
Societal context: Larger governing bodies including policies, mandates, and political climates that influence the local and institutional contexts	Pedagogic device: Relationship between the two. Sociological nature of pedagogic knowledge.	What larger context/ideas make this arrangement of knowledge and decision making possible? (cultural models/norms/member resources/ social practice)
	What makes this kind of communication/ phenomena possible?	Issues of style or ways of being

The concepts of text, discourse practice, and social practice referred to in Fairclough's CDA, and those of instructional discourse, regulative discourse, and pedagogic device (respectively) in Bernstein's work are combined in my use of CDA in critical policy analysis. For the ease of discussion, I will refer simply to text, discourse practice, and social practice throughout the rest of this chapter.

Fairclough and Bernstein's Frames in the Context of Critical Policy Analysis

In working to understand how policy and power fit together in creating change, Fairclough (1995a, 1995b) referred to cruces tension points as moments of crisis. These are times when things are changing or going wrong. What is significant about these moments is that they provide opportunities to deconstruct the various aspects of practices, particularly language practices, that are often naturalized and therefore difficult to notice. In this regard, important sites for investigation include policy documents, well-circulated documents that serve to redefine current thinking, and specific events where particular voices, ideas, or agendas are brought to the front and acted on. These texts have the potential to direct our attention away from the more complex sites of political tension where issues of equity and justice reside. For analysis, I will now turn to the reading policy changes in California between 1995 and 1997. This account and inquiry will serve as a springboard for continued critical policy analysis in education, including the most recent Race to the Top, and is designed to go beyond describing and interpreting these changes to explaining them through the use of CDA.

Inquiry Context

I selected California as the site for this inquiry for several reasons. First, the state of California has the largest population in the United States, with 5 million elementary and middle-school-age students currently being affected by the reading policies recently put into place. Second, California is the second largest textbook adoption state. The textbook market is a fiercely competitive one. Whichever publishers win California adoption typically win a huge chunk of the national textbook market (Manzo, 1997). Therefore, the legislated reading policies passed in California inevitably find their way into textbooks and thousands of classrooms across the nation. Students and teachers across the entire country are affected by California's policies by default. Third, California provides an extremely visible account of considerable policy change over a relatively short period of time, thereby facilitating critical conversations around change— questions ignored in the functional analysis of policy. Basing my sampling strategy on cases of political importance (Kuzel, 1992; Patton, 1990) affords a particular advantage in making explicit how policy can be used as a means to create social change with respect to teaching and literacy learning, and how terms like "systematic, explicit phonics" and "phonemic awareness instruction" have influenced the way reading is to be taught in California and elsewhere, ultimately influencing students' apprenticeships into literacy (Collins, 1995; Egan-Robertson, 1998; Ferdman, 1990; Gee, 1996; Mahiri & Godley, 1998; Mertz, 1996; Vygotsky, 1978).

Data

The data for this study included formal and informal documents, and written and oral texts, including legislated policy documents, official state education agency documents, professional listserve and private correspondence, newspaper articles, and documents from popular media sources with high circulation rates such as Time and Newsweek. Related discourse practices were also included in the data set. Historical context data were drawn from significant events that took place in California around this body of policy. These historical events included electoral events, shifts in the organization of educational decision-making procedures specific to California's governance system, temporal links between various documents, and legislative hearings (videotapes) where consistent and influential voices were present. Situating fine-grained discourse analysis in political and cultural context allows researchers to both explore cultural models and how they interact with moments of change, and to examine how educational processes and practices are constructed across time and how discourse processes and practices shape what counts as knowing, doing, and being within and across events (Fairclough, 2003; Gee, 1996, 1999; Gee & Green, 1998; Rogers, 2003). Steeped in this collection process, I maintained detailed field notes and research journals to record analytical decisions and explanations of social practices over time, and in order to register my ongoing reflections. Fairclough (1995a) noted that this third level of analysis is the most explanatory and thus requires such a system of accountability.

Analysis of Text

Fairclough (1992) suggested that the analysis of spoken and written texts can be organized under four main headings: vocabulary, grammar, cohesion, and text structure. His more recent work (2003) focuses more elaborately on genres (ways of acting), discourses (ways of representing), and styles (ways of being). Particularly interesting in the critical analysis of policy are features of text that speak to the genre (Chouliaraki & Fairclough, 1999; Fairclough, 2003) of policy, including the vocabulary used while presenting new rules about the way people function and the way in which policies are written so as to produce cohesion. Here authoritative sentence structure in the introducing of new information and the intertextual features of the text work together to create cohesion (which is a property of neither the text nor the interpreter, but rather the intersection of the two).

For this analysis, I have broken the selected texts into information units (Halliday, 1994) and identified theme and rheme in the sentence structure to interpret their structural role in the introduction of new information. As one analyzes spoken and written texts in CDA, one is at the same time addressing questions of form and meaning. I also looked at the nonstructural features of text that contribute to particular interpretations of text and social change. Specifically, I made note of the use of determiners in establishing authority and facts as well as the consistency of vocabulary in contributing to the cohesion of the overall text. How, during a time of policy change, did the policymakers make use of language to construct a perceived consensus among and between outsiders and insiders?

Analysis of Discourse

Practice With the tools and methods of CDA, I saw that policies were layered on top of one another to create cohesive collections of policy. When the discourses of policymakers are repeated over and over again, when policymakers talk about them collectively as "the final word" or "the most authoritative version," these texts come to be established as fact or normal when, in fact, they are simply individual texts bundled rhetorically. Also important in studying the production, distribution, and consumptions of these texts is the social and political context from which they come. In this study, I point to the opening of policy windows in California and the way in which new policies and text are strategically linked to established texts to promote minimal resistance. Further, I interpret the ways in which people are actually forced to consume the policy through mandatory and monitored professional development experiences.

Analysis of Social Practice

I have paid particular attention to the way in which consensus was actually crafted by influential policy professionals both in the context of legislative policymaking and in the popular media. Here we are able to explain levels of participation in the construction of new knowledge and think about how that new knowledge gets presented. In looking at the legislative and public contexts, we can begin to explain how particular individuals and research were strategic in the development of legislative policy and the preparation of the public for these policies through the popular media. Being able to then turn these understandings back on the prior analyses of texts and discourse practices in relationship to one another, as Bernstein's frame allows, strengthens my analysis of social practices and how people come to be positioned in various ways. Having introduced critical policy analysis into the frame of CDA, now let us explore one such case study of policy.

The Language Of Politics And The Politics Of Language In California Reading Policy

As I analyze the changes that took place throughout California's reading policies, it is interesting to watch the ways that a seemingly small assumption grows and hardens into mandated teacher practices and instructional materials. The first of the five policies presented "the fundamental skills required" in reading, a construct that would become the stem from which basic instructional materials and current and confirmed research would be named.3 As each of these policies gained speed individually and collectively, the restrictive nature of the policy increased, further narrowing decision-making processes and the definition of reading, teaching, and learning. By engaging in this close analysis of changes that took place over time, I am able to not only describe the changes, but push further to explain how these changes occurred.

Text

Texts and Themes in the CDA of California's Reading Policies In January 1995, the California state Assembly introduced the first of five bills that would later redefine reading instruction in California. Given this surge of California legislation and the tremendous impact it had in creating radical changes in California's state documents, instructional materials, and professional development experiences, these legislative documents are key data in the critical analysis of California policy. These policies (individually and collectively) represent radical changes in how California named reading in K to 3 and also the underlying assumptions about teaching and learning.

Making the Unfamiliar Familiar Through Text Structure

The bills inscribe an underlying assumption or assertion (no small difference there) that there were some predetermined "fundamental skills required" in reading. This language was first introduced (and mandated) through Assembly Bill 170 (1995a), Instructional Materials. Fairclough (1992) highlighted that "it is always worth attending to what is placed initially in clauses and sentences, because that can give insight into assumptions and strategies which may at no point be made explicit" (p. 184). In the analysis of the semantic relationship between information structure and thematic structure, Halliday (1994) noted that generally a speaker will "choose the Theme from within what is Given and locate the focus, the climax of the New, somewhere within the Rheme" (p. 299). Theme can most easily be defined as the initial part of a clause, whereas rheme is the later. This particular type of writing—where new information is linked with given, more familiar information in legislation—is important because it provides a set of conditions that exploit the potential of the new information being presented. New information here does not necessarily mean brand-new methods of instruction or definitions of reading. To be sure, California has experienced several cycles of more and less phonics-based methods of reading and instruction throughout its educational history. Rather, "new" in this analysis means new with respect to its presence in the given conversation: for example, in 1987, "these details [phonics, word-attack skills, vocabulary, and the conventions of language], when taught, should be in context and not in isolation" (Honig, 1991, p. 110). In the 1999 framework, however, "students first learn to apply and practice decoding and word-attack skills in carefully controlled, decodable texts" (California Department of Education, 1999, p. 4). A significant shift has taken place with respect to how reading, teaching, and learning were being presented in California's framework. The phonics and word recognition approach is considered "new" because it provides such a contrast to the previous framework, which emphasized meaning. How the given and new information of the first bill (A. B. 170, 1995a) information was positioned within the text ensured particular interpretations.4

1. 600200.4. (a) The State Board of Education shall ensure that the basic instructional materials that it adopts for mathematics and reading in Grades 1 to 8, inclusive, are based on the fundamental skills required by these subjects, including, but not limited to, systematic, explicit phonics, spelling, and basic computational skills.

2. (b) It is the intent of the Legislature that the fundamental skills of all subject areas, including systematic, explicit phonics, spelling, and basic computational skills, be included in the adopted curriculum frameworks and that these skills and related tasks increase in depth and complexity from year to year.

3. It is the intent of the Legislature that the instructional materials adopted by the State Board of Education meet the provisions of this section.

We can see specific patterns in how tensions between language and language structure present opportunities to make the unfamiliar familiar. These ultimately represent struggles over meaning and truth. The first information unit begins with a theme possessing a given:

1. "The State Board of Education shall ensure that the basic instructional materials that it adopts for mathematics and reading in Grades 1 to 8, inclusive . . ."

California has long been a textbook adoption state (Honig, 1991; Manzo, 1997). The State Board of Education is the governing force in this process. Therefore, the given information in the initial positioning of this sentence refers to this long-standing policy of textbook adoption. The new information is then presented in the final position of the sentence:

1. are based on the fundamental skills required by these subjects, including, but not limited to, systematic, explicit phonics, spelling, and basic computational skills.

The way in which this new information follows an already established fact relays to the reader a sense of order and logic. Here new ideas are attached to more familiar ideas, thus naturalizing the new concept at hand (Fairclough, 1992, 1995b). In the next sentence, this new information is picked up and placed in the initial position, thus relaying that it is now given information and used to introduce additional new information:

2. (b) It is the intent of the Legislature that the fundamental skills of all subject areas, including systematic, explicit phonics, spelling, and basic computational skills, be included in the adopted curriculum frameworks and that these skills and related tasks increase in depth and complexity from year

to year.

Here, policymakers strategically link yet another established policy (curriculum frameworks) with the newly introduced "systematic, explicit phonics." However, specific attention was also being given to the order and sequence of skills to be taught ("increase in depth and complexity"), which again marks a change from previous legislative authority. These maneuvers typically feel obvious and natural to the reader given their flow and reference to already established policies. They have come to be naturalized. In essence, however, they represent the privileging of particular ideologies and paradigmatic commitments. Finally, the authors of A. B. 170 use the last information unit in this sample to reiterate the purpose of the document:

3. It is the intent of the Legislature that the instructional materials adopted by the State Board of Education meet the provisions of this section.

In summarizing new information in this way, the authors make what was initially unfamiliar familiar. The information that sounded new at the outset of this policy ("the fundamental skills required," "systematic, explicit phonics," sequential "depth and complexity") is now established as fact ("the provisions of this section"; italics added). Although views about reading, teaching, and learning are manipulated via theme and rheme, later in the 1999 framework these same principles of order and complexity attain the status of fact claiming "the reality that standards in the earlier grades are building blocks for proficiency in the later grades" (California Department of Education, 1999, p. viii)—a significant shift.

p. viii)—a significant shift. In part through the structuring of the text, the elected officials have come to naturalize new information that was not present in California's reading policies immediately prior to that time, thus changing the language being used in conversations around reading and reading instruction. In essence, they are claiming a moral high ground of sorts from which they are able to establish moral order as a given. Whereas the analysis of theme/rheme and the structuring of given/new information inform our understanding of how meaning is organized at the elemental level, the analysis of lexical cohesion offers an understanding of the ways in which continuity is established in text via the use of key words, their repetition, and other words that are used as synonyms. Analyses of these nonstructural features are important in that they also can give any passage of text the status of fact—an important tool in influencing the readers' construction of text.

Lexical Cohesion: Fact or Foe

One discourse practice often present during times of change in educational policy is the use of specific new terms to name what is important or of value in the given policy (Fairclough, 1995a). These terms are often difficult to identify because they are presented with such authority and ofcourseness that we tend to pass over them. For example, "systematic explicit phonics instruction" is repeated time and time again throughout California's reading policies between 1995 and 1997. This phrase is repeated in documents from state education agencies as well as the popular media. These terms are used as places where particular views of reading, teaching, and learning are systematically mandated.

In the first information unit described earlier, the fundamental skills required for reading were introduced. This new information is then repeated in each of the subsequent information units5 that follow and warrants our attention in terms of how it is used to mandate new definitions of reading and instructional materials. Significant in the phrase "the fundamental skills required" (italics added) is the presence of the word the. In this case, the is a determiner (Gee, 1999), which serves as a cohesive devise communicating that there is some finite and stable set of skills that have been identified that correlate with reading achievement. Although the is a tiny word, it carries with it a tremendous amount of power. It serves in this context to signal some universal agreement on how reading is acquired. It assigns the status of fact to phonics as the fundamental or primary skill required in learning to read. In keeping with the previous analysis of text, such specific skills would typically be introduced earlier in the document, and then the determiner the would link back to them. This would indicate that that information was assumed to be predictable or known on the basis of the preceding sentences. Here, however, the fundamental skills is only defined later by the newly introduced systematic, explicit phonics with respect to reading, thus marking the introduction of new and favored information. It is as if the fundamental skills is used to initially arrange a general commonsense agreement among the audience members and is then returned to later and used interchangeably with systematic, explicit phonics. It is a discourse practice that has a quiet way of nursing the audience along in your way of thinking.

The intertextual nature of such structuring of change through various influential policy documents (formal and informal) necessitates the close analysis of text in understanding how new information comes to be established as fact. Particularly important in the intertextual chains throughout California's policy changes is the genre of policy. Specifically, the use of grammar and vocabulary in claiming authority while reducing resistance was significant. Together the use of grammar and vocabulary contributed to cohesion through consistency as new information became fact in these policies.

Differences in Discourse

We see as we begin to engage in the interpretive analysis of discourse practice in the changes taking place that California policy in mandating systematic, explicit phonics placed restrictive measures on teachers' professional development and knowledge. California legislation went so far as to mandate that "systematic explicit phonics instruction does not mean 'embedded phonics instruction' which is ad hoc instruction in phonics based on a random selection of sound and word elements" (A. B. 1086, 1997, p. 5; italics added). This means that the professional development that embraced or even entertained such a perspective would not (and did not) receive state funding, which is a huge regulative and restrictive exercise in power affecting how people are positioned. In this case, the opportunities to actually explore differences in discourse and how educators deal with difference are minimized, leaving the opportunity for a metadiscourse about change defunct (see Toll, 2002).

Discourse Practice

The analysis of discourse practice necessarily involves processes of text production, distribution, and consumption. By investigating these processes, we come to see how various member resources (Fairclough, 1992, 2003) are drawn on and how. As Fairclough suggested, pin-pointing the context of situation in terms of this mental map provides two bodies of information relevant to determining how context affects the interpretation of text in any particular case: a reading of the situation which foregrounds certain elements, backgrounds others, and relates elements to each other in certain ways; and a specification of which discursive types are likely to be relevant. (Fairclough, 1992, p. 83). In other words, understanding how texts are produced, distributed, and consumed informs our understanding of how authors work to ensure particular interpretations of text and how this engages our various member resources

Discourse Practices and Themes in the CDA of California's Reading Policies

During this period of change in California's legislative and state policies, larger political changes were also taking place. In November 1994, California Republicans gained control of the State Assembly, the majority of the nation's governors were Republican for the first time in decades, and bipartisan agreement over issues of education began (Carlos & Kirst, 1997).

As California's new reading policies were being mandated, California's system of educational decision making was reorganized. Traditionally, the State

Department of Education (CDE) had been the governmental unit charged with turning legislative policy into local policy, with the State Superintendent, Bill Honig, acting as overseer in this process. However, dismal test scores, fiscal improprieties, and bipartisan agreement with a back-to-basics agenda presented a unique window for policy change. Honig resigned, and power consequently shifted from the CDE to the State Board of Education (SBE). Important in California's educational governance system is the fact that members of the SBE are appointed by the governor. This meant that with the shift in control from the CDE to the SBE came more top-down power and political influence from elected officials via the governor's influence over the SBE. Instead of CDE members turning policies into action, now members of the SBE, handpicked by the governor, held this power. Also important is that this change took place in the context of fear and disbelief among the larger public in California. Again this represents another narrowing of decision making among a governing body that is responsible for much of the translating of legislation into local-level policy and instruction ultimately affecting California's teachers and students.

Assigning "Current and Confirmed Research"

One month after the introduction of the first reading bill, the Assembly introduced a second one, A. B. 1504 (1995b—Instructional Materials: Spelling). This bill was introduced by the same legislators (Burton, Alpert, and Conroy) and was designed with the legislative intent of ensuring the adoption of "basic instructional materials."

In this second bill, legislators specified the criteria for the adoption of instructional materials mandating that:

The submitted basic instructional materials are consistent with the criteria and the standards of quality prescribed in the state board's adopted curriculum framework. In making this determination, the state board shall consider both the framework and the submitted instructional materials as a whole.

The submitted instructional materials are factually accurate and incorporate principals of instruction reflective of current and confirmed research. (A. B. 1504, 1995b, p. 2)

There are two different features of this policy text that warrant our attention with respect to the institutional shaping of discourse. First, in this policy, legislators have made an explicit link between the frameworks that were, at that time, under revision and the textbooks that the SBE could approve. Aligning instructional materials in this way with "the state's educational philosophy, theory, current research, and best practices teachers are to follow" (Chrispeels, 1997, p. 459) is a pedagogic maneuver influencing both how reading is defined and how it is to be taught. Such legislated policy serves to place power over many among a small number of elected and appointed officials. It also reduces access to the naming of reading and reading instruction because fewer people are making decisions. Because of this decision-making structure or pedagogic device, there is little room for debate or conflict. Decision-making information is not provided, and public voice is not welcomed. The legislators mandating this link with a curriculum framework, which is ultimately, although implicitly, subjective and ideological, creates an understanding of and a compliance with a social order that, in this case, positions elected and appointed officials as authority.

The second feature of this policy sample is that "principles of instruction reflective of current and confirmed research" are introduced and named as criteria for selecting textbooks. Here "principles of instruction reflective of current and confirmed research" represent an intrinsic logic and favored agenda. This bill was making its way through the Legislature at the same time that dismal scores from the National Assessment of Educational Progress (NAEP) and California Learning Assessment System (CLAS) were being reported and local and national newspapers were riddled with conversations about America falling behind, "scientific research," America Reads, and reading on grade level by third grade. Gee (1999) suggested that such understandings are simplifications about the world that leave out many complexities. Problematic is that cultural models like this can do harm by "implanting in thought and action unfair, dismissive, or derogatory assumptions" (p. 59).

As systematic, explicit phonics, spelling, and basic computational skills were boldly named among the fundamental skills in mathematics and reading in the first ABC bill (A. B. 170, 1995a) without explicit and grounded logic, so we see instruction being linked with current and confirmed research here in this policy. Although legislators go no further than to define the research that instruction is to be based on as "current and confirmed" in this particular policy, later this principle was extended and transformed considerably. Two years later in A. B. 1086: Reading Instruction (1997), current and confirmed research would be further defined:

(j) ... "Current" research is research that has been conducted and is reported a manner consistent with contemporary standards of scientific investigation. "Confirmed" research is research that has been replicated and the results duplicated. "Replicable" research is research with a structure and design that can be reproduced. "Generalizable" research is research in which samples have been used so that the results can be said to be true for the population from which the sample was drawn. (A. B. 1086, 1997; italics added)6

Control over such discourse defining reading and how it is to be taught creates the rules of social order in educational decision making. This is a process of recontextualzation—of redefining knowledge with respect to reading, teaching, and learning. It is the process of regulations being placed on the formation of a specific pedagogic discourse. This legislation serves to eliminate entire bodies of quality research, including qualitative research that reports by means different from the replicable, generalizable "contemporary standards of investigation." Such a maneuver is a significant tool in naming what is thinkable and unthinkable in California's teaching of reading. As Bernstein (2000) suggested, it attempts to regulate those who have access to this site and in this way control alternative possibilities. We see this being done in the naming of instructional principles based on current, confirmed research complying with contemporary standards of scientific investigation in California's reading policies.7

Eliminating Resistance: A. B. 3482 and A. B. 1086—California's Teacher Training Bills

Up to this point, we have been talking about policy documents as if there is a direct relationship between policy and practice. Of course, this is not necessarily true, and policymakers know this. To ensure the success of policy, one must engage in discourse practices that eliminate as much resistance as possible. This can take many forms. In California it took the form of mandatory and heavily screened professional development for teachers. Less than a year after both Instructional Materials had been passed (A. B. 170, 1995a; A. B. 1504, 1995b), a third bill came along (Education: Teacher Reading Instruction [A. B. 3482, 1996]). This was the first of two bills dedicated entirely to influencing teacher inservice training. It mandated that:

44756. To be eligible for funds pursuant to this chapter, a school district shall certify to the State Department of Education that not less than 90 percent of its certificated employees who provide direct instructional services to pupils enrolled in Kindergarten or any of grades 1 to 3, inclusive, have received the type of inservice training described in [the policy].

Whereas the prior bills had targeted instructional materials primarily, this legislation mandated that the vast majority of California's K to 3 teachers receive specified inservice training in how to teach reading. A fourth bill, A. B. 1086, specified that teachers must abide by developmental progressions and that their instruction must be direct, systematic, and explicit. Embedded phonics instruction was not to be taught in these service training sessions because it was deemed by policymakers to be "ad hoc instruction in phonics based on a random selection of sound and word elements." This policy was followed by the last of the California reading mandates: Reading Instruction (A. B. 1086,

1997). This final bill provided explicit details about the specific criteria for the teacher inservice training sessions mandated in A. B. 3482 (1996). One year later, the State Superintendent of Public Instruction, the SBE, and the California Commission on Teacher Credentialing collectively authored and published the advisory report Teaching Reading: A Balanced, Comprehensive Approach to Teaching Reading in Prekindergarten.

Through Grade 3 (Reading Program Advisory, 1996). The report was designed to "provide the policy direction and instructional guidance needed to support the improvement of reading achievement in California" (p. v).8 Recognized as being influential in the content provided were 10 of the 27 authors of the earlier Task Force report issued the year before. Tracing the authors in this way is an important part of critical policy analysis because it enables us to further explore which voices are influential and which power sources dominate. For instance, the State Superintendency is an elected position in California, as is the office of governor. The SBE and this taskforce, however, were appointed positions controlled by Governor Wilson and State Superintendent Eastin at that time. Making explicit the pedagogic device, who controls knowledge, and how control over time, text, and space come to exist (Bernstein, 1990) is essential in the critical analysis of policy. Given that these reports were intended to inform policy and resulted in more prescriptive policies, we see how increased control over issues of educational content and instruction were situated among a relatively small number of elected and appointed officials. Again these connections represent the naming and distribution of influential ideas and ideologies about reading and reading instruction in California.

Teaching Reading was in direct response to the recommendations outlined in the report of the Superintendent's Reading Task Force, Every Child a Reader (September 1995). It was also designed to support two new statutes known as the ABC bills (Assembly Bill 170, Chapter 765, Statutes of 1995, and Assembly Bill 15, Chapter 764, Statutes of 1995), which required, in part, that the SBE adopt materials in grades 1 through 8 that include "systematic, explicit phonics, spelling, and basic computational skills." The advisory amplified both the recommendations of the Reading Task Force report as well as the new requirements in law, and it was offered as a policy statement rather than a "how-to manual" (Reading Program Advisory, 1996). Particularly interesting in our inquiry here are (a) the intertextual link and "support" for the previous ABC bill, and (b) the statement that Teaching Reading was not intended to be a "how-to manual." Because it was distributed to all of the schools in the state, the Reading Program Advisory was the intertextual link with the ABC bills and its support for such policy, Teaching Reading served to add to the cohesiveness of this movement in reading ideology toward systematic, explicit phonics instruction and current and confirmed research. The second feature—the statement that Teaching Reading was not intended to be a how-to manual—extends beyond intertextual to intratextual relations (Bernstein, 2000, p. 53) Although its authors express that Teaching Reading was not intended to be a how-to manual, we find, in the same text, the contradictory intent that it will "provide the policy direction and instructional guidance needed to support the improvement of reading achievement in California" (Reading Program Advisory, 1996, p. v). These two intentions are in conflict with one another. Although the Task Force states that it is not intended to be a how-to manual, they did state their intent that it provide "policy direction and instructional guidance." The recommendations from this document would

later be found in the subsequent legislative policy (A. B. 1086, 1997). Here we see a discourse practice being used that leads readers to believe that this report is something that it is not, creating dissonance between what is being articulated and what is actually being carried out. Bernstein (2000) referred to this as the carrier versus what is carried. This makes manifest the institutional power that elected and appointed officials have in producing new information and ideas via such influential documents and legislation.

Institutional Arrangement and Power

As particular concepts such as current and confirmed research come to be privileged and defined in more detail and by fewer people, we witness an example of Bernstein's (2000) regulative discourse. Understanding this shifting of power and the ways in which it changes the larger discourse is key in moving beyond recognizing the presence of power to understanding how such political power constructs and is constructed by larger social practices.

Social Practice

While understanding how texts are produced, distributed, and consumed informs our understanding of how authors work to ensure particular interpretations of text, the analysis of social practices makes explicit the connections between the discourse practices and the social practices of which they are a part (Fairclough, 1992). Fairclough's more recent work suggests that "social practices can be thought of as ways of controlling the selection of certain structural possibilities and the exclusion of others" (2003, p. 23). This dialectical ordering of discourse reinforces the fact that discourse as a political practice is not only a site of power struggle, but also a stake in power struggle: Discursive practice draws on conventions that naturalize particular power relations and ideologies, and these conventions and the ways in which they are articulated are a focus of struggle (Fairclough, 1992).

The Role of the Expert in Influencing the Policymaking Forum and Building Consensus

Immediately following the first of the [teacher bills] (A. B. 3482, 1996), a special Hearing on Reading of the Education Committee of the California State Assembly was held on May 8, 1996 (Honig, 1996). During this hearing, former State Superintendent Bill Honig was called on to provide expert testimony. Throughout Honig's testimony, one of his main messages was that of a need for consensus: this research that you are about to hear [NICHD research]. It's very powerful stuff. I think it backs up this consensus position. It shouldn't be a right, or left, or moderate, or at all. It really is what works with youngsters and if enough of us get behind it I think we're going to make a difference in California. (italics added).

During his testimony, Honig made several references to the "convergence of research and best practice," "the secret to getting a consensus position," "fashioning a message," "singing the same tune on this position," and the need for major players such as the State Board, Department of Education, legislators, governor, and educators to "get behind" this consensus message. His message was clear to the Assembly Education Committee: Together, they were crafting a consensus (Allington, 1999) for the educational institution and larger public to consume. Also during this hearing, G. Reid Lyon of the National Institute of Health (NIH), then acting chief of the division of Child Health and Development, was invited to provide expert testimony with respect to reading research. Lyon emphasized that phonemic awareness, phonics, and high-interest, decodable texts are necessary to ensure the "fast, accurate decoding of words." Lyon manipulated his testimony to best persuade his audience with respect to what is rational and what is not in terms of reading and reading instruction (thinkable and unthinkable in Bernstein's terms). Via Lyon's title, and supported by the cultural assumptions about "science and research" that he presents as commonsense to the Assembly, he pain nted a simple picture of what reading is and how best to go about teaching it. The Education Committee assembled was chaired by Assemblyman Steve Baldwin with Committee Vice Chairwoman Mazzoni. Nine months later, they would become first and second authors of California's most restrictive professional development bill yet, A. B. 1086.

During this special hearing, Assemblyman Baldwin introduced Lyon to the rest of the Assembly as clearly being the authority figure on reading. Lyon initially established his credibility to the Assembly member quorum by linking himself with real science (e.g., neurobiologist neophysiologist, biomedical research, genetics).

He then emphasized that he was "recruited" by the federal government to develop the research he was about to share. This discourse practice is effective in appealing to the Assembly members present and positioning himself as expert. Further, he emphasized that the NIH oversees 12 research sites around the country that are studying "the reading issue" to which Baldwin referred. He offered that the annual budget for NIH reading research is $14 million, and "since 1983 the cumulative budget looking at these issues that I'll talk with you about today is about $104 million dollars." Despite his deep investment in this particular collection of research, however, he strategically positioned himself as being "unbiased"—another important discourse practice in establishing credibility. Lyon: You won't hear me endorse any reading approach today or any reading method. That's not the job of the NIH. The job of the NIH is to distill the information so we understand "what does a human being have to do to be able to read?"

To be sure, Lyon has a vested interest in maintaining the health of the NIH research budget—his own paycheck depends on it. Yet he claimed to remove himself politically and ideologically from the testimony he was about to give— he was only there to provide the distilled information and inform policy. This image of distilled information relayed a message to the audience that they were about to receive "facts" about the "reading issue" from the authority figure in the field of reading in their most pure and unbiased form. This, of course, is misleading because with any kind of inquiry come choices about which information is valued and which is dismissed. One of the more recent and visible examples of this is the Congressionally commissioned National Reading Panel and their distillation process. That panel, in attempts to "build on the recently announced findings presented by the National Research Council's Committee on the Prevention of Reading Difficulties in Young Children," limited the research that they reviewed and that would be used to "identify gaps in the knowledge base for reading instruction and the best ways to close these gaps" (National Research Council's Committee on the Prevention of Reading Difficulties in Young Children, 1998).

Lyon later appealed to the Assembly members present with the agenda of improving reading education by claiming what he believed to be an irrefutable truth: "If you don't learn to read, you simply don't make it in life." Such a declarative moral and causal statement fanned the flames of existing fears and tuned the ear of his captive Assembly member audience. After all, the Assembly members' job is to serve the people and preserve the peace. Surely finding a way to ensure that we "make it in life" qualifies as an agenda for immediate action. It primed the Assembly and positioned them as recipients for the distilled information and research provided in Lyon's testimony. He linked illiteracy with those who do not finish school, end up in prison, and become unwed mothers. Such presuppositions are effective ways to manipulate people because they are so difficult to challenge (Fairclough, 1992, 2003). Here they are presented as fact and in causal relationship. There is little room in Lyon's discourse practice here to challenge these assumptions because he distilled the information, insisting that he does not want to "belabor or bore" the Assembly with the "technical issues." Ultimately, this means they are not able to evaluate the information firsthand, but rather are forced to go on his own expert interpretation. There is little room for debate because of the moral high ground laced throughout his argument. As such, anyone who would get in the way of policy intended to "help children learn to read" would be seen as ultimately getting in the way of children and success. This is a moral battleground that few are willing to enter—especially those who are publicly elected and rely on people's votes.

Despite Lyon's admission that he is the lead person within the federal government by way of the time he spends in it versus his knowledge, he offered and claimed the authority to name reading as "fast, rapid, automatic decoding and recognizing of words" and "fast, accurate decoding of single words." He then identified phonological or phonemic awareness as the solution, which in just 9 short months would be found in the final policy and criteria for mandated inservice providers, affecting at least 90% of all California's primary teachers and their students.

The Role of the Expert in Influencing the Larger Public and Building Consensus This consensus was also portrayed throughout the popular media during California's changes in reading and instruction policies. October 27, 1997, was a particularly interesting day in popular print media with respect to education and, more specifically, reading education. On this day, both Time and Newsweek, two of the most widely circulated and accessible print media sources, ran feature articles specific to how children learn to read. These feature articles were distributed the week prior to when the Reading Excellence Act (1998) was to pass through Congress, reinforcing the consensus position that Honig referred to earlier (see Coles, 2000; Taylor, 1998). The Newsweek (Wingert & Kantrowitz, 1997) reporter reported that:

Researchers have identified four distinct steps in learning to read; breakdowns anywhere in this process can explain severe reading problems. G. Reid Lyon, acting chief of the child-development and behavior branch of the National Institutes of Child and Human Development, says that reading for all children begins with phonological awareness. (p. 60; italics added)

Note that it is the reporter and not G. Reid Lyon speaking himself—an interesting reporting style because it removes the reader from the original source of information. We saw the same authorial move by Lyon in his testimony when he said things like, "I don't want to belabor or bore you" with the technical details (p. 7). We also experienced this in Honig's testimony when he made broad claims about the NICHD research as being "powerful stuff." We also hear this in many, many different arenas as people claim "the research shows" yet do not provide the original research so that the intended audience can decide for themselves. This Newsweek quote goes on to complete the list of four steps that include linking sounds with specific letters, becoming fast readers, and finally concentrating on the meaning of the words. This information is the same that Lyon presented in his testimony before the Assembly.

It is interesting to note that, in this article, Lyon's voice consumes more space than those of any of the other experts or researchers referenced throughout the article. Also Lyon is introduced with the long and authoritative title of "acting chief of the child-development and behavior branch of the National Institutes of Child and Human Development" attached to his name. This use of status, as in the prior legislative hearing, lends him credibility as an expert throughout this article.

In the Time (Collins, 1997) article, Lyon is again referenced directly—this time on the heels of two other well-known researchers. The reporter in this article foregrounded similar steps to learning to read via these researchers, and then added:

As the 1990s progressed, more verification of the importance of phonemic awareness came from studies conducted by the National Institute of Child Health and Human Development at the National Institutes of Health. Under the direction of Reid Lyon, researchers have found that problems with phonemic awareness correlate extremely closely with reading failure. Other NICHD studies have reaffirmed the conclusions reached by Chall and Adams—that programs with some systematic phonics instruction lead to better outcomes. (p. 80; italics added)

Both of these reports actively construct a perceived consensus in terms of both the problem at hand and the solution. The first is the authority given to research. Throughout the prior texts, research identifies, verifies, finds, and reaffirms conclusions. These are powerful and uncontested actions in this context. From these claims specific assumptions about reading, teaching, and learning are advanced. As we saw in the legislative changes discussed earlier in this chapter, such claims have significant impacts on how children come to experience reading and reading instruction in the classroom. Understanding the specific ways by which policymakers and scientific research are placed in positions of authority and how they relay certain understandings about knowledge and our role in the production and consumption of knowledge is essential because it is constitutive (Bourdieu, 1991, p. 52).

What we see through these discourse practices is the naturalization and consolidation of the message that both Honig and Lyon conveyed in their expert testimony before the Education Committee of the California State Assembly. In naming reading as a series of set steps and in explicitly focusing on a narrow body of research, reading in California was redefined and recontextualized. These ideologies and agendas were then effectively distributed through what would be the last of California's reading bills at that time. These points are important because they push our thinking about the intersection between the text and the reader. Understanding this relationship offers us the opportunity to explain the ways in which learning takes place throughout the many facets of policymaking (e.g., participation in policymaking, the way in which participation—limited or not—positions people, and the structural power that that contributes to in the policymaking process and, in this case, the power of few over many).

Gee suggested that we do not have a reading crisis in our schools. Rather, we have an affiliation crisis. To affiliate with particular people, practices, institutions, methods, and so on is to "participate fully in the attitudes, values, and norms the practice requires" (Gee, 2001, p. xviii). This is not realistic for many students coming in contact with legislated and one-size-fits-all policy, curricula, and assessments. We need to find ways to engage in larger dialogue and systematic research about how the ways in which literacy-related social practices do and do not recruit children's affiliation (Gee, 2001).

Current Policy Impacting Literacy Education Today

Since the first edition of this book was published, the Presidential administration has changed, the costly "War on Terrorism" continues, and the economic crisis looms large. To date, the U.S. carries a national debt of $12.5 trillion and a national unemployment rate of 9.7% (U.S. Department of Labor). NCLB's Reading First was initially authorized for FYs 2002–2007. It was then extended with significantly less financial support. Now the reauthorization of the ESEA is on the horizon once again. It is certainly welcomed at a time when resources are scarce and schools feel more accountability pressure than ever before. However, many schools are also anxious about what the reauthorization will require and how responsive it will be to the genuine challenges faced by children and schools gripped by poverty, changing family dynamics, and often times increasingly contrastive home and school experiences. NCLB was scorned for what seemed to many education practitioners an overly simplistic approach to assessing Annual Yearly Progress (AYP). Teachers and administrators remain thoughtful as to how English Language Learners and Special Education Students will fit within the legal parameters of the next wave of legislation.

California has also experienced changes of its own to be considered in this changing political climate. It now serves more than 6.2 million students. Currently approximately half of the state's students come from low-income families, a quarter of them are ESL students, and about one in 10 requires Special Education services (EdSource). Finally, the state has made more than $17 billion in cuts to education in the past two years and is likely to cut more in the near future (ABC News). This means a potential loss of more than 19,000 teachers, which certainly presents daunting challenges for the nation's most populous state.populous state. Most recently, the federal economic stimulus package channeled 4.35 billion dollars to the U.S. Department of Education for a competition called "Race to the Top." This competition fund is targeted specifically for education reform and is of obvious interest to both California and all other states in a time of such economic stress.

Arne Duncan, U.S. Secretary of Education, communicated the competitive nature of the "race" on the U.S. Department of Education website:the president and I want to send a message to everyone: governors and mayors, school board members and teachers, parents and students; businesses and non-profi ts. We all need to work together to win this race so that our students can outcompete any worker in the world. To win the race, states have to have standards and tests that prepare students to succeed in college and careers. They'll need to recruit and reward excellent teachers and principals. They must have data systems to track students' progress and to identify effective teachers. They must identify their lowest-performing schools and take dramatic action to turn them around.

In addition to the "Race to the Top" competition, the administration

has another $5 billion available to targeted efforts to reform schools.

We have the resources at the federal level to drive reform. Now all of us

need to take this challenge on and work together to reform our schools.

(http://www.ed.gov/blog/2009/07/race-to-the-top-begins/)

There are many assumptions embedded within this text, discourse practice, and social practice. Words such as win, race, and outcompete name values and norms that you must buy into if you are to participate in the race (and who can afford not to?). College is lifted up as a commonsense practice when the reality in today's economic crunch is that many cannot afford the burgeoning costs associated with college. These assumptions represent but one particular set of ideas about how to set education policy or conceptualize reform. In terms of school reform in Duncan's comments, teacher effectiveness is bound with student progress with little or no regard for the challenges that states like California are currently facing. Also, the call to identify "lowestperforming schools and take dramatic action to turn them around" implies a very top heavy approach to school reform. Decades of school reform literature makes explicit that lasting school change is an inside out process. Fullan (2001) observed, "Educational change is technically simple and socially complex" (p. 69). The perception that children and schools can be "turned" is simplistic. Instead, struggling schools must be given support that meets them where they are in their development and guides them forward with urgency and accelerated learning toward equity and ever narrowing achievement gaps.

While California did compete for funds for the "Race to the Top," the state did not receive support in the first of two rounds of applications. As often happens when demonstrating a perceived consensus is important for approval, finger pointing increases and scope of vision decreases. A reporter from the San Francisco Gate (March 6, 2010) reported:

> One thing that definitely went wrong [with California's "Race to the Top" application for funds] was the attitude of the state teachers' unions. Union leaders fought the reform legislation at every turn and managed to water down the [application] package that eventually passed in January. Marty Hittelman, president of the California Federation of Teachers, even said he wasn't sorry that California lost the first round. And in part because of these kinds of feuds within the education community, lots of California school districts opted out of participation in Race to the Top. In Kentucky, every single school district signed on.

The tenor of this text is blame—frustration with losing the first round of the "race." While Hittelman is blasted for not being sorry that California lost the first round, the unwritten text is why he wasn't sorry. Were the differences of opinion really "feuds within the education community"? Were they perhaps deeper, more experienced commitments to lines that he was not willing to cross

in terms of what is best for children and their learning? Did the compromises required to be successful in this application mean a bigger compromise that some students would excel while others would be further pushed to the margin? Recognizing the exercise of power that is embedded with federal funding is important. Most grant-funded activities require applicants to endorse the funder's assumptions as the point of departure and provide limited flexibility for one's own agenda or context. These are the larger issues that are important to unpack in both written and unwritten texts present in all federal policy documents and subsequent state and local responses. These difficult locales are where questions of power and authority lie waiting to be pulled apart and put back together again in more equitable and just ways.

Discussion

Extending critical analyses of policy to include explanations of how political power constructs and is constructed by larger social practices is an important process because policy is constitutive. It serves not only to distribute, but to mandate such ideals across a much larger forum—the educational institution and its members. This is particularly important as we consider larger social issues and trend data reflecting social injustices linked with literacy education, children and families of poverty, and second language learners. As we have seen here, the close analysis of text, discourse practice, and social practice through CDA extended by Bernstein's theory of relationships makes explicit the ways in which text, discourse practice, and social practice come together to foster social change. Across all three of these dimensions was the drive to create consensus and restrict potential resistance.

Typical to information structures, we saw in California's policies the ways in which text was structured to ensure particular interpretations. In the close analysis of particular texts in context, we saw how informational units were structured so that given information preceded the new. Structuring text in this way contributes to what is known as the "good reason" principle (Halliday, 1994, p. 308; see also Habermas, 1996, for a more thorough discussion) and ultimately constitutes the internal resources for structuring the clause as a logical, grounded message. This contributes to the process of naturalization (Fairclough, 1992; 2003). Analyzing this process of naturalization in the structural analysis of text, we understand the ways in which ideologies are embedded in discursive practices and made more effective by becoming naturalized. When this happens, the ideologies and discourse practices attain the status of common sense and become difficult to recognize or push against. Naturalization takes place not only in the structural elements of text, but also in the nonstructural elements. Lexical cohesion through consistent vocabulary or reference to "current and confirmed research" also builds cohesion and helps naturalize a text. Regardless of whether there is intrinsic logic to "current and confirmed research," the ways in which it is promoted and imposed on the educational institution are what Bernstein (2000) called social facts. In transmitting this particular idea about how things are and should be, policymakers are positioning themselves in a rather dictatorial way, which means that others must be more passive and receptive. At the core of this naming of what counts and what does not is a power relation between dominant and passive participants, thus influencing principles of selection.

As elected and appointed officials force changes in the terms that we use, the focus of our attention changes, creating similar conversations among larger populations and thus altering what is perceived as normal. By doing this, resistant readings of the policy are reduced by way of anchoring new and often vague terms against specific bodies of research, proclaimed experts, and instructional materials. In changing which instructional resources are to be made available and prohibited, we not only further influence what practices and conversations are likely to take place, but also the potential content and pedagogical knowledge made available to teachers. The implications of such positioning mean that such discourse methods actually gather steam from the people being systematically eliminated from them in the first place. Also important is that the readers contribute to this unknowingly because the text is structured to be seamless and naturalized. Again, this ultimately creates a distraction from the larger social issues that are at the root of imbalances of power and representation.

Understanding the shift in California's system of educational decision making in power (CDE to SBE), we must also look at how the ideologies and agendas represented by influential players were advanced both within the policymaking forum and among the larger public. Studying the relationship between power and ideology in this way extends Fairclough's attention to text and context via CDA. "Particular interpretive principles come to be associated in a naturalized way with particular discourse types, and such linkages are worth investigating for the light they shed on the important ideological functions of coherence in interpellating subjects" (Fairclough, 1992, p. 84).

The presence of the NICHD research in these policy development forums, as well as the ways in which it is naturalized and effectively distributed, cannot be ignored. It represents a body of research that was hand picked by the federal government and policymakers, which many have been passively selected as the authoritative source on reading and reading instruction. Influential reviews (sometimes including second- and third-generation published research) as well as the physical presence of NICHD researchers and staff members in legislative sessions have influenced how reading has come to be defined and taught via legislation in California.

As reflexive and critical discourse analysts, we must make decisions about how to interpret, describe, and explain texts, discourse practices, and social practices. Bringing Bernstein's pedagogic device to CDA offers us the opportunity to understand how text, discourse practice, and social practice represent the elements of social analyses that Fairclough highlighted (i.e., social matrix, orders of discourse, and the ideological and political effects of discourse). In placing text and discourse practice in relation to one another in this way, we come to see not only the function of language in change, but also the social network that underlies the degree of success or failure to impact change that language and discourse practices can have.

Concluding

Thoughts Political discourse, by its very nature, is designed to influence people's representations of cultural norms and the principles of classification which underlie them. "The power of political discourse depends upon its capacity to constitute and mobilize those social forces that are capable of carrying into reality its promises of a new reality, in its very formulation of this new reality" (Fairclough, 1995a, p. 182). Throughout this analysis we have used critical discourse analysis to make sense of reading policy in public schools. This analysis of California policy between 1995 and 1997 makes explicit the ways in which policy is constitutive and can have a lasting impact reaching social systems far and wide. It presents specific examples of cruces for analysts of educational policy to examine to identify the deeper social practices at hand. As a result, we are left with urgent questions for continued critical analysis: What are the new realities presented in today's policies? What principles of classification are being defined, mandated, and used across diverse populations with complex and varying needs? Here we see that there are procedural changes that take place with policy implementation (i.e., reading curriculum and policy) but that there are also social changes that require close analysis if we are to truly understand the social practices and the relationship between instructional and regulative discourses (Woodside-Jiron & Gehsmann, 2009). In taking a critical approach to policy analysis in this way we are better equipped to understand the intended and unintended consequences of policy-induced change in schools. Schools are democratic institutions and as such require reorienting of our means of policy inquiry (Fischer, 2009). Critical discourse analysis offers one such means of doing so with its multidimensional approach to both inquiry and analysis.

Fundamental to critical policy analysis is the explicit analysis of the process of naturalization in policy development, policy communication, and policy implementation. This is especially important because the procedures and practices may be politically and ideologically invested and because these procedures and practices position people in specific ways. In this naturalization processes or shaping of cultural models, some norms are brought to the center and others are pushed to the margin. In the case of policymaking around reading in education, select policy players and policy informants took center stage while parents, teachers, administrators, taxpayers, and students were pushed to the margin. How people participate in the language and power of policy shapes their surrounding social structures, social relations, and agendas. Often this is an invisible process that strengthens the language, power, and participation processes. This is particularly problematic when participating in this way continues to push some people to the margin and silence them from the conversation. Such hegemonic processes must be not only brought to light, but aggressively pushed against and restructured. As researchers and leaders in education, it is essential that we become better at communicating such practices to the larger public being supplied with these crafted consensuses around such constructs as scientific research, reading crisis, and one-size-fits-all solutions like systematic, explicit instruction. Such balances of power and orders of discourse have serious implications. Such manipulative (discursive) practices shape our children and their literacy learning experiences. CDA as a framework for analyzing power and cultural models offers a promising means to better understand the links between policy and those who experience policy firsthand and offers a social lens for change.

Notes

(1)   The authorization for the program was automatically extended for one additional fiscal year (through FY 2008) under section 422(a) of the General Education Provisions Act (GEPA) (20 U.S.C. § 1226a(a)) but at a significantly lower rate.

(2)   This period of change in California is particularly illustrative of this process given the presentation of popular media and political power at that time. Further still, the unusual size of the state and its subsequent impact on the larger educational publishing industry is signifi cant.

(3)   This later extended to the federal level as NCLB legislation linked increased funding to "scientifically proven methods of reading instruc-tion" (NCLB, 2003, p. 2).

(4)   Note that these have been broken into information units (Halliday, 1994).

(5)   Here the provisions of this section refers to the fundamental skill fur-ther defined as "systematic, explicit phonics, spelling, and basic com-putational skills."

(6)   It is interesting that these terms are all present in G. Reid Lyon's testi-mony before the Assembly Education Committee Hearing on Reading on May 8, 1996.

(7)   At the national level, we see this being done through the Congres-

sionally mandated review of research by the National Reading Panel. Their review included a restrictive screening process by which whole bodies of research were systematically eliminated.

(8)   Baldwin referenced this report as if looking forward to it in a policy decision in the May 1996 hearing.

LOCATING THE ROLE OF THE CRITICAL DISCOURSE ANALYST

Historically, Critical Discourse Analysis (CDA) first involved analysis of language and its ideological echoes in public speeches and platforms, with the analyst functioning as a conduit between the public and the ideologies conveyed through language by public office holders. For example, Norman Fairclough, a foundational author of both uses and methodological structures of CDA, has used CDA (2000) to explore the neoliberal ideologies enacted through public speeches by British Prime Minister Margaret Thatcher and United States President Ronald Reagan. In uses such as these, the direct interface between the analyst and the speaker is limited, with the analyst examining language that was readily available to and heard by others and publishing the analysis to academic and public audiences.

Across the use of CDA in educational research, two trends have emerged. First is a trend largely in keeping, relationally speaking, with CDA's first analyses of public speech, in the form of critical policy analysis using CDA to explore educational policies' ideologies and positions (e.g., Dworin & Bomer, 2008; Jones, 2009; Liasidou, 2008; Stevens, 2003). A second trend is characterized by CDA used in situations where the researcher and the speaker are in close relational proximity to each other, with the analyst working with and/or researching teachers, students, and parents' uses of language (e.g., Rogers & Mosley, 2008; Sieg, 2008; Tuten, 2007). This proximity brings to bear altogether different questions of power and responsibility, particularly pressing for researchers and study participants.

Some of the questions instigated by an up-close use of CDA include: What responsibilities and roles do educational researchers using CDA hold in school settings? How does the public intellectual, who holds the explicit role of analysis and exploration of ideologies, work in settings where the researcher and participant work together closely? How does this role of the public intellectual fluctuate within structured and informal relationships where power slips and glides across interactions? In these types of settings, what promise is held by CDA as both an exploration of potentially harmful discourses and social relations and as potentially transformative of those social practices?

These questions are not unique to CDA but carry with them a disturbingly opportunistic legacy of educational research in school settings. Educational research has been conducted, published and fed academic knowledge that has diminutized and then pathologized 'at-risk' populations (Stevens, 2009). This trend emanates not from malicious intents but more so of a mismatch between the pursuit of 'scientific' and objective knowledge and a more humanistic and engaged praxis (Freire, 1970; Bartolome, 1994). Similarly, some educational research, particularly qualitative research that is conducted in classrooms and schools, has a tendency of being less than forthright about intents (Newkirk, 1996). Again, this mismatch can be mapped to the intents of academic pursuits and the responsibility researchers have to participants, not just to academic publishing. Critical inquiry into language holds both the potential to re-enact these opportunistic trends and the possibility to recraft the presence and use of critical language awareness in educational research.

In this chapter, I draw upon my own uses of CDA and critical linguistics from educational praxis and research settings to explore these questions and the potential possibilities of shared critical discussions about language and ideology in educational settings. In particular, I describe and analyze my uses of CDA as a researcher with teachers. In relation to the data I present here, I held various institutional positions as a literacy specialist, a co-teacher, and a researcher. Common to these positions was my explicit interest in the ways that language practices can be better understood to shed light on the dynamics of power and identity in educational spaces. However, as I moved from literacy specialist and collaborator to researcher and critical discourse analyst, my dialogic exchanges with teachers became more complicated, contested, and, arguably, better. In this chapter, I share some of these conversations and what they portend for educational researchers using critical linguistic approaches in the field. In particular, I articulate two key concepts crucial to the exploration of this role: reflexivity and answerability.

From the fields of sociology and psychology, reflexivity is defined as an act of self-reference where examination or action bends back on itself, refers to, and affects the entity instigating the action. Social theorist Margaret Archer (2007) refers to reflexivity as "the regular exercise of the mental ability, shared by all normal people, to consider themselves in relation to their social contexts and vice versa" (p. 11). Archer elaborates upon this definition to describe the internal conversations that humans have with themselves, explaining, justifying, interrogating themselves and others in the social world. Thus, as we bring CDA into the field and use it in direct action with participants, we engage in acts of reflexivity, bring internal conversations into the realm of the interpersonal, with potential affects on all participants, including ourselves.

In moving internal conversations into the realm of the spoken and interpersonal and prompting this shift, we also engage in dialogic exchanges with research participants never broached by analysts of Thatcher's speeches. These interpersonal exchanges hold, as with any dialogic exchange, the promise and portend of answering each others' invitations to engage, what philosopher and semiotician Mikhael Bakhtin called answerability (1990). Bakhtin described every utterance as answerable, as it is part of a dialogue with another who is part of our dialogic exchange, an interlocutor. Those are the rules of illocutionary discourse but interlocutors feel those moments of dialogic promises and responsibilities to respond in immediate and subsequent exchanges. In that sense, conducting CDA in schools with/on participants brings to bear questions of answerability that are different in analyses conducted from afar. In the following, I share my research approach, particularly the steps in my methodology that magnified questions of reflexivity and answerability.

Shifting roles as interlocutor

In my research approach, I endeavored to share my uses of Critical Discourse Analysis with my participants, to seek their perspectives as ways of better understanding possible interpretations of classroom practices. Using CDA in educational settings with participants, as opposed to on participants, requires high levels of trust and the willingness of both parties to engage in an exploration of plausible descriptions and interpretations of discourse. In the data that I present, I had different shared sets of inquiry stances with the participants over time. The work here was drawn from my dual relationship as a researcher and literacy specialist working with a sixth-grade science teacher. Within the study, I paid attention to, and the participants paid differential attention, to the ways that language enacted ideologies.

Working as a Literacy Specialist

When I was a literacy specialist working at a middle school, I worked primarily with the school's content area teachers, modeling effective literacy strategies and lessons in their classrooms and mentoring their use of the literacy practices. Within that middle school context, I worked with all of the school's teachers, and my goal was to support how language and literacy were leveraged and used within their content area teaching. With other teachers in the school, there was a shared interest in developing and using metalanguage to identify how language, both semantically and syntactically, represents worldviews (Halliday, 1985). With some teachers, these exchanges were closely connected to a textcentered literacy strategy used to engage students with content, and the conversations that I examine in this chapter draw from such a collaboration.

Throughout my work as a literacy specialist and transitioning into my doctoral research, collected at the same school, I worked with Dawn Scolari (pseudonym), an experienced sixth-grade life science teacher. Dawn was a thoroughly pragmatic teacher, interested in her students achieving well on district and state assessments. Dawn was the science department's chairperson, a veteran teacher with 15 years' experience at the time of our pedagogical and research collaboration, and she held the reputation of a teacher who covered well her Earth Science curriculum. When I was a literacy specialist assigned to the school where Dawn worked, our interactions typically went something like following:

Dawn: Hey, Lisa, that vocab strategy worked really well the rest of the day. The kids seemed to like it a lot.

Lisa: Great. They should be used to adding the pictures and sentences, since

we already practiced that with the vocab cards.

Dawn: Mmhmm. I'll save some samples so you can see their work.

Lisa: OK, cool. Hey, I've got another strategy that has the kids do the same thing, except they take more of the lead in picking words they don't know well.

Dawn: Yeah?

Lisa: Yeah. I'll drop a copy in your box. And maybe I can come back in to demo it.

Dawn: Sounds good. See you later.

What is superficially a simple exchange about both past and present interactions contains nuances of our different educational roles. From a discourse analysis view (Gee, 1996) of this exchange, there are clearly defined differentiations in our roles, although we share a few key identity kit aspects being female and teachers at the same middle school. Another view of the interaction, with some critical discourse analysis notations, shows more clearly the shades of distinction between our roles. The italicized comments are notes about the dialogic positions taken up within the exchange. The underlined text shows the style choices, the particular language choices to position the speaker, and the italicized text shows the genre, or mode of interaction taken up in the exchange.

Dawn: Hey, Lisa, that vocab strategy worked really well the rest of the day.

The kids seemed to like it a lot. Review, Report of last interaction and reference to student response as indicator of success.

Lisa: Great. They [the students] should be used to adding the pictures and sentences, since we already practiced that with the vocab cards. Confirmation

of report and connection to previous work conducted. Use of we to promote collaborative stance

Dawn: Mmhmm. I'll save some samples so you can see their work. Offer of access to the students' work to an outsider. Reference to student work as another source of support.

Lisa: OK, cool. Hey, I've got another strategy that has the kids do the same

thing, except they take more of the lead in picking words they don't know well. Offer of similar activity follow-up, with slight modification.

Working within the style of what has already occurred in the collaboration

Dawn: Yeah? Expression of interest.

Lisa: Yeah. I'll drop a copy in your box. And maybe I can come back in to demo it. Reiteration of follow-up and offer for assistance.

Dawn: Sounds good. See you later.

Within our interaction between literacy specialist and classroom teacher, Dawn assumed the role of reporting back to me, and I used modalities such as maybe to offer support for her report and for offering an additional team teaching situation while resisting directives and other strongly worded viewpoints.

As the literacy specialist for the school, I was still a teacher on the same professional level as Dawn, but also responsible for mentoring and coaching teachers in their literacy practices. This was a challenge in several ways: being younger yet being in the role of a coach when not all the teachers in the school felt they wanted a coach. My professional role was to mentor them, ideally through team teaching in their classrooms, and nurture a professional learning community. I was responsible for mentoring but beholden to the teachers to allow me access to their practices, and in some cases, to their beliefs about teaching and learning through language.

During one year of my doctoral work, I resigned from my literacy specialist role in the school and focused full time on graduate studies, with emphasis on gathering empirical data, at this same school, about the shape of literacy practices in science teaching. Again, I appealed to the collaborative generosity of colleagues to provide me access to their classrooms and pedagogical practices and beliefs. Certainly throughout my roles as a literacy specialist and through the initial months I came back to the school as a researcher, Dawn and I did not necessarily share the same critical theoretical perspective on language. Our respective roles of classroom teacher and literacy specialist were more closely knitted to discourses of what works, what is effective, for classroom learning of science content. Our genre of conversation had tended to revolve around planning and reviewing classroom strategies, but stylistically our linguistic choices in terms of words and syntax reflected an experienced classroom teacher and a younger, academically leaning specialist.

The patterns of discourse are particularly notable in my appropriation of Dawn's pragmatic view of teaching and learning (what works), in a way to establish intersubjectivity and somewhat shared understandings. Subtext to this discussion was the more tenuous relationships of mentor and learner, more experienced and less experienced teacher, older and younger women. In our discussions, these roles and identities were backgrounded and our exchanges more cleanly reflected the roles of classroom teacher and literacy specialist.

Working as a Researcher

However, these dimensions of subjectivity (Stevens, 2005), or more accurately their surface performances, were further complicated when Dawn participated in a year-long professional development project centered on content area literacy, which I facilitated. The dimensions were further deepened and transformed in the immediate when I returned to Dawn's classroom as a researcher using ethnographic and discourse analysis to study secondary science teachers' beliefs and practices about literacy.

As a literacy researcher, and one using CDA (Fairclough, 1989, 1992) as a framework and methodology, I navigated different territory with Dawn than I had as a literacy specialist. I chose to use CDA as a way to analyze how language.was reflection and enacting ideologies and beliefs within the science classroom. This stance was, and continues to be for me, informed by sociological views of literacy and education (Bourdieu, 1991; Luke, 2008).

However, this was a different role than the one I held as literacy specialist with some of the school's teachers, including Dawn. Visiting her classroom on a weekly basis for 1 year, I found the role of the critical discourse analyst in an educational setting to be much more complex, tentative, rewarding, revealing, and fraught with confrontation than that of a literacy specialist whose primary concern was access to teachers' classroom. As I used CDA as a set of tools to examine the relationship between knowledge, power, and identity in her science classroom, I also began to share my findings and perspectives with Dawn. I shared my field notes, transcriptions of interviews, and first sets of analyses not in an effort to triangulate or arrive at a shared truth, but rather, to be explicit about the research, to put it "on the stage" (Anfara, Brown, & Mangione, 2002, p. 28). In this sense, CDA became a tool for discussions about her classroom, the school context, and society. Dawn and I shared interactions that touched on much deeper issues than we had previously, including our differing positions and epistemologies as educators. These conversations, in which we used a metalanguage to talk about the discursive and ideological choices made by both Dawn and myself, also brought forth an opportunity to explore the potentially transformative nature of CDA. Although the precise use of the term critical in this setting evokes, for me, the dialectical relationship between language processes and social worlds, it also holds in a Freirian sense the possibility of analyzing and exploring discourse as a mediational tactic to understanding and transforming these social relations. It is within that definition that CDA holds great promise to be reflexive and answerable to those who use it.

As Dawn and I discussed my CDA of her practice, I found that our interactions marked a different sort of dialogic process around the ideologies of education, literacy, and young people. In other words, it was only through sharing the CDA and more so, sharing a common metalanguage, that we were able to see the patterns in our talk and interactions and engage, often disagreeing, about those patterns and what they meant.

The Research Methodologies

For the discourse analysis, I used Gee's (1996) explication of social linguistics and discourses, as well as Fairclough's (1989, 1992) CDA as both frameworks and methodologies. From the perspective of these frameworks, language works to construct us as much as we use language to construct possible worlds (Foucault, 1999). Related, language both embodies and constructs ideologies (Fairclough, chap. 6, this volume). However, for a study examining literacy practices and beliefs in a largely textually mediated setting, CDA provided an appropriate perspective and methodology. Further, my desire to address close dialectic between language and social relations necessitated the critical perspective that Fairclough's (1989) work lent.

Working with these frameworks, I positioned the form and function of language in relation to Dawn's literacy practices. Using Fairclough's orders of discourse (Fairclough, chap. 10, this volume), I analyzed the study participants' words, including Dawn's during class and interviews for the genres, discourses, and styles used to create and constrict literate possibilities for their students.

I transcribed and analyzed classroom and out-of-classroom discussions between myself and the study participants for elements of (a) genre, the loosely configured relations typically associated with a type of exchange; (b) discourse, the systematic clusters of themes; and (c), style, the ways of being taken up within a dialogic exchange. In analyzing the transcripts shared in this chapter, I paid particular attention to the ways in which style choices complicated the genres of research and pedagogical conversations.

In the study, I used these analyses to draw conclusions about the various societal discourses, or clusters of ideologies (Gee, 1996), about adolescents and literacy that were operationalized in classroom practices. The overall purpose of these approaches was to provide a continual mediation between interpersonal uses of language and its reflection and creation of social relations. During the weekly classroom visits, participant observation techniques (Merriam, 1998) were used to document the literacy activities in the classroom. I sat in the back portion of the room and recorded field notes on a computer, noting the classroom environs, activities, physical factors, and particularly the discourses during the class sessions. After the field notes were collected, I immediately transcribed them all into detailed descriptions. Additionally, class sessions were audiotaped, occasionally videotaped, and later transcribed for discourse analysis.

Sharing the Analyses

Each week I created a one-page summary of my observations and analyses and sent it to Dawn. These one-page summaries were first developed to gain feedback from Dawn and ultimately became one of the key tools used to mediate our discussions about her beliefs and practices and my discourse analysis. These one-page summaries became pivotal because they served as the initial launch pads for the conversations that Dawn and I had about my analyses of her literacy practices.

Interviews—both structured and unstructured—were conducted to inquire about specific literacy practices, general notions of literacy in the content classroom, and perceptions of the staff development project and its components. Unstructured interviews, which occurred primarily directly before and after each classroom observation, were noted using field notes and followed the same transcription process as the observation field notes. At first, I shared the one-page summaries of interviews and observations out of advice from another qualitative researcher and to be somewhat consistent with the open and forthright relationship that Dawn and I had known as colleagues working in the same school. However, both of these premises for sharing back qualitative notes proved remarkably shallow for navigating the issues of answerability and reflexivity that surfaced.

Although I knew Dawn would not restrict me from making my own analyses and to a certain extent could not, I was also relatively certain that I would not gain validation in the form of a member check, as is sometimes sought from participants in ethnographic studies. In many cases, member checks are used as a form of triangulation, a method of ensuring validity of the study. In fact, since the publication of the first edition of this edited volume, triangulation has regained once critiqued ground (Blaiki, 1991) as a mechanism of establishing validity across quantitative and qualitative approaches (e.g., Kadushin et al., 2008). However, I was interested in a method that would help me to be explicit about my subjective interpretations in Dawn's classroom, and I hoped that sharing my research would help me move more fluidly between the reflection and realism for which reflexivity calls, and more so, make these subjective analyses more explicit and traceable to others (Luttrell, 2000). Sharing the analyses and findings with Dawn proved complex. Discussions of her discourse and how it often supported what literacy researchers would deem less than desirable ideologies about teaching and learning were difficult topics for discussion. Using discourse analysis revealed much about Dawn's literacy practices and ideologies, but it also raised questions of how to conduct research in ways that are reflexive to all parties and how to be answerable to field participants.

Shifting Roles

Contrasted with the pragmatic identity that I enacted with Dawn as an onsite literacy specialist, my purpose as a critical discourse analyst marked an indelible departure from the seemingly apolitical relationship we had previously cultivated. Although many ethnographic and qualitative researchers (e.g., Merriam, 1998; Spradley, 1980) have documented the challenge of working with research participants in qualitative inquiries, the prospect of entering Dawn's classroom to explicitly investigate local, institutional, and societal enactments of ideology in language required more than just gaining access to her physical classroom. Beyond access to her room, I also needed access to her beliefs and practices, and although analyzing her classroom discourse revealed much about her beliefs, I found it necessary to debrief with Dawn after each classroom observation. These discussions marked the first turn we took toward discourse analyst and participant. After one classroom visit, I was talking with Dawn about the schoolwide emphasis on organization. All students were expected to keep a three-ring binder, with one section for each class. In many classes, teachers did spot checks of the binders, including Dawn. She directed her students to number the pages in their binders as a way to make sure that the students all had the same notes, handouts, and worksheets in their science binders. After a classroom observation in November 2000, Dawn and I were discussing this highly structured use of notebooks with her sixth graders:

Lisa: I wonder if this school-wide emphasis on organization can even be somewhat stifling for the students who don't, um, value that way of learning. Dawn: Maybe, but that's what they need to get through the system and be successful, don't you think?

Lisa: Without a doubt. I think what I'd like to question, though, is how the system might be too narrow in how it defines success for all students.

Dawn: Yeah, maybe.

Dawn: (after a pause) But that is the system we're working on, and that is what these kids need for college, isn't it?

Lisa: Yeah, to a certain extent, but also to a certain extent not, 'cause I'm not sure this is the one and best way of getting there. Does that make sense?

Dawn: Um, not really. Until they develop their own systems of organizing their stuff, they need to be shown how to do it.

Within this exchange, Dawn and I are making an explicit turn in our previous patterns of discussion of 'what works,' beginning to discusses the underlying purposes and functions of classroom practices like maintaining a uniformly organized binder. In this conversation, I make judicious use of modalities (Halliday, 1985)—words and phrases like I wonder, I'd like to, might, if, I'm not sure, and does that make sense. These are all modalities used to soften my stance that the monochromatic practice of organizing information prioritized certain types and stances towards knowledge. The use of these modalities also echoes a mismatch between my discourses as an emerging researcher using sociological lenses and that of both my former role as a literacy specialist and Dawn's epistemological stance as a science teacher. This mismatch is on the surface in this conversation across all of those subjectivities. Of note here also is the contrast between this conversation and the conversation at the start of the chapter, where I used some but far fewer modalities, and my and Dawn's style choices matched more closely.

The genre of our conversation had also shifted significantly, in that we were no longer working within the genre of evaluating a classroom strategy and making room for another one. In the latter conversation, our genre shifted significantly to discussing not what works but more so for what purposes and intents, and what the side effects might be of classroom strategies that work more so to maintain order than to result in learning. As we moved into this genre, I made some stylistic turns in how I interacted, most notably through the markedly increased use of modalities as I etched out a different theoretical stance on the binders than Dawn. One interpretation of my usage of these modalities is that as a linguistic researcher, I am at once analytical of the discourse but also interested in opening possibilities for conversation around alternative views. Looking back, I used these modalities both to strive for a dialogic exchange and out of my own hesitations at taking up considerable representational power and not yet fully grasping how to name and claim my own subjectivities within the study as a first step, and as next and more important steps, how to share findings in ways that make the dialogue accessible and meaningful for all involved. In short, how to make it answerable. When I am responding from an overly academic style—one that stems from a critical orientation—I am enacting an answerability that is not a shared order of discourse between myself and Dawn. This, then, undercuts the potential for shifts in reflexivity, or at least for those shifts to be part of the shared language and shared discourses of the interlocutors. It is actually with the refractive view that CDA provides of this interaction that I was able to discern an increase in modalities on my part. I might have suspected that, due to the long-range nature of my relationship with Dawn, I would be more forthright and less guarded about my viewpoints, but the analysis done with CDA shows just the opposite. Although other grounded theories and discourse analyses might offer insights into the conversational pattern, CDA helps provide the metalinguistic tools of style, genre and discourse to highlight this compelling example of the mismatch in discourses across exchanges over time. What is also of note is Dawn's ease and willingness to disagree with me and, more largely construed, my then affiliation with a university. It may seem probable that the professional relationship we maintained, as specialist (or grant facilitator, or researcher) and classroom teacher, would reflect the power dynamics in which the specialist (now researcher) maintains a more expert position in educational systems where higher education is positioned as more advanced than secondary contexts. This is far from the case in this and reflects a more nuanced understanding of power than as residing easily within institutional roles. Rather, Dawn's clarity about her philosophy of teaching, her goals for her students, and her identity as a teacher remained relatively fixed over the course of our professional relationship, where my role shifted from literacy specialist and teacher to researcher. For example, although Dawn occupies what could be viewed as a lower status position of being a teacher in juxtaposition to a university-affiliated researcher, she uses phrases like don't you think so and isn't it as openings and markers for me to take up part or all of what she has just said, exerting her own position and authority as a practicing teacher—one who is in the trenches and interacts with theories and research from a practical level. Pursuant to this more fluid and fluctuating power footing is Dawn's strongly established identity as an experienced and successful teacher of 22 years, her position as department chairperson in the school, and our previous relationship in which she chose what she found useful from what I had to offer as a literacy specialist. In short, in the social field of the school, Dawn had a tremendous amount of status, of cultural and social capital. She could take up what she found useful from my offerings as a literacy specialist, focusing on text-based strategies, and leave behind other themes such as critical approaches to language and schooling.

Also relevant to these types of exchanges was the relationship we had formed over several years of working together. Dawn and I enjoyed a high level of mutual professional regard. This was not born out of closely overlapping ideologies, but instead came out of multiple successful partnerships as teachers, working alongside each other with both her sixth graders and the rest of the science faculty. This collegial regard carried over into my presence in her classroom as a critical discourse analyst, but not without some explicit references to the shift in my roles, as is demonstrated in the following excerpt. While Dawn and I were debriefing a typical one-page summary in which I posed some questions about school-sanctioned literacies versus other types of literacies, she and I had the following exchange:

Dawn: What did you mean here by "dichotomy between in-school literacies vs. out-of-school literacies?"

Lisa: Well, what I was getting at was that in all of the stuff that I'm listening to, it's just about the kinds of reading, writing, listening and speaking

that's found in schools. And not so much all of the things that we might do well outside of school, like digital literacies, you know, like the Internet, visual literacies. That kind of stuff.

Dawn: (slight laugh). I must be missing the point here. Aren't we supposed to teach them the stuff they need for school?

Lisa: Well, yes and no. It's kind of like the question that kids ask: When am I ever going to use the stuff that you're teaching today? Um, I guess

what I am saying is that seems to be a pretty valid question in today's world. And I'm, uh, wondering about all the literacies our kids have,

maybe even some of our struggling kids, that don't ever get acknowledged.

Ya know?

Dawn: Hmmmm. I guess you have more time to think about that kind of stuff now, huh?

Lisa: Yeah, that's definitely true. But I was thinking about some of this stuff when I was still here.

In this conversation, Dawn and I are again providing different interpretations to the core purpose of schooling, and the purpose of literacy and language pedagogy within that purpose. Coupled with this difference in viewpoint is Dawn's interpretation that I bring up these observations at this juncture in my professional trajectory because, as a doctoral student, I must have more time for these observations. These points are expressed both explicitly through the content that is discussed but also through stylistic choices made by both of us. In this exchange, we find the same types of modalities used by me and the same types of attempts for shared understandings from Dawn. Yet what is perhaps most compelling is Dawn's mention of the shift in my role from teacher to researcher with far more flexibility with time than the typical teacher enjoys. Dawn's message is spot on and speaks strongly to the institutional roles and responsibilities that differ strongly from school to university. From a classroom teacher's

perspective, researchers and discourse analysts obviously enjoy great luxuries of time to review myriad nuances of classrooms, including language, the use of which seems as automatic as the intake of oxygen. Therefore, the development and use of a metalanguage for the analysis of something so automatic and pervasive can seem frivolous and indulgent. It was out of this perception of discourse analysis as something for academics, Dawn's curiosity, and the promise of Critical Discourse Analysis as transformative (Fairclough, 1989) that I began to share more of my discourse analysis with her. What is most compelling to me here is Dawn's gradual uptake of the metalanguage used in my analysis. Antithetically, although Dawn quite cogently levels an implicit critique of the luxury of discourse analysis, she is able to do so from the vantage of acquiring and learning some of those very skills and processes. In other words, Dawn engages in a conversation about the types of literacies that are sanctioned by school, a conversation spun into motion from the presence of a researcher, and then is able to critique the conversation for its dabbling into less pressing matters, like out of school literacy practices. This instance gives a point of reflection on the role of learning in these interactions. First, drawing from Gee's (1996) work, we must first try to distinguish between learning and acquisition in this situation. I spoke explicitly to Dawn about the methodologies I was using, but we also began to use terms like literacies, metalanguage, sanction, and power in our conversations. In this way, we can see nuances of both acquisitions (through use) and learning (through explicit explanation) of this metalanguage. As we gradually began to share a metalanguage, Dawn and I were able to discuss the connections that I was making between some of her discourses and the social relations in her classroom and in broader contexts, as seen in the following example about Dawn's discourse about young people. Within these exchanges, though, my reflexivity went through unexpected and important challenges. I needed to be answerable to Dawn's critique of my shifting role, and more so, to her critique of the relevancy of academic research to classroom practice, a consistent discourse across many of our conversations. I found it to be fairly easy to engage with these her in instances where we negotiated differing interpretations, but when there was a stronger disconnect between worldviews, as with our views of adolescents, our exchanges demonstrated stronger gaps in answerability and engagement.

Differing perspectives on youth

The discourse of adolescent as bundle of raging hormones was readily apparent in Dawn's instruction. A large and pervasive societal discourse of youth characterizes them as bundles of raging hormones, virtually devoid of rational thought, as they are at the will of their changing physiologies. This discourse is present not only as a commonly held notion, but also goes largely unchallenged in educational settings (Finders, 1998; Lesko, 2001). Ascribing to this notion that adolescence is a life stage that amounts to little more than a hormonally induced confusion contains common sense, almost teleological, implications for instruction, including positioning the teacher as agent of control in the classroom, choosing activities that allow for minimal student interaction, and using unidirectional, didactic instructional strategies. In keeping with the purposes of CDA and also stemming from a sociological analysis, I spent time in the study participants' classrooms, noting how their conceptions of youth were enacted in their classroom interactions. Using the discourse analysis to note turn-taking patterns, the overwhelming predominance of Dawn's turn taking (Fairclough, 1989) and the series of unidirectional directives underscores Dawn's consistent role as decision maker in her classroom. The discourse is also apparent in the highly structured routine and formatting that her students followed. There was little or no room for students' individual identities to have voice in her classroom, the implication perhaps being that as bundles of raging hormones the adolescents had little sense of identity to offer; this stance was expressed in her classroom interactions and in our conversations about her teaching, as seen in the last conversation analyzed in this chapter. In conversations about teaching sixth graders, Dawn often referred to her duty to train them, including showing them how to organize their notebooks according to her system and teaching them how to behave in middle and high school classrooms. Expected behaviors included only speaking during the course of a lesson and only after raising their hands, asking the teacher only those questions deemed by the teacher pertinent to the daily lessons, and following teacher-given directions (Field notes, 3/26/00, 4/ 15/00, 8/28/00, and 10/12/00). During an interview in March 2000, Dawn also used several metaphors that described the characteristics of her sixth graders as animals:

Dawn: It takes me a good month or two to just rein them in.Lisa: Um, can you tell me a little more of what you mean by that?

Dawn: Well, you know, they come not knowing anything, not how to organize their backpacks, what forms to use, where the bathroom is (laughter), anything!

Lisa: So, they have to be reined in to learn those things?

Dawn: Exactly. I get them under control, herded up, and then we get onto the business of learning, reading and writing.

In my summaries of observations and interviews such as these, I included comments about the pervasive discourse regarding young people. For these analyses, I paid particular attention to the content in Dawn's talk, such as the need for organization, the imperative to discipline, and an ethos of business. As Dawn reviewed her talk, she became increasingly aware of her language choices that, in turn, prompted her interest in the relationship between her discourse and classroom interactions. She was alternately bothered by and defensive of her characterization of young people as overly hormone-driven. When she and I sat down to review the last excerpt, we had the following conversation:

Dawn: Geez. That seems kind of bad, doesn't it?

Lisa: What do you think? Is it bad to talk about kids that way?

Dawn: Well, it seems harmless enough and pretty accurate, if you watch them for a while, but what's bugging me is that you think that there's a link between how I teach and how I view them.

Lisa: Yeah, I think so.

Dawn: So what's the alternative?

Lisa: Well, if you were teaching a group of adults, would you do things in the same way?

Dawn: No, but I wouldn't have to.

Lisa: Right. So. There seems to be a kind of link between seeing adolescents as kind of out of control and how you teach them. Does that make sense?

Dawn: It does, but the more I think about it, the more I'm sure that if I didn't do it this way, it would be chaos. Just look at Brian [a seventh-grade Earth Science teacher down the hall from Dawn]. His kids are totally out of control.

Lisa: And do you think that's because he thinks about adolescents differently that you do?

Dawn: I think it's because he doesn't know how to control them.

Through debriefing discussions such as this, Dawn and I figured out quickly that we could agree implicitly that her language and actions in her classroom communicated certain viewpoints, and this could be plausibly certain. However, we could also agree and disagree to varying extents, and from instant to instant, as to how appropriate and justified these viewpoints were for the benefit of the sixth graders and to what extent these viewpoints reflected, rejected, and/or transformed dominant ideologies about youth, schooling, and literacy. In this way, Dawn and I enjoyed a joint investigation into the highly complex and layered nature of discourses and explored multiple interpretations. We developed a "self-consciousness about the rootedness of discourse" (Fairclough, 1989, p. 167). In this sense, the one-page summaries and debriefing conversations never accomplished the goal of triangulating the analysis—a misapplied notion from the irreconcilable viewpoint of quantitative research. Instead these conversations served to textualize my analysis and make me answerable to Dawn's practitioner-based responses to my analyses. The conversations also served to reconstruct the texts, breaking from a potentially nihilistic cycle in which texts are only deconstructed without reconstruction or revisioning of alternate texts. Sharing and talking about the discourse with Dawn also created space for different variations on our roles, more appropriately wrestling with and exploring various hybrid forms of representation and identity (Luke, 2002).

Last, this example also points to the potentially transformative promise of CDA in educational settings. As Dawn and I used a shared metalanguage to discuss the flows between language and ideologies, Dawn showed an impermanent awareness of the connections between some of her language choices and the social relations in her classrooms. Although there is no empirical evidence in this study as to whether this resulted in change in Dawn's practice, such an investigation might be too narrow to fully engage the interpretive and symbolic analysis that a focus on discourse potentially holds (Fairclough, 1989). The use of CDA holds great promise as a mediational tactic to be used in educational settings, but should not be saddled with teleological transformative responsibilities because no unilateral and foregone connection exists between discourses and social worlds. Instead public intellectuals can look to CDA as a way to mediate their responsibilities to be an agent of social and political justice (Said, 1996), to help them to be answerable to their interlocutors and to engage in regular reflexivity about the responsibility and relevancy of their research. Because the use of CDA has largely occurred outside of direct contact with the participants, using this framework and methodology in educational settings with participants requires deep consideration of the analyst's responsibilities.

How then should critical discourse analysts proceed in working with research participants? From my experiences with Dawn and other teachers, I have come to believe that the answer to this lies within the explicit self-naming of the analyst's perspectives and subjectivities (reflexivity) and, in a collaborative stance, one that allows for mediation and negotiation of power and knowledge from the onset by both the researcher and participant. This collaboration was marked by both participants being willing to be explicit about their beliefs and, in fact, staying in conversations where their beliefs were challenged and probed by the other person. Over the time of the research project, our collaboration opened the door to a shared inquiry into teaching and learning, and the discourse analysis was a deepened aspect of this pattern. In that we held shared ground of purpose. However, as my purpose in her classroom and with her shifted to one of more research colleague than teaching colleague, our exchanges reflected more areas of disconnect and more explicit negotiations of agency and power, reflected in language choices. These language choices also point to areas of answerability that are far from quickly resolved.answerability that are far from quickly resolved.

The conversation we had about Dawn's appropriation of a dominant discourse about adolescents made me, and probably Dawn, uncomfortable. At the time, I misjudged my discomfort to be from feeling that I needed to objectively justify my analysis. On reflection, I now believe the reason for my uneasiness was a nagging realization that I was perhaps revealing to Dawn an aspect of her discourse and ideology that served a real and possibly justified purpose in her identity kit as a teacher. I was hesitant that I was asking her to question an aspect of her ideology that she did not want to question—and what right did I have to do that? In those moments, I felt uncomfortably like I had somehow stepped into the role of a psychoanalyst rather than a critical discourse analyst working in education. This slip, in essence, was one of answerability. I was working and researching from a stance where my research answerability was held accountable not by Dawn but by the doctoral committee that would approve my dissertation. From that realm of answerability, it was appropriate and expected for me to elucidate my findings of ideologies enacted through classroom practice. However, sharing research, let alone conducting research with participants, begs a wholly different answerability.

Often discourse analysts avoid this complication by working with the discourse of people far removed from themselves—that of politicians, advertisers, and others who do not participate in weekly interactions about the discourse analysis. However, Dawn and I faced this challenge of using her discourse as a refracted image of her beliefs and practices. In so doing, the analyses also engendered refractions of my role as a researcher, my beliefs about education which largely had been previously unspoken to Dawn, and my practices as a professional educator who valued and continues to value work with teachers in school settings. Just as I was cautious about exposing aspects of Dawn's discourse and ideology to her, I was equally hesitant about superimposing a false sense of knowledge of what was acceptable to share with her and what was not. Because of Dawn's confidence as a teacher and her experience as a teacherresearcher, I could not arbitrarily decide which discourse analyses to share with her. She needed access to all of them, but she then also assumed the responsibility of determining what she wanted to further understand, what she wanted to question, and what she saw as inconsequential or inaccurate.

The Possibilities of Critical Discourse Analysis to Enhance Learning

The exploration of what theory of learning can be used as a lens to understanding the interactions between a critical discourse analyst and participants in an educational setting must first be cautioned with who is doing the learning. As with our previous interactions, Dawn and I enjoyed a dialogic exchange (Freire, 1970), in which roles of teacher and learner were blurred. Although I offered descriptions, interpretations, and analyses of her discourse, she texturized these reactions with reflections from her vantage point. Also at work in our interactions was a theory of learning about language that differentiates between acquisition and learning (Krashen, 1985; cited in Gee, 1996). Although Dawn had acquired primary and secondary discourses (Gee, 1996) as a teacher, department chairperson, scientist, and middle school educator, our work together engendered a learning situation about language and ideologies. This is not to say that Dawn was learning a discourse. Rather, Dawn—through her interactions with a critical discourse analyst— was learning a metalanguage for discussing how her practices as a sixth-grade life science teacher shaped and were shaped by ideologies. This learning is similar to the aspects of critical literacy that are all but missing from traditional educational notions of reading and literacy found in the United States (Freebody & Luke, 1990). This overall lack of acknowledgment of the highly political, historical, and social nature of language and its role in ideology is part of what made CDA seem at first to Dawn so foreign, and then so compelling once she was able to enter into interpretations.

This type of inquiry is a good first step to making classroom talk a portal for analysis of ideologies and cultural practices in classrooms—one that could be engaged to move beyond the traditionally stultifying ways in which practitioners are shaped and reinforced as rugged individualists with little to no time for reflection (Britzman, 1991; Lortie, 2002). CDA encourages educators to push beyond the surface layers of language and note the ideological work accomplished through language. In this way, researchers and teachers can further understand the ways in which certain cultural models of teaching and learning are reproduced and reinforced and other cultural models ignored. Also the use of the tools and social theories behind CDA by users such as teachers and students would serve the larger and much needed purpose of opening of

CDA as a metalanguage to unpack and name the ways that language enacts ideologies (Luke, 2004).

Engaging educators in this type of analysis is easily done and facilitated using nonidentified samples of discourse and language. However, engendering on this type of inquiry with a teacher's own discourses requires an altogether different type of relationship. The exchanges between Dawn and me proved to be successful from the standpoint of achieving shared understandings and maintaining respect for divergent opinions because of the high level of trust and forthright conversations. This type of relationship must be cultivated and constantly remediated for the various hegemonic underpinnings of such an inquiry. Ample spaces of answerability and reflexivity must be co-negotiated by the discourse analyst and educator. In other words, all parties must be willing to claim their positions, speak from those positions, answer to others' positions, and reflexively re-engage in those roles (Hanrahan, 2006). In our situation, Dawn and I achieved those spaces by eventually blurring the lines between who was doing analysis. As Dawn and I furthered our interactions, she appropriated the language of discourse analysis and was able, at times, to coincide with my "read" of her discourse and at other times to challenge it.

The process provided myself and Dawn with opportunities to learn about language, opening up spaces for all-too-rare instances of analytic and ideological awareness. Dawn and I engaged in many conversations in which we were refracting the discourses used in her classroom, used in teacher education, and used in the school and district. We were in essence looking back on captured moments in time. Rather than characterize these backward looks as reflective of either the participants or the language, it is more appropriate to term them refractive, accounting for the altered ways in which subjectivities are performed.

This refraction, or negotiated reflection, is more closely attuned to reflexivity than more commonly understood notions of reflection found in the field of education. It is generally believed that reflection is an essential component of teachers' professional development and is commonly defined as an individual reflecting on their unique practices and beliefs as an educator (Risko, Roskos, & Vukelich, 1999). However, this type of definition, focusing on the sole practitioner and introspection, is contrary to the social situatedness of CDA and a dialogic understanding of interactions. Rather, as Chouliaraki and Fairclough (1999) discussed, CDA calls for a reckoning of historical and social positioning as crucial aspects and contexts of discourse, ideology, and habitus. The interactions between myself and Dawn demonstrate that in negotiating the various contexts, interpretations, and analyses, refractions of our positions, our interpretations, and our beliefs were explored.

This notion of refraction accounts for the appropriately altered interpretations offered, negotiated, and rejected throughout our discussions. In the end, both Dawn and I commented several times how fruitful it would be for teachers to have the intellectual space and support to reflect on the ideologies enacted in their classrooms. The more common use of reflection in educational research hegemonically positions the lone practitioner reflecting in order to modify practices, not necessarily to better understand ideologies at play in the classroom. In this sense, then, educational research, including CDA, must be answerable not just to maintaining teachers' prescribed roles but to opening up spaces and providing tools for reflexive interrogation. By situating the teacher-researcher interactions within the social fields of schooling and the academy, by using CDA as a tool to critical language and ideologies, and allowing for various refractions of representations, Dawn and I were able to move away from restrictive binaries that dominated content area literacy research: good/bad, what works/what doesn't, teacher/researcher, and, of course, teacher/student.

This also helped us move away from a potentially nihilistic presence of CDA and research in a larger sense in classrooms. In numerous locations around the world, relationships between schools and universities are strained as teachers and administrators have felt the sting of a research article that has characterized their work in negative portrayals or have been seduced and then betrayed by researchers' expressed interests (Newkirk, 1996).

Although a level of reflexivity in the researcher-participant collaboration does not and should not guard against research and discourse analysis that shows damaging aspects of education, it should offer an opportunity for a dialogic process between researcher and participant. It points to a possible way for critical discourse analysts who work in educational settings to be answerable to their participants, not to produce synchronized interpretations, but to flesh out better differing interpretations.

REFERENCES

1. Bakhtin, M. M. (1986). Speech genres and other late essays. Austin: University of Texas Press.
2. Bizzell, P. (1992). Academic discourse and critical consciousness. Pittsburgh: University of Pittsburgh Press.
3. Engeström, Y., Miettinen, R., & Punamäki, R.-L. (Eds.). (1999). Perspectives on activity theory. Cambridge, UK: Cambridge University Press.
4. Fillmore, C. (1975). An alternative to checklist theories of meaning. In

C. Cogen, H.

5.   Thompson, G. Thurgood, K. Whistler, & J. Wright (Eds.), Proceedings of the First Annual Meeting of the Berkeley Linguistics Society (pp. 123–131). Berkeley, CA: University of California at Berkeley.

6.   Gagnon, P. (1987). Democracy's untold story: What world history textbooks neglect. Washington, DC: American Federation of Teachers.

7.   Gee, J. P. (2004). Situated language and learning: A critique of traditional schooling. London: Routledge.

8.   Gee, J. P. (2005). An introduction to discourse analysis: Theory and method (2nd ed.).

9.   London: Routledge. Gee, J. P. (2007). Social linguistics and literacies: Ideology in Discourses (3rd ed.). London: Taylor & Francis.Gee, J. (2011). How to do discourse analysis: A tool kit. New York: Routledge.

10. Habermas, J. (1984). Theory of communicative action, Vol. 1 (T. McCarthy, Trans.).

11. London: Heinemann.Hacking, I. (1986). Making up people. In T. C. Heller, M. Sosna, & D. E. Wellbery (Eds.), Reconstructing individualism: Autonomy, individuality, and the self in Western thought(pp. 222–236). Stanford, CA: Stanford University Press.

12. Halliday, M. A. K. (1994). An introduction to functional grammar (2nd ed). London: Edward Arnold.

13. Halliday, M. A. K., & Hasan, R. (1989). Language, context, and text: Aspects of language as a social-semiotic perspective. Oxford: Oxford University Press.

14. Harkness, S., Super, C., & Keefer, C. H. (1992). Learning to be an American parent: How cultural models gain directive force. In R. D'Andrade & C. Strauss (Eds.), Human motives and cultural models (pp. 163–178). Cambridge, UK: Cambridge University Press.

15. Holland, D., Lachicotte, W., Skinner, D., & Cain, C. (1998). Identity and agency in cultural worlds. Cambridge, MA: Harvard University Press.

16. Labov, W. (1972a). Language in the inner city: Studies in Black English vernacular.

17. Philadelphia: University of Pennsylvania Press.

18. Labov, W. (1972b). Sociolinguistic patterns. Philadelphia: University of Pennsylvania Press.

19. Latour, B. (2004). Politics of nature: How to bring the sciences into democracy. Cambridge,MA: Harvard University Press.

20. Latour, B. (2005). Reassembling the social: An introduction to actor-network-theory. Oxford: Oxford University Press.

21. Lave, J., & E. Wenger. 1991. Situated learning: Legitimate peripheral participation. New York: Cambridge University Press.

22. Levinson, S. C. (2000). Presumptive meanings: The theory of generalized conversational implicature. Cambridge, MA: MIT Press.

23. Philipsen, G. (1975). Speaking "like a man" in Teamsterville: Culture patterns of role enactment in an urban neighborhood, Quarterly Journal of Speech, 61, 26–39.

24. Pomerantz, A., & Fehr, B. J. (1997). Conversation analysis: An approach to the study of social action as sense making practices. In T. A. van Dijk (Ed.), Discourse as social interaction: Discourse studies 2: A multidisciplinary introduction (pp. 64–91). London: Sage.

25. Street, B. (1995). Social literacies: Critical approaches to literacy in development, ethnography, and education. London: Longman.

26. Wieder, D. L., & Pratt, S. (1990). On being a recognizable Indian among Indians. In D. Carbaugh (Ed.), Cultural communication and intercultural contact (pp. 45–64). Hillsdale, NJ: Lawrence Erlbaum.

27. Álvarez, A. (2009). Comportamiento de la deserción y reprobación en el Colegio de Bachilleres del Estado de Baja California: Caso plantel Ensenada. Memoria del X Congreso Mexicano de Investigación Educativa. México: COMIE.

28. Amsterdam, A., & Bruner, J. (2000). Minding the law. Cambridge, MA: Harvard University Press.

29. Bakhtin, M. (1981). The dialogic imagination: Four essays by M. M. Bakhtin (M. E.Holquist, Ed.). Austin: University of Texas Press.

30. Bakhtin, M. (1986). Speech genres and other late essays. Austin: University of Texas Press.

31. Boaler, J. (2000). Mathematics from another world: Traditional communities and the alienation of learners. Journal of Mathematical Behavior, 18(4), 379–397.

32. Bourdieu, P. (1980). El sentido práctico (Ariel Danon, Trans.). Buenos Aires: Siglo XXI Editores. (Original title in French: Le sens practique) Bourdieu, P., & Passeron, J. C. (1994). Introduction: Language and relationship to language in the teaching situation. In P. Bourdieu, J. C. Passeron, & M. de Saint Martin,

33. Academic Discourse (pp. 1–34). Stanford, CA: Stanford University Press.

34. Bruner, J. (1986). Actual minds, possible worlds. Cambridge, MA: Harvard University Press.

35. Casey, K. (1995). The new narrative research in education. Review of Research in Education, 21, 211–253.

36. Coulter, C. A., & Smith, M. L. (2009). Discourse on narrative research. The construction zone: Literary elements in narrative research. Educational Researcher, 38(8), 577–590.

37. Fairclough, N. (1995). Critical discourse analysis: The critical study of language. London

38. & New York: Longman.

39. Gee, J. P. (1989). The narrativization of experience in the oral style. Journal of Education, 171, 75–96.

40. Gee, J. P. (1996). Social linguistics and literacies. Ideology in discourses (2nd ed.). London: Taylor and Francis.

41. Gee, J. P. (1999). An introduction to discourse analysis. Theory and method. New York: Routledge.

42. Gentili, P. (2009). Marchas y contramarchas. El derecho a la educación y las dinámicas de exclusión incluyente en América Latina (a sesenta años de la declaración universal de los derechos humanos). Revista Iberoamericana de Educación, 49, 19–57.

43. Holland, D., & Kipnis, A. (1994). Metaphors for embarrassment and stories of exposure:The not-so-egocentric self in American Culture. Ethos, 22(3), 316–342.

44. Holland, D., & Leander, K. (2004). Ethnographic studies of positioning and subjectivity: An introduction. Ethos, 32(2), 127–139.

45. Holland, D., Lachiotte, W., Skinner, D., & Cain, C. (1998). Identity and agency in cultural worlds. Cambridge, MA: Harvard University Press.

46. INEGI (2005). Anuario estadístico de los Estados Unidos Mexicanos. Edición 2005. Mexico: Author Instituto Nacional de Evaluación Educativa (INEE) (2006). Panorama educativo de México 2005. Indicadores del Sistema Educativo Nacional. México: Author.

47. Jameson, F. (1981). The political unconscious. Narrative as a socially symbolic act. Ithaca, NY: Cornell University Press.

48. Kress, G. (2001). "You've just got to learn how to see": Curriculum subjects, young people and schooled engagement with the world. Linguistics and Education, 11(4), 401–415.

49. Labov, W. (1972). Language in the inner city. Philadelphia: University of Philadelphia Press.

50. Labov, W., & Waletzky, J. (1967). Narrative analysis: Oral versions of personal experience.

51. In J. Helm (Ed.), Essays on the verbal and visual arts (pp. 12–44). Seattle: University of Washington Press.

52. Lave, J., & Wenger, E. (1991). Situated learning: Legitimate peripheral participation. Cambridge, UK: Cambridge University Press.

53. Miramontes, A. (2003). Conociendo el bachillerato: un estudio cualitativo sobre la práctica docente y fracaso escolar. Unpublished Master's Thesis. Universidad Autónoma de Baja California, Ensenada, Mexico.

54. Morson, G. S. (2004). The process of ideological becoming. In A. Ball & S. W. Freedman (Eds.), Bakhtinian Perspectives on language, literacy, and learning (pp. 317–331).Cambridge, UK: Cambridge University Press.

55. Romo, A., & Fresán, M. (2002). Los factores curriculares y académicos relacionados con el abandono y el rezago. México: ANUIES.

56. Skinner, D., Valsiner, J., & Holland, D. (2001). Discerning the dialogical self: A theoretical and methodological examination of a Nepali adolescent's narrative [34 paragraphs].

57. Forum Qualitative Sozialforschung / Forum: Qualitative SocialResearch, 2(3), Art. 18, http://nbnresolving.de/urn:nbn:de:0114-fqs0103187.

58. Villa, L. (2007). La educación media superior ¿Igualdad de oportunidades? Revista de Educación Superior, 26(141), 93–110.

59. Wenger, E. (1998). Communities of practice: Learning, meaning and identity. Cambridge, UK: Cambridge University Press.

60. Wertsch, J. (2002). Voices of collective remembering. Cambridge, UK: Cambridge University Press.

61. Zorrilla, J. F. (2008). El bachillerato mexicano: Un sistema académicamente precario.Causasy consecuencias. México: ISSUE.

62. Barthes, R. (1972). Mythologies (A. Lavers, Trans.). New York: Hill and Wang. (Original work published 1957) Barthes, R. (1977). Image-music-text. New York:

63. Hill and Wang. Benhabib, S. (2002). The claims of culture: Equality and diversity in the global era. Princeton: Princeton University Press.

64. Bhabha, H. K. (1990). DissemiNation: Time, narrative, and the margins of the modern nation. In H. K. Bhabha (Ed.), Nation and narration (pp. 291–322). New York:

65. Routledge. Bhabha, H. K. (1994). The location of culture. New York: Routledge . Bishop, R. S. (1990). Mirrors, windows and sliding glass

doors. *Perspectives, 6,* ix–xi.

66. Botelho, M. J., & Rudman, M. K. (2009). *Critical multicultural analysis of children's literature: Mirrors, windows, and doors.* New York: Routledge.

67. Childs, P., & Williams, P. (1997). *An introduction to post-colonial theory.* New York:Prentice Hall.

68. Eagleton, T. (1991). *Ideology: An introduction.* New York: Verso.

69. Eagleton, T. (2000). *The idea of culture.* Malden, MA: Blackwell.

70. Fairclough, N. (1992). *Discourse and social change.* Cambridge, UK: Polity.

71. Fairclough, N. (1995). *Critical discourse analysis: The critical study of language.* New York: Longman.

72. Fairclough, N. (2004). Semiotic aspects of social transformation and learning. In *An introduction to critical discourse analysis in education* (pp. 225–235). Mahwah, NJ: Lawrence Erlbaum.

73. Fowler, R. (1977). *Linguistics and the novel.* London: Methuen.

74. Fowler, R. (1981). *Literature as social discourse: The practice of linguistic criticism.* Bloomington, IN: Indiana University Press.

75. Gee, J. P. (2006). *An introduction to discourse analysis: theory and method* (2nd ed.). New York: Routledge Taylor and Francis. (Original work published 1999).

76. Gee, J. P. (2008). *Good video games + good learning: Collected essays on video games,*

77. learning and literacy. New York: Peter Lang.

78. Hadaway, N. L. (2007). Building bridges to understanding. In *Breaking boundaries with global literature: Celebrating diversity in K–12 classrooms* (pp. 1–6) [Introduction].

79. Newark, DE: International Reading Association.

80. Hodge, R. (1990). *Literature as discourse: Textual strategies in English and history.*

81. Baltimore: The Johns Hopkins University Press.

82. Hodge, R., & Kress, G. (1993). *Language as ideology.* New York: Routledge.

83. JanMohamed, A. (1986). The economy of Manichean allegory: The function of racial difference in colonialist literature. In H. L. Gates (Ed.), *Race, writing, and difference* (pp. 78–106). Chicago: University of Chicago Press.

84. Kapur, R. (2005). *Erotic justice: Law and the new politics of*

postcolonialism. Portland, OR: Cavendish.

85. Kress, G., & van Leeuwen, T. (1996). Reading images: The grammar of visual design. New York: Routledge.

86. Kress, G., & van Leeuwen, T. (2001). Multimodal discourse: The modes and media of contemporary communication. London: Oxford University Press.

87. Laclau, E. & Mouffe, C. (1985). Hegemony and socialist strategy: Towards a radical democratic politics (W. Moore & P. Cammack, Trans.). Thetford, Norfolk, UK: The Thetford Press.

88. Lakshmanan, M. (2009). Reading Canadian children's literature as models of international relations. Journal of Children's Literature, 3(1), 68–88.

89. Lave, J., & Wenger, E. (2002). Situated learning: Legitimate peripheral participation. New York: Cambridge University Press. (Original work published 1991)

90. Lepman, J. (1969). A bridge of children's books (E. McCormick, Trans.). Chicago: American Library Association.

91. Lewis, G. (2007). Fighting a crime that shames us all. In Speech by Mr. Gary Lewis, Representative, UNODC, South Asia at Commonwealth Parliamentary Association, New Delhi, 27 September 2007 [Speech]. Retrieved October 12, 2009, from United Nations Office on Drugs and Crime website: http://www.unodc.org/india/en/gl_

92. cwpa_27sept.html

93. McCormick, P. (n.d.). Author interview. In Patricia McCormick. Retrieved October 12,2009, from http://www.pattymccormick.com/index.php?mode=objectlist&section_ id=115&object_id=152

94. McCormick, P. (2006). Sold. New York: Hyperion.

95. McGillis, R. (2000). Introduction. In Voices of the other: Children's literature and the postcolonial context (pp. xix–xxxi). New York: Routledge.

96. McKenna, M. J. (2007). Transformative literature: A teaching/learning model for using global literature to positively influence our world. In M. J. McKenna & N. L. Hadaway (Eds.), Breaking boundaries with global literature (pp. (165–180)). Newark, DE: International Reading Association.

97. Mohanty, C. T. (2000). Under Western eyes: Feminist scholarship and colonial discourse.

98. In D. Brydon (Ed.), Postcolonialism: Critical concepts, Vol. 3 (pp. 1183–

1209).

99. New York: Routledge.

100. Said, E. W. (1979). Orientalism. New York: Vintage Books.

101. Said, E. W. (1994). Culture and imperialism. New York: Vintage Books.

102. Sontag, S. (2003). Regarding the pain of others. New York: Farrar, Straus and Giroux.

103. Spivak, G. C. (1990). The post-colonial critic: Interviews, strategies, dialogues (S. Harasym, Ed.). New York: Routledge.

104. Stan, S. (2002). Books as bridges. In S. Stan (Ed.), The world through children's books (pp. 27–37). Lanham, MD: The Scarecrow Press.

105. Stephens, J. (1992). Language and ideology in children's fiction. New York: Longman.

106. Tagg, J. (1988). The burden of representation. Amherst, MA: University of Massachusetts.

107. Torfing, J. (1999). New theories of discourse: Laclau, Mouffe and Žižek. Malden, MA: Blackwell.

108. Traugott, E. C., & Pratt, M. L. (1980). Linguistics for students of literature. New York:Harcourt Brace Jovanovich.

109. van Dijk, T. A. (1985). Discourse and literature. Philadelphia: John Benjamins.van Dijk, T. A. (1998). Ideology: A multidisciplinary approach. Thousand Oaks, CA:

110. Sage.

111. Wenger, E. (1998). Communities of practice: Learning, meaning, and identity. New York:Cambridge University Press.

112. Yokota, J., & Kolar, J. (2008, January/February). Advocating for peace and justice through children's literature. Social Studies and the Young Leaner, 22–26.

113. Young, R. J. (2003). Postcolonialism: A very short introduction. New York: Oxford University Press.

114. Zimmer, T. V. (n.d.). Sold [Discussion guide]. Retrieved October 12, 2009, from Hyperion website: http://www.hyperionbooksforchildren. com/data/books/dgpdf/ 07868517161686.pdf.

115. AAUW. (2009). Separated by sex: Title IX and single-sex education. Retrieved January 8, 2010 from http://www.aauw.org/advocacy/issue_ advocacy/actionpages/singlesex.

116. cfm

117. Alloway, N. (2007). Swimming against the tide: Boys, literacies, and

schooling—an Australian story. Canadian Journal of Education, 30(2), 582–605.

118. Arciniega, G. M., Anderson, T. C., Tovar-Blank, Z., & Tracey, T. (2008). Toward a fuller conception of machismo: Development of a traditional machismo and caballerismo scale. Journal of Counseling Psychology, 55(1), 19–33.

119. Beaupre, B. (2003, March 9). Boys, not girls, on worse end of education gap.

120. Chicago

121. Sun-Times. Retrieved March 13, 2003, from http://www.suntimes.com Blair, H.A., Sanford, K. (2004). Morphing literacy: Boys reshaping their school-based literacy practices. Language Arts, 81(6), 452–460.

122. Brozo, W. G. & Gaskins, C. (2009). Engaging texts and literacy practices for adolescent boys. In K. D. Wood & W. E. Blanton (Eds.), Literacy instruction for adolescents:

123. Research-based practice (pp. 170–186). New York: The Guilford Press.

124. Coles, T. (2009). Negotiating the fi eld of masculinity: The production and reproduction of multiple dominant masculinities. Men and Masculinities, 12, 30–44.

125. College Board (2007). Advanced placement report to the nation. Retrieved November 04,2007 from http://apcentral.collegeboard.com Connell, R. W. (1987). Gender and power: Society, the person and sexual politics. Stanford, CA: Stanford University Press.

126. Connell, R. W. (2005). Masculinities (2nd ed.). Berkeley, CA: University of California Press.

127. Cook, G. (2006). Boys at risk: The gender achievement gap. The American School Board

128. Journal, 193, 4–6. Downey, D. B., & Vogt-Yuan, A. S. (2005). Sex differences in school performance during

129. high school: Puzzling patterns and possible explanations. Sociological Quarterly, 46, 299–321.

130. Fairclough, N. (2003). Analysing discourse: Textual analysis for social research. New York:

131. Routledge.

132. Faludi, S. (1999). Stiffed: The betrayal of the American Man. New York: William Morrow.

133. Fonda, D. (2000, December 2). The male minority. TIME Magazine.

Retrieved March 13, 2003, from http://www.TIME.com

134. Gee, J. P. (1996). Social linguistics and literacies: Ideology in discourses (2nd ed.). Bristol, PA: Taylor & Francis.

135. Gee, J. P. (2005). An introduction to discourse analysis: Theory and method (2nd ed.).

136. London: Routledge.

137. Gee, J. P. (2007). Social linguistics and literacies: Ideology in discourses (3rd ed.). London: Taylor & Francis.

138. Gee, J. P. & Crawford, V. (1998). Two kinds of teenagers: Language, identity, and social class. In D. E. Alverman, K. A. Hinchman, D. W. Moore, S. F. Phelps, & D. R. Waff

139. (Eds.), Reconceptualizing the literacies in adolescents' lives (pp. 225–245). Hillsdale, NJ: Lawrence Erlbaum.

140. Goodman, E. (2002, September 4). What a surprise: College gender gap in deemed in crisis. Arizona Republic, p.B9.

141. Griffi th, A. T. (2009). A study of the literacy experiences and related life experiences of incarcerated black adolescent males (Doctoral dissertation, Arizona State University, 2009).

142. Dissertation Abstracts International, 70, 04. Hammett, R. & Sanford, K. (2008) Boys and girls and the myths of literacies and learning.

143. Toronto: Canadian Scholars Press.

144. Harris, I. M. (1995). Message men hear: Constructing masculinities. Bristol, PA: Taylor & Francis.

145. Hedges, L., & Nowell, A. (1995, July 7). Sex difference in mental test scores, variability, and numbers of high-scoring individuals. Science, 269, 41–45.

146. Institute of Oral History. (2001, April 14). Oral history workshop on the Web: Transcribing style guide. Retrieved January 31, 2003 from http://www.baylor.edu/Oral History/ Styleguide. html

147. Jackson, D., & Salisbury, J. (1996). Why should secondary schools take working with boys seriously? Gender and Education, 8, 103–115.

148. Kimmel, M. S. (2000). The gendered society. New York: Oxford University Press.

149. Klein, A. M. (2000). Dueling machos: Masculinity and sport in Mexican baseball. In J.McKay, M. Messner, & D. Sabo (Eds.), Masculinities, gender relations, and sport (pp.67–85). Thousand Oaks, CA: Sage.

150. Lesko, N. (2000). Masculinities at school. Thousand Oaks, CA: Sage.

151. Lloyd, S. C. (2007) Gender gap in graduation. Retrieved January 9, 2010 from http://www.edweek.org/rc/articles/2007/07/05/sow0707.h26.html.

152. Madill, L. (2009). Deconstructing gender: Realizing the possibilities. Canadian Journal of New Scholars in Education, 2(1), 1–12.

153. Martino, W. & Kehler, M. (2007). Gender-based literacy reform: A question of challenging or recuperating gender binaries. Canadian Journal of Education, 30(2), 406–431.

154. Mead, S. (2006). The evidence suggests otherwise: The truth about boys and girls. Washington, DC: Education Sector.

155. Myers, G. (1999). Functions of reported speech in group discussions. Applied Linguistics, m 20(3), 376–401.

156. National Center for Education Statistics. (2000). Trends in educational equity of girls and women. Washington, DC: U.S. Department of Education.

157. Reed, L. R. (1999). Troubling boys and disturbing discourses of masculinity and schooling: A feminist exploration of current debates and interventions concerning boys and

158. schools. Gender and Education, 11, 93–110.

159. Scieszka, J. (2003). Guys read. Retrieved June 24, 2003, from http://www. guysread.com Skelton, C. (1998). Schooling the boys: Masculinities and primary education. Philadelphia:

160. Open University Press.

161. Smith, M. W., & Wilhelm, J. D. (2002). "Reading don't fi x no Chevy's": Literacy in the lives of young men. Portsmouth, NH: Heinemann.

162. Sommers, C. H. (2000). The war against boys: How misguided feminism is harming our young men. New York: Simon & Schuster.

163. Tatum, Λ. W. (2008a) Literacy and African-American boys: Shifting the paradigm. Plenary address delivered at National Reading Conference annual conference, Orlando, FL. Retrieved January 9, 2010 from http:// nrconline.org/conference/conf08/videos.html

164. Tatum, A. W. (2008b). Toward a more anatomically complete model of literacy instruction: A focus on African American male adolescents and texts. Harvard Educational Review, 78(1), 155–180.

165. Tyack, D., & Hansot, E. (1990). Learning together: A history of coeducation in American

166. schools. New Haven, CT: Yale University Press.

167. Tyre, P. (2006, January 30). The trouble with boys. Newsweek. Retrieved

from http:// www.msnbc.msn.com/id/10965522/site/newsweek/

168. Young, J. P. (2000). Boy talk: Critical literacy and masculinities. Reading Research Quarterly, 35, 312–337.

169. Young, J. P., Hardenbrook, M., Esch, M., Hansen, K., & Griffi th, A. (2003). What's happening with/to boys in adolescent literacy classrooms? Unpublished manuscript.

170. Archer, M. (1995). Realist social theory: The morphogenetic approach. Cambridge, UK:Cambridge University Press.

171. Archer, M. (2000). Being human: The problem of agency. Cambridge, UK: Cambridge University Press.

172. Bernstein, B. (1990). The structuring of pedagogic discourse. London: Routledge.

173. Chiapello, E., & Fairclough, N. (2002). Understanding the new management ideology. A transdisciplinary contribution from critical discourse analysis and the new sociology of capitalism. Discourse and Society, 13(2), 185–208.

174. Chouliaraki, L., & Fairclough, N. (1999). Discourse in late modernity. Edinburgh: Edinburgh University Press.

175. Fairclough, N. (1992). Discourse and social change. Cambridge, UK: Polity.

176. Fairclough, N. (1993). Critical discourse analysis and the marketisation of public discourse: The universities. Discourse & Society, 4, 133–168.

177. Fairclough, N. (2000a). Discourse, social theory and social research: The case of welfare reform. Journal of Sociolinguistics, 4(2), 163–195.

178. Fairclough, N. (2000b). New Labour, new language? London: Routledge.

179. Fairclough, N. (2001). The dialectics of discourse. Textus, 14, 231–242.

180. Fairclough, N. (2003). Analysing discourse: Textual analysis for social research. London: Routledge.

181. Fairclough, N., Jessop, R., & Sayer, A. (2003). A critical realist interpretation of the effectivity of the production of meaning. In J. Roberts (Ed.), Critical realism, deconstruction and discourse. London: Routledge.

182. Fairclough, N., Jessop, R. & Sayer, A. (2004). Critical realism and semiosis. In J. Joseph & J. Roberts (Eds.), Realism, Discourse and Deconstruction (pp. 23–42). London: Routledge.

183. Halliday, M. (1978). Language as social semiotic. London: Edward Arnold.Halliday, M. (1994). Introduction to functional grammar. London:

Edward Arnold.

184. Harvey, D. (1996). Justice, nature and the geography of difference. Oxford: Blackwell.

185. Salskov-Iversen, D., Hansen, H., & Bislev, S. (2000). Governmentality, globalization and local practice: Transformations of a hegemonic discourse. Alternatives, 25, 183–222.

186. Sayer, A. (2000). Realism and the social sciences. London: Sage.

187. Achinstein, B. (2002). Conflict amid community: The micropolitics of teacher collaboration.

188. Teachers College Record, 104(3), 421–455.

189. Alvermann, D. E., Commeyras, M., Young, J. P., Randall, S., & Hinson, D. (1997). Interrupting gendered discursive practices in classroom talk about texts: Easy to think about, difficult to do. Journal of Literacy Research, 29(1), 73–104.

190. Bakhtin, M. (1981). The dialogic imagination: Four essays (Michael Holqiust, Ed.). Austin: University of Texas Press.

191. Bakhtin, M. (1986). Speech genres and other late essays (C. Emerson, Ed.). Austin: University of Texas Press.

192. Barrera. R. B. (1992). The culture gap in literature-based literacy instruction. Education and Urban Society. 23(2), 227–244.

193. Barton, D. & Hamilton, M. (2005). Literacy, reification and the dynamics of social interaction.

194. In D. Barton and K. Tusting (Eds.), Beyond communities of practice: Language, power and social context (pp. 14–35). Cambridge, UK: Cambridge University Press

195. Beach, R. (1997). Students' resistance to engagement with multicultural literature. In T. Rogers & A. O. Soter (Eds.), Reading across cultures: Teaching literature in a diverse society (pp. 69–94). New York: Teachers College Press.

196. Bonilla-Silva, E. (2001). White supremacy and racism in the post-civil rights era. Boulder, CO: Lynne Rienner Publishers.

197. ABC KGO-TV SanFrancisco, CA (n.d.) . Retrieved March 6, 2010, from http://abclocal.go.com/kgo/story?section=news/education&id=7311615

198. Allington, R. L. (1999). Crafting state educational policy: The slippery role of educational research and researchers. Journal of Literacy Research, 31, 457–482.

199. Allington, R. L. (2002). Big brother and the national reading curriculum.

Portsmouth, NH: Heinemann.

200. Allington, R. L., & Woodside-Jiron, H. (1999). The politics of literacy teaching: How "research" shaped educational policy. Educational Researcher, 28(8), 4–13.

201. Assembly Bill 170, Instructional materials, Chapter 765 (1995a).

202. Assembly Bill 1504, Instructional materials: Spelling, Chapter 764 (1995b).

203. Assembly Bill 3482, Education: Teacher reading instruction, Chapter 196 (1996).

204. Assembly Bill 1086, Reading instruction, Chapter 286 (1997).

205. Ball, D. L. (1990). Reflections and deflections of policy: The case of Carol Turner.

206. Educational Evaluation and Policy Analysis, 12(3), 247–259.

207. Bernstein, B. (1990) The structuring of pedagogic discourse. New York: Routledge.

208. Bernstein, B. (2000). Pedagogy symbolic control and identity: Theory, research, critique.

209. Bristol, PA: Taylor & Francis.

210. Bourdieu, P. (1991). Language and symbolic power. Cambridge, MA: Harvard University

211. Press.

212. California Department of Education. (1999). Reading/language arts framework for California public schools. Sacramento: Author.

213. Carlos, L., & Kirst, M. (1997). California curriculum policy in the 1990s: "We don't have to be in front to lead." Paper presented at the annual meeting of the American Educational Research Association, Chicago, IL.

214. Chouliaraki, L., & Fairclough, N. (1999). Discourse in late modernity: Rethinking critical discourse analysis. Edinburgh: Edinburgh University Press.

215. Chrispeels, J. H. (1997). Educational policy implementation in a shifting political climate: The California experience. American Educational Research Journal, 34(3),

216. 453–481.

217. Coles, G. (2000). Misreading reading: The bad science that hurts children. Portsmouth, NH: Heinemann.

218. Collins, J. (1995). Literacy and literacies. Annual Review of Anthropology, 24, 75–93.

219. Collins, J. (1997, October 27). How Johnny should read. Time, pp. 78–81.

220. Edmondson, J. (2000). America Reads: A critical policy analysis. Newark, DE: International Reading Association.

221. Edmondson, J. (2002). Asking different questions: Critical analyses and reading research.

222. Reading Research Quarterly, 37(1), 113–119.

223. EdSource. (n.d.). Retrieved April 17, 2010, from http://www.edsource.org/sys_students.

224. html

225. Egan-Robertson, A. (1998). Learning about culture, language, and power: Understanding relationships among personhood, literacy practices, and intertextuality. Journal of Literacy Research, 30(4), 449–487.

226. Fairclough, N. (1992). Discourse and social change. Cambridge, UK: Polity.

227. Fairclough, N. (1995a). Media discourse. London: Arnold.

228. Fairclough, N. (1995b). Critical discourse analysis: The critical study of language. New York: Longman.

229. Fairclough, N. (2003). Analyzing discourse: Textual analysis for social research. New York:

230. Routledge.

231. Ferdman, B. M. (1990). Literacy and cultural identity. Harvard Educational Review, 60, 181–203.

232. Fischer, F. (2009) Democracy & expertise: Reorienting policy inquiry. New York: Oxford University Press.

233. Fullan, M. (2001). The new meaning of educational change. New York: Teachers College Press.

234. Gee, J. P. (1996). Social linguistics and literacies: Ideology in discourses (2nd ed.). Bristol, PA: Falmer.

235. Gee, J. P. (1999). An introduction to discourse analysis theory and method. New York: Routledge.

236. Gee, J. P. (2001). Forward. In C. Lewis (Ed.), Literacy practices as social acts: Power, status, and cultural norms in the classroom (pp. xv–xix). Mahwah, NJ: Lawrence Erlbaum Associates.

237. Gee, J. P., & Green, J. L. (1998). Discourse analysis, learning, and social practice: A methodological study. In P. D. Pearson & A. Iran-Nejad (Eds.), Review of research in education. Washington, DC: American Educational Research Association.

Chapter 6

INTRODUCTION OF STUDENT TEACHERS IN TUNISIAN SECONDARY SCHOOLS: A DISCOURSE ANALYSIS OF COOPERATIVE TEACHER

Wadii Zayed[1,2], Naila Bali[1,2]

[1]High Institute of Sport and Physical Education, Ksar Saîd, University la Manouba, Tunis, Tunisia
[2]Tunisian Research Laboratory "Sport Performance Optimization", Tunis, Tunisia

ABSTRACT

In reference to professional training for trainee teachers, the tutor or cooperative teacher (CT) is considered as an alternation between two environments, academia and training, contributing to the training by the advice and support. Our research provides "support for physical education student teachers (PE-STs)" as determinants of teaching advice of CT. This study includes a qualitative analysis which aims to identify the advice of CTs to the student teachers for whom they are responsible for training. It's a descriptive/exploratory methodology based on observation and video recorded six (6) physical education (PE) sessions lasting one hour each and six semi structured interviews (30 minutes each) and gave CTs the opportunity to share their perspectives on broad topics such as professional training, teaching, and characteristics of the training environment and succinct topics such as training program and their preoccupation. Data were collected during 2 months of observations and interviews with six CTs during professional training of 12 PE-STs in Level 3 (third year, BAC+3). CTs justify their teaching by six categories in which we have grouped the different types of advice. The CTs are more interested by problems of organization and control students. They believe that educational content is worthless without a good control of the class.

INTRODUCTION

The analysis of the tutorial activity by professionals has been a growing interest both in the training area in the work (Dugal, 2003; Carlier & Clerx, 2012) and of High Institute of Sport and Physical Education (ISSEP) in Tunis (Bali & Zayed, 2014) . This interest is likely that the tutorial activity plays a joint role development of professional skills of trainee teachers (Darnis & Magendie, 2011) . According to Maela (2009) the term tutoring designs a defender, a protector and a guardian. It also inherits all practical accompanying an insertion referred to the professional life. Tutoring is situated at the crossroads of two logical productive and educational, and defined as training device in the workplace. Indeed, much research has demonstrated the importance of the accompaniment of the PE-ST on their practicum. In this context, the CT plays a fundamental role in facilitating their integration in the professional context (Lévesque & Gervais, 2000; Martineau, 2003; Perez-Roux, 2012) . However, Carlier (2000); Crinon (2003) ; Trohel et al. (2004) discussed the importance of exchange of scholarly knowledge, say that the CT would teach as it was taught and it's mainly based on his professional experience and teaching skills. Other research has provided contrasted results about the use the experience that is not enough to undertake the tasks of the trainer. Brau-Antony et al. (2011) report that tutoring is a difficult task. The CT share their professional time between a main teaching activity and a training PE-ST in practicum. According to Desbiens (2009)and Bali (2012, 2014) , there is considerable uncertainty as to the qualification, experience and skills required to be a CT. The objective of this study is to highlight the teaching practices of CT. we will define a first time to study the nature of post sessions speeches at welcome sessions and check in a second time to identify the opinions in a confrontational data collected across data crossing observations and semi-directive interviews.

What is learned in the "welcome session the trainee"? I will be interested in this question in the field of the introduction of the PE-ST in Tunisian secondary schools. In order to operationalize research questions, we have developed the following hypothesis: The discourse of the CT help the PE-ST to integrate in to the professional life and establishing a good relationship. The organization and the mastery of students occupy the great part of advice and support of the CT.

METHODOLOGY

Participants

To test our research hypotheses, we used a sample consisting of 06 CT from two secondary schools in the Tunis region very engaged in professional training. These teachers are training everyone two trainees teachers. The CT has professional experience about 12 years and experience in the formation of the PE-ES between 5 and 10 years. Each CT is filmed during his speech in "natural" situation. These teachers are training everyone two PE-ST (Table 1).

Three main reasons justified the choice of this sample: 1) an institutional reason: This study is part of the professional training of student teachers. The CT is considered a person of alternating between the university and the training environment. This justifies the choice of the masters of this course is dual affiliation will allow us to see the nature of that advice of CT. 2) a social reason: there is a social difference between the academic and professional. This allowed us to hypothesize the role of CT in the integration of PE-ST. This difference could influence the teaching practices of student teachers. And 3) an academic reason: the application of the aims and the official program of physical education. Enabled to us hypothesize of the nature of the post-session speech of CT should accord with its orientations and promote student learning. To maximize opportunities to cover teachers trainers intervention, we asked all teachers working in/at ISSEP to participate in this study. Our work sample meets these three parameters as indicated in the Table 1 below. The criteria for selection of training environments are the number and distribution of PE-STs.

Table 1: Sample of Tunisian CT

	CT
Filmed	06
Interviewed	06
Filmed and interviewed	06
Years of Experience	≥12 years
Years of tutorat practice	Between 5 and 10 years

The Interview Audio Post-Session

Two week after the video recording sessions observing teaching discourse of CT, a semi structured interview was conducted with each of CT observed and recorded. This interview was conducted with six CT working in Tunis. We then proceeded to the transcription of audio recordings of semi-structured interviews individually established after the observation of each CT to form the PE-STs and we have reported in the grid also developed by the researcher (step 1). This grid has allowed us to categorize the discourse of CT. Finally, the third step is the linking of analyzes from different investigative techniques. We crossed the data collected during the first two steps. This categorization allowed us to approach through what the CT said and done.

The Formation of the Corpus

Structured interviews: we used a dictaphone to record the responses of CT interviewed. The questions focus on teaching council previously filmed subjects interviewed in the first meeting with the PE-STs. Then the CT are interviewed while allowing them freedom of speech they can express themselves at their ease. Accordance with the principles of the semi structured interview (Mucchielli, 1979, 1983), the interview guide may change due to data collected by the observations of CT council in these subjects interviewed but without deviating from the main subject. The interview was scheduled for 30 minutes, according to the same considerations, the duration varied slightly from one subject to another.

Data Collection

Data collection was conducted in three phases. The first is an interview with the CT in order to have data that can be useful in this study as the number of years of experience and his career. At this meeting we presented to the teacher, the various stages of this research namely a video recording of the first meeting with the teacher followed by an interview semi directive representing the other two step of data collection.

RESULT AND DISCUSSION

Result

The contents of the speech of six CT during the welcome session, we conducted a coding after a didactic transcription. We developed six categories in which we have grouped the different types of advice: 1) "The behavior of PE-STs" whenever the CT talk about attendance, presentation and relationship to provide a model of the behavior of the CT. 2) "Documents and materials" whenever the CT states that the PE-STs must prepare a paper that contains essentially forms cyclic programming, instructional sheets, student assessment grids and observations between trainee teachers, have a notebook to keep track of absences, use of a notebook containing instructions on post sessions feedback and have a trousseau containing one or two whistles, a stopwatch, a double measuring tape, a watch. 3) "The organization" whenever CT talks about the management of infrastructure of the school and the equipment available, states that PE-STs must adapt to working conditions by sharing equipment with other teachers, pick up the equipment at the end of session so as not to lose, says to PE-STs must organize and control students. Make a disciplinary contract at the beginning of the school year and remind students of the rules disciplinary each session, impose disciplinary rules (to prohibit noise locker room, wearing jewelry, a mobile, the loss of its objects, tobacco, moving out of the classroom). They should not provoke or insult students, to not accept in case of successive delays. Punish them in a report, organize them into clubs and teaching level groups, accompany them to the locker room and the field. The PE-STs must manage the time of the session, advice the student to come on time and in uniform, not to waste time when dressing in the locker room, respect the time of the laying and does not release them late. The PE-STs must accountability agitated students, engage students in the organization of the session by transporting the materials and doing the markup ground, the observation and arbitration. 4) "The administrative tasks" whenever the CT states that PE-STs should making the call at the beginning and at the end of the session by noting and controlling. They should write in the call register with codes and track absentee and sick students throughout the cycles, talks about the different cases of the exclusion of the student, said that in case of accident, PE-STs must complete accident reports, talks about the different cases of the exclusion of the student. 5) "The interventions of PE-STs" whenever CT states that PE-STs must transmit knowledge, contribute to the regulation of the activity of students, have methods of intervention, and discover effective solutions to constraints. The PE-STs must use understandable language and do not make mistakes in pronunciation and no hesitation, listen to students. He must know the state of mind and problems of students at the beginning of the session, attract their attention, motivate and reward them to like the physical education field, ensure the security and health of students: no of intensive work. The CT says that PE-STs needs to student assessment; announce the results and the parameters taken into account in the note. Attribute the note and identify talent. 6) "The content taught" whenever the CT states that PE-STs must develop content to teach, programming situations by taking into consideration what the student loves their initial levels, the proofs of bac sport using game situations, the sport and physical activity program performed at training environment. Use knowledge disciplinary, doing documentary research, program from simple to complex. States that PE-ST must apply the objectives of physical education. ES should refer to the high program school. The PE-STs must develop theoretical lessons in bad weather. Every time the CT talks about student learning.

Discussion

The results reveal that the major concern of tutors seems to be the behavior of PE-STs (20.18%) indicated in the Table 2: some of CT said: "I prefer that you arrive early, be at school at 7:30", "each absence must be justified and signed by the ISSEP", "Your outfit should be presentable" (CT 2).

"When I go to the administration, I want to hear good things about the student teachers. They are effective. I do not want to hear that they are an additional problem", "we are here to give a good image of physical education. No one can speak and even if he talks, he will not say well of physical education. We, the physical education teachers, we need everyone respects us" (CT 5).

"Here, it has comments. This area is difficult; you have to taking precautions" (CT 4).

"About your relationship with the student, do not insult him or hit him or even touch. You should never call it with a nickname" (CT 2).

By referring to what is found in the literature, it could be said that this result is in accordance with all work of Levesque and Gervais (2000); Martineau (2000) ; Jorro (2007) ; Perez-Roux (2012) who spoke of the importance of the category "relationship" that occupies much of the volume advice interviews of CT. According to Martineau et al. (2010), the professional integration of teachers is a difficult time of life at work, during which the PE-ST is confronted with a multitude of experiences and new situations that must adapt quickly. Without support, it is very difficult for novice teachers to get through this crucial level of professional development. Perez- Roux (2012) identifies ethical recognition that values interpersonal skills of the individual and the moral principles underlying them. These elements are essential for CT and PE-ST to operate. The sharing of values among professionals in the Council constitutes a form of recognition, a report to the profession that organizes their daily activities. Apart from the relational that articulates the self-esteem and the recognition of others, the biographical dimension implies for the individual to be recognized for what it is and for what he has experienced/constructed previously. Also, PE-SToften feel lost because they do not know the functioning of the school or the habits of teachers in place and must adapt to these innovations (Martineau, 2010) . According to Martineau and Mukamurera (2012) to exercise a professional role in a given environment and be accepted as a member, it's essential that PE-ST appropriates operating rules, expectations and culture of this community. The introduction of PE-ST refers to the adaptation and mastery of the professional role by the development of knowledge and skills specific to this profession. This is the knowledge "teach the class", to become effective in the work according to professional skills expected. Ndoreraho and Martineau (2006)report that the difficulties experienced by PE-ST during their professional integration period such as stress in his functions and teaching in an unfavorable environment negatively affect their interest in applying the teaching profession. In the following, these difficulties are the cause of their profession abandonment.

Table 2: Analysis grid of discourse of CTs during the introduce session

Category	The items	Total	%
1- The behavior of PE-ST TOTAL: 221 20.18%	Assiduity absence and lateness	47	21.26
	presentation	23	10.40
	Discipline, serious	7	3.16
	Concentration	26	11.76
	Relationship	118	53.39
		221	20.18
2- Documents and materials TOTAL: 195 17.8%	Preparation of the class journal	148	75.89
	The workbook of the note	10	5.12
	The notebook of feedback	13	6.66
	Tool Kit of PE-ST	24	12.3
		195	17.8
3- The organization TOTAL: 326 29.77%	Management of resources	89	27.3
	Spatial planning	34	10.42
	Control of students	124	38.03
	Time Management	39	11.96
	Participation of students	40	12.26
		326	29.77
4- The administrative tasks TOTAL: 99 9.04%	Checking presence	89	89.89
	Exclusion of the students	6	6.06
	Filling the accident report	4	4.04
		99	9.04
5- The interventions of PE-ST TOTAL: 119 10.86%	Regulation of student activity	60	50.42
	communication skills	16	13.44
	Student motivation	21	17.64
	Safety and health of students	13	10.92
	Student assessment	9	7.56
		119	10.86
6- The content taught TOTAL: 135 12.32%	Choice of learning situations	89	65.92
	Application of the aims of the EPS	1	0.74
	Application of official programs	7	5.18
	Conception of the theory lessons	23	17.03
	Appropriations by students	15	11.11
		135	12.32
Total:		1095	

The documentary and equipment has preparing (17.8%) as indicated in the Table 2. One of them announced, "the pedagogy documentary are newspaper class, note book and notebook feedback" (CT 3).

The organization and control of the students (29.77%) indicated in the Table 2 have the large proportion of Advice tutors. Some of CT said: "With a good organization, we will not find problems," "it's not for one person to take all the equipment, you have to share. You have to manage according to the available material" (CT 1).

"You have to do tracing and marking the field, you prepare yourself for the session." "You have to accustom students to be disciplined, presence at time, properly dressed", "with discipline students can organize work for successful act of teaching" (CT 5).

"The student must invest in the session and allows interest to physical education", "you can give it a responsibility, the student is going to help you" (CT 2).

By referring to the literature, it could be said that this result is in accordance with all work of Dugal and Amade-Escot (2004) that showed a predominance of class "organization" that occupies much of the volume advice interviews of CT.

The other part is constituted by the administrative tasks (9.04%) indicated in the Table 2. Some of them have pronounced:

"The appeal is an administrative task; you must control the presence of students at the beginning and end of the meeting" (CT 1).

"The Call Register, this document is a link between you, the administration and the parent. The administration needs to know that such a student is absent, present or late" (CT 3).

"If there is accident, fill out the false statement, filed with the administration to protect oneself and student" (CT 6).

The result obtained in research is in agreement with the work of Dugal (2003) concluded that the organizational concerns of classroom management most often take the priority over the content taught. In recent literature, Rayou and Ria (2009) found that some teachers were convinced that the work with minimal instructions helps to reduce noise and control of the class. According toBremond (2013) , the CT said they did not understand what they could bring to PE-STs who experiencing difficulties to control her students. Whereas the CTs consider that PE-STs was leaving an education that develops the management class. Martineau et al. (2010) and Bali (2015) argue that the lack of experience of beginning teachers makes it difficult to solve everyday problems particularly the classroom management. The CT spell out that the problems with the organization are the symptom of a particular difficulty to the PE-ST that should be questioned. These results are justified by Dugal (2003) who asserts that the CT spontaneously want to help and secure the PE-ST they have the charge to accompany; which is reflected by preoccupations oriented to the organization and the classroom management as to the content to be taught.

The interventions of PE-ST (10.86%) indicated in the Table 2; One of them said: "the teacher is close to student, communication on the field or even way of speaking, that is to say in Arabic and French" (CT 2).

The content taught (12.32%) indicated in the Table 2, the application of the purposes of the EPS and official programs (5.92%) is second. One of CT said: "We will try to educate the student. Do not forget the purposes and programs of physical education" (CT 3).

Gervais and Desrosiers (2005) argue that tutor is an important component for teachers to implement in a real situation, what they learned during University studies. Boutet and Pharand (2008) add that student's teachers want to be guided and supervised. They want to take the initiative and accept that their errors are reported. Rayou and Ria (2009) argue that beginning teachers rarely have a clear awareness of the reasons for the failure or success in of their interventions.

The crossing of the content analysis of post sessions interviews and semi-structured interviews conducted with tutors brings us to clarify these results. The semi-structured interviews show that CT is more concerned with problems of organization and control students. They believe that teaching content is worth nothing without a good functioning of the class.

"I talked about the importance of discipline, more important than anything else. If students were undisciplined you could not do anything"

"You have to know how to organize and manage the classroom, how to choose the situations and program this is one will learn later" is the view expressed by (CT 3) in a semi structured interview.

According to Gervais and Desrosiers (2005), teacher training is undertaken by the school as a social responsibility. In a professional environment, the presence of PE-STs in education has high incidences on the daily work of the school staff, the executive team of the school teachers and non-teaching staff. They say they know little of the actual work of persons who introduce and accompany PE-STs to school as well as those who supervise them in the name of the training institution.

Gervais and Desrosiers (2005) report that the reasons to introduce PE-STs are of three types: professional development of PE-STs, in terms of opportunity for reflection, source of stimulation and satisfaction; the contribution to the renewal of the action in the classroom. Speaking of professional training, Gervais and Desrosiers (2005) propose to focus on the importance of naming the skills expected of PE-STs. They say that competence is constructed from a practice, in a real-professional context, is based on a set of personal resources (knowledge, skills, attitudes, other skills) and resources from the environment (colleagues, literature), develops gradually. Carlier (2009) claims when the CTs describe their didactic and relational intervention, they are located in the three supervision style defined by Brûlé (1983). The democratic style (support, confrontation, discussion, clarification) the most used in the post sessions speech. Advice on the selection of content refers to the didactic style, the more directive (management, provocation, evaluation, security, education, demonstration). When the CTs adopt a posture of listening, they are in the non-directive experiential style (interpersonal exploration, consultation, self-expression, laissez-faire).

According to Mouton (2009) and Bali et al. (2014), the organization and conduct of the internship that sets up the CT, diced his first contact with the trainees, it will influence their conceptions and their appropriations. At the end to clarify their reciprocal expectations, Carlier (2002) suggest doing as a guide of training. CT is supposed to take the lead in drawing up the contract: "I, master your internship, what are my strengths, my characteristics? What I can honestly and modestly made, that you will not find elsewhere?" (Carlier, 2002: p. 103). The concept of didactic contract according Amade-Escot (2003) is central, as a concept focusing presupposed or implicit rules that organize the relationship teacher/students/knowledge. It is the anchoring point from which can be structured didactic observation. For its part, the didactic environment is the environment in which the student is and integrates equipment device, objects of knowledge or expertise, previous acquisitions and memory of the class.

Gervais and Desrosiers (2005) add that traineeships are an important component of any program of teacher training. They were provided in training to allow intending PE-STs to implement in a real situation, what they had learned at university. Both authors spoke of the link between theory and practice, postulating that the theoretical knowledge was acquired outside school and that the contribution of the school was limited to the practical dimension. The internships also aimed at allowing to PE-STs to demonstrate their level of mastery of skills deemed essential for teaching. They add that in the current training programs, internships are rather approached as experiments to gain a realistic picture of the working environment and profession, develop progressively of professional skills by mobilizing various resources, including knowledge acquired in academia. The internship is a learning environment of multiple knowledge and fostering the awareness's and identification of requirements for knowledge.

Carlier (2009) shows that CTs are based on the most accessible resources to construct their profession. They refer primarily on their personal experience of teachers. According to Bremond (2013) and Bali et al. (2014), the training is approached as an interaction, the CT is an actor among others; it's not a holder of knowledge. The diffusion of knowledge is fundamentally tainted by the exchange in which she will set out. The CT aims is to transmit knowledge and not talking. He must register in the interaction without forgetting the unexpected and indefinite nature of professional situations they exchange.

In this approach, Leriche et al. (2010) and Bali et al. (2014) believe that internships are not sufficient to promote the development of professional teaching skills. The success of this company seems strongly associated with accompanying practices implemented by the CT. They postulate that the PE-ST is the central actor in his own training. It is not isolated with a CT, but surrounded by teachers, including other CT, in contact with members of the school including the school administration, with students and other trainees. The role of the CT is paramount in accompanying the PE-ST, but a large number of actors participating, formally or informally, for his training. In this orientation, Perrenoud (1994) argues that teaching is a profession that requires great flexibility, a practice engaged in uncertainty, where various dimensions of human relationships coexist.

Boutin and Camaraire (2001) state that if the criteria for selection of CTs based on the pole model (teaching experience, proven expertise, team spirit and sensitivity to the life of the school), the pole trainer of CT remains high (observation skills, analytical and critical thinking). Boutet (2002) lists some characteristics of a good CT: the experience, the confidence in its means, the openness to theoretical contributions and reflection, the coherence, the acceptance to question and to be questioned. To be a CT, one must be able to explain his thinking; to work in teams and to share tasks also have interpersonal skills, attention to each other and positive confrontation. For its part, Gosselin (2002) proposes various conceptions of what constitutes a CT. It uses six poles of Lang (1999) to represent these tendencies: the academic pole (an educated master who knows his subject); artisanal pole (the CT craftsman imitated by the apprentice observing); the pole of Applied Science and Technology (the emphasis is on the "how, knowledge in the laboratory); personality pole (the quality of the relationship, psychological maturity of the CT, the development of his own style of teaching); the pole of the social actor (the effort to develop critical thinking); professional pole (the reflective practitioner able to analyze what he does in terms of the effects produced) Bali (2013) .

Trohel et al. (2004) described the forms of joint commitments of the CT and the PE-ST during their interaction during post-lesson interviews, giving a privileged viewpoint of each actor involved in these interactions. They noticed that the CT is not or poorly trained in the role of tutor, they act on the basis of their professional experience and competence to teach physical education.

Recent studies Beau-Antony and all (2011) are moving in this direction, they study the characteristics of the professional activity of the CT to identify the difficulties encountered when supervising PE-ST. They showed that tutoring is a difficult function to perform because you have to engage the best in a mission for which most of the time it's poorly trained.

Boutin and Camaraire (2001) developed a guide for teachers who introduce the PE-STs. It notes the qualities required to their accompaniment: altruism, maturity, experience and communication skills, a willingness to share and to make discover. To play the role of a CT, the tutor should possess specific skills (Boudreau, 2009) . According to Carlier (2002) , the CT must have a style; develop a training contract, the mastery of interview techniques and the evaluation. Carlier (2002) proposes to bring the CT and PE-ST to exchange about academic knowledge and knowledge. Avoid introducing his trainee so: "Forget everything you learned in college" Carlier (2002: p. 104) . Carlier (2002) suggests to CT to recognize the existence of two types of knowledge and try to exploit them optimally. It presents two distinct worlds that everything seems to separate: the academic world on the one hand and professional reality, on the other. In addition, Carlier (2002) proposed to establish a communications contract with the trainee to guide the verbalization of his action. Through questioning that he put in place, the CT enters the psychic intimacy of the trainee.

Finally, Carlier (2002) wants the CT course could: first, increase the self-confidence of the PE-ST by allowing them to appropriate the content and models of appropriate behavior to interactive classroom management. Secondly, bring the PE-ST to analyze and evaluate his practice by directing it to the methods that allow for crossing the barrier between the experience and the experiential knowledge.

According to Faingold (2006) the most positive points in professional training are the quality of discussions, debates and the sincerity of the relationship between PE-ST and the CT. From session to session, this work makes sense and interest: listening quality and type of questions. It take distance from its practice promotes the sharing of experiences and modifies representations of the profession (students accept them as they are to be active and daring to express in his establishment; dialogue and work with colleagues).

Faingold (2006) suggests promoting the speaking the PE-ST, refraining from interfering to better listen and understanding his views on his practice. The CT should change posture. It must cease to be in a position to pass on knowledge to become accompanist appropriating a style intervention, assistance and conceptualization of experience.

Bali et al. (2014) confirm the difficulties encountered by the trainee teacher influences these behaviors and the tutor takes by responsibility see its role to clarify the objectives of the training.

It demonstrates the need for reflection on how the integration of PE-ST in schools in the hope of finding solutions to the con-constraints imposed on them in their professional environment. This requires reflection on the competence and CP response.

Escot (2004) questioned the impact of counseling on the didactic and the place given to the content taught. For this, three main categories were developed: the organization, the interventions with students and the content taught. Results of these studies show a predominance of class "organization" that takes up half the volume interviews advice of CT, the other half consisting of two other categories ("interventions for students" and "the content taught"). Mouton (2009) confirms that the nature of the counseling of and its contents depend on the environment co-constructed by the CT and PE-STs but also from the conception of the CT to introduce PE-ST into the profession.

Mouton (2009) finds that there is a great illusion to believe that CT is able to respond effectively to the requirements of a trainee engaged with a problem situation. He added that the CT is neither a scientist nor an expert, but a professional who organizes a training environment in a role to introduce PE-STs in the teaching profession.

Bremond (2013) suggests CT to reintroduce the dimension of the relationship with knowledge and position themselves active subject not just a catalyst. He asked the CTs to occupy a role that determines the exchange rather than the absolute neutrality.

According to Carlier (2009) the CTs extract from their practice the best knowledge of experience to make them available to the PE-STs in the profession they exercise. This expression of personal theories (Donnay and Charlier, 1996) is a first step in a reflexive approach, which is essential to the professionalization of the CT.

Vandercleyen et al. (2013) and Bali (2015) show that the success of the professional training depends largely on the type of intervention of the CT to the PE-ST, and the quality of the relationship between the two actors. They highlight in particular the dual role of the CT, to be able to explain their own pedagogical concepts to the PE-ST and help the latter to clarify his thoughts, his actions and his decisions.

Loizon (2008) reveals that counseling training must become a priority for all who are led to "give advice", or rather "hold advice" (Dugal, 2006). Loizon (2008) showed that training through research contributes to the development of the skills of counselors. To produce effects, training of CT must register in time and in confidence. These are the two major conditions that have allowed advisers say and write their feelings, their doubts, their remarks; this engagement in a real research work produced declared transformations and questioning of their consulting practices. The training generate a new question: "I give direct advice, but what effect does it have?"

CONCLUSION

The study of the accompanying practices of six CTs in two secondary schools practices, responding to a question: how CT introduces PE-ST into teaching practices through the first discourses post-sessions.

Globally the concerns of the tutors revolve around the acquisition of six professional skills that PE-ST should be used in the exercise of his profession: 1) acting in an ethical and responsible, 2) cooperate with school staff, parents, 3) working with members of the teaching staff, 4) communicate clearly and correctly in the teaching language, oral and written, 5) conceive teaching and learning situations, 6) control of teaching situations.

At the beginning of year, we found that the discourse of CT is more oriented to the professional identity and the school context that the act of teaching. For tutors, a PE-ST should be well behaved, prepared these documents, organizing his students accomplish administrative tasks, how to intervene and develop content to teach. These interpretations raise the question on the contribution of the Council to provide education, and the place given to the conception of the content taught and their appropriation by the student.

An important question that emerges from this study: Namely the evolution of councils of the CT in the professional training. We will discuss in the next article.

REFERENCES

1. Amade-Escot, Ch. (2003). Interactive Management of Didactic Contract in Volleyball. In C. Amade-Escot (Ed.) , Teaching of Physical Education: State of Research (pp. 255-278). Paris: EPS Review.

2. Amade-Escot, Ch. (2004). Study the Work of the Physical Education Teacher in the Classroom: Teaching Contribution to the Research Analysis of Actual Practices. In J.-F. Marcel (Ed.), Practice Teachers outside the Classroom (pp. 53-77). Paris: L'Harmattan.

3. Bali, N., et al. (2014). The Conceptions of Integration of Tunisian Physical Education Cooperative Teachers and Student Teachers. Creative Education, 5, 279-289.http://dx.doi.org/10.4236/ce.2014.54037

4. Bali, N. (2013). Teachers' Thought Processes: The Case of Tunisian Gymnastic University Teachers. Creative Education, 4, 77-84. http://dx.doi.org/10.4236/ce.2013.47A2020

5. Bali, N. (2015). The Tunisians Cooperative Teachers and Student Teachers' Conceptions about Class Management Skill. Creative Education, 6, 87-99.http://dx.doi.org/10.4236/ce.2015.61008

6. Bali, N., et al. (2012). The Conceptions of Authority of Tunisian Physical Education Cooperative Teachers and Student Teachers. Conference Proceedings of the 7th Biennial ARIS, Amiens.

7. Boudreau, P. (2009). For a Model of Supervision of Inductive Training in Supervising Tutors in Physical Education. Education and Francophonie, 1, 37.

8. Boutet, M., & Pharand, J. (2008). Concentrated Accompanying of Student Teachers. Quebec: PUQ.

9. Boutet, M., & Rousseau, N. (2002). The Challenges of Teaching Practicum Supervision. Quebec: PUQ.

10. Boutin, G., & Camaraire, L. (2001). Introduce and Mentor of Student Teacher. Practical Guide for Teacher-Trainer, Montreal, News Editions.

11. Brau-Antony, S., Mieusset, C., Lenfant, A., & Miot, C. (2011). Analyze the Work of Tutors Beginning Teachers. Continuing Education, 186, 175-185.

12. Bremond, C. (2013). The Trainer He Knows What He's Talking. New Review of Psychology, 1, 241-252.

13. Carlier, G. (2002). Supervise of Trainee in Physical Education: Tags for a Function in the Process of Professionalization. Louvain: Catholic University of Louvain, 96-111.

14. Carlier, G. (2009). Accompany and Training of Tutors in Physical Education. The Experience of the Catholic University of Louvain (Belgium). Education and Francophonie, 37, 68-88. http://dx.doi.org/10.7202/037653ar

15. Carlier, G., & Clerx, M. (2012). The Pleasure of Participating in Continuing Education Training. In: G. Carlier, C. Borges, M. Clerx, & C. Delens (Eds.), Professional Identity in Physical Education: Research in Teacher Education and Teaching (pp. 23-41). Leuven: Leuven University Press.

16. Crinon, J. (2003). Professional Teacher's Memory Observatory Practices and Leverage for Training. Harmattan.

17. Darnis, F., & Magendie, E. (2011). Teacher Training in Alternation:

Towards the Co-Construction of Pragmatic Concepts. Knowledge Magazine, 27, 63-83.

18. Desbiens, J. F., Borges, C., & Spallanzani, C. (2009). Educational Supervision in Physical Education. Education and Francophonie, 37, 1-5.

19. Dugal, J. P. (2003). Consulting Initial Teacher Training: Interest and the Pedagogic Knowledge for Mentoring Student Teachers in EPS. Doctoral Dissertation, PhD in Sports Science, Toulouse: Université Toulouse III—Paul Sabatier.

20. Dugal, J. P., & Amade-Escot, C. (2004). Consulting Initial Teacher Training: Interest and the Pedagogic Knowledge for Mentoring Student Teachers in EPS. Doctoral Dissertation, PhD in Sports Science, Toulouse: Université Toulouse III—Paul Sabatier.

21. Faingold, N. (2006). Training of Trainers in the Analysis of Practices. Research and Education, 51, 89-104.

22. Gervais, C., & Desrosiers, P. (2005). The School, Place of Teaching Training: Question and Marks and for Supervision of Trainees. Canada: The Laval University Press.

23. Jorro, A. (2007). The Alternation Research and Professional Training Ground. Research and Training, 54, 101-114.

24. Leriche, J., Desbiens, J. F., Dugal, J. P., & Amade-Escot, C. (2010). Analysis of the Accompanying Responsibility in Quebec and France: A Look at the Post-Lesson Interviews with the Ecology of the Classroom. Review e-JRIEPS, 71-98.

25. Lévesque, M., & Gervais, C. (2000). Professional Integration: A Step to Succeed in the Professionalization of Teaching. Education Canada, 40, 12-15.

26. Loizon, D. (2008). Training of Educational Adviser's First Degree by Research. Research and Education, 59, 105-119.

27. Maela, P. (2009). Around the Word Accompaniment. Research and Training, 62, 91-107.

28. Martineau, S., & Corriveau, G. (2000). Promoting an Understanding of the Sense of Professional Incompetence among Teachers in Secondary Vocational Integration. Training and Profession, 6, 5-8.

29. Martineau, S., & Mukamurera, J. (2012). Overview of Major Programs and Support Systems for Professional Integration in Education. Phronesis, 1, 45-62.http://dx.doi.org/10.7202/1009059ar

30. Martineau, S., & Presseau, A. (2003). The Sense of Professional Incompetence of Teachers Early in Their Careers and Support

Employability. Brock Education, 12, 2-6.

31. Martineau, S., Portelance, L., & Presseau, A. (2010). Mentoring as a Support System for the Employment of Teachers. Proceedings of the International Conference on Complex Thinking: Challenges and Opportunities for Education, Research and Organizations, 31, 2-8

32. Mouton, J. C. (2009). Form Analysis Consultancy Master Trainer Training of Accompanied Practice. Research and Education, 62, 65-76.

33. Ndoreraho, J. P., & Martineau, S. (2006). A Problematic Beginning of the Teaching Career. Retrieved November 20, 2009.

34. Perez-Roux, T. (2012). Identity Construction of New Teachers: What Recognition of Others to (Re) Known as a Professional? Educations & Research Journal, 7, 69-84.

35. Perrenoud, P. (1994). Teacher Training: Theory and Practice. Paris: L'Harmattan.

36. Rayou, P., & Ria, L. (2009). Train New Teachers. Various Statutes, Organization and Professional Knowledge. Education and corporate, 1, 79-90.

37. Trohel, J., et al. (2004). The Dynamic of Interactions Tutors Students Experiencing Educational Advice. Knowledge, 5, 119-140.

38. Vandercleyen, F., Delens, C., & Carlier, G. (2013). Supervision Styles of Tutors in Physical Education: Consideration of the Emotional Experiences of Trainees during a Post-Lesson Interview. EJRIEPS, 61-99.

Chapter 7

A BASIC DISCOURSE ON DISCIPLINE FOR NOVICE TEACHERS

Lucie Kucerova, Tereza Buchtova, Stefan Chudy, Pavel Neumeister

Olomouc Department, Faculty of Education, Palacky University, Olomouc, Czech Republic

ABSTRACT

This paper presents a research investigation focused on creating a basic discourse on discipline in novice teachers. The qualitatively-chosen methodology identifies, for a selected sample, how length of pedagogical experience and gender influence the creation and maintenance of a teacher's authority in the classroom. This research is a part of the project, which focuses on mapping the different approaches of education for novice teachers to PDF Palacky University in Olomouc. The aim is to highlight the possible theoretical and methodological approaches in addressing the issue of discipline than on specific statistical data.

INTRODUCTION

Discipline represents order, a procedure that is essential for students to be able to learn effectively. There is extensive literature on discipline in schools, which also includes a series of books that provide good practical information and advice. The problems and issues of discipline are thus one of the essential topics for pedagogical students, and one of the most essential areas of further education [1] .

Teachers' educational activities in the classroom can be relatively easily observed; but however, is this true for educational activities? Teachers do not talk about their individual conception of educational activities, but despite this they prepare themselves to teach and organize life in the classroom. Therefore, in order to carry out their educational activities, they need to have an awareness and knowledge of educational resources that will enable them to do so.

This group also includes planning, controlling and maintaining discipline in the classroom. Discipline is an important prerequisite not only for the functioning of a classroom, but also of society as a whole. This field is very demanding, whether for teachers with years of experience, and especially for novice teachers or student teachers. Novice teachers however, are not really concerned with this topic specifically—until they encounter a particular problem.

This contribution's aim is to shed especial light on particular theoretical issues in the form of a discourse on the concept of discipline as an educational resource for novice teachers; on the basis of a definition of discourse— understood as a statement about the functioning of human societies' established perceptions. Achievement of the main goal was conditional on the fulfilment of the specific subsidiary objectives where throughout the research process, this paper focuses only on the qualitative part of the collection and analysis of the data; and it only presents the main findings.

THEORETICAL BACKGROUND

The concept of discipline can be viewed from the perspective of multiple meanings. Each person perceives discipline differently—for example, simply as obedience, a set of rules of behaviour or habits acquired through education and/or training. These views are, to a greater or lesser extent, close to the truth [2] .

Discipline, as a complex phenomenon, affects people's lives every day. According to Bendl, discipline can be defined as: "conscious adherence to specified behaviour norms" [3] .

One such important aspect is pedagogical discipline, closely associated with education. Pedagogical discipline is focused on the child. Thereby, the given nature learns to subordinate itself to authority. If one talks about the goal of discipline, this is understood to mean that discipline has to create a useful member of the state from a student, and shall create a structured student life and teach them what the state needs from citizens; that is to say, obedience to the laws [4] .

Interpretations of discipline differ as do the different approaches of individual authors. The aforementioned Bendl, states that one can approach the interpretation of discipline according to areas like, the aim of discipline, and its function and content, the establishment of standards and norms, a sense of responsibility for discipline, and the further development of discipline and methods [5] . One can designate several phenomena as causes of indiscipline, or the syndrome of risky behaviour. These phenomena can include for instance things like substance abuse, and negative phenomena in the reproductive and psychosocial fields. Negative phenomena in the reproductive field include for example, overly early initiation of a sexual life or excessive changing of sexual partners. Negative phenomena in the psychosocial field include aggression, behaviour disorders, or depression [5] . Other causes of indiscipline include: the pedagogue, teaching activities, and aspects of behaviour, or emotional and physiological reasons, the environment as well as a student's personality and their relationship to the learning process. These causes of disorderly behaviours are those most often manifested.

One of the ways of maintaining discipline among students is that the teacher has authority—and it is precisely this authority of the teacher which is the prerequisite not only of teaching success, but also the observance of discipline. Authority can be divided as follows:

- Personal—primary, or also, natural.

- Functional—i.e. professional.

- Positional—i.e. secondary.

- Formal—resulting from one's position in the organisational chart.

- Informal—resulting from skills, talent, education, etc. [6] .

These types of authority work together; sometimes, one replaces another. The ideal situation is then, that a teacher had informal authority which flows from their control of their subject, the extent of their pedagogical competencies, and also—from a good relationship with their pupils. This is however, not as simple for example for novice teachers, because the pedagogical competence of maintaining discipline (i.e. the teacher has authority) is very complicated and teachers must work on it [6] . How then can a teacher build authority? This process is dependent on the expression of status, pedagogical competence, teachers themselves, and the effective and equitable resolution of situations where the teacher has to deal with pupils' undesirable behaviour as well as consistency between a teacher's words and actions. This listing is for a teaching assistant, on just how to build authority. Different influences affect the students and their inappropriate behaviour, and a teacher's authority is also one [6] .

One of the most important features in the creation of a positive climate in the classroom, which acts on pupils' discipline, is motivation. Just as teachers' authority is important, so too is it also important to motivate students to not even think of inappropriate behaviour. When motivating, it is important that pupils are motivated from several different directions. This involves their internal motivation, external motivation and pupils' expectations of success

[1] . Internal motivation includes the degree to which students participate in certain activities so as to meet their needs; these include curiosity, interest in the actual topic, and also to be able to gain skills and abilities. Extrinsic motivation can include their actual participation in activities so as to achieve the specifically defined goals. Internal and external motivations are often pitted against each other, but this does not mean that they are incompatible. The third motivation strength is their expectation of success. This expectation is associated with how students feel that the given activities can help them to achieve success [1] .

"Rules" or "Principles" exist, by means of which it is not only possible to resolve indiscipline, or at least to confront indiscipline and to fight it preventively. So how then does one deal with indiscipline and ensure the prevention of indiscipline? For example, the discovery of indiscipline or insubordination, exposing the causes of indiscipline, the use of a diverse range of educational resources, the introduction of lectures for pedagogues, and the inclusion of social pedagogues and school psychologists in schools and other establishments [7] .

RESEARCH QUESTIONS

The main research goal was to create a basic discourse on discipline in novice teachers, through the analysis and summarisation of the essential components of the disciplinary techniques by which pedagogues manage pupils' indiscipline in school classrooms. This investigation was carried out in several empirical stages. An important goal in the analysis process was just this creation of the aforementioned discourse on discipline in the educational activities novice teachers [8] . The empirical validation of the functionality of discourse served for these purposes.

The survey had to be implemented in several consecutive steps. Some of the basic theoretical analysis steps form the basis for the empirical investigation, and conversely, data from the empirical investigations assist in the creation of the perspectives and internal structure of this discourse. The chosen methodology serves as the basis for the optimalisation of the discourse. The main objective of the work was divided into sub-goals, which are readily seen in the form of the specific focus of the various stages of the work of creating and subsequently verifying the functionality of this discourse.

Analysis of the given sample and the respondents' typology in comparison with the theory as determined forms the basis of the validity and reliability of the research. This analysis is supplemented by the Cluster Analysis and Factor Analysis of data elements, which means that evaluation and inappropriate influences are eliminated from the empirical research (e.g. the randomness of answers, incorrect answers, and so on); and it also optimises the validated rating system data (i.e. the credibility of the data). The verification of the independence of the evaluations of respondents' preferences, and for instance, their attitudes, is resolved by using Non-parame- tric Tests for Ordinal Data Types in dual and multiple comparisons. The empirical research was realized in the following steps:

The selection of the sample and the identification of respondents.

- The elimination of undesirable elements (e.g. tendency to mediocrity, etc.).

- The establishment of the research assumptions.

- The specification, optimization and innovation of research tools.

- The modification of the research sample.

- The implementation of the empirical investigation.

- And, the verification of the independence of the optimized data system.

The context of the research investigation is based on factor and cluster analysis of elements to verify and determine the assumptions and hypotheses. It is precisely this use of factor analysis which does not allow the creation of classic hypotheses [9] . When applying this method, it is not possible to define classical hypotheses that the use of other statistical methods would allow [10] . With a view to these facts and the nature of the empirical data obtained, as well as for the content and purpose of creating this discourse—where the basic premise is the specification of the characteristic elements of the concept of discipline as a means of educationally-influencing novice teachers, it was decided to set the research assumption and verify it in the preliminary research stage and thereby to reduce variables to the desired number needed to specify the discourse with respect to the theoretical definition. Verification using Cluster Analysis is in line with the stated goal of this research.

One of the important characteristics for its use in practice is its clarity and use in the evaluation system's operations—i.e. its independence and support of important respondent characteristics. Other factors include gender and length of working experience. The research sample of novice teachers is subjected to simple Descriptive Statistics. In the context of the pilot study, assumptions were established and then were subsequently subjected to statistical verification, and further specified. Based on the preliminary research, the following hypotheses were created for the main empirical research:

- The length of working practice does not influence the formation and maintenance of teachers' authority in the classroom, this hypothesis monitors the difference between the length of working practice and, secondarily, also between sexes in the creation of authority (i.e. teacher rigor, maintaining order and quiet, re-seating pupils, insistence on compliance with the School Regulations, etc.).

- There is no statistically significant difference between men and women in their perception of disciplinary measures for maintaining the teacher's authority in the classroom, this hypothesis expresses an effort to uncover and describe the relationship between discipline and gender differences in the perception of disciplinary resources between men and women.

- Teachers, unlike lady teachers, perceive the importance of determining the precise rules in the classroom because of their importance for the observance of discipline, this hypothesis enables the tracking and revelation of the causes of such perceptions and the building of relationships between a teacher and a student; here, the interesting variables are gender and the seniority of the teachers.

- In the course of building teachers' responsibility towards their educational work in the classroom, length of practice does not play an important role, the aim is to describe the level of responsibility, which is expressed by the relationship between their profession; and, it is assumed that a significant difference exists in the length of individual respondents' working practice and their relationship to their profession.

- In the course of repeated violation of the disciplinary rules, compliance is required more by teachers with minimal experience, this hypothesis captures part of the discourse which expresses the methodological concept of discipline and focuses on building a relationship between a teacher and student in the sense of discipline as an educational element.

Differences exist in the creative creation of disciplinary techniques between men and women, this presupposes the use of creativity in teachers' work and for setting the rules for building a relationship between a teacher and pupil and follows the pupil's acceptance of disciplinary elements.

METHODOLOGY

Conceptual Mapping and Projection Techniques using Incomplete Sentences were used in the data collection phase, as well as to create a structure defining the basic aspects and concepts of the discourse method [11] . Conceptual Mapping (i.e. thought maps, mind mapping) was used as a data collection method for structuring concepts [12] , schematic concepts and depicting their mutual interrelationships. Conceptual mapping served for "uncovering" the "ontological structures" of thinking in students and novice teachers [13] . The clear structuring and reconstruction of the conceptual apparatus at different levels of generality, over a certain time interval, and on the basis of their own experience provides very suggestive material for the analysis of, and the creation of a concept and focus of the discourse. Thanks to this method we are able to understand changes in thinking and structuring concepts; processing style whether as graphomotoric expressions or constructivist deliberation and to capture the meaning of terms by using concepts, signs or symbols.

Janík, distinguishes two kinds of conceptual maps—structured and unstructured. Input variables expressed as a fixed list of terms are presented in the Structured Conceptual Maps. Unstructured mapping, presented by means of a central concept and whose purpose is to search for related concepts of content, sensory data, and the like [14] . In the context of this research investigation, the concept mapping focus is oriented on the scope and content of discourse; and thus, the creation of structures and related concepts that formed the imaginary boundary of a discourse. The creation of the structure of concepts of discipline and the concepts associated with it, are demonstrated in the conceptual maps presented herein in reflection of the clarification function, and for the visualisation and presentation of ontological structures. These maps illustrate novice teachers' perception of the conceptual apparatus and uncover the level of the ontological foundation of the concept of discipline and disciplinary techniques.

The Unfinished Sentences Method was utilized for further research. This is a method with a written character, used for its freedom in space and spontaneity of expression. It serves for the investigation of non-cognitive characteristics, attitudes, opinions and beliefs. Stimuli, in the form of words or phrases, evoke the possibility of creating answers. Space for answers is given by the bond to other inspirational phrases or words and the possibilities offered by writing is expressed by the size of the "room to respond" for the answer. These sentences in the investigation were formulated as incomplete statements—which respondents completed by finishing them. The resulting data is Incomplete Statements that are expressed in the overview tables and placed in the context of the discourse content. Thanks to this technique, extensive material was obtained (since the sample consisted of 190 novice teachers). Narrative Analysis was used in the course of analyzing the written responses of novice teachers, where their portfolio from their periods of study at the Faculty of Pedagogy formed a part. The sections that deal with discipline in schools were used as sources. Students were supposed to write—in different literary forms, their perceptions and experiences pertaining to discipline. The portfolio is supplemented with a new part, which contains the recollections of the qualities of a teacher in the classrooms in which the respondents participated in the role of pupils. Thanks to this analysis, it was possible to detect the hidden meanings of situations, perceptions and resolution of discipline issues.

Written responses are an excellent material source for analysis and are qualitative sources of empirical data. Novice teachers were thus able to choose their own descriptions of the situations and events which the researcher represented, who would have watched these situations themselves.

From the validity point-of-view, this has to do with an accurate description of the perceptions of the given sample of respondents and thus, the expression of the described phenomenon of perception, i.e. discipline. Narrative Analysis uses, due to the nature of the material, structural and thematic analysis components. While it thematically describes the answer to the question—what is said; it notes the structural answers to the question— how it is said.

RESEARCH INVESTIGATION RESULTS

An important step in the research investigation context was the representative sample, whose members would adequately and competently express themselves. In the course of defining the basic set of questions, the specific characters of the base file had to be specified [15] . The main criteria include: a minimum of working experience in a school environment, a minimal knowledge of the phenomena under investigation, personal experience with the management and organization of a classroom, a description of the subjective perception of the phenomenon being examined, and the assurance of maximum anonymity and willingness. In addition, the specification for the basic sample took place; that is to say, that the investigation would focus on fifth-year students in the Bachelor's Degree or the second-year of the Master's Degree programmes at UP PDF. Because the research was realized on PDF UP, home students were utilized as respondents who already have within a master's degree internship and fulfill the criteria chosen throughout the research.

In the initial stage of the analysis, the pilot-study sample consisted of 205 respondents. The research sample in the main phase of the research investigation was 130 respondents.

To better understand the broader context of the resolution of the problems and issues of discipline, and the concept of novice teachers in schools and classrooms in the form of discourse analysis, an analysis was performed of basic concepts and the reconstruction of the concept of discipline. The data collection methods included Unfinished Sentences, Conceptual Maps, Interviews, while the data analysis methods were Narrative and Content Analysis. The aim was to discover how the description of the basic definition of the concept of discipline forms the concept of discipline in a school environment. Novice teachers thus demonstrate that they can present the power elements of discipline in the character of its institutional and normative definitions. The key to creating a discourse on discipline as an educational resource is the fact that novice teachers expect the determination of the behaviour of the actors in the educational process in certain situations, require exact behaviour patterns and also determine the penalties for non-compliance.

The psycho-pedagogical aspects of the teacher—pupil relationship were investigated using Unfinished Sentences and their subsequent analysis. The results are processed in the form of a table (viz Appendix No. 1) Students were asked to complete Unfinished Statements (viz Appendix No. 2). Another of the activities was the discipline-building process in the form of self-discipline. Conceptual Maps served this purpose.

For novice teachers, building of "some form of relationship" is important. The discourse on discipline thus takes on the aspect of the creation of positive relationships and authority not based on formal institutionalized education elements. Another important role in the concept of discipline is also played by bad experience acquired in the role of a pupil. From novice teachers' responses, it became clear that bad experiences in the role of a student result in a turnaround in their perception of the role and status of teachers in the classroom.

Another sub-objective was the definition and specification of discipline as an educational resource oriented on the elements of the consolidation of power and power-relationships in the classroom.

From the information obtained above, it is clear that discipline is perceived as a component of educational activities in which reconciliation comes about between the teacher's ideas, objectives and the educational activities' content; and pupils' needs. The main objective of discipline is to optimise the environment and teacher-student interaction. The teacher thus uses their experience, personal potential, disciplinary techniques, and social control.

In order to create the discourse, the goal-description of the current state of discipline with a regard to the content and structure of discipline, was also set. The result is the implementation of disciplinary techniques in novice teachers' disciplinary concepts. For novice teachers, this is mainly about maintaining power over students, maintaining stereotypes in the course of the learning process, and coping with disciplinary educational activities as something that is already above and beyond the defined duties associated with teaching. If the basic aim of a teacher is to maintain their authority and position in the class, then they must make greater use of their use intellectual potential rather than their physical disposition. Discourse on discipline as an educational tool is formed in this way and takes on dimensions ranging from maintaining authority through the fulfilment of educational goals to the creation of the pupil-teacher relationship. This is done through disciplinary techniques.

The modality of resources is applied through many disciplinary techniques and strategies. Variability and creativity in the development, application and evaluation of disciplinary measures are well-known to novice teachers. The modality of classical and verified disciplinary techniques lies in different intensities and variations of words. Physical punishment is a rare phenomenon—but it does occur. Another element that strengthens the power relationship in the classroom is to create rules that are supported by the documents of the given institution. Most often, this process takes place through mutual consent, also complemented by penalties for non-com- pliance. The most common approach is that an individual teacher presents the internal regulations of the school (school rules) and subsequently enforces them by sanctions set by the school. It is less common for the approach to be that the teacher tries to solve the problem themselves, or with their parents.

The application of power relationships and power at the general level taken from the samples of the research material also point out that any application of power is also things from previous experience. The goal of discipline in the school environment is not only to maintain order and the effort to improve the quality of the teacher- student relationship, but also the exercise of power in the teacher-role and the compensation of certain physical and psychic phenomena, as well as the justification of their actions—in front of themselves and their colleagues (i.e. rationalization).

To check discipline, teachers frequently choose the observation method and subsequently, use gestures, e.g. not only a raised finger or facial mimicry, but verbal expressions like a shout, suggestive questions, commands, etc. A specific form of discipline is supervision, which requires a certain degree of observation skills from tea- chers. It also requires concentration and the maintenance of the rules, as well as a certain degree of empathy, and the effort to build a teacher-pupil relationship not only based on superiority and inferiority terms. Supervision is closely connected with sanctioning, determining sanctions, and ensuring compliance, which all play a positive role in the school discipline environment.

CONCLUSIONS

The aim of this research was the creation of the theoretical basis of a discourse on discipline in novice teachers. Content and discourse analysis elements served to meet this end, as did their self-reflection on practical experiences in the teacher role. Sub-goals helped to create the basic concept of power and the use of discipline in the school environment as an educational resource. This paper mainly deals with the theoretical basis of discipline and authority in novice teachers and provides a possible methodological approach; especially in the areas of data collection methods and their subsequent analysis. The research material was obtained and processed using methods like interviews, unfinished sentences, concept mapping and the analysis of the biographical written statements of the respondents. As part of this study were not presented results of a survey, but it was focused on theoretical and methodological approach that is only a partial part of the research project. By setting the theoretical concept of discipline as a means of education we have fulfilled the main objective of this paper. Options of processing empirical verification of a theoretical treatment are a matter for further discussion.

The results of this research clearly show that the gender-gap between the sexes exists, and is significant. This finding provides us with a clear answer to why school-managers prefer men over women teachers in teacher recruitment. The question remains, how many male teachers can last in the school environment and overcome the initial failures linked to discipline. For this reason, the questions were also oriented on the length of practice as a factor in the formation of the teacher-pupil relationship. Respondents positively appreciated the creativity, passion, and the so-called "learning to live with experience" of the profession. They did not take length of experience as being an important factor. The answers clearly show that when solving problems with discipline, respondents would prefer first of all to resolve the issue with the class themselves; and only after that, with the school management staff, and finally, with parents. From the results, we can also conclude that gender plays an important role in the selection of disciplinary techniques and, on the contrary, that length of service is not a significant factor in influencing creativity in the use of discipline as an educational resource activity. A positive factor for novice teachers is that students take normative discipline means as something that is necessary and normal in schools.

ACKNOWLEDGEMENTS

Internal grant of PDF UP: From subjective implicit theories of education to teaching knowledge. The process of constitution of a cognitive framework sciences education in the national and international context.

IGA PdF 2014004: Mapping Approaches to describe fragments and constructs training for new teachers at Faculty of Education on UP in Olomouc.

The VOICE of European TeacherS (VOICES), 526613-LLP-2012-NL-Comenius—CNW.

REFERENCES

1. Kyriacou, Ch. (1996) Klíčové dovednosti učitele. Portál, Praha, 82, 95.

2. Makarenko, A.S. (1957) O výchově dětí v rodině. 7. vyd. SPN, Praha, 31.

3. Bendl, S. (2004) Jak předcházet nekázni, aneb, Káze?ské prostředky. ISV, Praha, 23.

4. Uher, J. (1924) Problém kázně. Dědictví Komenského, Praha, 24.

5. Bendl, S. (2011) Káze?ské problémy ve škole. Triton, Praha, 29, 34, 35.

6. Podlahová, L. (2004) První kroky učitele. Triton, Praha, 89, 90.

7. Bendl, S. (2001) Školní káze?. Metody a strategie. ISV, Praha.

8. Haining, R. (1990) Spatial Data Analysis in the Social and Environmental Science. University Press, Cambridge. http://dx.doi.org/10.1017/CBO9780511623356

9. Hendl, J. (2004) Přehled statistických metod zpracování dat. Portál, Praha.

10. Macdonald, R.P. (1991) Faktorová analýza a příbuzné metody v psychologii. Academia, Praha.

11. Skalková, J. (1983) Úvod do metodologie a metod pedagogického výzkumu. SPN, Praha.

12. Buzan, T. (2007) Mentální mapování. Portál, Praha.

13. Bendl, S. and Vo?ková, H. (2010) Využití pojmových map ve výuce pedagogiky. IN: Pedagogická orientace, r. 20, č. 1, 16-38.

14. Janík, T. (2005) Znalost jako klíčová kategorie učitelského vzdělávání. Paido, Brno.

15. Gavora, P.(2009) Stanovení výzkumného vzorku. In: ŠVEC, Š., Ed., Metodologie věd o výchově, Paido, Brno.

CITATION

CHAPTER 1

Nobrega, J. (2014). Discourse Analysis: Ronald Reagan's Evil Empire Speech. Open Journal of Modern Linguistics, 4, 166-181. doi: 10.4236/ojml.2014.41014.

CHAPTER 2

Paniago, M. and Silva, K. (2015) The Participation in a Research and Study Group: A Collective Discourse Perspective. Creative Education, 6, 2325-2332. doi: 10.4236/ce.2015.622239.

CHAPTER 3

Yang, G. and Chen, Y. (2015) Investigating the English Proficiency of Learners: A Corpus-Based Study of Contrastive Discourse Markers in China. Open Journal of Modern Linguistics, 5, 281-290. doi: 10.4236/ojml.2015.53025.

CHAPTER 4

Oute, J. , Huniche, L. , Nielsen, C. and Petersen, A. (2015) The Politics of Mental Illness and Involvement—A Discourse Analysis of Danish Anti-Stigma and Social Inclusion Campaigns. Advances in Applied Sociology, 5, 273-285. doi: 10.4236/aasoci.2015.511026.

CHAPTER 6

Zayed, W. and Bali, N. (2015) Introduction of Student Teachers in Tunisian Secondary Schools: A Discourse Analysis of Cooperative Teacher. Creative Education, 6, 359-368. doi: 10.4236/ce.2015.63034.

CHAPTER 7

Kucerova, L. , Buchtova, T. , Chudy, S. and Neumeister, P. (2015) A Basic Discourse on Discipline for Novice Teachers. Open Journal of Social Sciences, 3, 88-95. doi: 10.4236/jss.2015.32012.

INDEX